STUDIES IN SCRIPTURE IN EARLY JUDAISM AND CHRISTIANITY

Edited by
Craig A. Evans
Volume 22

PUBLISHED UNDER

JEWISH AND CHRISTIAN TEXTS IN
CONTEXTS AND RELATED STUDIES

Executive Editor
James H. Charlesworth

Editorial Board of Advisors
Motti Aviam, Michael Davis, Casey Elledge, Craig Evans, Loren Johns, Amy-Jill
Levine, Lee McDonald, Lidija Novakovic, Gerbern Oegema, Henry Rietz,
Brent Strawn

Volume 34

VISIONS AND VIOLENCE IN THE PSEUDEPIGRAPHA

Edited by
Craig A. Evans, Brian LePort, and Paul T. Sloan

LONDON • NEW YORK • OXFORD • NEW DELHI • SYDNEY

T&T CLARK

Bloomsbury Publishing Plc

50 Bedford Square, London, WC1B 3DP, UK
1385 Broadway, New York, NY 10018, USA
29 Earlsfort Terrace, Dublin 2, Ireland

BLOOMSBURY, T&T CLARK and the T&T Clark logo are trademarks of Bloomsbury Publishing Plc

First published in Great Britain 2022
Paperback edition published 2023

Copyright © Craig A. Evans, Brian LePort, Paul T. Sloan and contributors, 2022

Craig A. Evans, Brian LePort, Paul T. Sloan have asserted their right under
the Copyright, Designs and Patents Act, 1988, to be identified as Editors of this work.

Cover design: Charlotte James

All rights reserved. No part of this publication may be reproduced or
transmitted in any form or by any means, electronic or mechanical, including
photocopying, recording, or any information storage or retrieval system,
without prior permission in writing from the publishers.

Bloomsbury Publishing Plc does not have any control over, or responsibility for,
any third-party websites referred to or in this book. All internet addresses given
in this book were correct at the time of going to press. The author and publisher
regret any inconvenience caused if addresses have changed or sites have
ceased to exist, but can accept no responsibility for any such changes.

A catalogue record for this book is available from the British Library.

Library of Congress Cataloging-in-Publication Data

Names: Evans, Craig A., editor. | LePort, Brian, editor. |
Sloan, Paul (Religious educator), editor.
Title: Visions and violence in the Pseudepigrapha / edited by Craig A. Evans,
Brian LePort, and Paul T. Sloan.
Description: New York : T&T Clark, 2021. | Series: Jewish and Christian texts in contexts and related
studies ; volume 22 | Includes bibliographical references and index. |
Identifiers: LCCN 2021031252 (print) | LCCN 2021031253 (ebook) |
ISBN 9780567703217 (hardback) | ISBN 9780567703248 (epub) | ISBN 9780567703224 (pdf)
Subjects: LCSH: Apocryphal books (Old Testament)–Criticism,
interpretation, etc. | Vision–Biblical teaching. | Violence–Biblical teaching.
Classification: LCC BS1700 .V57 2021 (print) | LCC BS1700 (ebook) | DDC 229/.9106–dc23
LC record available at https://lccn.loc.gov/2021031252
LC ebook record available at https://lccn.loc.gov/2021031253

ISBN:	HB:	978-0-5677-0321-7
	PB:	978-0-5677-0325-5
	ePDF:	978-0-5677-0322-4
	ePUB:	978-0-5677-0324-8

Series: Jewish and Christian Texts, volume 34

Typeset by Integra Software Services Pvt. Ltd.

To find out more about our authors and books visit www.bloomsbury.com
and sign up for our newsletters.

*This book is dedicated to the memory of
Professor James A. Sanders*

Contents

Preface	ix
List of Abbreviations	x
List of Contributors	xv
Introducing Biblical Themes and Traditions in the Pseudepigrapha	1

Part I
Expanded and Visionary Tradition in the Pseudepigrapha

Chapter 1
THE LEGACY OF SOLOMON THE SAGE FROM QOHELET TO JOSEPHUS
   Torleif Elgvin   5

Chapter 2
VENEREAE DAEMONIORUM: EROTIC DEMONS, EGYPTIAN MONASTICISM, AND THE *TESTAMENT OF SOLOMON*
   Blake A. Jurgens   29

Chapter 3
A NEW *TESTAMENT OF ADAM* IN THE SYRIAC *REVELATION OF THE MAGI*?
   Bradley N. Rice   51

Chapter 4
THE *SHEPHERD OF HERMAS*' APOCALYPTIC VISIONS AND ANGELIC INTERMEDIARIES IN AND IN LIGHT OF CLEMENT OF ALEXANDRIA
   Christopher S. Atkins   67

Part II
Violence and Polemic in the Pseudepigrapha

Chapter 5
VIOLENCE AND DIVINE FAVOR IN *LIBER ANTIQUITATUM BIBLICARUM*
   Benjamin J. Lappenga   83

Chapter 6
"CLEAR EYES, FULL HEARTS, CAN'T LOSE": THE RHETORIC OF VIOLENCE
IN THE *ANIMAL APOCALYPSE*
    John Garza   95

Chapter 7
THE POWER OF POLEMICS: JEWISH SLANDER AGAINST SAMARITANS
IN LATE SECOND TEMPLE PERIOD LITERATURE
    Tim Wardle   107

Chapter 8
ESCHATOLOGICAL EXPECTATION AND REVOLUTIONARY VIOLENCE:
ISRAEL'S PAST AS INDICATIVE OF ITS FUTURE IN 1QM AND JOSEPHUS'
JEWISH WAR
    Jesse P. Nickel   123

Chapter 9
THE FIERY ORIGINS OF GEHENNA IN ISAIAH, ENOCH, JESUS,
AND BEYOND
    Craig A. Evans   141

Chapter 10
VIOLENCE AND "MAGIC" TRADITION
    Matthias R. Hoffmann   171

Bibliography   198
Index of References   229
Index of Modern Names   251

Preface

The series Studies in Scripture in Early Judaism and Christianity (SSEJC) was founded almost thirty years ago by Craig A. Evans and James A. Sanders. More than twenty volumes have been published to date. Many of them have focused on the function of Israel's sacred Scripture in early Christian writings, whether in those eventually recognized as canonical or in those not so recognized. Most of these volumes have appeared in the "blue series," that is, the Library of New Testament Studies (LNTS). Some volumes have focused on the artifacts of Scripture (such as LSTS 70 and LSTS 94, both in the "red series"); others, like the present one, have focused on texts loosely grouped together under the heading of "pseudepigrapha." The editors are grateful to Professor James H. Charlesworth for accepting the present collection of studies in the "yellow series," that is, the Jewish and Christian Texts (JCT) series.

The editors of the present SSEJC volume are grateful to Professor Randall Chesnutt who at the outset provided counsel and vetted a number of papers and to Professor Loren Stuckenbruck who at a later stage also provided assistance. The editors are very grateful, of course, to the contributors, who in various ways seek to break new ground. Their chapters are gathered into two parts. The first is focused on how sacred tradition is expanded and interpreted in the Pseudepigrapha, especially through vision. The second part focuses more narrowly on themes of violence, polemic, and judgment—both "historical" and eschatological—in the Pseudepigrapha. Both parts of chapters show in what ways ancient Scripture informs and inspires the writers of later times who in various ways seek to address new challenges and new questions. The Introduction will say more about the individual chapters.

We dedicate this book to the memory of James A. Sanders (1927–2020), who founded the Ancient Biblical Manuscript Center in Claremont, co-founded the SSEJC series, and throughout his long and distinguished career championed the intertextuality of the sacred tradition.

Craig A. Evans
Brian LePort
Paul T. Sloan

ABBREVIATIONS

AB	Anchor Bible (Commentary)
ABD	D. N. Freedman (ed.), *Anchor Bible Dictionary*
ABRL	Anchor Bible Reference Library
AfRG	*Archiv für Religionsgeschichte*
AGJU	Arbeiten zur Geschichte des antiken Judentums und des Urchristentums
ALGHJ	Arbeiten zur Literatur und Geschichte des hellenistischen Judentums
ANF	Ante-Nicene Fathers
AnOx	Anecdota Oxoniensia
ANRW	*Aufstieg und Niedergang der römischen Welt*
APF	*Archiv für Papyrusforschung und verwandte Gebiete*
APOT	R. H. Charles (ed.), *Apocrypha and Pseudepigrapha of the Old Testament*
ArBib	Aramaic Bible
ARG	*Archiv für Religionsgeschichte*
ARW	*Archiv für Religionswissenschaft*
ASE	*Annali di storia dell'esegesi*
AthR	*Anglican Theological Review*
Aug	*Augustinianum*
AUUSSU	Acta Universitatis Upsaliensis: Studia Semitica Upsaliensia
BA	*The Biblical Archaeologist*
BASP	*Bulletin of the American Society of Papyrologists*
BDAG	*Greek-English Lexicon of the New Testament*
BDB	Brown-Driver-Briggs, *A Hebrew and English Lexicon of the Old Testament*
BibInt	*Biblical Interpretation*
BibInt	Biblical Interpretation Series
BibSem	The Biblical Seminar
BJS	Brown Judaic Studies
BMI	The Bible and Its Modern Interpreters
BN	*Biblische Notizen*
CBET	Contributions to Biblical Exegesis and Theology
CBQ	*Catholic Biblical Quarterly*
CCSL	Corpus Christianorum: Series Latina

CEJL	Commentaries on Early Jewish Literature
CHANE	Culture and History of the Ancient Near East
CJAS	Christianity and Judaism in Antiquity Series
ClAnt	*Classical Antiquity*
CNI	Carsten Niebuhr Institut (Copenhagen)
CRINT	Compendia Rerum Iudaicarum ad Novum Testamentum
CSCO	Corpus Scriptorum Christianorum Orientalium
CSCT	Columbia Studies in the Classical Tradition
CSS	Cistercian Studies Series
CurBR	*Currents in Biblical Research*
DCL	Deuterocanonical and Cognate Literature Studies
DCLY	Deuterocanonical and Cognate Literature Yearbook
DDD	K. van der Toorn, B. Becking, and P. W. van der Horst (eds.), *Dictionary of Deities and Demons in the Bible*
DJD	Discoveries in the Judaean Desert
DSD	*Dead Sea Discoveries*
DT	*Defixionum Tabellae*
DTA	*Defixionum Tabellae Atticae*
EJL	Early Judaism and Its Literature
FRLANT	Forschungen zur Religion und Literatur des Alten und Neuen Testaments
GCS	Die griechischen christlichen Schriftsteller der ersten drei Jahrhunderte
GECS	Gorgias Eastern Christianity Studies
GNS	Good News Studies
HALOT	Koehler-Baumgarten-Stamm, *The Hebrew and Aramaic Lexicon of the Old Testament*
HdO	Handbuch der Orientalistik
HDR	Harvard Dissertations in Religion
HKAT	Handkommentar zum Alten Testament
HTR	*Harvard Theological Review*
HUCA	*Hebrew Union College Annual*
Hug	*Hugoye: Journal of Syriac Studies*
IAA	Israel Antiquities Authority
ICC	International Critical Commentary
Int	*Interpretation*
JAAR	*Journal of the American Academy of Religion*
JAJSup	Journal of Ancient Judaism Supplements
JBL	*Journal of Biblical Literature*

JCPS	*Jewish and Christian Perspectives Series*
JCT	*Jewish and Christian Texts*
JECS	*Journal of Early Christian Studies*
JH	*Jewish History*
JJS	*Journal of Jewish Studies*
JNES	*Journal of Near Eastern Studies*
JQR	*Jewish Quarterly Review*
JRS	*Journal of Roman Studies*
JSJ	*Journal for the Study of Judaism in the Persian, Hellenistic and Roman Period*
JSJSup	Supplements to the Journal for the Study of Judaism
JSNT	*Journal for the Study of the New Testament*
JSNTSup	Journal for the Study of the New Testament Supplements
JSOTSup	Journal for the Study of the Old Testament Supplements
JSP	*Journal for the Study of the Pseudepigrapha*
JSPSup	Supplements to the Journal for the Study of the Pseudepigrapha
JSS	*Journal of Semitic Studies*
JSSSup	Journal of Semitic Studies, Supplements
JTS	*Journal of Theological Studies*
KlT	Kleine Texte
LBS	Linguistic Biblical Studies
LCL	Loeb Classical Library
LNTS	Library of New Testament Studies
LSJ	Liddell-Scott-Jones, *A Greek-English Lexicon*
LSTS	Library of Second Temple Studies
MHNH	μήνη ("moon") series
MKS	Münchener kirchenhistorische Studien
MRLLA	Magical and Religious Literature of Late Antiquity
NHC	Nag Hammadi Codex
NHMS	Nag Hammadi and Manichaean Studies
NHS	Nag Hammadi Studies
NICNT	New International Commentary on the New Testament
NovT	*Novum Testamentum*
NovTSup	Novum Testamentum Supplements
NTGF	New Testament in the Greek Fathers
NTOA	Novum Testamentum et Orbis Antiquus
NTS	*New Testament Studies*
OECS	Oxford Early Christian Studies

Or	*Orientalia*
ORA	Orientalische Religionen in der Antike
OrChrAn	*Orientalia Christiana Analecta*
OTL	Old Testament Library
OTP	J. H. Charlesworth (ed.), *Old Testament Pseudepigrapha*
PG	J.-P. Migne (ed.), Patrologia Graeca
PGM	K. Preisendanz and A. Henrichs, *Papyrae Graecae Magicae*
PRSt	*Perspectives in Religious Studies*
PVTG	Pseudepigrapha Veteris Testamenti Graece
RAC	T. Klauser et al. (eds.), *Reallexikon für Antike und Christentum*
RB	*Revue biblique*
RevQ	*Revue de Qumrân*
RGA-E	*Das Reallexikon der Germanischen Altertumskunde—Ergänzungsbände zum Reallexikon*
RGRW	Religions in the Graeco-Roman World
RSR	*Recherches de science religieuse*
RSV	Revised Standard Version (of the Bible)
RSVA	Revised Standard Version Apocrypha
RVV	Religionsgeschichtliche Versuche und Vorarbeiten
SBL	Society of Biblical Literature
SBLDS	Society of Biblical Literature Dissertation Series
SBLEJL	Society of Biblical Literature Early Judaism and Its Literature
SBLSCS	Society of Biblical Literature Septuagint and Cognate Studies
SBLSP	Society of Biblical Literature Seminar Papers
SBLSymS	Society of Biblical Literature Symposium Series
SBLTT	Soceity of Biblical Literature Texts and Translations
SC	Sources chrétiennes
SE	*Studia Evangelica*
SEÅ	*Svensk exegetisk årsbok*
SEAug	Studia Ephemeridis Augustinianum
SecCent	*Second Century*
SEG	*Supplementum epigraphicum graecum*
SGD	*Survey of Greek Defixiones*
SJ	Studia Judaica
SNTSMS	Society for New Testament Studies Monograph Series
SSEJC	Studies in Scripture in Early Judaism and Christianity
SSS	Semitic Study Series

STAC	Studien und Texte zu Antike und Christentum
StPB	Studia Post-biblica
STDJ	Studies on the Texts of the Desert of Judah
StPatr	*Studia Patristica*
StT	Studi e testi
SUNT	Studien zur Umwelt des Neuen Testaments
SVTP	Studia in Veteris Testamenti Pseudepigraphica
SVTQ	*St. Vladimir's Theological Quarterly*
TA	Theologische Akzente
TBN	Themes in Biblical Narrative
TENTS	Texts and editions for New Testament Study
TSAJ	Texte und Studien zum antiken Judentum
TSMJ	Texts and Studies in Medieval and Early Modern Judaism
TUAT	Texte aus der Umwelt des Alten Testaments
TUGAL	Texte und Untersuchungen zur Geschichte der altchristlichen Literatur
UF	*Ugarit-Forschungen*
UTB	Uni-Taschenbuch
VC	*Vigiliae Christianae*
VCSup	Vigiliae Christianae Supplements
VT	*Vetus Testamentum*
VTP	Veteris Testamenti Pseudepigrapha
VTSup	Vetus Testamentum Supplements
WBC	Word Biblical Commentary
WUNT	Wissenschaftliche Untersuchungen zum Neuen Testament
ZAC	*Zeitschrift für antikes Christentum*
ZDPV	*Zeitschrift des deutschen Palästina-Vereins*
ZMKA	*Zetemata: Monographien zur klassischen Altertumswissenschaft*
ZNW	*Zeitschrift für die neutestamentliche Wissenschaft*
ZPE	*Zeitschrift für Papyrologie und Epigraphik*
ZWT	*Zeitschrift für wissenschaftliche Theologie*

CONTRIBUTORS

Christopher S. Atkins	Yale University
Torleif Elgvin	NLA University College, Oslo
Craig A. Evans	Houston Baptist University
John Garza	Fordham University
Matthias R. Hoffmann	Carl von Ossietzky Universität Oldenburg, Germany
Blake A. Jurgens	Florida State University
Brian LePort	TMI Episcopal, San Antonio
Benjamin J. Lappenga	Formerly Associate Professor of New Testament at Dordt University
Jesse P. Nickel	Columbia Bible College
Bradley N. Rice	McGill University
Paul T. Sloan	Houston Baptist University
Tim Wardle	Furman University

INTRODUCING BIBLICAL THEMES AND TRADITIONS
IN THE PSEUDEPIGRAPHA

The chapters in the first part of the present volume focus on how sacred tradition is expanded in some of the extra-canonical writings, usually associated with the somewhat amorphous collection known as the Pseudepigrapha. The unifying feature of these studies is vision, or revelation. Torleif Elgvin reviews the intriguing history, or legacy, of "Solomon the sage" from Qohelet to Josephus. Along the way he looks at 1 Maccabeees, *Psalms of Solomon*, Wisdom of Solomon, and Qumran's Canticle Scrolls, among others. Elgvin finds that the legacy of Solomon was viewed from different perspectives. Indeed the sectarian texts of Qumran hold the famous monarch at arm's length, perhaps because of his exploitation in pro-Hasmonean literature. Blake Jurgens extends the discussion in his analysis of Solomon in the *Testament of Solomon*. Jurgens views the *Testament* as a Christian pseudepigraphic narrative. He undertakes an original investigation of the erotic element in the text's demonology by offering a comparison with the literature associated with Egyptian monasticism (with special attention given John Cassian). From this comparison Jurgens thinks the *Testament of Solomon* should not be dated earlier than the third century CE and that its place of origin could well have been Egypt.

Bradley Rice explores the possibility of a link between the *Testament of Adam to Seth* and the recently discovered and published *Revelation of the Magi*. Rice concludes that the *Testament* at one time circulated as a composition in its own right, probably composed in Syriac sometime between the second and fourth centuries and then later incorporated into the *Revelation*, which was itself later incorporated into the *Chronicle of Zuqnin*. Christopher Atkins concludes the first part with an chapter that investigates in what ways the *Shepherd of Hermas* was utilized by Clement of Alexandria. Atkins notes that in contrast to other contemporary Fathers (such as Irenaeus), Clement quotes and alludes to all three major sections of *Hermas*. Atkins concludes that whereas Irenaeus accords some authority to *Hermas*, Clement seems to accord a greater degree of authority to this work, probably because of its visions said to have been given by divine "powers."

The chapters of the second part focus more narrowly on themes of polemic and violence in the Pseudepigrapha. The violence envisioned in these works could be temporal, or it could be eschatological. Benjamin Lappenga investigates the alternating themes of violence and divine favor in the *Liber Antiquitatum Biblicarum*. The author of this work, usually called Pseudo-Philo, engages in narrative retelling to understand, perhaps even justify, God's actions. Lappenga finds that Pseudo-Philo's retellings are crafted to avoid facile propositions in favor of invitations to close and careful readings that open the reader to new patterns of living. John Garza focuses on the *Animal Apocalypse* imbedded in the book of Enoch (= *1 Enoch* 85-90). He argues that this apocalyptic material uses the interplay between sight and blindness to create an expectation of deliverance that, though initially fulfilled in the Exodus, only finds fulfillment in the Hasmonean-led revolt.

According to Tim Wardle the second century BCE proved a pivotal one in the relationship between Jews and Samaritans. Following a discussion of the Jewish and Samaritan temples and John Hyrcanus' destruction of the Samaritan temple on Mount Gerizim, his paper explores the rising Jewish polemic directed against Samaritans in Jewish literature from the second and first centuries BCE, how this polemical rhetoric served to first create and then reinforce the political realities of separateness between Jews and Samaritans, and the manner in which rhetoric can give birth to violence in the right circumstances.

Jesse P. Nickel explores an important element of typology in Qumran's *War Scroll*. He believes this text understands Israel's future in light of Israel's past. Israel's enemies will hold to the same misguided assumptions they entertained long ago, completely underestimating the power of Israel's God. Nickel also takes into account Josephus' critique of the Jewish revolt in his day, in which in his speech outside the walls of Jerusalem, he offers the Jewish people an alternative interpretation of Israel's past. Craig Evans investigates the origin and meaning of Gehenna, especially as it relates to the last two verses of Isaiah (i.e., Isa 66:23-24). Evans believes that Isaiah's graphic imagery of undying worm and unquenchable fire, which probably dates to about 200 CE, was a major contributor to the emergence of the concept of fiery Gehenna, the place where the wicked will suffer punishment.

The volume concludes with Matthias Hoffmann's interesting study of violence and the magic tradition. He notes the reciprocity of violence in magic, in which practitioners of magic were often violently attacked and in which the magic itself was sometimes used to inflict violence against others. Hoffmann adds that even prayers for vengeance against enemies or persecutors could be seen as examples of violence (or at least hoped for violence).

Part I

EXPANDED AND VISIONARY TRADITION
IN THE PSEUDEPIGRAPHA

Chapter 1

THE LEGACY OF SOLOMON THE SAGE FROM QOHELET TO JOSEPHUS

Torleif Elgvin

Solomon from Qohelet to the Hasmoneans

During most of biblical history, Solomon remained in the shadow of his father. The expected ideal king, whether close at hand or far into the future, would be a "son of David." During the growth and growing-together of psalm scrolls during the post-exilic period, one can observe a growing Davidization of the Psalter.[1] Solomon remains as originator or honoree of one psalm only, the royal-messianic Ps 72, and as the unnamed king in the wedding scene of Ps 45:11-16, preceded

---

[1] On the importance of the David tradition in the structuring of the Book of Psalms, see Bernard Gosse, *David and Abraham. Persian Period Traditions*. SupTranseuphratène 16 (Pendé: Gabalda, 2010), 73–118, 195–9; idem, *L'espérance messianique davidique et la structuration du Psautier*. SupTranseuphratène 21 (Pendé: Gabalda, 2015), 137. By 130 BCE, the prologue to Ben Sira lists "the Law and the Prophets and the others that followed them," with no mention of "David." However, the early-first-century translation of 151 psalms into Greek would show that the collection then had reached it full size, and that the Davidic Psalter was considered among the important books of the fathers. Slightly later, the conclusion of the halakḥic letter from Qumran includes the Davidic Psalter among the books of authority: " … the book of Moses [and] the books[of the p]rophets and Davi[d and the books of events] of ages past" (4QMMT, C 10-11, the last group may refer to Joshua–Kings). The following factors suggest a first-century dating for MMT: (1) the manuscripts are early- or mid-Herodian; (2) "sacrifice for the gentiles" in the temple (B 8) primarily makes sense in the early Roman period (63–37 BCE); (3) the language of MMT is the closest we come to Mishnaic Hebrew among Qumran writings: Shlomo Morag, "Language and Style in Miqsat Maase Ha-Torah: Did Moreh ha-Sedeq Write this Document?" (in Hebrew), *Tarbiz* 65 (1996): 209–23.

by a court poet's lofty address to the king (vv. 2-10).² In Ptolemaic times, when a mighty king ruled from Egypt, Solomon would appear from the shadows—in the book of Qohelet, chapters 1-2 play on Solomon's memory without mentioning his name.

By the early second century, Ben Sira remembered Solomon for his wealth, his wisdom, and his relationships with women. The latter had led him away from the right path and brought judgment and division upon the kingdom (Sir 47:12-22). Verses 14-17 attribute wisdom and understanding to Solomon, the originator of songs (ᾠδαῖς), proverbs, parables, and explanations. The Book of Proverbs is definitely in view, but it is questionable whether these verses also relate to Qohelet. Solomon is remembered as a songster in 1 Kgs 4:32, with 1,005 songs ascribed to him. The ᾠδαῖς of Sir 47 refer to these traditions. The love songs of Canticles are not remembered, which indicates that the Song of Songs was not written by 190 BCE—noted by A. Th. Hartmann in his brilliant 1829 article on the Song of Songs.³

Ben Sira gives his perspective from Seleucid Jerusalem, a small town in the tiny province of Yehud. Priesthood and temple play a significant role in his Jerusalem, both in the present and in hope for the future. The Davidic line is less important.⁴ Ben Sira's eschatological poem about Zion (36:1-19) does not mention a Davidic ruler at all, only the coming renewal of Jerusalem and the temple. The same is true for the concluding Zion hymn in the contemporary book of Tobit (13:8-17).

---

² In Ps 72, vv. 8–11, 15, 17b are likely post-exilic "messianic" additions to a pre-exilic royal psalm. The superscript לִשְׁלֹמֹה was added in a late redaction. The Greek rendering, Εἰς Σαλωμων, may be read as "on Solomon." Seen together with the concluding colophon, "End of the prayers of David, son of Jesse," it suggests that the psalm then was read as a prayer by David for his son: Frank-Lothar Hossfeld and Erich Zenger, *Psalms 2: A Commentary on Psalms 51–100* (Minneapolis: Fortress, 2005), 207–8, 211, 219. The wedding scene of Ps 45:11-16 is a post-exilic extension of the preceding court scene, inspired by the legacy of Solomon. Juxtaposed with the wedding scene, Solomon would also be the king addressed in vv. 2–10. Cf. Frank-Lothar Hossfeld and Erich Zenger, *Die Psalmen I* (Würzburg: Echter, 1993), 278–9.

³ "Und nun klärt sich auch auf, warum das Buch Sirach, welches das Lob des gefeierten Israelitischen Königes Kap. 47, 12 ff. mit den glänzendsten Farben ausmahlt, zwar V. 17. vgl. mit K. 39,2.3 der Sprüchwörter, Denksprüche und Räthsel gedenkt die Salomo's Ruhm verkündigen, aber über das reizende Lied der Liebe das tiefste Stillschweigen beobachtet": A. Th. Hartmann, "Über Charakter und Auslegung des Hohenliedes," *ZWT* 3 (1829): 397–448 (437). Hartmann dated Canticles to the early Hasmonean period.

⁴ Sir 50:1-4 portrays the high priest Simon acting as the leader of the people. Cf. William Horbury, *Messianism among Jews and Christians. Biblical and Historical Studies* (London: T&T Clark, 2003), 43–50. According to Sir 45:24-26, the covenant with Aaron is greater than that with David. The Hebrew version of v. 25 limits the Davidic promise to Solomon, while the covenant with Aaron is lasting: "And there is also a covenant with David, son of Isai, from the tribe of Judah; the inheritance of a man [i.e., David] is to his son alone, the inheritance of Aaron is also to his seed" (MS B, translation Horbury); Greek "an inheritance

1. The Legacy of Solomon the Sage

Solomon would play different roles in the subsequent centuries. Many perspectives changed with the Hasmoneans coming to power and the rapid expansion of Judea under Hyrcanus, with a renewed interest in David and Solomon coming to the surface. The Hasmonean state expanded significantly in the north, east, and south between 130 and 85 BCE,[5] the military conquests of John Hyrcanus (135–105 BCE), Aristobulus (105–104 BCE), and Alexander Yanneus (103–76 BCE) creating an Israelite state that would match the biblical accounts of David and Solomon's kingdom (cf. Figure 1.1). According to historians and archeologists, the new state by far superseded the entity ruled by David and Solomon or the combined ninth-century northern and southern kingdoms.

With a priestly dynasty coming to power in Judea, both pro-Hasmonean and anti-Hasmonean circles could call upon the son of David *par excellence* in support for their cause. Scribal allies of the Hasmoneans would see the rapid expansion of Judea as a fulfillment of biblical prophecies and a re-establishment of the legendary Solomonic kingdom of the Bible. In contrast, critical circles such as the *Yahad* would challenge the Hasmonean merging of priestly and royal power, evident, for example, in 4QTestimonia, which foresees the coming of a priestly, a royal, and a prophetic figure. Writings or collections as different as Canticles, the *Psalms of Solomon*, and the Wisdom of Solomon ended up carrying the name of the famous king.

1 Maccabees: The Hasmonean Dynasty in the Image of David and Solomon

One would expect a new priestly dynasty to seek legitimation by appealing both to priestly prerogatives and to David and Solomon. And this is what we find in 1 Maccabees, our prime example of pro-Hasmonean apologetics.

The Hasmoneans are declared elect deliverers of the Judean nation. "By their hand was deliverance given to Israel" (1 Macc 5:62, an echo of 2 Sam 2:17, in which deliverance is entrusted to David). By their deeds, they have established themselves as rulers and legitimate high priests of Israel. 1 Macc 2:24-28 sets Phinehas' zeal for the purity of Israel as a paradigmatic ideal. By repeating the deeds of "Phinehas our father" (2:54), Mattathias and his sons earn God's favor: "and

---

of the king for son from son only." The panegyric praise of Simon in chapter 50 hardly allows for a Davidic ruler alongside the priest. However, the section on David and Solomon in Ben Sira's praise of the fathers could suggest a possible future fulfillment of Davidic promises: "The Lord … exalted his [i.e., David's] horn forever; he gave him a royal covenant and a glorious throne in Israel … But the Lord would not go back on his mercy, or undo any of his words, he would not obliterate the issue of his elect, nor destroy the stock of the man who loved him; and he granted a remnant to Jacob, and to David a root springing from him" (Sir 47:11, 22).

[5] Josephus, *Ant.* 13.256-258; 13.318-319; 13.395-397; *J.W.* 1.63.

Figure 1.1 The growth of the Hasmonean State.

he became zealous in the law as Phinehas had done" (2:26). The covenant of Phinehas, which gave legitimacy to the high priesthood of the house of Zadok, is superseded by the new covenant with the house of the Hasmoneans.[6] Through

---

[6] John J. Collins, "The Zeal of Phinehas, the Bible, and the Legitimation of Violence," *JBL* 122 (2003): 3–22, esp. 12–13.

their actions, the Maccabees restored the righteousness and independence of Israel.

Appealing to Solomon the temple builder would make sense in the generations following the rededication of the temple in 164 BCE. The Hasmonean building projects in Jerusalem (1 Macc 10:10-11; 12:36; 13:52; 14:10), which included renovation of the extended Temple Mount platform,[7] may have amplified the "messianic" connotations associated with the early Hasmonean rulers and drawn renewed attention to the temple and its builder. Later, the rapid expansion of the Hasmonean state and its capital under Hyrcanus would serve as an appropriate context for adducing Solomon as the ideal and *typos* for the ruling dynasty (cf. Figure 1.2).

The powers the Judean assembly gave to Simon around 140 BCE authorize the dual office of the new dynasty:

τοῦ εἶναι αὐτῶν Σιμωνα ἡγούμενον καὶ ἀρχιερέα εἰς τὸν αἰῶνα ἕως τοῦ ἀναστῆναι προφήτην πιστόν, "Simon should be their leader and high priest forever until a trustworthy prophet should arise." (1 Macc 14:41 [my translation])

The words ἀρχιερέα εἰς τὸν αἰῶνα echo the royal/messianic Psalm 110, σὺ εἶ ἱερεὺς εἰς τὸν αἰῶνα κατὰ τὴν τάξιν Μελχισεδεκ (Ps 110:4=109:4𝔊).

Two poetic eulogies honoring respectively Judah Maccabee and Simon after their death (1 Macc 3:3-9; 14:4-15) evince that Hasmonean rulers used David and Solomon as *typoi* as part of their attempt to legitimize their rule, regarding themselves as the heirs of David and Solomon, the son of David *par excellence*.[8] These poems may predate the composition of 1 Maccabees (in the 120s BCE), as their poetic form stands out from the context. The two passages contain recurring key words taken from various messianic passages, including Gen 49:9; 1 Sam 17:5, 38; 1 Kgs 5:3-5; 8:13; Isa 11:4; Mic 4:4; 5:3-5; Zech 9:10; and Ps 2:10; 45:18[17]; 72:4, 17-19; 110:5-6.

The declarations that "his memory will be a blessing for ever" and "his name was known to the ends of the earth" (1 Macc 3:7, 9) recall the Solomonic Ps 72: "May he have dominion from sea to sea, and from the River to the ends of the earth" (v. 8); "May his name endure forever, his fame continue as long as the sun. May all nations be blessed in him" (v. 17). When Simon made Jaffa "an entrance way to the islands of the sea ... and widened the borders of his nation" (1 Macc 14:5-6), he fulfilled prophecies according to which the future Davidic rule would

---

[7] Torleif Elgvin, *The Literary Growth of the Song of Songs during the Hasmonean and Early-Herodian Periods*, CBET 89 (Leuven: Peeters, 2018), 125–7.

[8] See my more detailed argument in "Texts on Messianic Reign from the Hasmonean Period: 4Q521 as Interpretation of Daniel 7," in L. Grabbe and G. Boccaccini (eds.), *The Seleucid and Hasmonean Periods and the Apocalyptic Worldview* (London: Bloomsbury T&T Clark, 2016), 169–78; and "Violence, Apologetics, and Resistance," in Kipp Davis et al. (eds.), *The War Scroll, Violence, War and Peace in the Dead Sea Scrolls and Related Literature*, STDJ 115 (Leiden: Brill, 2016), 319–40, 325–7.

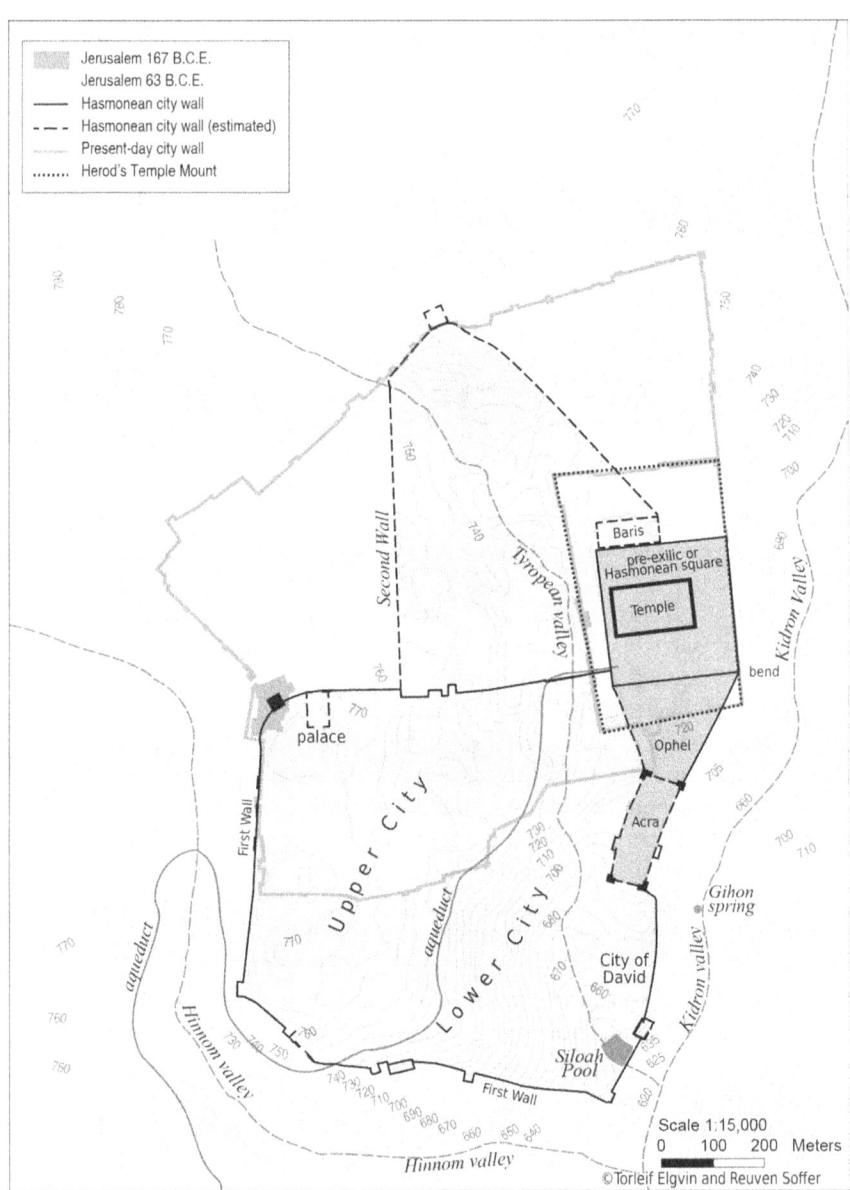

Figure 1.2 The growth of Hasmonean Jerusalem.

reach "from the sea to the sea" (Ps 72:8) and "from the River to the sea" (Zech 9:10; cf. Ps 89:26[25]). The notations "they were farming their land in peace," "everyone sat under their own vine and their own fig tree," and "he made peace in the land" (1 Macc 14:8, 11, 12) allude to Mic 4:4—"they shall all sit under their own vines and under their own fig trees, and no one shall make them afraid"—and the Davidic prophecy of Mic 5:4-5: "And they shall live secure, for he shall be great to the borders of the land; and he is peace."

The statement, "Anyone fighting them disappeared in the land, and the kings were crushed in those days" (1 Macc 14:13), recalls Ps 2:9, "You shall break them with a rod of iron, and dash them in pieces like a potter's vessel," and 110:2, 5, "Rule in the midst of your foes … The Lord is at your right hand, he will shatter kings on the day of his wrath." The statement, "he supported all the humble among his people" (1 Macc 14:14), alludes to Isa 11:4, "with righteousness he shall judge the poor, and decide with equity for the meek of the earth." Simon's glorification of the holy places and multiplication of the vessels therein (1 Macc 14:15) calls to mind David's instructions to Solomon regarding the temple equipment in 1 Chr 28:11-18, Solomon's dedication of the temple, and the listing of the temple vessels in Ezra 1:7-10.

In these passages the anointed priestly rulers are hailed as quasi-messiahs, having partially fulfilled Davidic prophecies and others relating to the days of salvation. One could talk of a combined present and future eschatology—salvation has come to Israel (1 Macc 5:62), God has sent anointed successors of David and Solomon, although the final redemption, and the human tools God will then send to his people, still lies in the future (cf. the clause "until a trustworthy prophet should arise," 1 Macc 14:41).

The Psalms of Solomon: *A Dissident Community Calling upon Solomon*

The first-century BCE collection the *Psalms of Solomon* represents a community critical of the luxurious and lascivious lifestyle of the Hasmonean rulers.[9] The community included deposed priests and dissident scribes. Prayer and fasting are seen as a means of atonement, which led earlier scholars to link the community to Pharisaic circles.[10] Most of the psalms are written in the years following the Roman takeover of Judea in 63 BCE.[11] Only two of the psalms (*Pss. Sol.* 17:4-6,

---

[9] See the various contributions in E. Bons and P. Pouchelle (eds.), *The Psalms of Solomon: Language, History, Theology* (Atlanta: Society of Biblical Literature, 2015).

[10] Rodney A. Werline, "The Psalms of Solomon and the Ideology of Rule," in L. M. Wills and B. G. Wright (eds.), *Conflicted Boundaries in Wisdom and Apocalypticism*, SBLSymS 35 (Atlanta: Society of Biblical Literature, 2005), 69–88; Kenneth Atkinson, "Perception of the Temple Priests in the Psalms of Solomon," in *Psalms of Solomon: Language, History, Theology*, 79–96.

[11] The text is preserved in Greek and Syriac. J. Joosten has challenged the traditional view of a Hebrew original, arguing that the psalms were written in a style of Greek heavily influenced by the LXX by a Judean author with connections to the diaspora: "Reflections on the Original Language of the Psalms of Solomon," *Psalms of Solomon. Language, History, Theology*, 31–47. In his response, Kenneth Atkinson maintains that a Hebrew *Vorlage* best explains some of the linguistic features, while some passages probably were written in Greek: *Psalms of Solomon. Language, History, Theology*, 177–81.

21-46; 18:1-9) describe and praise the Davidic messiah, so it is noteworthy that the full collection ended up carrying Solomon's name. Apart from the first psalm, all the others carry Solomon's name in the superscription, mostly as "A psalm of Solomon," ψαλμὸς τῷ Σαλωμων (a translation of מזמור לשלמה).[12] As liturgical texts, the psalms were formative community texts with transformative power upon the individual.[13]

The contents of *Pss. Sol.* 1-16 by itself hardly call for an ascription to Solomon. However, Jerusalem is in focus in a number of the psalms: *Pss. Sol.* 1, 2, 7, and 8 deplore the sins and impure deeds of the city's inhabitants, priests, and leaders. Some verses lament the impurity and destiny of the Temple (1:8; 2:2-3, 19-21; 7:1; 8:11-12, 22). *Pss. Sol.* 9:1-2 sees Israel's sins as cause for the exile—a destiny foreseen by Solomon at the dedication of the Temple (1 Kgs 8:46-52). In contrast, in hymnic phrases reminiscent of Second Isaiah, *Pss. Sol.* 11 describes the return of the dispersed Israelites from the north, east, and west to Zion, probably referring to the influx of Judean immigrants into the Hasmonean kingdom in the early first century BCE. Different from other psalms in the collection, this hymn does not signal any criticism of the Jewish rulers of the land.

The full collection opens with two Jerusalem laments and concludes with two Davidic-messianic hymns. Thus, the framing of the collection could invite an ascription to Solomon, the temple builder and son of David *par excellence*. The ascription of the individual psalms and the full collection to Solomon should not be read in any authorial sense; the allusions and references to Hasmonean rulers and Pompey show that many psalms present themselves as testimonies of the first century BCE. τῷ Σαλωμων/לשלמה should be read as "of Solomon." The ascription to Solomon of a collection with many Hasmonean-critical passages may be a silent protest against Hasmonean use of Solomon as *typos* for their rule and dynasty. Brad Embry suggests that an author with a prophetic self-understanding utilized the image of Solomon as a prophetic figure to convey his vision of a Davidic restoration of Israel.[14]

The two last psalms describe and praise the Davidic messiah (17:4, 21-46; 18:1-9). After a proclamation of the covenant with David, *Pss. Sol.* 17 continues with God's judgment on the Hasmoneans by the hand of Pompey.

⁴Lord, you chose David to be king over Israel

---

[12] *Pss. Sol.* 2, 3, 5, 13, 15, 17, 18 are designated ψαλμος, and 10, 14, and 16 υμνος.

[13] Atkinson, "Perception of the Temple Priests," 93–6; Rodney A. Werline, "The Formation of the Pious Person in the Psalms of Solomon," in *Psalms of Solomon. Language, History, Theology*, 133–54.

[14] Brad Embry, "Some Thoughts on and Implications from Genre Categorization in the Psalms of Solomon," in *Psalms of Solomon. Language, History, Theology*, 59–78, p. 63 n. 7; cf. idem, "Solomon's Name as a Prophetic Hallmark in Jewish and Christian Texts," *Henoch* 28 (2006): 47–62.

and swore to him about his descendants forever,
that his kingdom should not fail before you.
⁵Those to whom you did not make a promise they took away by force,
those who had not honored your glorious name.
⁶With pomp they had set up a haughty monarchy,
they despoiled the throne of David with arrogant shouting.
⁷But you, O God, overthrew them, and uprooted their descendants from the earth, for against them rose a man from the nations …
⁹According to their deeds, God showed no mercy to them,
he hunted down their descendants and did not let even one of them go.

The psalm then continues with a lament of the decay under the last Hasmonean rulers, and concludes with a long messianic hymn.

Some passages in the *Psalms of Solomon* can be contrasted with another late second temple collection, the Song of Songs, a composition to which we will return below. Some passages may constitute a negative mirror of lascivious scenes depicted in Canticles:

They set up the sons of Jerusalem for derision because of her prostitutes.
Everyone passing by entered in broad daylight …

And the daughters of Jerusalem[15] were available to all because they defiled themselves with improper intercourse (2:11, 13).

His eyes are on every woman indiscriminately …
With his eyes he speaks to every woman of illicit
affairs (4:4, 5).

In secret places underground was their
provoking lawbreaking, Son involved with
mother and father with daughter,
everyone committed adultery with his neighbor's wife (8:9-10).

Restrain me, O God, from sordid sin, and from every evil woman who seduces the foolish.
And may the beauty of a criminal woman not deceive me,
nor anyone subject to useless sin (16:7-8).

The Wisdom of Solomon

The Greek Wisdom of Solomon (Egypt, C1 BCE) demonstrates that also diaspora Jews could attribute a sapiential composition to the legendary king. In chapters

---

[15] The designation "daughters of Jerusalem" recurs in Canticles.

1–6 and 11–19, the book presents itself as a parenetic book on wisdom from above and the ways of the righteous and ungodly, with chapters 11–19 being formed as a parenetic midrash on the Exodus.

Lady Wisdom, residing at God's side, is portrayed in 1:4; 6:12-24; 7:22–11:4. The righteous are exhorted to partner with the divine Wisdom. Wis 6:1-25 (cf. 1:1) is an exhortation to kings and rulers, to partner with Wisdom and follow her advice. The teacher of this passage does not cloth himself in a royal robe. But following this exhortation to kings, Solomon enters the scene. Chapter 8 employs language that recalls the sensuality of Ben Sira's love poem to Lady Wisdom (Sir 51:13-21; cf. the more sensual version in 11QPs[a]) and the Song of Songs. Solomon is the speaker.

> [Wisdom] reaches mightily from one end of the
> earth to the other, and she orders all things well.
>
> I loved her and sought her from my youth;
> I desired to take her for my bride and became enamored of her beauty.
> She glorifies her noble birth by living with God, and the Lord of all loves her.
>
> For she is an initiate in the knowledge of God
> and an associate in his works. (8:1-4)
> I determined then to take her to live with me,
> knowing that she would be a good
> counselor for me and a comfort in
> cares and grief.
> Because of her, I will have glory among the multitudes and honor in the presence of elders, although I am young (8:9-10)
> When I enter my house, I will find rest with her,
> for companionship with her has no bitterness, and living with her no grief,
> rather gladness and joy.
> When I considered these things in myself and
> pondered in my heart that in kinship with wisdom
> is immortality
> and in friendship with her pure delight and in the labors of her hands unfailing wealth
> and in training in intimate companionship with her
> understanding and great renown in conversing with her,
> I went about seeking how I might
> take her to myself. I was a naturally
> clever child, and I obtained a good
> soul as my lot, or rather, being good,
> I entered an undefiled body.
> But knowing that I would not otherwise gain
> possession of her unless God gave her to me …
> (8:16-21)

In chapters 7–9 (and only here), the pseudepigraphic foil is carried fully through: here Solomon (his name not mentioned) speaks in the first person as originator of chapters 6–9 (or 6–10), closely echoing passages from 1 Kings. Indeed, among sages from the Hebrew Bible Solomon would be the ideal candidate to authorize a book on divinely given wisdom.

Without its superscription the full book does not present itself clearly as written by or originating with Solomon; it does not open with his name or allusions to him as do Proverbs and the final recension of Canticles (see below). The "royal chapters" 6–9, 10 bridge the instruction of chapters 1–5 with the midrashic exhortation of chapters 11–19. With its admonition to walk with Wisdom and the presence of chapters devoted to Solomon, the book would easily invite a superscription that made Solomon the originator of the book as such. However, we do not know how early the superscription σοφια σαλωμωνος, present (with slight variation) in the LXX codices, was added.

The Song of Songs: A Collection of Love Songs from Hasmonean Jerusalem

The Territory and Culture of Hasmonean Judea

In a recent monograph I demonstrate how a number of features of the Song of Songs are easier understood during the Hasmonean reign than in any previous period.[16] The urban culture of Hasmonean Jerusalem, which for the first time in history could be called a cosmopolitan city, allowed for more open gender relations than possible in the closely controlled environment in which young girls lived in rural contexts and more ancient Israelite society. The songs of Canticles reflect the culture of this cosmopolitan and Hellenistically influenced Jerusalem, with scribes well versed in both Hebrew and Greek literature.[17]

The singers and editors represented in this collection stand at a distance from both the Hasmonean establishment and the circles behind the *Psalms of Solomon*.[18] Heinevetter argues that Canticles exhibits an editorial *Tendenz*

---

[16] Elgvin, *Literary Growth*. For an update and detailed investigation of the literary growth, see T. Elgvin, "Chasing the Hasmonean and Herodian Editors of the Song of Songs," in Pierre Van Hecke (ed.), *The Song of Songs in Its Context. Words for Love, Love for Words*. BETL 310 (Leuven: Peeters, 2020), 71–98.

[17] Already Heinrich Graetz (*Schir Ha-Schirim oder das salomonische Hohelied* [Wien: Braumüller, 1871], 68–73) demonstrated the influence of Theocritus' pastoral poetry on Canticles.

[18] Michael V. Fox posits a milieu at some distance from the wealthy upper class: "The young people themselves do not live in special luxury, and most of the valuable items referred to in the Song are mentioned only for the sake of comparison and not as the property of the lovers": *Song of Songs and the Ancient Egyptian Love Songs* (Madison, Wisconsin: University of Wisconsin Press, 1985), 187.

critical of the (imagined) customs prevalent in Solomon's court.[19] Such a critique may constitute a covert condemnation of the top echelon of the Hasmonean "Solomonic" dynasty and Yanneus' luxurious lifestyle and dictatorial policies (cf. 3:7-11; 8:11-12).[20]

Hasmonean and Herodian Jerusalem came to be surrounded by a circle of agricultural villages at a 4–6-km distance, supporting the needs of the city.[21] The gardens, orchards, and vineyards described in Canticles best relate to these settlements that grew and flourished as Hasmonean Jerusalem expanded, cf., in particular Cant 7:12-13, "Come, my lover, let us go forth into the fields and lodge in the villages, let us go out early to the vineyards."[22]

Toponyms refer to Israelite sites that for the first time in centuries are under Judean rule (Sharon [2:1], Tirza [6:4], and Heshbon [7:5]). The reference to Hermon, Amana, and Senir (4:8) is easily understood in the light of the Hasmonean presence in the Galilee and Golan, the snow-topped Mount Hermon being the crown of the north. The hills of Gilead (4:1) came into close sight when Hyrcanus conquered Scythopolis in 108 BCE. Subsequently, Gilead and Carmel (7:6) were incorporated in Judea for a brief time period under Yanneus (cf. Figure 1.1).

With large territories conquered and settled by Judeans, the presence in old biblical lands could easily lead to the "land romanticism" reflected in many songs. The "vineyards of Ein Gedi" (1:14) and "the garden with beds of spices" (6:2) point to the terraces and intensive agricultural farming developing there after Hyrcanus' conquest of Idumea in 107 BCE.[23] The well-watered fruit and spice garden described in 4:13-15 also fits Hasmonean Ein Gedi more than any other location: "Your trees—an orchard of pomegranates with choice fruits, henna with nard. Ye, nard and saffron, calamus and cinnamon, with all the trees of

---

[19] Hans-Josef Heinevetter, "Komm nun, mein Liebster, dein Garten ruft dich!" *Das Hohelied als programmatische Komposition* (Athenäums Monografien; Königstein im Taunus: Athenäum, 1988). He notes the contrast in 3:6-11 between the mythical description of the maiden and the critical attitude evident toward Solomon's court: "Während mit der Frau Attribute des Heiligen verbunden wurden, steht der beschriebene Prunk Salomos hier eher für eine gewisse dekadente Überfeinerung" (113).

[20] Cf. *Ant.* 13:380: while feasting with his concubines in Jerusalem, Yanneus crucified 800 of his opponents.

[21] David Amit, "Remains of Jewish Settlements from the Second Temple Period near Teddy Stadium, Jerusalem," *Eretz-Israel* 28 (2007): 152–8.

[22] I translate the repeated דודי as "my lover" and דודים as "lovemaking" (1:2; 4:10; 5:1-4; 7:13). Ezek 16:8, 17; 23:17; Prov 7:18 evince that דודים means "lovemaking" rather than "love" as usually translated. Ehrlich notes, "דוד (kann) nur heissen Freund in erotischen Sinne": Arnold B. Ehrlich, *Randglossen zum Alten Testament. Textkritisches, Sprachliches und Sachliches*. vol. 7. (Hildesheim: Georg Olms Verlagsbuchhandlung, 1914), 11. Fox concurs, for stylistic reasons he translates דודים as "caresses" (*Song of Songs*, 97, 313).

[23] Yizhar Hirschfeld, *En-Gedi Excavations II. Final Report (1996–2002)* (Jerusalem: Israel Exploration Society, 2007), 9–11.

fragrance, myrrh and aloes, with all the best spices—there is a fountain that feeds orchards, a well of living water, flowing streams of Lebanon."

The praise of the "pools of Heshbon" only gave meaning after 60 BCE, when Heshbon developed into a town. Becoming part of Judea around 129 BCE, Heshbon remained a tiny settlement until the early Roman period—according to the archeologists there were no pools in Heshbon between the seventh and the first century.[24] The frequent mention of Jerusalem (eight times) may reflect the rapid growth of Jerusalem during the Hasmonean period (from around 1,000 to 6,000 inhabitants, cf. Figure 1.2).[25]

I have postulated a gradual literary growth of this collection of love songs throughout the first century BCE, followed by an ultimate "Solomonization" of the final product around the turn of the era. To understand these processes a study of the Qumran Canticles scrolls is necessary.

The Qumran Canticles Scrolls

A careful study of the Canticles scrolls on the Leon Levy website, and digital microscopic images made in the IAA scrollery have revealed a large number of previously unnoticed textual variants. Many of these represent *lectiones difficiliores* compared to 𝔐, and likely belong to pre-𝔐 stages of the collection(s) that ended up as the Solomonic Song of Songs. Further, two of the scrolls preserve short recensions that represent specific stages in the literary growth of Canticles.

4QCant^b is a somewhat sloppy scroll, paleographically dated to around 30 BCE, which from the outset had four columns only. The physical form of the fragments allows for a reconstruction of the circumventions and rolling of this scroll, which opened in 2:9b (with a variant text) and ended in 5:1, in fact preserving one of the larger literary subsections that scholars since Herder (1778) have recognized within the Song of Songs.[26] Col. I was a single sheet ca. 11-cm wide, with skin of

---

[24] Paul J. Ray, *Tell Hesban and Vicinity in the Iron Age* (Berrien Springs, MI: Andrews University Press, 2001), 98–100, 107, 123, 130–4, 168. During the late Hellenistic period (198–63 BCE) the large Iron Age II reservoir was filled in and used as a dump, the village thus having no pools during these years. See David Merling, "The 'Pools of Heshbon': As Discovered by the Heshbon Expedition," in D. Merling and L. T. Geraty (eds.), *Hesban after 25 Years* (Berrien Springs, MI: Andrews University, 1994), 211–23 (215–16). Two huge pools were subsequently constructed in the wadis east and west of the settlement, probably during the early-Roman period (oral communication from the excavator Oystein LaBianca).

[25] Hillel Geva, "Estimating Jerusalem's Population in Antiquity: A Minimalist View" (in Hebrew), *Eretz-Israel* 28 (2007): 50–65; idem, "Jerusalem in the Light of Archaeology – Notes on Urban Topography" (in Hebrew), *Eretz-Israel* 31 (2015): 57–75, 184*.

[26] Heinevetter identifies 2:8-5:1 as a separate section (*Kleinsammlung*) divided into subsections (2:8-17, 3:1-5, 3:6-11, 4:1-7, 4:8-5:1), 5:1b appearing to be a *conclusio* (*Schlusswort*).

better quality than the following sheet. There were fifteen lines in col. I, twelve lines in col. II, thirteen lines in col. III, and twelve lines in the final column IV (col. IV reconstructed from the 𝔐 text). Such a difference between the columns is highly unusual among the Qumran scrolls, and suggests that the scribe used leftover sheets of skin available to him.

In the section 3:2–4:1, 4QCant^b II not only jumps from 3:2a (in a version different from 𝔐) to 3:6, it contains a version of 3:7-11 different from the other witnesses.

4QCant^a, paleographically dated around the turn of the era, is a high-quality scroll. The preserved section starts with a variant text of 3:2-5. A tentative reconstruction based on column size evinces that the scroll could not have contained the full 𝔐 text of 1:1–3:1. With two columns preceding that of frg. 1, there would be space for a somewhat shorter text of Canticles 1–2. Alternatively, with only one preceding column, it may have opened with 2:1 and contained a shorter version of 2:1-17.

In the last preserved column, the text jumps from 4:7 to 6:11. This column ends with 7:7. The ending of the scroll is unknown, but since we also here deal with a pre-canonical literary recension it is unlikely that the scroll contained the full chapter 8. The scroll may have ended with 8:6aβb, a wisdom saying carrying the stamp of a *Schlusswort*.[27]

6QCant, from around 50 CE, preserves the beginning of a high-quality scroll that contains substantial parts of 1:1-7 in two columns, including the title ["The Song of] Songs that [is for Solom]on." 6QCant is carefully formatted as a small-sized scroll with large letters, drawn in an elegant late-Herodian hand. Also here we encounter an independent text compared with (the later) 𝔐. Although very few full words have survived in this scroll, 6QCant preserves three substantial variants from 𝔐, a fourth being reconstructed based on the length of the lacuna, and some other letter remains incompatible with 𝔐 or 𝔊. The scroll may solve a scholarly crux: how one should read and interpret 1:3.[28]

6QCant is the first witness to preserve 1:1, which belongs to the final editorial stage. 6QCant's late date and careful design suggest that it probably contained more or less the same amount of text as its contemporary, the LXX

---

[27] The love songs 8:1-3, 5b-6aα and 8:8-10 do not provide a fitting end to the book; 8:4 and 8:5a represent editorial bridges, 8:11-12 belong to the latest Solomonic polishing of the book (together with 1:1). 8:13-14 is a final editorial addition echoing 2:8, 2:17, and 4:6.

[28] The understanding that 1:2b-3a (among the last additions to the collection) is a recast of the earlier verse 4:10 suggests the emendation of the unexpected שְׁמֶךָ "your name" in v. 3 to שֶׁמֶנָ "your oil," or rather (supported by 6QCant) to בְשָׂמְךָ "your perfume" 6QCant I 3 should be reconstructed, ורי[ח שמנים טובים בש[מי] מוז[ל] ב]שמך על] כן עלמו[ת אהבוך "[{rich in} sce]nt of fragrant oils is my [perfu]me, your perfu[me is flowing freely(?)], there[fore the maide]ns love you." For the suggested מוזל בשמך cf. 4:16 יזלו בשמיו (Elgvin, "Hasmonean and Herodian Editors," 92).

Vorlage. From the first century, the full canonical recension is only known from the Greek translation, made in Judea in the first generation following the fall of the temple.[29]

The Literary Growth of Canticles

The role played by Solomon is "a-changin" throughout the growth of Judean love songs into a Solomonic composition. I have proposed a process of literary growth that can be illustrated graphically as follows: A = *Grundschrift* (pre-4QCant^{b,a}); B = 4QCant^b; C = 4QCant^a; D = hypothetical turn-of-the-era recension; E = early first-century recension leading to 6QCant, 𝔊 Vorlage, 𝔐.

```
                              1:1 (E)
                     1:5-17; 1:2-4 (D)
                         2:7, 8-9a (D)
                 2:1-6 (C)
             3:2b–4.5 (C= 4QCantᵃ)
  2:9b-14, 16-17; 4:1-7 + 3:1-2a; 3:6 (A)
         3:7-11* (B = 4QCantᵇ)
         4:8-5:1 (B)
               6:11-7:13 (C)
        8:1-3, 5b, 6aα; 8:4; 8:5a; 8:6aβb (C?)
                    5:2–6:10 (D)
                    8:7, 8-10 (D)
                              8:11-12; 8:13-14 (E)
```

I have suggested that 4QCant^b and 4QCant^a represent early literary witnesses to a growing collection, 4QCant^b preserving an early literary source of Canticles. Comparison of the two texts suggests that they are based on a common *Grundschrift*: (a) 2:9b-14, 16-17; 4:1-7; (b) 3:1-2a; 3:6. The small beginning was the spring song in dialogue between the two lovers (2:9b-14, 16-17), followed by the

---

[29] Dominique Barthélemy suggested that the Greek translations of Lamentations, Ruth, and Canticles, all of which belong to the καίγε-Theodotion-group, come from the same milieu in (late?) first century CE Judea: *Les Devanciers d'Aquila* (VTSup 10; Leiden: Brill, 1963), 47, 158–60. Isabelle Assan-Dhôte and Philip Alexander maintain that only the fall of the Temple prompted the translation of Lamentations, providing Greek-speaking synagogues a liturgical text for use on the 9 of Ab. According to Assan-Dhôte, several Lamentations passages—2:7, 8, 18, 3:5—hint at the destruction of the Second Temple: Isabelle Assan-Dhôte and J. Moatti-Fine, *Baruch, Lamentations, Lettre de Jérémie* (La Bible d'Alexandrie 25.2; Paris: Editions du Cerf, 2005), 168–74, 221–2; Philip S. Alexander, "The Cultural History of the Ancient Bible Versions: The Case of Lamentations," in N. de Lange, J. de Krivoruchko, and C. Boyd-Taylor (eds.), *Jewish Reception of Greek Bible Versions*, TSMJ 23 (Tübingen: Mohr Siebeck, 2009), 78–102 (80–91).

young man's love song with colorful description of her body (4:1-7)—perhaps two songs performed at weddings.[30]

The earliest growth is represented by the addition of 3:1-2a, 3:6.[31] The short unit 3:1-2a was added to the preceding song, thus letting this song end with the maiden's longing for her soul's beloved without any reunion. Here we do not encounter the daring דודי "my lover," but the more moderate את שאהבה נפשי "my soul's beloved." 3:6 is an enigmatic responsorium, describing a female figure *coming up* from the wilderness (i.e., coming up to Jerusalem), with connotations of God's mobile presence (column of smoke) and temple service (myrrh and frankincense)—typical of the many allusions to biblical texts interwoven in the love songs.

> Who is she coming up from the wilderness,
> like a column of smoke,
> perfumed with myrrh and frankincense,
> with all the fragrant powders of the merchant?

The responsorium would bridge the two songs 2:9b–3:2a and 4:1-7. The question "Who is she?" would then relate to the maiden roaming around seeking her beloved. 3:6 would resonate with 4:6, subtly connecting the sexual encounter (4:5-6) with temple service and God's presence during the wilderness wanderings.

4QCant[b] evinces the next two extensions (stage B): the Solomon poem 3:7-11 would separate the love songs in 2:9b–3:2a, 6 from 4:1-7.[32] This addition does not make the collection a Solomonic one. I rather sense a hidden critique of Yanneus' lifestyle in this ironic poem on the procession with Solomon's palanquin.[33] When juxtaposed with the Solomon poem 3:7-11, the mythological verse 3:6 could easily be reinterpreted as a reference to Solomon's procession into the city with his bodyguard, concubines, singers, and slave girls.

---

[30] The single verse 2:15 (the foxes ravishing the blossoming vineyards) is a later addition; the motif is drawn from Theocritus.

[31] In 4QCant[b], 3:1-2a is directly followed by 3:6, and then by 3:7-11: *Literary Growth*, 38–49.

[32] In both scrolls, 3:7-11 is followed by 4:1-7 (while 4QCant[b] closes the second song with 4:3). In 4QCant[b], the text of 3:10b is longer than 𝔐 by two words. 4QCant[a] contains a variant text of 3:10b, which replaces "from the daughters of Jerusalem" with "from the virgin Jerusalem," reflecting the work of a moderating editorial hand.

[33] The description of Solomon's palanquin closes with the words, תּוֹכוֹ רָצוּף אַהֲבָה מִבְּנוֹת יְרוּשָׁלָם, "Its interior was inlaid with love from the daughters of Jerusalem" (3:10). Zakovitch comments, "Der Dichter will anscheinend zu verstehen geben, der Fussboden des königlichen Tragsessels sei voller junger Mädchen gewesen … Wenn wir annehmen wollen, dass in *rizpa* auch die Nebenbedeutung dieser Vokabel, 'Glühstein' (vgl. Jes 6, 6) mitschwingt, würde daraus hervorgehen, dass das Innere von Salomos Tragsessel von der Liebe der Jerusalemerinnen glühte": Yair Zakovitch, *Das Hohelied* (Freiburg: Herder, 2004), 178. The Greek moderates the sensuality of the Hebrew: ἐντὸς αὐτοῦ λιθόστρωτον, ἀγάπην ἀπὸ θυγατέρων Ιερουσαλημ, "its interior was inlaid with stone, a love gift from Jerusalem's daughters."

In 4QCant^b, 3:7-11; 4:1-3 is followed by the "my sister, my bride" song (4:8–5:1). This song would mitigate the expressed sensuality in the earlier songs (the lover feeding between her lilies and leaping as a stag over her cleft hills, 2:16-17). 4:8–5:1 would signal that the daring young couple in fact are newlywed. This editorial hand also omitted the last verses of 4:1-7 to avoid the sensual verses 5-6.

4QCant^a shows the next stage of growth (C): the section 2:9b-17; 3:1-2a was expanded by the addition of 3:2b-4 and the refrain 3:5. The maiden's search for her beloved continues with her encounter with the city guard. Vv. 4b and 5 mitigate earlier references to lovemaking. The refrain warns against prematurely awakening sexual desire, in v. 4b the maiden dreams about her soul's beloved (not דודי, "my lover") meeting her parents, thereby formalizing their relationship. A reconstruction of the missing column(s) before 4QCant^a frg. 1 (preserving a variant text of 3:2-5) indicates that the scroll at least contained 2:1-6, 9b-14, 16-17.

5:2–6:10 is present in neither 4QCant^a nor 4QCant^b. This section (with the sub-units 5:2–6:3; 6:4-7, 8-9, 10) thus belongs to a post-4QCant^a editorial layer (D). 5:2–6:10 did not develop independently as a separate collection but was probably added in successive stages to an earlier collection (2:1–5:1?), since this section contains repetitions of material from chapters 2–4: the itinerant city guard from 2:4 recurring in 5:7, the description of the maiden's hair as a "herd of goats, streaming down the hills of Gilead" (6:5) repeating 4:1. The recitative dialogue between the maiden and the daughters of Jerusalem (1:5; 2:7; 3:5) recurs in 5:8-9, 16 and 6:1. The exclamation 2:16, "My lover is mine and I am his, he pastures among the lilies," is repeated in 6:3.

At this stage the scroll possibly extended from 1:2 to 8:6, with the wisdom saying on love as fire (8:6aβb) concluding both 5:2–8:6 and the book as a whole.[34] All through we encounter recitative dialogues with the daughters of Jerusalem (1:5; 2:7; 3:5; 5:8-9, 16; 8:4).

The last editorial stage is represented by 1:1 and 8:7-14.[35] Building upon the presence of two Solomon poems (3:7-11 and 6:8-9) and the maiden's use of "king" for her lover (1:4, 12; 7:5), an editor framed the book with a Solomon text at the end (8:11-12) and the opening title. The addition of three short units after the earlier *Schlusswort* made it necessary to add another final touch, the dialogue of 8:13-14. Earlier themes are repeated in the final section: the lover leaping over the mountains

---

[34] For Heinevetter, 8:6 is a *Schlusswort* inserted by the main editor, closing both the section (*Kleinsammlung*) 5:2–8:6 and the collection 1:2–8:6, similar to 5:1b as *conclusio* to 2:8–5:1: *"Komm nun, mein Liebster,"* 161–6.

[35] 8:7-14 may have been added together (thus Heinevetter) or in two stages (as suggested above): the wisdom saying of 8:7 faces and supplements the preceding one that closed 1:2–8:6. While some scholars incorporate Canticles in the biblical wisdom tradition, I see these two sayings as the only distinct sapiential elements in the book.

of spices like a stag (8:14) echoes 2:8, 17;³⁶ the vineyard (8:12) alluding to earlier images and the comparison of the maiden to a garden (1:13-14; 4:13, 16; 5:1; 6:2).

The repetends added throughout the growth of the book demonstrate conscious literary editing, some possibly reflecting parallel growth of love songs with common roots. The book contains two "Who is she … ?" refrains imbued with mythological terminology—3:6 and 8:5 (3:6 alludes to 4:6, the climax of the young man's love song of 4:1-7).

By the mid-first century CE, 6QCant and the LXX Vorlage testify to the addition of 1:1 as the title of the full collection. Considering its late date and elaborate format, 6QCant likely contained an 𝔐-like recension concluding with 8:6 or 8:7–14.

The Role of Solomon in the Collection

Canonical Canticles contains three "Solomon poems," 3:7-11; 6:8-9; and 8:11-12. The first (with its ironic critique of the king) is present in all three Cave 4 scrolls (even if the tiny piece 4QCantᶜ only preserves [remnants of] three words from 3:7-8). Neither 4QCantᵇ nor 4QCantᵃ contained 6:8-9, which I have ascribed to a later editorial stage. The description of a Solomonic wedding in Ps 45:10-15 (cf. 1 Kgs 11:2-3) inspired 6:8-9, where the unnamed Solomon plays a rhetorical role:

> There are sixty queens and eighty concubines, and maidens without number. Only one is my dove, my perfect one, the only one of her mother, a delight of the one who bore her. Maidens saw her and called her happy, queens and concubines praised her.

The presence of one (ironic) Solomon poem in the collection from stage B onward would hardly give the book a Solomonic flavor, neither would another Solomon poem from stage D. The designation of the male lover as "king" in 1:4, 12; 7:5b should not be read as a royal title; rather, it serves as a term of affection between lovers in the tradition of Egyptian love songs.³⁷

The last Solomon text is 8:11-12.

> Solomon entrusted a vineyard to a wealthy steward,³⁸
> and he (in turn) entrusted the vineyard to keepers,
> each one was to bring for its fruit a thousand pieces of silver.

---

³⁶ Canticles' terminology is often ambiguous. The concluding exhortation "Make haste, my lover, like a gazelle or a young stag upon the mountains of spices!" may be read as a direct invitation to a sexual encounter—cp. 4:5-6, "Your breasts are like two fawns, twins of a gazelle, feeding among the lilies. Until the day breathes, and the shadows flee, I will hasten to the mountain of myrrh and the hill of frankincense."

³⁷ Fox, *Song of Songs*, 98.

³⁸ With Tur-Sinai I translate "baal-hamon" not as a toponym, but "wealthy steward": *Die Heilige Schrift. Ins Deutsche übertragen* von Naftali Herz Tur-Sinai (1935, repr. Holzgerlingen: Hänssler, 1993), 1168.

> My vineyard, my very own, is for myself,
> you, Solomon, may have the thousand,
> and the keepers of the fruit two hundred!

Here, the maiden's one and only vineyard symbolizes her chastity, which she should have guarded, while "the thousand" of Solomon symbolizes his many women. This is no praise of the legendary king, Solomon plays only a rhetorical role in the poem, and Fox even senses a mocking touch here.

Fox comments on Solomon's role in the book:

> Solomon is not the speaker, the subject, or the center of interest in this poem, nor is there anything in the Song itself imputing authorship to him. Solomon is mentioned only incidentally, as an example or byword (for 1:4, 12 and 3:7, 9, 11, see ad loc.), or even the object of mockery (8:11-12). The title is the first known step in the appropriation of the book to religion, for it associates the poem with an ancient wiseman who was believed to have written other works in the Holy Spirit. Yet the title is not in itself evidence for an allegorical interpretation or even for an understanding of the Song as wisdom. Solomon was the logical candidate for the authorship of the book because his name is mentioned in it and because he was famous both for the number of his wives and for his songs.[39]

In his 2015 monograph, Martin Ravndal Hauge interprets Canticles as fashioned deliberately on a Solomonic pattern, drawing primarily on Proverbs 2-7.[40] As noted above, the Solomonic flavor of the book is in fact much more limited. The insertion of three poems about Solomon or referring to him in a growing collection of love poems is nonetheless unsurprising in light of Solomon's reputation as the king of many wives (1 Kgs 11:2-3).

The two Solomon texts inserted into the collection in stages B and D may well have led to the ultimate addition of 1:1. Only the editorially added title in 1:1 makes the collection as such a Solomonic book, and 8:11-12 was probably added at the same time. The insertion of the title, "The Song of Songs that is for Solomon," before "the king and I-section" (1:2-4) served to "Solomonize" the collection as a whole, the singular שיר in the title indicating the final editor's perception of the text as a unified whole rather than a loose collection of songs.[41]

The title may also evince another contributive element to the Solomonization of the collection. When the sexual activity described in the songs is attributed to Solomon's reign, they are removed from the readers' own life and times, thus softening their impact. The final editor, well aware of the recent origin of the songs, hints through the title that the collection is representative of Solomon's life and times. Henceforth the book would be "The Song of Songs that is Solomon's."

---

[39] Fox, *Song of Songs*, 95.
[40] Martin Ravndal Hauge, *Solomon the Lover and the Shape of the Song of Songs* (Sheffield: Sheffield Phoenix Press, 2015).
[41] Heinevetter, *"Komm nun, mein Liebster,"* 68–70.

Following this hermeneutical intervention, the references to the king (1:4, 12; 7:5b) would easily be linked with Solomon, and שלמה in 1:5 being read as "Shlomo" rather than desert tribe Salmah, appearing in parallel with Kedar (cf. σαλωμων).

The tendency to extol Solomon may also be reflected in the romanticizing of the land in Canticles. Although Mahanaim, Hermon, Gilead, and Carmel did not form part of the Hasmonean state proper (the two latter regions were included for a short time period under Yanneus), they lay within close reach and belonged to the legendary Solomonic kingdom described in earlier biblical texts, texts that may reflect memories of the large ninth-century Omride state and seventh-century Judea. Songs speaking of the beloved people in a land imbued with Solomonic color and fragrance might have led to the later ascription of the full collection to Solomon.

The insertion of 1:1 would in time contribute to the legitimation of the collection as a treasured composition of the fathers, a Solomonic book alongside Proverbs (and Qohelet—another Solomonic book being accepted as a book of authority in the early second century). The ascription of these songs to Solomon may form part of the Second Temple tendency to associate texts with foundational figures.[42]

The Septuagint translation of Psalms—probably made in Alexandria in the early first century BCE—indicates that "David," i.e., the full book of 150/151 psalms (formatted in two scrolls), already belonged to the growing collection of authoritative writings.[43] The inclusion of this Davidic book might well have drawn "Solomon" with it, particularly in light of the recognition of Proverbs as an ancient book of the fathers.[44] This, in turn, could have paved the way for the acceptance of

---

[42] "Understanding Ezra's ascription of legal innovation to Moses can also help us to understand practices of pseudepigraphy and rewriting the Bible—practices that continued throughout the Second Temple period and even beyond"; "these Second Temple authors [of Jubilees] … must have considered it insufficient to ground their interpretations and laws in a contemporaneous activity of interpretation or experience of prophecy. Clearly, they thought they had to ground their interpretations and laws in the preexilic past: in the Mosaic origins of the nation": Hindy Najman, *Past Renewals: Interpretative Authority, Renewed Revelation and the Quest for Perfection in Jewish Antiquity*, JSJSup 53 (Leiden: Brill, 2010), 86, 66. Cf. her discussion on the attribution of new texts to Moses: Najman, *Seconding Sinai: The Development of Mosaic Discourse in Second Temple Judaism*, JSJSup 77 (Leiden: Brill, 2003), 1–40, 63–9, 100–6; *Past Renewals*, 63–7, 73–86, 234–42; and Davis' arguments for the existence of a "Jeremiad discourse" in the final centuries BCE: Kipp Davis, *The Cave 4 Apocryphon of Jeremiah and the Qumran Jeremianic Traditions: Prophetic Persona and the Construction of Community Identity*, STDJ 111 (Leiden: Brill, 2014), 1–9, 26–9, 37–45, 234–53, 267–307.

[43] Arie van der Kooij argues for the early first century: "On the place of Origin of the Old Greek of Psalms," *VT* 33 (1983):67–74. The phrasing of Judean domination over Moab and Edom in LXX Ps 59(60):9–10 and 107(108):9–10 indicates that the translation was made after the conquest of northern Moab (ca. 129 BCE) and Edom (107 BCE).

[44] (Alleged) antiquity played an important role in establishing the status of books. See Arie van der Kooij, "Authoritative Scriptures and Scribal Culture," in M. Popovic (ed.), *Authoritative Scriptures in Ancient Judaism*, JSJSup 141 (Leiden: Brill, 2010), 5–71.

other books associated with David (Ruth) and Solomon (Canticles and Qohelet). Once more, this process may have been aided by the description of Solomon's wisdom in 1 Kgs 3:5-28, his being identified as a songster in 1 Kgs 4:32, and as author or honoree of the royal-messianic Ps 72.

Solomon the Magician

According to 1 Kgs 5:9-14[5:29-34] Solomon had unsurpassed knowledge of nature, including trees, animals, birds, and fishes. Wis. Sol. 7:17-22 elaborates:

> For he himself gave me an unerring knowledge of the things that exist, to know the constitution of the world and the activity of the elements, the beginning and end and middle of times, the alterations of the solstices and the changes of the seasons, the cycles of the year and the constellations of the stars, natures of animals and the tempers of wild animals, the violent forces of spirits and the thoughts of human beings, the varieties of plants and the powers of roots, and all things, both what is secret and what is manifest, I learned, for she that is the fashioner of all things taught me, namely wisdom.

There is a short step from a knowledge of spirits and hidden things to magic. 11Q11 (11QapocrPs) was copied in the first century CE, but likely contains older prayers and invocations, ascribed to Solomon and David. 11Q11 II 2-7 may be the earliest text according to which Solomon was given gifts of healing and exorcism. Consequently he is considered the originator of magical invocations.

> ²[…] Solomon, and invok[ed …] ³[… against all the spi]rits and demons [… ⁴] these are [the de]mons, and the pri[nce of Maste]mah … ⁷] with Him is healing [… the upright] leans [on] Your name and inv[okes

How should we interpret the first preserved words, "] Solomon, and invok[ed …"⁴⁵ Since Solomon is not introduced by the preposition *le-*, it is not an authorial

---

⁴⁵ The text reads ויקר[א שלומה [. The reconstruction of ויקר[א should not be doubted, even though only the lower part of *resh* is preserved before the lacuna. *Pace DJD* 23:189–90, there is no trace of any final *he* before the word space preceding שלומה. The editors have mistakenly perceived the irregular edge of the fragment as ink fitting traces of *he*, cf. PAM 44.113. A tentative reconstruction of the opening line could be על הפגועים השביע שלומה ויקר[א, "Solomon [adjured the possessed,] and invoke[d … " (the terms פגועים ("afflicted," "possessed") and *hiphil* of שבע ("adjure," "invoke") are used elsewhere in 11Q11). ויקרא could alternatively be read as referring to the performer: "[The adjuration taught by] Solomon: thus he should invok[e … "

ascription. More probably we have an apotropaic text that consciously places itself in the tradition from Solomon, cf. the below text from Josephus, where after praising Solomon's knowledge of all elements of nature, he continues:

> God also enabled him to learn that skill which expels demons, which is a science useful and sanative to men. He composed such incantations also by which distempers are alleviated. And he left behind him the manner of using exorcisms, by which they drive away demons, so that they never return, and this method of cure is of great force unto this day ... The manner of the cure was this: He (an exorcist known by Josephus) put a ring that had a root of one of those sorts mentioned by Solomon to the nostrils of the demoniac, after which he drew out the demon through his nostrils, and when the man fell down immediately, he adjured him to return into him no more, making still mention of Solomon, and reciting the incantations which he composed. (*Ant.* 8.44-45)

The tradition of Solomon as magician became widespread in Middle Eastern traditions.[46] In *Biblical Antiquities* 60, Pseudo-Philo portrays King David in the role of exorcist, taking control over the evil spirit that plagued Saul. David's song concludes, "let the new womb from which I was born rebuke you, from which after my time one born from my loins will rule over you," probably a prophecy alluding to Solomon's powers. We find the same tradition in the *Testament of Solomon*, the Nag Hammadi *Apocalypse of Adam*, and in Aramaic incantation bowls, which often refer to Solomon's seal or seal ring.[47] Later, the tradition of Solomon the magician found its way into the Quran, sura 34, and the Hadith. Early Islamic traditions on Solomon may be influenced by the *umma*'s relations to the Christians of Ethiopia and Sheba—Solomon plays a central role in the etiology of the Ethiopian kingdom.

Other Sources

1. The Septuagint version of 1 Kings, 3 Kingdoms, is built on a Hebrew *Vorlage* that thoroughly reworked a proto-𝔐 text. 3 Kingdoms portrays Solomon

---

[46] D. C. Duling, "Testament of Solomon," in J. H. Charlesworth (ed.), *The Old Testament Pseudepigrapha*, ABRL (New York: Doubleday, 1983), vol. 1, 935–87 (945–56); Klaus Berger, "Die königlichen Messiastraditionen des Neuen Testaments," *NTS* 20 (1974): 1–44 (5–9).

[47] Gideon Bohak, *Ancient Jewish Magic: A History* (Cambridge: Cambridge University Press, 2007), 93–105; Raanan Boustan and Michael Beshay, *Sealing the Demons, Once and For All: The Ring of Solomon, the Cross of Christ, and the Power of Biblical Kingship* (Berlin: de Gruyter, 2015), 99–130; Nils Hallvard Korsvoll, *Reconsidering "Christian:" Context and Categorisation in the Study of Syriac Amulets and Incantation Bowls* (PhD dissertation; Oslo: MF Norwegian School of Theology, 2017), 106–8.

in a more favorable light than 𝔐, enhancing his wisdom. According to Gooding, the first ten chapters were rewritten around Solomon's wisdom and included the whitewashing of his sins.[48] This Hebrew *Vorlage* can hardly be later than the early second century BCE.

2. I have argued that a central passage in the presectarian 4QInstruction (likely C2 BCE) reinterprets God's promises to the elect: the divine sonship awarded to the Davidic king (Solomon being the son of David *par excellence*) is now the share of the elect individual. Prominent in its lofty, poetic language, 4Q418 81 identifies the partaker of the end-time community as God's firstborn son ("He made you a firstborn son to him," 4Q418 81 5).[49] It also echoes Solomon's prayer for wisdom and God's promise to him in 1 Kgs 3:5-15.[50] The eschatological wisdom imputed to the elect in this section of 4QInstruction thus possesses Solomonic overtones.

3. In contrast, there is a silence on Solomon in texts authored in the *Yahad*, a silence reflecting the movement's anti-Hasmonean stance. Of eight references in the non-biblical texts, the only positive statement from a text close to the *Yahad* is the halakhic letter MMT, where the epilogue talks about "[the bles]sin[gs] came […] in the days of Solomon the son of David. Indeed, the curses came from the days of Jeroboam … " (4QMMT C 18–19, 4Q398 11-13 1–2).

---

[48] Emanuel Tov, "Three Strange Books of the LXX: 1 Kings, Esther, and Daniel Compared with Similar Rewritten Compositions from Qumran and Elsewhere," *Hebrew Bible, Greek Bible, and Qumran: Collected Essays* (Tübingen: Mohr Siebeck, 2008), 283–305, 371–7; David W. Gooding, "Problems of Text and Midrash in the Third Book of Reigns," *Textus* 7 (1969): 1–29.

[49] Torleif Elgvin, *An Analysis of 4QInstruction* [PhD dissertation, The Hebrew University of Jerusalem, 1997], 75, 137–45.

[50] For echoes of 1 Kings 3 and Psalm 89 in this 4QInstruction passage, cf. 1 Kgs 3:6 "you have kept for your servant David my father great and steadfast love … and have given him a son to sit on his throne today"; 1 Kgs 3:13 "I give you also what you have not asked, both riches and honor"; Ps 89:28 "I will make him a firstborn, the highest of the kings of the earth"; 4Q418 81 6 "and my favour I will give you"; 4Q418 81 5 "He cast your lot and greatly increased your glory, and set you as his firstborn amo[ng"; 1 Kgs 3:9, 11-12 "Give your servant therefore an understanding heart to govern your people, to discern between good and evil … since you have asked for yourself understanding to discern what is right, I now do according to your word. Indeed, I give you a wise and discerning heart"; 4Q418 81 9 "And for you he opened insight," as well as the sentence recurring in 4QInstruction, "He opened your ear for the mystery to come." "Discerning between good and evil" recurs in a farmer section in another copy of 4QInstruction (4Q423 5 5–6): "As a farmer,[you] should observe the seasons of the summer harvest and gather your crops at the right time. Throughout [the year keep watch and pay at]tention to all your crops, to unders[tand (the outcome of)] your work. [Then you will discern what is] good and what is bad (in the ingathered crops)." I am indebted to Shlomi Efrati for the reconstruction of the underlying Hebrew text of 4Q423 5.

4. In the gospels, Solomon does play a more positive role. In his 1974 article Berger demonstrates the influence of Solomon traditions (son of David, healer, exorcist) on the Christology of the gospels.[51] Solomon is mentioned nine times in the gospels (and as temple builder in Acts 7:47). The Q tradition knows of his glory, "Even Solomon in all his glory was not clothed like one of these [lilies]" (Matt 6:29//Luke 12:22), but boldly proclaims "The queen of the south … came from the ends of the earth to listen to the wisdom of Solomon, and see, something greater than Solomon is here!" (Matt 12:42//Luke 11:31).

   The earliest references to passages from Canticles as inspired text may be found in early Semitic gospel tradition: Mark 13:28-29 may allude to Cant 2:10-13; John 4:10-15; 7:37-38 to Cant 4:15; Matt 13:52 to Cant 7:14; and John 12:1-8//Mark 14:3-72; Matt 25:1-12//Luke 12:35-36 to Cant 1:3, 12; 5:2. "The bridegroom's voice" (John 3:28-30) may allude to "the voice of my beloved" (Cant 2:8 and 5:2) and the maiden's companions listening to her voice (Cant 8:13). These allusions and echoes have been explored in a recent study by Peter J. Tomson.[52] However, if these allusions go back to the historical Jesus, was he alluding to an authoritative Solomonic book, or rather to weddings songs he knew from Galilee?

Concluding: in spite of being the builder of the Temple, Solomon was not given the role of ideal king in the scriptures that became the Hebrew Bible. However, a notable Solomonic "renaissance" can be observed from the second century onward, possibly coming to the surface with the Hasmoneans and their restoration of Jerusalem and the Temple compound. In the subsequent century, his name attracted collections such as the *Psalms of Solomon* and the Wisdom of Solomon. In the first century BCE, when a collection of love songs would grow and develop, Solomon was initially the object of irony in the poem of Cant 3:7-11. However, at the end he would appear as honorable originator of a collection that rabbis and bishops later insisted should be read allegorically.[53] And from the first century BCE onward, Solomon the magician would remain prominent for centuries.

---

[51] Berger, "Die königlichen Messiastraditionen".

[52] Peter J. Tomson, "The Song of Songs in the Teachings of Jesus and the Development of the Exposition on the Song," NTS 61 (2015): 429–47.

[53] Akiba's saying "He who warbles the Song of Songs in a banquet-hall and makes it into a kind of love-song has no portion in the world to come" (t. Sanh. 12.10) may hit the mark as to the origin of some of the songs as wedding recitals, and evinces that some of his contemporaries viewed Canticles as a collection of earthly love songs.

Chapter 2

VENEREAE DAEMONIORUM: EROTIC DEMONS, EGYPTIAN MONASTICISM, AND THE *TESTAMENT OF SOLOMON*

Blake A. Jurgens

—The pencil of the Holy Ghost hath labored more in describing the afflictions of Job than the felicities of Solomon.

Francis Bacon, *On Adversity*

In terms of traditional expansion and elaboration, very few biblical characters have undergone as florid or dramatic a transformation as the figure of Solomon. From the Second Temple Period onward, an array of traditions emerged which developed and augmented features of Solomon's *persona* ranging from his architectural genius and lavish wealth to his unprecedented wisdom and mastery of the arcane arts.[1] One of these emerging trajectories was the association of Solomon with apotropaic and exorcistic power.[2] Noteworthy in this regard is the *Testament of Solomon*, a Christian pseudepigraphic narrative written in Greek where the eponymous royal describes his subjugation of various demons by means of a magical ring. Unlike earlier Jewish and Christian accounts of demons, which often depict them as a hazy clan of invisible evil spirits, the *Testament of*

---

[1] For a summary of these traditions, see Blake Jurgens, "The Figure of Solomon," in M. Goff and S. L. Adams (eds.), *The Wiley Blackwell Companion to Wisdom Literature* (West Sussex: Blackwell, 2020), 159–76; Pablo A. Torijano, *Solomon the Esoteric King: From King to Magus, Development of a Tradition*, JSJSup 73 (Leiden: Brill, 2002).

[2] For example, Sarah Iles Johnston, "The Testament of Solomon from Late Antiquity to the Renaissance," in J. N. Bremmer and J. R. Veenstra (eds.), *The Metamorphosis of Magic from Late Antiquity to the Modern Period* (Leuven: Peeters, 2002), 35–50; Augusto Cosentino, "La tradizione del re Salomone come mago ed esorcista," in A. Mastrocinque (ed.), *Atti dell'incontro di studio: Gemme gonstiche e cultura ellenistica* (Bologna: Pàtron Editore, 2002), 41–59; Sarit Shalev-Eyni, "Solomon, His Demons and Jongleurs: The Meeting of Islamic, Judaic and Christian Culture," *Al-Masāq* 18 (2006): 145–60. See also the contribution by Torleif Elgvin in the present volume.

Solomon offers an exceedingly colorful portrait of its demons replete with vivid descriptions of their monstrous bodies, their ominous origins, and their ghastly preoccupations. One after another, Solomon experiences first-hand the grotesque particulars of each individual demon, procuring the apotropaic ritual or angelic name, which can properly stymie them before condemning them to hard labor on the Jerusalem Temple.

One particular element of the robust demonic worldview of the *Testament* which stands out in comparison to other early Jewish and Christian texts is its tendency to depict its malevolent entities as rogue erotic spirits. Indeed, several of the demons of the *Testament* claim either to commit wanton acts of sexual violence or to induce their victims to engage in such carnal acts themselves. This association of the demonic with venereal affliction and temptation has not gone unnoticed by scholars. Following his analysis of the *Testament*, William Loader concludes that "sexual wrongdoing is one of the major manifestations of the demonic" in the *Testament*, a point echoed by Todd Klutz among others.[3] Surprisingly, one comparative avenue which has not received due attention is the eroticized depiction of demons in the *Testament* vis-à-vis the literature associated with Egyptian monasticism.[4] Much like the *Testament*, numerous desert fathers speak of unsightly demons of fornication, highlighting their ascetic battles against these lustful spirits. The goal of this study is to illustrate some of these specific shared features of the sexualized demonologies of the *Testament* and Egyptian monastic literature, as well as cautiously segue from these observations into two of the most tenuous topics in the scholarship of the *Testament*: its date and provenance.

---

[3] See Todd E. Klutz, *Rewriting the Testament of Solomon: Tradition, Conflict and Identity in a Late Antique Pseudepigraphon*, LSTS 53 (London: T&T Clark, 2005), 50, 109; William Loader, *The Pseudepigrapha on Sexuality: Attitudes towards Sexuality in Apocalypses, Testaments, Wisdom, and Related Literature* (Grand Rapids: Eerdmans, 2011), 136–45 (quote on p. 145); Cf. also Thomas Cason who states that "sexual vice proves the real craving du jour of these fiends" on p. 268 of "Cultural Features: Monstrosity and the Construction of Human Identity in the *Testament of Solomon*," *CBQ* 77 (2015): 263–79.

[4] In this study, I have tried to confine my sources to either literature composed by monks from Egypt or accounts composed by individuals who exhibit some degree of contact with Egypt (e.g., John Cassian). My particular focus upon Egyptian monastic literature does not seek to accurately describe historical events, so much as it seeks to analyze how people who were, or interacted with, Egyptian monks understood how sex, the body, society, and the demonic related to one another. For more on the tricky nature of historiography and Egyptian monastic literature, see Mark Sheridan, "The Modern Historiography of Early Egyptian Monasticism," in M. Bielawski and D. Hombergen (eds.), *Il Monachesimo tra Eredità e Aperture. Atti del simposio « Testi e temi nella tradizione del monachesimo cristiano » per il 50 anniversario dell'Instituto Monastico di Sant'Anselmo* (Rome: Pontificio Ateneo S. Anselmo, 2004), 197–220.

Erotic Demons in Ancient Judaism and Early Christianity: A Brief Survey

In order to properly gauge the distinctiveness of the visualized venereal demons of the *Testament*, it is crucial to first advance a basic understanding of how ancient Jews and Christians from the Second Temple period until the third century CE apprehended the relationship between evil spiritual entities and sexuality. During the Second Temple period, we begin to see certain evil entities linked to sexual misconduct and temptation, although in most cases this relationship is fairly peripheral. For example, although inordinate sexual activity plays a central role in the myth of the fallen angels found in the *Book of the Watchers* of *1 Enoch* and the book of *Jubilees*, neither of these works actually attribute sexual immorality to the gigantic offspring begotten through the Watchers and human women.[5] While these evil spirits, the disembodied Giants, are described as the *product* of the improper sexual liaison of angels and humans, at no point do they actually *inflict* sexual temptation or savagery. Rather, the disembodied spirits of the Giants are ruthless ruffians who cause disobedience, violence, and disease to spread across the face of the earth.[6]

In the same vein as *1 Enoch* and *Jubilees*, many treatments of demons coming out of the Second Temple period tend to depict evil spirits as causing disease, physical pain, or general sin and impurity.[7] Nevertheless, there are a handful of cases where evil entities are portrayed as having at least some connection to sexual sin, although it is often unclear in what capacity.[8] The *Damascus Document*, for instance, mentions the three nets of Belial meant to entrap Israel: "fornication

---

[5] More specifically, both the angels (e.g., *1 En.* 6:1; 15:4; 19:1; *Jub.* 5:1) and human women (e.g., *1 En.* 8:1-2) are accused of sexual immorality, although in both *1 Enoch* and *Jubilees* the Watchers are the subject of a majority of the blame.

[6] The role of evil spirits spreading violence and destruction is predicated upon their infliction of similar violent acts prior to their own destruction and disembodiment (see esp. *1 En.* 7:3-6; cf. 19:1). Similarly, in *Jubilees* these disembodied Giants continue to harm humanity by leading them astray (*Jub.* 7:27; 10:1; 11:4; cf. 12:20) and afflicting them with violence and/or causing them to commit violent acts (10:2, 3, 7-8; 11:5). For more on the nature of the deeds of the offspring of the Watchers, see Matthew Goff, "Warriors, Cannibals and Teachers of Evil: The Sons of the Angels in Genesis 6, the Book of the Watchers and the Book of Jubilees," *SEÅ* 80 (2015): 67–85.

[7] For example, the *Prayer of Nabonidus* (4Q242); *Songs of the Maskil* (4Q510 1.5); 4Q560.

[8] One other evil spirit which could also be put into this category is the רוח באישא in *Genesis Apocryphon* 20.16-32. While the spirit is associated with sex, in that it assails Pharaoh with an "affliction" preventing the king from having sexual intercourse with Sarai, the fact that the evil spirit was sent by God to prevent Sarai's defilement, and thus does not actually engage or cause any inappropriate sexual activity, in many ways problematizes an analysis of the spirit as a proper evil demon.

(זנות), avarice, and the defilement of the sanctuary" (CD 4.13-18).[9] Likewise, the Treatise of the Two Spirits describes the "spirit of deceit" as the power behind multiple vices including "shameless zeal for abominable works in a spirit of fornication" (1QS 4.10).[10] Unfortunately, both the *Damascus Document* and the Treatise offer no further explanatory details regarding these fairly terse allusions. Arguably, the most cited association of the demonic with sex found in Second Temple Jewish literature is the demon Asmodeus who in the book of Tobit infamously kills the suitors of the heroine Sarah before they can consummate their marriage. On the one hand, some scholars have interpreted Asmodeus' proclivity for assassinating Sarah's suitors as an indication of his own libidinous infatuation with Sarah; several of the manuscripts of Tobit even depict Tobias confiding in Azariah/Raphael his worry regarding Sarah since "a demon loves her and harms no one except those who approach her" (Tob. 6:15).[11] On the other hand, however, this interpretation reads quite a bit into the actual narrative. At no point in Tobit does Asmodeus himself make any actual sexual advances toward Sarah, much less express any intense longing for her. In fact, the only major act committed by Asmodeus' in the narrative is his violent murdering of the suitors. Moreover, Asmodeus never erotically assaults Sarah, and his killing of the suitors actually prevents her from entering into a non-endogamous marriage, thus (ironically) preserving her for Tobias, her kinsman and proper spouse.[12] Along these lines,

---

[9] For more on the three nets, see Hanan Eshel, "The Damascus Document's 'Three Nets of Belial': A Reference to the Aramaic Levi Document?" in L. LiDonnici and A. Lieber (eds.), *Heavenly Tablets: Interpretation, Identity and Tradition in Ancient Judaism*, JSJSup 119 (Leiden: Brill, 2007), 243–55.

[10] See Mladen Popović, "Anthropology, Pneumatology, and Demonology in Early Judaism: The Two Spirits Treatise (1QS 3:13–4:26) and Other Texts from the Dead Sea Scrolls," in J. Baden, H. Najman, and E. Tigchelaar (eds.), *Sibyls, Scriptures, and Scrolls: John Collins at Seventy*, JSJSup 175 (Leiden: Brill, 2016), 1029–67 (esp. 1052–57).

[11] This appears in the long recension of the Greek (Ms. Sinaiticus), the Vetus Latina, which often follows the long recension, and is plausibly restored in the Aramaic of 4Q197 4 ii.9 in Joseph Fitzmyer, "Tobit," *Qumran Cave 4: XIV. Parabiblical Texts, Part 2*, DJD 19 (Oxford: Clarendon, 1995), 1–76. For an interpretation of Asmodeus as a jealous and lovesick demon, in part because of this variant, see Beate Ego, "'Denn er liebt sie' (Tob 6, 15 Ms. 139). Zur Rolle des Dämons Asmodäus in der Tobit-Erzählung," in A. Lange, H. Lichtenberger, and K. F. Diethard Römheld (eds.), *Die Dämonen – Demons: The Demonology of Israelite-Jewish and Early Christian Literature in Context of Their Environment* (Tübingen: Mohr Siebeck, 2003), 309–17.

[12] Thus, Tobias all along is the ideal spouse for Sarah, while the suitors are suitable, but less attractive. Among others making this point, see Joseph Fitzmyer, *Tobit*, CEJL (Berlin: de Gruyter, 2003), 217. Ida Fröhlich also echoes this sentiment, noting that Asmodeus should not be equated with an *incubus* in that his "only function … is to impede Sarah's sexual relations with any other man, and that is the reason for killing her bridegrooms." See "Evil in Second Temple Texts," in I. Fröhlich and E. Koskenniemi (eds.), *Evil and the Devil*, LNTS 481 (London: T&T Clark, 2013), 23–50 (see p. 38).

then, Asmodeus may be best characterized in Tobit as a vicious assassin rather than a rampant sex fiend.[13]

Turning to early Christian literature, the Gospels uniformly eschew any coherent association of evil spirits or demons with sexual temptation or assault, and instead emphasize their possession of human bodies and triggering of erratic behaviors and various maladies (e.g., Matt 9:32; Mark 5:3; 9:14-18; Luke 4:27; 9:37-42).[14] Outside of the Gospels, the New Testament describes demons as the recipients of idolatrous sacrifices (1 Cor 10:20-21), the hidden force behind deceitful teachings (1 Tim 4:1), and the provocateurs of kings (Rev 16:14). The two places where evil spiritual beings are perhaps most clearly associated with sexual perversion come in Rev 18:2-3 and 1 Cor 7:5. In the former, the desolate and fallen city of Babylon (i.e., Rome) is described as a habitation of δαιμονίων due to "the wine of the wrath of her fornication (πορνείας)."[15] While demons and sexual perversity are found side-by-side here, it is important to note that the language here is symbolically charged, and at no point do the demons themselves play any tangible role in the rampant fornication.[16] More promising is Paul's terse warning in 1 Cor 7:5 that married couples should not deprive themselves of intercourse in order that "Satan may not tempt (πειράζῃ) you because of your lack of self-control (ἀκρασίαν)." According to Dale Martin, Paul's prescription of marriage and marital relations in 1 Cor 7 functions as a "prophylaxis" for the weak meant to prevent Satan from manipulating their uninhibited passions via temptation.[17] In this manner, the popular role of Satan as the adversarial tempter is modified to explicitly include sexual peril. While there is certainly a link drawn between Satan and erotic temptation in 1 Cor 7:5, Paul does not develop this idea further, and consequentially reveals nothing else regarding Satan's particular approach to arousing sexual longing among dissatisfied spouses.[18]

---

[13] This also fits several theories regarding Asmodeus' name, which most scholars derive from the Avestan *aēšma-daēuua* "demon of wrath." Thus, even Asmodeus' name implies his role as an inflictor of violence rather than sexual torment.

[14] For an overview of the role of possession and exorcism in the New Testament, see Eric Sorensen, *Possession and Exorcism in the New Testament and Early Christianity*, WUNT II/157 (Tübingen: Mohr Siebeck, 2002).

[15] The image of Babylon as a deserted ruin inhabited by wild (and demonic) beasts is borrowed from the prophecies of Isaiah (13:21-22) and Jeremiah (50:39; 51:37).

[16] The very concept of *porneia* in Revelation usually functions symbolically to describe general unfaithfulness to God rather than actual sexual misconduct. See for example Craig R. Koester, *Revelation: A New Translation with Introduction and Commentary*, AB 38A (New Haven: Yale University Press, 2014), 228–9, 697–8.

[17] Dale Martin, *The Corinthian Body* (New Haven: Yale University Press, 1995), 209, 217. Cf. Derek Brown, *The God of This Age: Satan in the Churches and Letters of the Apostle Paul*, WUNT II/409 (Tübingen: Mohr Siebeck, 2015), esp. 151–7.

[18] The next closest reference to Satan and sex is found earlier in 1 Cor. 5:5 where Paul also mentions that those who commit acts of πορνεία will be handed over to Satan "for the destruction of the flesh." However, this claim does not so much warn that Satan is the cause of sexual immorality in as much as it asserts that those who engage in such improper activities will be cast out and subsequently tormented by Satan.

A much more pronounced link between evil spirits and sex emerges in the *Testaments of the Twelve Patriarchs*, a collection of pseudepigraphic dialogues dating to the last half of the second century CE.[19] Unlike the New Testament and the Apostolic Fathers, both of which say very little about the demonic and sexuality,[20] several of the ethically driven deathbed testimonies of the patriarchs bemoan evil spirits under the jurisdiction of Beliar who assail humans with erotic temptation.[21] The *Testament of Reuben*, for example, depicts "the spirit of procreation and intercourse" (σπορᾶς καὶ συνουσίας), accompanied by the sin of "fondness for pleasure" (φιληδονίας), as the last of the "seven spirits of deceit" governed by Beliar which mislead the youth of humanity (*T. Reu.* 2.1-9). The "spirit of sexual immorality" (πορνείας), mentioned immediately after in *T. Reu.* 3.3, is even said to reside "in the nature and in the senses" of people (ἐν τῇ φύσει καὶ ταῖς αἰσθήσεσιν).[22] As Ishay Rosen-Zvi has shown, the *Testament of Reuben* views sexual temptation as a dynamic process in which the external provocations of the spirits of Beliar corrupt the internal and sensory parts of the soul. To effectively quell erotic enticement and stymie the influence of deceitful spirits then, one must be in full control of their perception and their desires.[23] Several other patriarchs also express similar warnings regarding the conjoined danger of deceitful spirits and the sensory. The *Testament of Issachar* proclaims that the single-minded man cannot be overpowered by the spirits of deceit if he avoids glancing at the beauty of the female physique.[24] Similarly, in his testament Judah hubristically recalls boasting of his fortitude to ignore the visual allure of "the face of a comely woman" only to have the "spirit of envy and sexual immorality (πορνείας)" successfully entice him into laying with the Canaanite Bathshua and with Tamar (*T. Jud.* 13.3).

---

[19] In my opinion, the *Testaments of the Twelve Patriarchs* reflect a second-century Christian community gradually emerging out of a Jewish *milieu*. For a similar assessment, see Joel Marcus, "The *Testaments of the Twelve Patriarchs* and the *Didascalia Apostolorum*: A Common Jewish Christian Milieu?" *JTS* 61 (2010): 596–626.

[20] Arguably, the most concrete allusion to the demonic and sexuality occurs in *Herm.* 36:5 [Mandate 6:2] where the indwelling of the spirit/angel of wickedness brings about bouts of drinking, greed, and "desires for women" (ἐπιθυμία γυναικῶν).

[21] Cf. also the *Martyrdom of Isaiah* 2:4 and 3:28 which link fornication and sexual error to "spirits of error."

[22] This emphasis upon the visual and sensual is tied to Reuben's own faltering due to the appearance of Bilhah (vv. 10–15). It is also *porneia* which is said to provide Beliar a foothold to cause humans to stumble (*T. Reu.* 4:7; cf. v. 11) and, in the antediluvian era, led to women seducing the Watchers (*T. Reu.* 5.5-6).

[23] Ishay Rosen-Zvi, "Bilhah the Temptress: The Testament of Reuben and 'The Birth of Sexuality,'" *JQR* 96 (2006): 65–94; cf. Tom de Bruin, *The Great Controversy: The Individual's Struggle between Good and Evil in the Testaments of the Twelve* Patriarchs *and in their Jewish and Christian Contexts*, NTOA/SUNT 106 (Göttingen: Vandenhoeck & Ruprecht, 2015), 97–163, esp. 162–3.

[24] *T. Issa.* 4.4: "The spirits of deceit have no power against him, for he does not look to witness feminine beauty, lest he defile his mind with perversion."

The emphasis upon diabolical entities as inveiglers of illicit sexuality found in the *Testaments* persists through the works of the second- and third-century apologists, albeit inconsistently. One of the most explicit is Justin Martyr. In his first *Apology*, Justin claims that the unrestrained and licentious sexual mores of the Romans are the product of the instigation of evil demons (δαιμόνων φαύλων)" (*1 Apol.* 5.1).[25] According to Justin, these demons "sexually despoiled women and corrupted boys" (*1 Apol.* 5), actively promoted inordinate sexual exploits by parading themselves as lascivious deities (*1 Apol.* 25),[26] and even enslaved those who venerated them as gods into *porneia* (*1 Apol.* 14.2; cf. *2 Apol.* 5).[27] By masquerading as gods, Justin argues, these demons were able to successfully dupe the Romans into abandoning reason (λόγος) and thereby cause their irrational appetites to improperly dictate both the conduct of their lives and their exercise of political authority.[28]

Besides the apologists, other Christian texts composed in the third and fourth centuries link the demonic to sexual danger. Like the examples treated above, some of these are little more than cursory allusions to a spirit of fornication, while others are more pronounced in their portrayals of demons as agents of erotic deception or danger. For instance, in a fourth-century Sahidic papyrus—most likely an excerpt from a copy of the *Acts of Andrew*—the apostle speaks of a renowned ascetic virgin tormented by a certain infatuated magician who conjures up some demons in order to tempt her into intercourse.[29] More visual is the third- or fourth-century Valentinian *Gospel of Philip* (NHC II,3) which, in similar fashion to Paul, advocates

---

[25] See especially the excellent work of Jennifer Wright Knust, *Abandoned to Lust: Sexual Slander and Ancient Christianity* (New York: Columbia University Press, 2005).

[26] Justin in particular highlights Dionysus and Apollo for their reputation for homosexual relations (οἵ δι' ἔρωτας ἀρσένων) and Persephone and Aphrodite who were "maddened with love" for Adonis.

[27] Cf. *1 Apol.* 12. In the following section (*1 Apol.* 15) Justin explains in further detail just what *porneia* consists of in contrast to the chastity (σώφρων) of Christians as prescribed through Jesus, including inappropriate looking at women, acts of adultery, and marrying only once. See Knust, *Abandoned to Lust*, 99. Later, in *1 Apol.* 26 Justin also decries various heresies who, because of their affiliation with demons and devils, commit shameful deeds including "immoral sex" (μίξεις), and in *1 Apol.* 27-28 Justin associates the prolific use of pederastic sex and prostitution among the Romans with their worship of the serpent, whom he identifies as Satan.

[28] In particular, Justin calls out Roman imperial attitudes and practices toward prostitution, pederastic sex, and homosexuality (esp. Hadrian and Antoninus).

[29] While this episode is not found in either of the major Greek manuscripts of the *Acts of Andrew*, a shorter version of the story is found in the epitome of Gregory of Tours. The use of demons here by the unnamed magician mechanically corresponds to various incantations, which instruct how to acquire a lover by means of a demonic helper. See Jan Bremmer, "Man, Magic, and Martyrdom in the Acts of Andrew," in J. N. Bremmer (ed.), *The Apocryphal Acts of Andrew* (Leuven: Peeters, 2000), 15-34.

for the marital union of man and woman as a prophylactic against the wiles of male and female unclean spirits.[30] These dangerous spirits in the *Gospel of Philip* are said to take on gendered forms in order to sexually assault single individuals devoid of their spousal counterpart.[31] Thus, the ribald female demon, witnessing a solitary man, might "leap down upon him and play with him and defile him" while the lecherous male demon, after gazing upon a beautiful woman, might "seduce her and compel her, wishing to defile her" (*Gos. Phil.* 65.13-19).

Some of the most vibrant accounts of erotic demons occur in the third-century *Acts of Thomas*. One of the pervasive themes of the *Acts of Thomas* is the renunciation of marital relationships and the corruptive intercourse accompanying it.[32] In a couple of places this point is expressed through Judas Thomas' encounters with demons. In act 3, a fearsome black serpent claims responsibility for the murder of a handsome youth, a deed committed after voyeuristically witnessing the young man engaging in sexual acts with an attractive young maiden (*Acts Thom.* 30-33).[33] In the fifth act (*Acts Thom.* 42-50) a young woman testifies to Thomas how, after leaving the public bath, a young man appeared before her, lewdly declaring that "I and you shall be in one love, and you have intercourse with me as a man and a woman have intercourse."[34] Over the next five years, the demon visits the woman in a "terrible form" in order to engage her in "filthy intercourse." In both of these episodes, the demons express desire for human women which drives them to either wantonly rape the objects of their affections or violently murder those who stand in their way. Unlike most of the sources already encountered, these

---

[30] For similarities between the *Gospel of Philip* and Paul regarding marriage, see Karen L. King, "The Place of the *Gospel of Philip* in the Context of Early Christian Claims about Jesus' Marital Status," *NTS* 59 (2013): 565–87.

[31] *Gos. Phil.* 65.1-12 reads "The forms of unclean spirits include male ones and female ones. The male (spirits) are those which unite with the (human) souls which inhabit a female form, but the female (spirits) are those which are mingled with those in a male form, though one who was disobedient. And no one shall be able to escape them, since they detain him if he does not receive a male power or a female power, the bridegroom and the bride. One receives them from the mirrored bridal chamber." Translation adapted from that of Wesley W. Isenberg, "The Gospel of Philip," in Bentley Layton (ed.), *Nag Hammadi Codex II, 2–7*, NHS 20 (Leiden: Brill, 1989), 141–60.

[32] For example, see Andrew S. Jacobs, "A Family Affair: Marriage, Class, and Ethics in the Apocryphal Acts of the Apostles," *JECS* 7 (1999): 105–38 (esp. 133–6).

[33] For more on the black serpent, see Tamás Adamik, "The Serpent in the *Acts of Thomas*," in J. N. Bremmer (ed.), *The Apocryphal Acts of Thomas* (Leuven: Peeters, 2001), 115–24. For more on demons in the *Acts of Thomas*, see István Czachesz, *The Grotesque Body in Early Christian Discourse: Hell, Scatology, and Metamorphosis* (Routledge: London, 2014), 56–77.

[34] Translation by A. F. J. Klijn, *The Acts of Thomas: Introduction, Text, and Commentary*, NovTSup 58 (2nd ed., Leiden: Brill, 2003). Later in *Acts Thom.* 44 it is revealed the demon has the ability to shape-shift.

demons are also explicitly visible entities with terrifying and enthralling forms which directly indicate their demonic nature.[35]

To summarize, while earlier Jewish and Christian texts are generally quite laconic regarding the relationship between demons and sexuality, by the third century at least some authors voiced a more developed understanding of evil spirits and demons as evokers of sexual sin. Texts like the *Testaments of the Twelve Patriarchs* and Justin's first *Apology* in particular emphasize the capability of demons to entice humans toward inordinate sexual behaviors through psychological manipulation. In addition, works such as the *Acts of Thomas* and the *Gospel of Philip* not only articulate a belief in the demonic as a source of both sexual danger and temptation, but also describe these demons as beings who can manifest themselves in various forms and appearances, including taking on human genders. Many of these latter features appear in the *Testament of Solomon* and in the literature of Egyptian monasticism, to which we shall now turn.

Egyptian Monastic Literature, the Testament of Solomon, and Sex Demons

As mentioned in the introduction to this chapter, both the *Testament of Solomon* and texts related to Egyptian monasticism yield a joint concern regarding the demonic and inordinate sexual activity. For Egyptian monks and ascetics, the suppression of erotic desire stood as one of the keynote exercises defining both the individual quest for virtue and the shape of monastic communities. As Caroline Schroeder has shown, inordinate sexual desire of various forms was one of the most common body confrontations undertaken by the desert monk.[36] More specifically, the act and practice of sexual renunciation for monks, both within and without organized communities, served as a prevalent means of boundary construction, delineating through bodily performance the world of the monk from the world outside the desert or the monastery.[37] The pervasive and ongoing effect of sexual desire, not to mention its ubiquity, quickly came to shape the very language of the ascetic life, with important figures such as Shenoute commonly appropriating the

---

[35] The ability for the demonic body to shape-shift, an ability predicated upon the fine pneumatic composition of their body, is expressed by several ancient authors. For more on this and demonic bodies in general, see Gregory A. Smith, "How Thin is a Demon?" *JECS* 16 (2008): 479–512.

[36] See for example "Prophecy and *Porneia* in Shenoute's Letters: The Rhetoric of Sexuality in a Late Antique Egyptian Monastery," *JNES* 65 (2006): 81–97. See also the excellent article by Elizabeth Clark, "Foucault, The Fathers, and Sex," *JAAR* 56 (1988): 619–41.

[37] As Peter Brown writes, "among the monks of Egypt, the problems of sexual temptation were most often seen in terms of the massive antithesis of 'desert' and 'world.'" See the classic work by Peter Brown, *The Body and Society: Men, Women, and Sexual Renunciation in Early Christianity* (New York: Columbia University Press, 1988), esp. pp. 213–58 (quote on p. 217).

erotic lingo of allure and danger to describe the constant threat of sin in general, going as far as metaphorically construing the monastic community as the female body vulnerable to sin's polluting enticement.[38]

The role of fornication, lust, and the monastic body in the shaping and boundary-demarcating of the world was facilitated in many ways by the relationship of the monk to the demonic. As David Brakke has lucidly shown, the demon played a crucial role in the construction of monastic identity in antique Egypt, embodying not only the incredible exterior danger of sin besetting the monk, but also engendering the inner anxiety of the desert fathers (and mothers) in their pursuits of holiness and ascent.[39] For many monks, Satan and the demons were nefarious forces whose perpetual presence could, at any time, potentially jeopardize their purity by manipulating anything from the female body to one's own thoughts. Thus, Shenoute, abbot of the famed White Monastery, in his homily *I See Your Eagerness* emphatically warns of demonic foes subduing female virgins and causing them to forego their vows of chastity in order to tempt well-meaning monks into deeds of sexual pleasure.[40] Likewise, in Athanasius' *Life of Antony* the young monk Antony is confronted by demons who attempt to spoil him through filthy thoughts, titillations of the body, and the projection of the sexually illicit images.[41] The demonic use of images to whet the carnal appetites is addressed extensively by the late-fourth-century Evagrius, who describes fornication as the most visual among all the demons' odious temptations, noting that demons will show obscene images of woman and perform "unspeakable acts" to unsuspecting monks.[42] Indeed, the hagiographic accounts of various desert monks often include enthralling anecdotes which recall colorful dialogues between pious ascetics and demonic interlocutors, many of which arrive in the forms of young women, black-skinned boys, and even chimeric beasts of terrifying forms. In other words, for the desert fathers demons were opportunistic denizens of sexual yearning whose

---

[38] See esp. chapters 1 and 2 of Caroline Schroeder, *Monastic Bodies: Discipline and Salvation in Shenoute of Atripe* (Philadelphia: University of Pennsylvania Press, 2007).

[39] David Brakke, *Demons and the Making of the Monk: Spiritual Conflict in Early Christianity* (Cambridge: Harvard University Press, 2009).

[40] Many times, Shenoute associates the female body, due to its increased materiality and irrationality, as being especially susceptible to the sexual temptations of demons. For more on the female body and Shenoute, see Rebecca Krawiec, *Shenoute & the Women of the White Monastery: Egyptian Monasticism in Late Antiquity* (Oxford: Oxford University Press, 2002).

[41] *Life of Antony* 5–6. David Brakke goes into great detail regarding the demonic use of images to tempt Antony. He also notes that the first to propose that demons are associated with particular vices, including lust, was Origen (e.g., *Homilies on Joshua* 15; *Homilies on Ezekiel* 6). See *Demons and the Making of the Monk*, 23–47 (esp. 26–30).

[42] Among other places, see Evagrius, *Praktikos* 8; *Eight Spirits* 4–6; *Eulogios* 13, 16, 27; *Excerpts* 9. See also Brakke, *Demons and the Making of the Monk*, 60–1. The visual force of the demon of fornication is especially pronounced in Book 2 of Evagrius' *Talking Back*.

methods ranged from promoting the "benefits" of the married life to taking on the physical forms of lewd women with the hopes of engaging seduced monks in intercourse.

In comparison to earlier Jewish and Christian accounts of demons, the literature of Egyptian monasticism presents a flamboyant picture of the demonic. Most of the demons encountered by monks not only engage them in lively discussion and debate, but also take on a variety of seductive and/or terrifying apparitions. Much like the literature of Egyptian monasticism, the *Testament* also reflects a pronounced concern regarding the ability of demons to cause sexual dysfunction and impurity through both temptation and assault. In several instances, the venereal disorders inflicted by demons in the *Testament* resonate with the experiences of Egyptian monks and their combat against their demonic foes. This can be seen early on in chapter 2 of the *Testament*, where the demon Ornias reveals to Solomon several features of his character explicitly linked to the sexual defilement of human beings. In *T. Sol.* 2:2 Ornias informs Solomon that he physically torments men associated with the constellation Aquarius "because of their desire (δι' ἐπιθυμίαν) for women" who reside beneath the zodiac sign Virgo.[43] More fascinating is the version of this episode found in MS E, where Ornias also informs Solomon that one of his other devious deeds is to assume the phantasmic form of a woman and cause men to sin in their sleep.[44] The dual act of Ornias taking on the form of a woman and nocturnally appearing before a man with the intent of causing sin draws several salient points of comparison with the desert fathers and their accounts regarding the danger of erotic dreams. As noted earlier, figures like Evagrius warned ascetics of the ability of demons to exploit sensual images meant to derail monastic abstinence.[45] One of the most susceptible occasions for demons to threaten the chastity of even the most vigilant of monks was during their dreams. The widely known capability of the fine-material demonic body to infiltrate dreams appears in monastic literature, with several accounts recalling demons taking on the form of beautiful women as a way of triggering the filthy

---

[43] As Klutz rightly points out, the mention of people residing under a zodiac sign reflects chorographic astrology which was not uncommon in the Greco-Roman world. In this sense, Ornias' physical wrath is inflicted upon men who lust after women who do live in the same region of the earth, which is under the auspice of the constellation Aquarius (which Ornias seems also to be associated with). See Klutz "The Archer and the Cross: Chorographic Astrology and Literary Design in the *Testament of Solomon*," in T. Klutz (ed.), *Magic in the Biblical World: From the Rod of Aaron to the Ring of Solomon*, JSNTSup 245 (London: T&T Clark, 2003), 219–44. See also Kocku von Stuckrad, *Das Ringen um die Astrologie: Judische und christliche Beitrage zum antiken Zeitverstandnis* (Berlin: de Gruyter, 2000), esp. pp. 397, 409–15.

[44] The Greek reads καὶ πότε ὡσὰν γυναῖκα ἔμορφη φαντάζομαι εἰς τὸν ὕπνον τους [ἀνθρώπους] καὶ ἁμαρτάνουν (MS E 3:2).

[45] Cf. the *Testament of the Twelve Patriarchs* and Origen, who also hold a similar view regarding the role of *phantasia* which shows some dependence upon Stoicism.

desires of a slumbering target, sometimes even causing nocturnal emissions. As David Brakke has shown, monks both in and outside of Egypt understood the racy images of such dreams to be a precarious threat to the sexual purity of the monastic body.[46] The fact that the dream *phantasia* was facilitated by the animalistic soul of the human, and thus fell outside the jurisdiction of the rational faculty, meant that moments of sleep exponentially increased the susceptibility of the ascetic body to the erotic influence of female images.[47] According to John Cassian, even the most chaste of monks was vulnerable to the "images of women" (*fantasmata feminarum*) produced during dreams.[48] In many ways, the claim of the demon Ornias from the *Testament* to φαντάζομαι female forms before men at night in order to cause them to sin embodies the exact same sense of anxiety articulated by Evagrius and other desert fathers. Much like the nocturnal demons feared by the monks, Ornias too uses female apparitions in order to cause men to surrender to erogenous error in their sleep, where their inhibitions are most exposed.[49]

Without question, however, the most degenerate and disturbing feature of Ornias is his proclivity to take the form of a man who lusts after (ἔχων ἐπιθυμίαν) the bodies of effeminate boys and subsequently causes them great pain when he engages them in intercourse.[50] Besides striking a generally terrifying image of demonic rape, Ornias' lecherous transformation conveys a sense of anxiety

---

[46] David Brakke, "The Problematization of Nocturnal Emissions in Early Christian Syria, Egypt, and Gaul," *JECS* 3 (1995): 419–60. Indeed, the use of the verb φαντάζομαι evokes the language used by Dioscorus in the Greek text of the *Historia Monarchorum* 20 where the monk declares that anyone who has witnessed the "image" (φαντασία) of a woman during their sleep avoid the Eucharist, lest they have a nocturnal emission due to the image. Note also Evagrius, *Talking Back* 2.15 where Evagrius cites 1 Kgs 2:4-5 as scripture to counteract the demon of fornication who appeared to him at night in the form of a woman (cf. 2.19, 22–23, 32).

[47] See Leslie Dossey, "Watchful Greeks and Lazy Romans: Disciplining Sleep in Late Antiquity," *JECS* 21 (2013): 208–39.

[48] In book 12 of his *Conferences*, John Cassian categorizes chastity into six ascending classes, with the lowest being avoiding carnal deeds while awake, and the highest degree of chastity being avoiding the images of women during sleep (12.7.4). For more on Cassian and erotic dreams, see Simon Lienyuah Wei, "The Absence of Sin in Sexual Dreams in the Writings of Augustine and Cassian," *VC* 66 (2012): 362–78 (see pp. 367–76).

[49] In many ways, this fits the pre-established *modus operandi* of the demon, as in chapter 1 Ornias is seen sucking the life out of one of Solomon's workers while he sleeps.

[50] *T. Sol.* 2:3: ποτὲ μὲν ὡς ἄνθρωπος ἔχων ἐπιθυμίαν εἴδους παιδίων θηλυκῶν ἀνήβων καὶ ἁπτομένου μου ἀλγῶσι πάνυ. Duling in *OTP* translates this as "Sometimes I am a man who craves the bodies of effeminate boys and when I touch them, they suffer great pain." The participle ἁπτομένου literally means "to touch" but as Duling notes can be used to also describe sexual contact. Loader (*The Pseudepigrapha on Sexuality*, 137) finds it most likely that παιδίων θηλυκῶν ἀνήβων refers to young effeminate boys rather than young girls, thus making this a scene of "pederastic rape."

similar to that expressed in monastic communities. Homosexual and pederastic sex was viewed as a threat to the celibacy of cenobitic communities, many of which were exclusively or predominately male.[51] In one of his letters Shenoute disparages monks from engaging in several activities with boys which induce "desire" (*epithumia* in Coptic), some of which include kissing, co-bathing, and even touching.[52] At times, demons even transformed their appearances to look like effeminate youths or used young boys as a means of overwhelming the ascetic's virtuous fortitude. In the *Life of Antony*, a demon takes the form of a feminized Ethiopian boy before the tormented Antony, a visual token of sexual vulnerability used by the spirit of whoredom and lust.[53] The *Sayings of the Desert Fathers* tells of an episode attributed to Abba John the Persian where an old monk witnessed a brother falling prey to the seductive prowess of a boy possessed by a demon.[54] Much like his embodiment of the nocturnal images of lust, Ornias' form as a wanton molester of boys in the *Testament* demonizes the same sexual anxieties experienced by the desert fathers regarding the sensuous trap of pederastic sex, a demonic mirror image of desire gone amok.

After subduing Beelzeboul, the prince of demons, in chapter 3, the next demon Solomon encounters spreads much of the same sexual danger as Ornias. In chapter 4, the demon Onoskelis appears to Solomon as a woman with an extravagantly beautiful form (μορφὴν … περικαλλῆ) and a fair bodily constitution (δέμας … εὐχώρτου), albeit donning a pair of donkey legs (*T. Sol.* 4:2).[55] The physical description of Onoskelis found in the *Testament* contains several elements,

---

[51] See Caroline Schroeder, "Queer Eye for the Ascetic Guy? Homoeroticism, Children, and the Making of Monks in Late Antique Egypt," *JAAR* 77 (2009): 333–47; cf. also Terry G. Wilfong, "'Friendship and Physical Desire': The Discourse of Female Homoeroticism in Fifth-Century CE Egypt," in N. Sorkin Rabinowitz and L. Auanger (eds.), *Among Women: From the Homosocial to the Homoerotic in the Ancient World* (Austin: University of Texas Press, 2002), 304–29.

[52] See Schroeder, "Queer Eye for the Ascetic Guy?" esp. pp. 341–3. Schroeder here cites an unpublished Coptic letter from the Austrian National Library (AT-NB K9101).

[53] *Life of Antony* 6.

[54] "A demoniac boy came one day to be healed, and some brothers from an Egyptian monastery arrived. As one old man was coming out to meet them he saw a brother sinning with the boy, but he did not accuse him; he said, 'If God who has made them sees them and does not burn them, who am I to blame them?'" Translation by Benedicta Ward, *The Sayings of the Desert Fathers*, CSS 59 (Kalamazoo: Cistercian Publications, 1975), 107. Abba Isaac of the Cells in the *Sayings* expresses a similar sentiment when he commands not to bring young boys due to their penchant for causing churches to disassemble.

[55] MS T of the Greek contains this aside: κνήμας δὲ ἡμιόνου lit. "(her) legs were half-ass." Many of the other manuscripts do not contain any explicit description of her ass-like features (MS P adds that Onoskelis possessed horns on her head [κερατίζουσα τὴν κεφαλὴν]), although very meaning of the name Onoskelis "ass-legged" would perhaps suggest as much for readers.

which convey a sense of sexual anxiety and danger. The gendering of Onoskelis as a comely female in and of itself exudes a latent erotic anxiety, which finds many correspondences in monastic literature.[56] In addition, as both Busch and Loader highlight, the asinine features of Onoskelis' lower body recall the story of Aristonymus whose copulation with a mule led to the birth of "the comely maiden Onoskelis."[57] Besides potential connotations of bestial coitus and procreation, the appearance of Onoskelis also draws comparison to the succubus Empousa, infamous for her seduction of young men and subsequent consumption of their blood and flesh.[58] Much like the Empousa, Onoskelis in the *Testament* possesses both the attractiveness to allure men and the aspiration to batter these men both physically through strangulation and psychologically by perverting their true natures (*T. Sol.* 4:5). The erotically monstrous appearance of Onoskelis, and its apparent overlaps with other satyr-like figures notorious for inordinate sexuality and danger, situates her as the dangerous demonic embodiment of unrestrained lust, a spiritual foe not unlike those encountered by various desert monks.[59] In fact, some monastic literature even attests to monks coming across satyr-like demons similar in appearance to Onoskelis. In the *Life of Antony*, for example, a beastly demon visits Antony, which has the appearance of a human, save for its legs, which were those of an ass (ὄνῳ).[60] As Brakke points out, the form of this demon—the final demonic trial of Antony—mimics the appearance of the god Pan/Min who was especially popular in Upper Egypt where a high concentration of monks settled.[61] Shenoute in particular exemplifies this same antagonism to Pan/Min in his polemicization of the temple and shrines of the fertility god,

---

[56] For a full treatment of the issue, see Gáspár Parlagi, "The City without (?) Women: Approach to the Female in Early Monastic Literature," in G. G. Xeravits (ed.), *Religion and Female Body in Ancient Judaism and Its Environments* (Berlin: de Gruyter, 2015), 246–62.

[57] Loader, *The Pseudepigrapha on Sexuality*, p. 137; Peter Busch, *Das Testament Salomos: Die Älteste Christliche Dämonologie, Kommentiert und in Deutscher Erstübersetzung*, TUGAL 153 (Berlin: de Gruyter, 2006), 111. Other references to the Onoskelia include that of Lucian, *Vera Historia* 2.46, and Plutarch, *Parallela minora* 29.

[58] For more on the Empousa see Sarah Iles Johnston, *Restless Dead: Encounters between the Living and the Dead in Ancient Greece* (Berkeley: University of California Press, 1999), 133–9; Maria Patera, *Figures grecques de l'épouvante de l'antiquité au présent: peurs enfantines et adultes*, Mnemosyne Supplements 376 (Leiden: Brill, 2014), 249–90. Unlike Onoskelis, however, Empousa possessed only one donkey leg made of bronze.

[59] Note also the detail given by Onoskelis that her residential domain are caves, cliffs, and ravines (*T. Sol.* 4:5-6), isolated locations which happen to be the same locales where anachorite and cenobitic monks situated themselves.

[60] Cf. also chapter 8 of the *Vita Pauli* of Jerome which tells how Antony came into contact with a satyr in the desert. See especially A. H. Merrills, "Monks, Monsters, and Barbarians: Re-defining the African Periphery in Late Antiquity," *JECS* 12 (2004): 217–44.

[61] *Life of Antony* 53; cf. Brakke, *Demons and the Making of the Monk*, 34–5.

whose iconography was often donned with an enlarged phallus.⁶² Altogether then, much like Ornias, the demoness Onoskelis manifests several major anxieties which would have held relevance for Egyptian monks. Her monstrous appearance and name both recall legendary female fiends known for their erotic appetites and partiality for violence, and iconographically her resemblance to the fertility god Pan/Min is reminiscent of monastic encounters with demonic satyrs.

The next demon Solomon comes across is none other than the infamous Asmodeus.⁶³ While the depiction of Asmodeus in the book of Tobit, as noted earlier, does not explicitly ascribe the demon a partiality toward sexual temptation or violence, the author of the *Testament* emphasizes latent elements of Asmodeus' character which imply as much.⁶⁴ Besides revealing to Solomon his constellation and origins as the spawn of a human mother and an angelic father (cf. the *Book of the Watchers*), Asmodeus describes himself as one who "schemes against newlyweds" and "spoils the beauty of virgins and causes (their) hearts to change" (παρθένων κάλλος ἀφανίζω καὶ καρδίας ἀλλοιῶ) (*T. Sol.* 5:7). Like his character in Tobit, Asmodeus in the *Testament* is associated with causing problems for newlyweds.⁶⁵ In addition, however, Asmodeus also perverts the beauty of virgins and causes them to have a change in heart. In most versions of Tobit, while Sarah presumably has saved her marital purity for wedlock, at no point do we see her explicitly called a virgin, making this an exegetically motivated addition

---

⁶² See, esp., pp. 170-2. The worship of Pan in Stephen Emmel, "Shenoute of Atripe and the Christian Destruction of Temple in Egypt: Rhetoric and Reality," in J. Hahn, S. Emmel, and U. Gotter (eds.), *From Temple to Church: Destruction and Renewal of Local Cultic Topography in Late Antiquity*, RGRW 163 (Leiden: Brill, 2008), 161-202. Pan/Min was especially prominent in Upper Egypt, including near monastic communities.

⁶³ It seems likely that most Egyptian Christians (and Jews) would have been familiar with Asmodeus. By the fourth century, the book of Tobit appears to have not only circulated Egypt in Greek, but may have also been translated into Coptic, as exhibited by the fragments of Coptic Tobit found in the Bodmer papyri, which date from the fourth to the seventh centuries. In addition, Athanasius includes Tobit in the canon list found in his Festal Letter 39.

⁶⁴ In contrast, later Jewish traditions regarding Ashmedai, such as the lengthy narrative found in *b. Git.* 68a, do not dramatically overemphasize the demon's erotic nature. See Richard Kalmin, *Migrating Tales: The Talmud's Migrating Tales: The Talmud's Narratives and Their Historical Context* (Oakland: University of California Press, 2014), 95-129.

⁶⁵ MS P in particular elaborates that Asmodeus prevents newlyweds from sleeping with one another (συμμιγῆναι). Besides causing problems for newlyweds, other affinities shared between Tobit and the *Testament* in their depictions of Asmodeus include his aversion to Raphael and the use of the burning of fish organs to thwart him (see *T. Sol.* 5:9-11). In addition, the book of Tobit notes in chapter 8 and once Asmodeus is expelled from the presence of Sarah, Raphael pursues him all the way into Egypt before binding him (Tob 8:3).

to the Asmodeus storyline.⁶⁶ While the language is admittedly unclear here in the *Testament*, one potential interpretation is that Asmodeus causes virgins to abandon their abstinence and thereby despoil their beauty. Asmodeus' danger to the beauty of the παρθένων recalls several instances where chaste female monks are described as beautiful even in old age.⁶⁷ One particular virgin, Amma Sarah, is said in the *Sayings of the Desert Fathers* to have strived against the demon of fornication for thirteen years, ultimately defeating the tempting spirit, and the fifth-century account of Syncletica likewise depicts its virginal subject instructing her followers to avoid the erotic foils of the devil.⁶⁸ Unfortunately, not all virgins were so successful in their pious endeavors. In one of his homilies, Shenoute chastises former virgins who abandoned their vows, going as far as to accuse them of being seduced by, and having intercourse with, Satan himself.⁶⁹ In this fashion, Asmodeus' marring of virginal beauty and his changing of their hearts could reflect a similar situation where sexual purity is forsaken by ascetic women due to the meddlesome work of a demon.⁷⁰

A few other demons in the *Testament* likewise proclaim to commit acts of sexual temptation or violence. The Winged Dragon demon in chapter 14 paints an especially disturbing self-portrait when he declares to Solomon that his primary activity is copulating with beautiful women in the buttock and that one of his female victims even died giving birth to his offspring—the god Eros (*T. Sol.* 14:4).⁷¹ In chapter 17, Solomon meets a shadowy spirit with glowing eyes who describes himself as "a lecherous spirit of a giant man who had died in the massacre of

---

⁶⁶ In fact, only in Jerome's fairly free rendering of Tobit in the Vulgate do we see the word *virgo* applied to Sarah. Another interesting feature of the depiction of Asmodeus in the *Testament* is that while Tobit does not state whether Asmodeus is a serial offender of violently killing potential suitors, in the *Testament* his malevolent work has been expanded to include multiple newlyweds and virgins.

⁶⁷ In the *Lausaic History*, for example, we find Asella (16.4), Taor (59.2), and the virgin who hid Athanasius (63).

⁶⁸ For a translation and assessment of the life of Syncletica, see Elizabeth Bryson Bongie (translation) and Mary Schaffer, *The Life and Regimen of the Blessed and Holy Syncletica*, 2 vols. (Eugene, OR: Wipf and Stock, 2005).

⁶⁹ Shenoute, *I See Your Eagerness*. For more on all of these examples, see Brakke, *Demons and the Making of the Monk*, 184–97. For more on virgins and female monks in Egypt, see Susanna Elm, '*Virgins of God': The Making of Asceticism in Late Antiquity* (Oxford: Clarendon Press, 1994), 227–372.

⁷⁰ Cf. Klutz, *Rewriting the Testament of Solomon*, 142–3. In addition to his manipulation of virgins, Asmodeus claims to "spread madness about women (θηλυμανίας) through the stars" (*T. Sol.* 5:8), suggesting that the demon disseminates lustful insanity among young men.

⁷¹ Busch (*Das Testament Salomos*, 193–200) intriguingly associates this detail with the Eros myth from books 4 and 5 of Apuleius' *The Golden Ass* where Amor, the father of Eros, is depicted as a dragon (4.33.1-2; 5.17; 5.22.2).

the time of the giants."⁷² In chapter 6, we also witness Beelzeboul, the "prince of demons" declaring his own affinity for inflicting sexual disorder among other dastardly deeds:

> I [Solomon] said to him, "What are your activities?" He [Beelzeboul] replied, "I bring destruction by means of tyrants; I cause the demons to be worshiped alongside men; and I arouse desire in holy men and select priests (καὶ τοὺς ἁγίους καὶ τοὺς ἐκλεκτοὺς ἱερεῖς εἰς ἐπιθυμίαν ἐγείρω). I bring about jealousies and murders in a country, and I instigate wars." (*T. Sol.* 6:4; trans. Duling)

Besides bringing about unrest, violence, and the worship of demons among humans, Beelzeboul professes to rouse up ἐπιθυμίαν (cf. Ornias and Onoskelis) in holy individuals and certain priests.⁷³ This particular reference to holy men and select priests is fairly protuberant and unexpected in the immediate context of Beelzeboul's speech, as he gives no prior indication to Solomon that he afflicts humans with desire.⁷⁴ What may perhaps make more sense of this unanticipated statement is the frequent portrayal of demons and the devil as a constant source of lustful danger among various Egyptian holy men, clerics, and monks. In the *Sayings of the Desert Fathers* we see several monks, such as Isiodore, Macarius the Great, and John the Dwarf, who are ordained as priests. Additionally, a number of monks took on the roles of holy men during the fourth and fifth centuries, an occupation which largely arose in response to the ritual expectations and needs of their native communities. Many times, these monks functioned in much the same way as their pagan counterparts, issuing amulets and incantations,⁷⁵ and

---

⁷² Cf. also Kunopegos who in chapter 16 of the *Testament* claims to "desire the bodies" (εἰμὶ ἐπιθυμῶν σωμάτων) of seafaring men (*T. Sol.* 16:2). It is unclear, however, whether Kunopegos lusts after these bodies, or desires them (i.e., wants a human body). The surrounding context of *T. Sol.* 16 does not explicitly reveal the demon's motivation for his desire.

⁷³ MS P contains a longer reading of this section and includes sodomy among these sins. The sorts of disorders caused by Beelzeboul here may bear some relationship to his statement in *T. Sol.* 6:2-3 that he was the highest ranking of the angels who fell from heaven (*T. Sol.* 6:2-3). Much like the Enochic watchers, Beelzeboul induces insurrection, violence, and demon-worship among humans, and his association with inappropriate sexual activity recalls the fallen angels' own sexual manipulation of human women. Cf. Matthew Goff, "The Diabolical Wisdom of Solomon: Assessing the Jewishness of the Testament of Solomon," in F. Albrecht and J. Dochhorn (eds.), *Testamentum Salomonis. Editiones studiaque collegerunt edideruntque*, Parabiblica 1 (Tübingen: Mohr Siebeck) (forthcoming).

⁷⁴ According to Loader (*The Pseudepigrapha on Sexuality*, 138) Beelzeboul's use of desire "most probably refers to sexual desire" and links its association with traditions which reflect hostility toward the priest establishment (i.e., *1 Enoch*, *Jubilees*, the *Psalms of Solomon*, etc.).

⁷⁵ For example, see Theodore de Bruyn and Jitse H. F. Dijkstra, "Greek Amulets and Formularies from Egypt Containing Christian Elements: A Checklist of Papyri, Parchments, Ostraka, and Tablets," *BASP* 48 (2011): 163–216.

even counteracting the ill-effects of love-spells.⁷⁶ As such, this particular reference to the susceptibility of priests and holy men to Beelzeboul may once again reflect a sense of anxiety regarding the demonic partiality toward sexual temptation.

Out of Egypt? Implications and Conclusions

As this study has shown, the demons of the *Testament* share a pronounced affinity for sexual misconduct and sin with the demons found in the literature of Egyptian monasticism. Both the *Testament* and Egyptian monastic accounts contain detailed portraits of evil entities, replete with vivid descriptions of their appearances. These demons commonly use the projection of images as a way of misleading humans into lustful deeds, including priests and holy men, and at times even go as far as to sexually assault unwary victims. In comparison to earlier Jewish and Christian demonologies, both the *Testament* and the works composed by, or about, figures such as Antony, Evagrius, and Shenoute, stand out in all of these regards, and draw close comparison to texts such as the *Acts of Thomas* and the *Gospel of Philip*.⁷⁷

To conclude, I would like to draw out two potential implications this study may hold for future analysis of the *Testament of Solomon* regarding the date of its composition and its provenance. First, in terms of dating the *Testament*, scholars have inconclusively proposed a variety of possible dates ranging from the first century CE⁷⁸ to the late Byzantine period.⁷⁹ The recent work of Todd Klutz concludes that while the final form of the *Testament* (as witnessed in MS P) ultimately came to be around the third century CE, chapters 1–15 and 18 are considerably older and may date to a first-century, pre-Christian stratum.⁸⁰ Contrarily, in her dissertation

---

⁷⁶ See David Frankfurter, "The Perils of Love: Magic and Countermagic in Coptic Egypt," *Journal of the History of Sexuality* 10 (2001): 480–500.

⁷⁷ In addition, it is worth noting that the conclusion of the *Testament* depicts the downfall of Solomon as a consequence of his unquenchable lust. Thus, even one of the central and ongoing themes of the *Testament* is Solomon succumbing to the powers of sexual temptation.

⁷⁸ For example, Frederick C. Conybeare, "The Testament of Solomon," *JQR* 11 (1898): 1–45. In his assessment, C. C. McCown proposed that some of the recensions of the *Testament*, most notably his reconstructed recension *d*, probably dated to the first century CE due to the use of Koine Greek and the preservation of "pre-Talmudic" Judaism. See *The Testament of Solomon* (Leipzig: J. C. Hinrichs, 1922), 105–9.

⁷⁹ For example, Ferdinand Florens Fleck, "Testamentum Salomonis: Bibliothecae Regiae Parisinae ineditum," in F. F. Fleck (ed.), *Wissenschaftliche Reise durch das südliche Deutschland, Italien, Sicilien und Frank-reich 2,3* (Leipzig: Barth, 1837), 111–40; V. M. Istrin, "Grieceski Spiski Zabesania Solomona," *Lietopis istoriko-philologetscheskago Obtchestva* 7 (1899): 49–98.

⁸⁰ Klutz, *Rewriting the Testament of Solomon*, 108–9. More specifically, Klutz sees *T. Sol.* 1-15 as being the earliest stratum of the *Testament* (besides the decan chapter of *T. Sol.* 18) and roughly dates it to between 75 and 125 CE.

Sarah Schwarz argues that while portions of the *Testament* may indeed date to the first several centuries of the Common Era, the final form of the *Testament* most likely did not arise until the Byzantine period.[81] Bridging the gap between Klutz and Schwarz, Peter Busch has proposed that several features of the *Testament* hint at a mid to late fourth-century date sometime after the death of Constantine.[82]

While the results of this study certainly cannot pinpoint the exact time when the *Testament* was composed, the fact that the demonology of the *Testament* and its association of the demonic with wanton sexuality bear much more in common with Egyptian monasticism than first- or second-century Jewish or Christian literature does perhaps offer some insight regarding a possible *terminus post quem*. In fact, as the following pages have exposed, it is not until the third century that we see any depictions of the demonic which even vaguely compare to the *Testament* in either the descriptive portrayal of these evil entities or their expressed tendency to cause amatory bedlam. As such, this study suggests that any dating of the *Testament*, which extends earlier than the third century CE, is most likely overstating the antiquity of the text.[83]

Second, arguably the most tendentious topic regarding the *Testament* has been its provenance. Chester McCown, the original editor of the text, all but ignored the subject in his 1922 volume, declaring that "no certain conclusion can be reached,"[84] and it was not until Dennis Duling's work in the 1980s that the subject reemerged.[85] A number of scholars have made fairly detailed arguments supporting a Judaean provenance. Duling concludes that Palestine is the most likely location fostering the composition of the *Testament*, noting the prolific amount of material coming

---

[81] Sarah L. Schwarz, "Building a Book of Spells: The So-called Testament of Solomon Reconsidered" (PhD dissertation; Philadelphia: University of Pennsylvania, 2005); Cf. also eadem, "Reconsidering the Testament of Solomon," *JSP* 16 (2007): 203–37. Much of Schwarz's argument depends upon reading the *Testament* as a Byzantine *grimoire*, an observation she bases largely on the composite nature of the *Testament* and the varied constitution of the available manuscripts, not to mention their late dating. Similar points regarding the *Testament* as a spellbook are also made by Philip Alexander in "Contextualizing the Demonology of the Testament of Solomon," in *Die Dämonen—Demons*, 613–35.

[82] Peter Busch, "Solomon as a True Exorcist: The Testament of Solomon in Its Cultural Setting," in J. Verheyden (ed.), *The Figure of Solomon in Jewish, Christian and Islamic Tradition: King, Sage and Architect*, TBN 16 (Leiden: Brill, 2013), 183–95.

[83] Cf. Goff, "The Diabolical Wisdom of Solomon" who arrives at a similar conclusion by noting that nothing in the *Testament* concretely proves that it preserves any explicitly, non-Christian material, thus dissembling the Jewish *Urschrift* theory of previous scholars.

[84] McCown, *The Testament of Solomon*, 109–11. McCown ultimately concluded that Asia Minor, Egypt, and Jerusalem, in descending order, were the most probable locations where the *Testament* was composed.

[85] Dennis C. Duling, "The Testament of Solomon," in J. H. Charlesworth (ed.), *The Old Testament Pseudepigrapha*, 2 vols., ABRL (Garden City: Doubleday, 1983–1985), 1.935-87; idem, "The Testament of Solomon: Retrospect and Prospect," *JSP* 2 (1988): 87–112.

out of the region which describes Solomon's power over demons.[86] Peter Busch likewise supports Jerusalem as the most probable *milieu* for the composition of the *Testament*, arguing that the *Testament*'s depiction of Solomon's magical ring and his God-given authority over the demonic reflects the "lokalkolorit," topography, and socio-cultural situation of the religious establishment of Jerusalem and the Church of the Holy Seplucher.[87]

Besides Palestine, a few scholars have proposed Egypt as a potential location from which the *Testament* may have been produced,[88] a suggestion most certainly affirmed by this study. Besides the shared demonological features highlighted above, a number of the Nag Hammadi manuscripts reference Solomon and his power over the demons, suggesting that by the third and fourth centuries traditions regarding Solomon's demonological abilities were present in Egypt.[89] The portrayal of the thirty-six decans found in chapter 18 of the *Testament* likewise draws several striking parallels to decanal *melothesia* (a form of astrological medicine) as found in Roman Egypt.[90] In addition, several Coptic and Arabic manuscripts from Egypt contain narratival episodes, which may have derived from, or had been based upon, stories found in the *Testament*.[91]

Perhaps the most concrete evidence for locating the *Testament* in Egypt is the citation of Solomon's διαθήκη found in the *Dialogue of Timothy and Aquila*—an anonymous Jewish-Christian dialogue dated to fifth- or sixth-century Alexandria.[92]

---

[86] Duling, *OTP*, 943-44; idem, "The Testament of Solomon," 96-7. These include Wis 7:20; Josephus, *Antiquities*, 8.42-49; Pseudo-Philo, *L.A.B.* 60; and column 2 of 11Q11 as well as the *Sepher Ha-Razim* and a second- or third-century CE Jewish foil amulet which refers to a "seal of Solomon."

[87] See esp. Busch, *Das Testament Salomos*, 17-30; idem, "Solomon as a True Exorcist," 193-4. Among other elements connoting a Jerusalem provenance, Busch reads the references to pillars in *T. Sol.* 12:4 and 24:5 as etiological narratives referring to the statues constructed by Hadrian on the Temple mount and Golgotha, respectively, and takes pilgrimage accounts (such as *Itinerarium Egeriae*, the *Breviarius*, and the Pilgrim of Bordeaux) as evidence that Solomon's ring was a prominent icon in Jerusalem during the fourth century.

[88] Most notable here is Klutz, *Rewriting the Testament of Solomon*, 104-10; see also 35-6, 50.

[89] For a summary, see Jacques van der Vliet, "Solomon in Egyptian Gnosticism," in *The Figure of Solomon in Jewish, Christian and Islamic Tradition*, 197-218.

[90] For a detailed analysis of *T. Sol.* 18 as reflecting Roman Egyptian astrology, see my forthcoming publication "Demonic Decans: An Analysis of Chapter 18 of the *Testament of Solomon*," in *Testamentum Salomonis. Editiones studiaque collegerunt edideruntque*.

[91] For example, see Slavomír Čéplö, "Testament of Solomon and Other Pseudepigraphical Material in Aḥkām Sulaymān (Judgment of Solomon)," in V. S. Hovhanessian (ed.), *The Canon of the Bible and the Apocrypha in the Churches of the East* (New York: Peter Lang, 2012), 21-37.

[92] Supporting an Egyptian provenance are R. G. Robertson, "The Dialogue of Timothy and Aquila: A Critical Text, Introduction to the Manuscript Evidence, and an Inquiry into the Sources and Literary Relationships" (Th.D. Dissertation; Harvard University, 1986), 345-71; Jacqueline Z. Pastis, "Dating the Dialogue of Timothy and Aquila: Revisiting the Earlier Vorlage Hypothesis," *HTR* 95 (2002): 169-95.

In chapter 9, the Christian Timothy argues against the Jew Aquila regarding whether Jesus or Solomon is the true fulfillment of Ps 2:7. Among several other arguments, Timothy retorts his Jewish interlocutor by stating:

"Know, O Jew, that he [Solomon] worshipped and sacrificed grasshoppers to the idols" (προσεκύνησεν καὶ ἀκρίδα ἔσφαξεν τοῖς γλυπτοῖς). The Jew said: "He did not sacrifice, but he crushed them in his hand unwillingly (οὐκ ἔσφαξεν ἀλλὰ ἔθλασεν ἐν τῇ χειρὶ ἀκουσίως). But the Book of Kings does not contain these things, but they have been written in his Testament" (ἐν τῇ διαθήκῃ αὐτοῦ) (*Dialogue* 9.11-13).[93]

Timothy's statement shows a lucid resemblance to chapter 26 of the *Testament* which also depicts Solomon "sacrificing" (σφάξαι) grasshoppers to idols (*T. Sol.* 26:4 MSS H and N) and "worshipping" (προσκυνῆσαι) these foreign gods (*T. Sol.* 26:2-3).[94] Moreover, the *Dialogue* even explicitly attributes this narrative to Solomon's διαθήκη, suggesting the author at a minimum knew the version of the story found in the *Testament*, if not possessed a copy of it. Along these lines, then, the similarities drawn between the *Testament* and Egyptian monastic literature stand as further proof supporting a fourth- or fifth-century Egyptian provenance for the *Testament*.

However, before jumping the proverbial gun here, it is important to keep in mind that, despite the substantial evidence supporting an Egyptian provenance for the *Testament*, the manuscript attestation of the *Testament* does severely curtail any definitive efforts to date or locate the *Testament*. Indeed, a majority of these

---

[93] Text and translation taken from William Varner, *Ancient Jewish-Christian Dialogues: Athanasius and Zacchaeus, Simon and Theophilus, Timothy and Aquila* (Lewiston/Queenston/Lampeter: Edwin Mellen Press, 2004). Most scholars compare this to *T. Sol.* 26:5: "So because I [Solomon] loved the girl—she was in full bloom and I was out of my senses—I accepted as nothing the custom (of sacrificing) the blood of the locusts. I took them in my hands and sacrificed in the name of Raphan and Molech to idols, and I took the maiden to the palace of my kingdom" (trans. Duling, *OTP*).

[94] One other point supporting the *Dialogue*'s reliance upon the *Testament* here lies in the atypical nature of the actual event. As far as I know, there are no other instances in ancient Jewish, Christian, and Greco-Roman literature where grasshoppers or locusts are actually sacrificed to a deity or idol. The closest parallel is that of Rabbi Ishmael in *Gen. Rab.* 53.11, where he states that Sarah's catching of Ishmael "making sport" (מצחק) in Gen. 21:8 refers to Ishmael play-sacrificing grasshoppers on a mud altar. However, this anecdote seems to reflect the use of grasshoppers as play items, a somewhat common thing in the Roman world, rather than as actual objects of sacrifice, per Solomon in the *Testament*. See Ronit Nikolsky, "Ishmael Sacrificed Grasshoppers," in M. Goodman, G. H. Van Kooten, and J. T. A. G. M. Van Ruiten (eds.), *Abraham, the Nations, the Hagarites: Jewish, Christian, and Islamic Perspectives on Kinship with Abraham*, TBN 13 (Leiden: Brill, 2010), 243–62. Solomon is also seen sacrificing grasshoppers in the Islamic *Stories of the Prophets* by Al-Kisa'i and chapter 63 of the Ethiopian *Kebra Negest*, both of which are much later than the *Testament*.

manuscripts date to around the fifteenth century, with many of them displaying a frustrating amount of variance between one another. As Ra'anan Boustan and Michael Beshay have aptly shown in a recent article, to even speak of the *Testament* as a concrete "text" ignores the modularity and plasticity of its polymorphic manuscript tradition.[95] Rather than understand the *Testament* as a pristine and stable text, it is more correct, based upon the manuscript evidence, to view it as an ongoing collection of traditions, which freely integrated new material into its preservation of Solomonic lore. While certain episodes and narrative portions show a higher consistency of preservation and adaptation in these manuscripts, other episodes vary more frequently both in terms of their configuration in the various manuscripts and in their general presence. As such, to speak of a "date" and "provenance" for the *Testament* entails the question what we exactly mean when we speak of a "*Testament of Solomon*" in the first place. While the case can be made that many of the manuscript variances and components could be located in Egyptian scribal contexts, the lack of any older manuscript portions (save for chapter 18) does complicate any concrete attempts to front an entirely certain argument. Indeed, while Egyptian monasticism certainly was prone to depicting demons as graphic sexual assailants, by no means were Athanasius, Evagrius, and Shenoute alone in this regard. By the fifth century, prominent Christian authorities across the Mediterranean, including those in monastic communities, offered similar portraits of the demonic which accentuated both their appropriation of grotesque images and apparitions, and their fondness for causing erotic temptation. Such pictures of the demonic persisted well into the Byzantine and Medieval period through accounts of incubi and succubi. In this sense, while the comparison of the *Testament* to Egyptian monastic literature does provide some helpful insights into larger questions regarding the date and provenance of this fascinating compendium, such benefits do encounter some limits due to its multifaceted and complex literary history and flexible transmission.

---

[95] Ra'anan Boustan and Michael Beshay, "Sealing the Demons, Once and for All: The Ring of Solomon, the Cross of Christ, and the Power of Biblical Kingship," *AfRG* 16 (2015): 99–130 (see esp. 103–5).

Chapter 3

A NEW *TESTAMENT OF ADAM* IN THE SYRIAC *REVELATION OF THE MAGI*?

Bradley N. Rice

In recent years, a remarkable yet little-known Christian apocryphon in Syriac has come to light called the *Revelation of the Magi* (*RevMagi*).[1] It recounts the story of the Magi, those mysterious foreigners from the distant East who came

---

A version of this chapter was presented in the Pseudepigrapha Section at the annual meeting of the Society of Biblical Literature in San Antonio, Texas, on November 19, 2016.

[1] The *Revelation of the Magi* is attested in a single Syriac manuscript (Vat. syr. 162), where it forms part of the *Chronicle of Zuqnin*, a chronicle describing the history of the world from its creation up to 775/776 CE. Editions of the *Chronicle* have been published by Otto F. Tullberg (*Dionysii Telmahharensis Chronici liber primus: Textum e codice ms. syriaco Bibliothecae Vaticanae* [Uppsala: Regiae Academiae Typographi, 1850]) and Jean-Baptiste Chabot (*Chronicon anonymum Pseudo-Dionysianum vulgo dictum* [CSCO 91: Scriptores Syri 3.1; Paris: E Typographeo Reipublicae, 1927]). A new edition of *RevMagi* is currently being prepared by Brent Landau for the Corpus Christianorum Series Apocryphorum; the preliminary form of his edition may be found in "The Sages and the Star-Child: An Introduction to the *Revelation of the Magi*, An Ancient Christian Apocryphon" (Th.D. Dissertation, Harvard Divinity School, 2008), 23–74. Landau also offers the first English translation of the text, for which see "Sages and the Star-Child," 75–136; Landau, *Revelation of the Magi: The Lost Tale of the Wise Men's Journey to Bethlehem* (New York: HarperOne, 2010), 35–88. Although *RevMagi* is only preserved in Syriac, a Latin summary of the text has long been known from the *Opus imperfectum in Matthaeum* (*OIM*), an Arian commentary on the Gospel of Matthew dating to the fifth century; see Joop Van Banning, *Opus imperfectum in Matthaeum: Praefatio* (CCSL 87B; Turnhout: Brepols, 1988). Since Van Banning's edition has not yet appeared, for the Latin text one must still consult Jacques Paul Migne, *Joannis Chrysostomi opera omnia quae exstant* (PG 56; Paris, 1859), cols. 637–638. For an English translation of the *OIM* summary, see James A. Kellerman, *Incomplete Commentary on Matthew* (Opus imperfectum), 2 vols., Ancient Christian Texts (Downers Grove, IL: IVP Academic, 2010), 1:32; Alexander Toepel, "The Apocryphon of Seth: A New Translation and Introduction," in Richard Bauckham, James R. Davila, and Alexander Panayotov (eds.), *Old Testament Pseudepigrapha: More Noncanonical Scriptures* (Grand Rapids, MI: Eerdmans, 2013), 33–9.

to Bethlehem to pay homage to the newborn king of the Jews (Matt 2:1-12)—but it does so from the perspective of the Magi themselves. In the *Revelation of the Magi* we discover that the Magi do not come from Persia, Babylon, Arabia, or any other known country,[2] but from a faraway land called "Shir," situated on the eastern edge of the world near paradise (chapters 1–2).[3] They trace their lineage to Adam's son Seth, who received from his father a prophecy about the coming of a star that would signify the birth of Christ. This prophecy was recorded by Seth and carefully passed down through the generations (2–4). In anticipation of the star, the Magi regularly ascend a certain mountain in Shir called the "Mount of Victories" and read from writings found in the "Cave of Treasures of Hidden Mysteries" (4–10). At a pivotal moment in the story of *RevMagi*, the star finally appears to the Magi, and it turns out that the star is none other than Christ himself (11–15), who then proceeds to guide their lengthy journey to Bethlehem (16–18). In Bethlehem, they discover a cave resembling the cave on the Mount of Victories, and there they see the star transform itself into a luminous infant (18–21). After a brief encounter with Mary and Joseph (18–25), the Magi return to Shir and share their experiences with its inhabitants (26–28). Finally, the apostle Judas Thomas arrives in Shir, baptizes the Magi, and commissions them to preach (29–32).[4]

One of the more striking features of the *Revelation of the Magi* is its description of how the Magi knew about the star. It was not through astrology, as the tantalizingly terse account of the Magi in Matthew's gospel (2:1-12) would suggest. Indeed, the possibility that Matthew's infancy narrative was an endorsement of astrology proved troubling to most early Christians, who swiftly connected the Magi's knowledge of the star with the messianic prophecy of Balaam in Num 24:17: "a star shall come out of Jacob, and a scepter shall rise out of Israel."[5] Rather, the *Revelation of the Magi* suggests that the Magi learned of the star through a still more ancient prophecy, one uttered by Adam himself at the beginning of time. In this "Testament of Adam to Seth" (= *TAS*),[6] Adam tells Seth about his fall from

---

[2] On these options, see Raymond E. Brown, *The Birth of the Messiah: A Commentary on the Infancy Narratives in the Gospels of Matthew and Luke*, ABRL (New York: Doubleday, 1993), 168–70.

[3] For more on the location of Shir, see Bradley N. Rice, "From the Watchers to the Sethites to the Magi: Reinterpretations of Genesis in the Syriac *Revelation of the Magi*," *Henoch* 41 (2019): 226–42.

[4] For a more detailed summary of *RevMagi*, see Landau, "The *Revelation of the Magi*: A Summary and Introduction," in Tony Burke and Brent Landau (eds.), *New Testament Apocrypha: More Noncanonical Scriptures* (Grand Rapids, MI: Eerdmans, 2016), 19–38.

[5] On the popularity of this approach, see Tim Hegedus, *Early Christianity and Ancient Astrology* (Patristic Studies 6; New York: Lang, 2007), 203–6.

[6] The title for this otherwise unknown testament is a tentative one, intended to distinguish it from the more well-known *Testament of Adam*. On my reasons for identifying this text as a "testament," see the discussion under the heading "The *Testament of Adam to Seth* among the Pseudepigrapha" below.

glory and about how he failed to comprehend his lofty position within paradise; he foretells the idolatry and apostasy that will occur at the end of time; and he exhorts his son to avoid temptation and seek righteousness. Seth records the testament in the world's first book (*RevMagi* 3.2-3), and the book is carefully passed down over the centuries until the time of the Magi themselves.

A Summary of the Testament of Adam to Seth (TAS)

The *Revelation of the Magi* purports to offer an extract from the *Testament of Adam to Seth* in chapters 6–10. At this point in the narrative, the Magi have ascended the Mount of Victories and entered the Cave of Treasures to read from certain books that contain "every word that our father Adam, chief of our great lineage, spoke with his son Seth" (6.1). Adam begins by telling Seth about the coming of the Star of Bethlehem, which he himself had seen standing over the Tree of Life in the Garden of Eden, casting light over the entire garden (6.2). After Adam disobeyed the commandment not to eat from the Tree of Knowledge, he was expelled from the garden and could no longer see the light of the star (6.3). Adam then mourns over his "foolishness" and warns Seth to pursue righteousness "that he might find mercy before the Father of Majesty" (6.4).

What follows is a kind of haggadic midrash, replete with wordplays and metaphors, on Adam's fall from his glorious position within paradise and the familiar role that Eve played in his demise. Adam tells Seth that succeeding generations will tell stories about him (7.1), saying such things as "every kingdom that is divided against itself shall not stand." This is said to be "fulfilled" about Adam himself, for he "doubted" the royal majesty that he enjoyed in his kingdom of paradise (7.2). Adam says that the rib removed from his side became a thorn that put out his eye (7.3), and that Eve was appropriately called "time" because she became a stumbling block (7.4). Adam then cautions Seth not to listen to his mother, for though she was created as a helper (7.6), she became a hindrance and the ultimate cause of his expulsion from Eden (7.7).

Adam then reflects on how he failed to realize how good he had it in paradise, and praises God for his boundless mercy (8.1). Adam tells Seth that God judged him for his disobedience "like a kind father whose mercy is combined with discipline" (8.2-3), and that all creation remains under his—i.e., Adam's—authority (8.4). Adam then describes his encounter with the serpent, here called the "Evil One," who deceived him because he wished to be free from Adam's dominion (8.5). As punishment for the serpent's deception, God filled his mouth with dust and tore off his feet (8.6). And, of course, Eve is blamed for all of it (8.7), and Adam therefore warns Seth not, under any circumstances, to listen to his mother (8.8). Adam goes on to say that honorable people will be found among his descendants, those who will recite "the mysteries of the majesty" (9.1). But at the end of time they will be rebellious and blaspheme against heaven (9.2), making idols and serving the sun and moon (9.3), prompted by the "cunning deceiver" (9.4) and given over to all sorts of debauchery (9.5-6).

Adam then again reflects on his time in paradise and on how he was fooled by the serpent (10.1-2). Yet he also professes that his "kind savior and merciful master" will have mercy on him at the end of days (10.2) and will raise him again from the dust (10.3). Looking back again to that astral light that shone in Eden, Adam then reveals how the savior will descend into the darkness and illumine his eyes as he had once before when giving him the breath of life (10.4). Finally, the extract concludes with Adam's assurance to Seth that he too shall find mercy, for the merciful savior does not reckon the father's sins against the son (10.5-6). Adam further says that the maker and savior "does not neglect in his great mercy anyone who loves him and walks in justice before him. Even to those who offend him, he gives opportunity for repentance, and is gracious to them if they repent and seek (it) from him, because his mercy upon his world is great" (10.7).[7]

The Testament of Adam to Seth *as an Independent Composition*

Although there are some points of contact with the broader narrative of the *Revelation of the Magi*, to some extent the *Testament of Adam to Seth* sits uncomfortably with the rest of the story. If it were removed, one might not even notice that it was missing. Was it an independent composition that was later integrated into *RevMagi*? The question has received scant attention in scholarship. This is partly because most of the previous studies of *RevMagi* were devoted to demonstrating an Iranian and/or Zoroastrian influence on the text,[8] and partly because *RevMagi* was only accessible in Latin, Italian, and Polish translation until fairly recently.[9] To my knowledge, the first scholar to address this question was

---

[7] Trans. Landau.

[8] See, e.g., Geo Widengren, *Iranisch-semitische Kulturbegegnung in parthischer Zeit*, Arbeitsgemeinschaft für Forschung des Landes Nordrhein-Westfalen: Geisteswissenschaften, Heft 70 (Cologne: Westdeutscher Verlag, 1960), 62–86; Anders Hultgård, "The Magi and the Star—the Persian Background in Texts and Iconography," in Peter Schalk and Michael Stausberg (eds.), *Being Religious and Living through the Eyes: Studies in Religious Iconography and Iconology*, Acta Universitatis Upsaliensis: Historia religionum 14 (Uppsala: Uppsala University Library, 1998), 215–25; Toepel, "Apocryphon of Seth," 36–7; Toepel, *Die Adam- und Seth-Legenden im Syrischen Buch der Schatzhöhle: Eine quellenkritische Untersuchung*, CSCO 618: Subsidia 119 (Louvain: Peeters, 2006), 172–5. See also Landau's discussions of previous scholarship in "Sages and the Star-Child," 10–16, 216–17; Landau, "The *Revelation of the Magi*: A Summary and Introduction," 24.

[9] Latin: Jean-Baptiste Chabot, *Incerti auctoris Chronicon Pseudo-Dionysianum vulgo dictum*, CSCO 121: Scriptores Syri 3.1 (Louvain: L. Durbecq, 1949); Italian translation: Ugo Monneret de Villard, *Le leggende orientali sui Magi evangelici*, trans. Giorgio Levi Della Vida, StT 163 (Vatican City: Biblioteca Apostolica Vaticana, 1952), 27–49; Polish translation: Witold Witakowski, "Syryjska *Opowieść o Magach* (OpMag)," in Marek Starowieyski (ed.), *Apokryfy Nowego Testamentu*, 3 vols. (Krakow: Wydawnictwo WAM, 2003–8), 1: 352–83.

Gerrit Reinink, who in a brief discussion of *RevMagi* suggested that the text was composed of three sources: a story about the Magi told in the first person (a "we-testimony"); a "revelation of Adam to Seth" ("eine Offenbarung Adams an Seth"); and a story about Judas Thomas.[10] However, Reinink did not offer any substantive argument for his position, other than to note that the "revelation of Adam to Seth" differs in content and interrupts the first-person narration of the Magi. Brent Landau, who to date has published the most detailed studies of the *Revelation of the Magi*, maintains that "there is no evidence that chapters 6–10 had a prior written existence independent of *Rev. Magi*."[11] The matter is far from resolved, and in what follows I would like to consider some of the reasons why this otherwise unknown testament is likely to have been an independent composition.

One of the first reasons is what Landau has called the "Judas Thomas Episode" (JTE), found at the end of the *Revelation of the Magi* (chapters 29–32).[12] At this point in the narrative, the Magi have returned to their native land of Shir and told its inhabitants about all the wonders they witnessed at Christ's birth and on their journey to Bethlehem, and the people of the land have been enjoying various visions of Christ in multiple forms (chapters 27–28). What then follows is peculiar: Judas Thomas, apostle of the East, arrives in Shir (29.1). The Magi welcome him and tell him about what they saw (29.2-3), which prompts Thomas to recount

---

[10] Gerrit J. Reinink, "Das Land 'Seiris' (Šir) und das Volk der Serer in jüdischen und christlichen Traditionen," *JSJ* 6 (1975): 72–85. "Obwohl der Abschnitt grösstenteils dargestellt wird als eine Geschichte, die von den Magiern erzählt wird, erweist sie sich nicht ganz und gar einheitlich. Plötzlich fangen die Magier an zu reden (Chabot, S. 59) und ebenso plötzlich wird der "Wir-Bericht" unterbrochen durch die Offenbarung Adams an Seth, die eingeleitet wird mit den Worten: 'wiederum aus den Büchern, die sich in der Schatzhöhle befanden' (Chabot, S. 62-65). Auch im Schlussteil findet eine Verschiebung statt. Die Erzähler sind nicht mehr die Magier in der Geschichte von ihrer Begegnung mit Judas Thomas (Chabot, S. 86ff). Das Ganze erweckt den Eindruck, es sei zusammengesetzt aus mehreren Quellen (u.a. eine Magier-Geschichte im 'Wir-Stil', eine Offenbarung Adams an Seth und eine Judas Thomas-Geschichte)" (p. 75, n. 13). Jean-Claude Haelewyck ("Le nombre des Rois Mages: Les hésitations de la tradition syriaque," in Jean-Marc Vercruysse (ed.), *Les (Rois) Mages*, Graphè 20 [Arras: Artois presses université, 2011], 25–37) also suggests that *RevMagi* is "sans doute composite" (p. 34, n. 33), yet offers no supporting arguments.

[11] Landau, "The *Revelation of the Magi*: A Summary and Introduction," 31, n. b; Landau, "Sages and the Star-Child," 13–14. Landau does admit, however, that chapters 6–10 contain much material that is at best "only peripherally related to the content of the *Revelation of the Magi*" ("Sages and the Star-Child," 89, n. a) and acknowledges the presence of older traditions.

[12] Landau, "Sages and the Star-Child," 176–91; Landau, "The *Revelation of the Magi* in the *Chronicle of Zuqnin*," *Apocrypha* 19 (2008): 182–201 (195–96). For a more extensive summary of the JTE, see Landau, "The *Revelation of the Magi*: A Summary and Introduction," 37–8; Landau, "Sages and the Star-Child," 176–8.

his own time with Jesus (29.4). Thomas' lofty description of Christ inspires the Magi to request baptism from his hand (29.5-6). Thomas then leads the Magi to a spring (30.1), utters a prayer over baptismal oil (30.2-9), and baptizes them (31.1). Upon emerging from the water, the Magi see a luminous child, who then proceeds to administer the Eucharist (31.1-3). Thomas again praises Christ's many forms (31.4-7), the Magi give thanks (31.8-9), and Thomas commissions the Magi to preach (31.10). This they do, going on to perform miracles and healings through the Holy Spirit (32.1) and proclaiming that only "the wings of the Lord Jesus" will provide refuge from the coming judgment of fire (32.2-3).

Landau has argued—I think convincingly—that the Judas Thomas Episode is a later addition to the *Revelation of the Magi*. He offers several reasons for thinking so. First, there is an awkward shift from the first to the third person in the two chapters preceding the JTE (27-28), together with several odd transitions between direct and indirect speech.[13] In the first clear instance of third-person narration, the Magi are seemingly reintroduced: "And there was great joy in the entire land of the East, and the nobles, and the poor, and women, and children from the entire land were gathered together in the love of our Lord before those nobles who were called Magi."[14] Landau observes that the Magi are called "nobles" (ܪܘܪܒܢܐ) and "brethren" (ܐܚܐ) throughout the JTE, as opposed to the designation "magi" (ܡܓܘܫܐ) found earlier in *RevMagi*.[15] Indeed, the second reason is the different vocabulary seen in the JTE, such as the frequent use of "our Lord Jesus Christ" in different combinations—something curiously absent in the remainder of *RevMagi*, which prefers titles such as "son," "guide," and "savior."[16] In the prayer that Thomas says over the baptismal oil (30.2-9), there is an athletic terminology which is often used in Syriac literature for ascetic accomplishments, and which is much more at home in the *Acts of Thomas* than in *RevMagi*.[17] Third, the JTE is superfluous to the narrative. Before Thomas arrives in Shir to baptize the Magi, the Magi have *already* witnessed the fulfillment of Adam's prophecy of the star and brought the

---

[13] Landau, "Sages and the Star-Child," 180–2. Landau observes that the first chapters of *RevMagi* are also narrated in the third person (1.1-3.6), though he finds that the redactor had a far less heavy hand here than in chapters 27–32 ("Sages and the Star-Child," 182–4).

[14] *RevMagi* 28.4 (trans. Landau).

[15] Landau, "Sages and the Star-Child," 186.

[16] Landau, "Sages and the Star-Child," 184–5. Landau counts no fewer than eighteen instances where "Jesus," "Christ," and/or "our Lord" occur in the JTE (p. 185). The remainder of *RevMagi* contains a particularly rich christological vocabulary heavily informed by the Gospel of John; see Landau, "Sages and the Star-Child," 233–8.

[17] For example, "athlete" (ܐܬܠܝܛܐ), "contest" (ܐܓܘܢܐ), and "to crown" (ܟܠܠ); Landau, "Sages and the Star-Child," 185. On the similarities between this prayer and the prayers seen in the *Acts of Thomas*, see Sebastian P. Brock, "An Archaic Syriac Prayer over Baptismal Oil," in Francis M. Young, Mark J. Edwards, and Paul M. Parvis (eds.), *Studia Patristica: Papers Presented at the Fourteenth International Congress on Patristic Studies Held in Oxford 2003* (Leuven: Peeters, 2006), 3–12, here 7–11; Landau, "Sages and the Star-Child," 191–6.

inhabitants of Shir to faith in Christ.[18] According to Landau, the JTE was appended because there was "a concern for officially integrating the Magi into the broader Christian church through an apostolic visit and baptism."[19]

If Landau is correct that the Judas Thomas Episode is an interpolation into the *Revelation of the Magi*, it stands to reason that there may be others.[20] Employing similar criteria, a reasonable case can be made that the *Testament of Adam to Seth* (6.1–10.9) is also an interpolation. Like the JTE, the *TAS* appears to be superfluous to the narrative, and one would hardly notice its absence. It interrupts the narrative flow of *RevMagi*, as can be seen already at 6.1. The sentence begins with the Syriac adverb ܬܘܒ, which is often used to indicate the start of a new section: "Now (ܬܘܒ) from the books which were in the Cave of Treasures … " We find that ܬܘܒ is used similarly at the beginning of the JTE: "Now (ܬܘܒ) when Judas Thomas went down there … " (29.1).[21] Seth is also introduced in 6.1 as though he had not been previously mentioned, although his name is found no fewer than eight times in chapters 1–5: "Every word that our father Adam, chief of our great lineage, spoke with his son Seth, whom he had after the death of Abel, whom Cain his brother killed and over whom his father Adam mourned" (6.1).

There is also an awkward transition at the end of the *Testament of Adam to Seth*. After the conclusion of Adam's words in 10.7, we read: "And Seth heard everything that his father Adam commanded him, commandments more numerous than these, and wrote them down with diligence, and we found them in the books that were placed in the Cave of Treasures of Hidden Mysteries. He also commanded and added to them" (10.8-9a).[22] Landau rightly notices the awkwardness of 10.9a,[23] which shifts abruptly back to the third person without specifying the subject, who appears to be Seth, as we learn in 10.10: "Seth also commanded these mysteries to his sons." Thus 6.1 and 10.9a appear to be the editorial seams revealing the beginning and end of the *TAS*.

A more complicated question, however, is how 6.1–6.4—which appears to be a précis of the *TAS*—relates to Adam's own account in 7.1–10.7. In 6.1–6.4, the story continues to be told from the perspective of the Magi, as seen from the first-person plural possessives: "our father Adam" (6.1), "our great lineage" (6.1), and "Adam our father" (6.4). It is only at 7.1 that Adam tells his own story in the first person, and this continues until 10.7. The first-person narration of the Magi then resumes in 10.8, with an awkward shift back to the third person at 10.9a. Thus there is a shift in narrative perspective, but it is one that would be expected for a revelation

---

[18] Landau, "Sages and the Star-Child," 186–8; Landau, "The *Revelation of the Magi* in the *Chronicle of Zuqnin*," 195.

[19] Landau, "The *Revelation of the Magi*: A Summary and Introduction," 21.

[20] For instance, Landau proposes that the list of names for the Magi (2.3) is also a later addition, based on its presence in other Syriac sources ("Sages and the Star-Child," 78, n. b.).

[21] Thus Tullberg's emendation; on the textual uncertainty here, see Landau, "Sages and the Star-Child," 67.

[22] Trans. Landau.

[23] Landau, "Sages and the Star-Child," 96, n. d.

given by Adam; by contrast, the Judas Thomas Episode speaks of the Magi in the third person where one would expect the first.

At the same time, this shift in perspective seems to offer our first clues concerning how 6.1–6.4 relates to the rest of the *Testament of Adam to Seth*. Landau had argued that there was editorial tampering in the two chapters (27–28) preceding the Judas Thomas Episode (29–32), and it may be that 6.1–6.4 is also the result of editorial tampering—that is, this section should be understood as a redactor's introduction to the *TAS*. On the one hand, the vocabulary of 6.1–6.4 has more in common with the main narrative of *RevMagi* than it does with 7.1–10.7. For instance, in the latter Adam regularly speaks of his creator as "my master,"[24] whereas the remainder of *RevMagi* speaks with great frequency of the "Father of Majesty" or "Father of Heavenly Majesty."[25] On the other hand, 6.1–6.4 contains episodes not seen in 7.1–10.7. Much of 6.1–6.4 tells how Adam had seen the star and its glory over the Tree of Life in Eden, and how the sight of it was removed when Adam sinned (6.2-3)—yet this does not figure into Adam's own account of his sin and fall.[26]

There is thus good reason to think that 6.1–6.4 constitute a redactor's introduction to the testament itself in 7.1–10.7. This would account for both the abrupt transition in 6.1 and the differences in vocabulary and content seen between chapter 6 and chapters 7–10. At first blush, it is tempting to attribute the phrase "Now from the books which were in the Cave of Treasures" (6.1) to the author of the *Chronicle of Zuqnin*, for it parallels several other instances in which the chronicler has added a comment on the origins of his sources.[27] At the

---

[24] The title "my master" (ܪܒܝ) is used no less than six times (*RevMagi* 7.6; 8.1, 5, 8; 10.1–2), always paired with one or more adjectives: "kind master" (ܪܒܝ ܒܣܝܡܐ): 8.5, 8; 10.1–2; "merciful master" (ܪܒܝ ܚܢܢܐ): 10.4; "my holy master" (ܪܒܝ ܩܕܝܫܐ): 8.1. Adam also refers to his maker as "my kind savior" (ܦܪܘܩܝ ܒܣܝܡܐ; 10.4) and likens him to a "kind father" (ܐܒܐ ܒܣܝܡܐ; 8.1).

[25] "Father of majesty" (ܐܒܐ ܕܪܒܘܬܐ): *RevMagi* 6.4; 13.1; 15.3–5; 19.1, 9; 21.6, 8; 21.10; 27.7; "Father of heavenly majesty" (ܐܒܐ ܕܪܒܘܬܐ ܫܡܝܢܝܬܐ): 6.2; 10.9; 11.7; 13.1; 27.3. This also happens to be an epithet commonly found in Manichaeism; see Widengren, *Iranisch-semitische Kulturbegegnung*, 74; John C. Reeves, *Heralds of That Good Realm: Syro-Mesopotamian Gnosis and Jewish Traditions*, NHMS 41 (Leiden: Brill, 1996), 121; Brock, "An Archaic Syriac Prayer," 12. The question of whether *RevMagi* is a Manichaean text has not yet been sufficiently addressed. It certainly has some features that could be classed as "gnostic," for which see Widengren, *Iranisch-semitische Kulturbegegnung*, 73-9; Landau, "Sages and the Star-Child," 105.

[26] Of course, the author of 6.1–6.4 may be summarizing content seen elsewhere in the *TAS*, since it is otherwise hard to explain why the star is absent.

[27] See Witakowski's discussion of the chronicler's "metahistoriographic remarks," for which he gives the following example: "Now from [ܡܢ ܗܟܝܠ] the book of Socrates, another history in brief"; *The Syriac Chronicle of Pseudo-Dionysius of Tel-Mahre: A Study in the History of Historiography*, Acta Universitatis Upsaliensis: Studia Semitica Upsaliensia 9 (Uppsala: Uppsala University Press, 1987), 116.

same time, however, the chronicler does tend to reproduce his sources faithfully and frequently verbatim.[28] For longer extracts, the chronicler usually provides a title—often in red ink—and sometimes also a conclusion.[29] Thus the *Revelation of the Magi* begins with the heading, "On the revelation of the Magi, their coming to Jerusalem, and the gifts that they brought to Christ" (1.1), and it concludes with the comment, "The account of the Magi and their gifts has finished" (32.4).[30] This means that the *TAS* together with its introduction probably entered the *Revelation of the Magi* before coming into the hands of the chronicler.

Date and Original Language of the Testament of Adam to Seth

Precisely when the *Testament of Adam to Seth* was interpolated into the *Revelation of the Magi* is more difficult to say. A firm terminus ante quem is established by the composition of the *Chronicle of Zuqnin* in the late eighth century (ca. 775). It is less clear, however, whether the testament was found in the version of *RevMagi* referred to in the fifth-century *Opus imperfectum in Matthaeum*. Here we find the following:

> Apocryphal book in the name of Seth [*Liber apocryphus nomine Seth*]—Victorious Mountain. I have heard some referring to a certain writing [*quadam scriptura*] that, even if not authentic, does not destroy the faith, but rather delights [*etsi non certa, tamen non destruente fidem, sed potius delectante*], that there was a certain people located in the furthermost east, next to Ocean, among whom there was said to be a certain writing in the name of Seth [*quaedam scriptura, inscripta nomine Seth*], concerning the appearance of this star, and concerning the gifts and such to be offered him, which was thought to have been passed down, from fathers to their sons, by generations of diligent men.[31]

In the second part of the extract, the "writing penned in Seth's name" (*quaedam scriptura, inscripta nomine Seth*) clearly refers to a book of Seth in the possession of the Magi. The "certain writing of dubious authenticity" (*quadam scriptura, etsi non certa*) in the first part of the extract, however, more likely refers to the narrative of *RevMagi* as a whole.[32] In this case, the phrase *etsi non certa, tamen non destruente fidem, sed potius delectante* should probably be taken as the author's way of saying

---

[28] Witakowski, *The Syriac Chronicle*, 124–36; Amir Harrak, *The Chronicle of Zuqnīn: Parts III and IV: A.D. 488–775*, Mediaeval Sources in Translation 36 (Toronto: Pontifical Institute of Mediaeval Studies, 1999), 21–4.
[29] Witakowski, *The Syriac Chronicle*, 114.
[30] Landau, "Sages and the Star-Child," 75, n. b.; 136, n. d.
[31] PG 56:637 (Second Homily on Matthew 2).
[32] So also Landau, "Sages and the Star-Child," 146–7; cf. Toepel, "Apocryphon of Seth," 34.

that *RevMagi* is a charming tale, albeit a fictitious one. Moreover, there is nothing in this summary that could not have been drawn from the beginning of *RevMagi*, since there we also find a description of how Adam told Seth about the arrival of the star, and how Seth recorded it in a book that was passed down from generation to generation.[33]

If there is no clear indication that the *TAS* was present in the version of *RevMagi* available to the author of the *Opus imperfectum in Matthaeum*, the *Chronicle of Zuqnin* remains our terminus ante quem. The terminus a quo for the insertion of the *TAS* depends, of course, on the date of the *Revelation of the Magi*, which has been dated anywhere between the late second and early sixth centuries. On the early end of this range is Landau, who has attempted to push the date as early as the late second or early third century.[34] His dating is based partly on his thesis that *RevMagi* is a piece of Christian apologetic, partly on Christ's polymorphy in *RevMagi*, and partly on his reconstruction of the redactional history of *RevMagi*, in which his argument that the JTE is a later addition figures prominently. Some of Landau's arguments for an early date are questionable, however, and the recent responses to his work situate the text more comfortably in the fourth or fifth century.[35] On the later end of the spectrum is Monneret de Villard, who suggested that *RevMagi* probably emerged around the start of the sixth century, under the

---

[33] The parallels to the *OIM* in *RevMagi* are as follows (I offer here the text of the *OIM*, with the *RevMagi* parallels in parentheses): "There was a certain people located in the furthermost east, next to Ocean (2.4), among whom there was said to be a certain writing in the name of Seth concerning the appearance of this star (4.2-3, 7, 10; 5.1, 10) and concerning the gifts and such to be offered him (4.7-9), which was thought to have been passed down, from fathers to their sons, by generations of diligent men" (2.5-6; 3.1-7; 4.2-3, 10; 5.1, 9-10).

[34] Landau, "Sages and the Star-Child," 175–220. For summaries of the arguments, see "The *Revelation of the Magi*: A Summary and Introduction," 21–3.

[35] Kristian S. Heal, review of Brent Landau, *Revelation of the Magi: The Lost Tale of the Wise Men's Journey to Bethlehem*, in *Hug* 14.2 (2011): 294–8, here 297–8; Annette Yoshiko Reed, review of *Revelation of the Magi: The Lost Tale of the Wise Men's Journey to Bethlehem* by Brent Landau, in *Sino-Platonic Papers* 208 (2011): Reviews 13, pp. 43–7; Pierluigi Piovanelli, "Scriptural Trajectories Through Early Christianity, Late Antiquity, and Beyond: Christian Memorial Traditions in the *longue durée*," in Tony Burke (ed.), *Forbidden Texts on the Western Frontier: Christian Apocrypha in North American Perspectives: Proceedings from the 2013 York University Christian Apocrypha Symposium* (Eugene, OR: Cascade, 2015), 100–1. Piovanelli, for instance, points out that Christ's polymorphy, while seemingly archaic, does not necessarily "betray the antiquity of a given text" (101, n. 30). Piovanelli draws attention to Pseudo-Cyril's homily *On the Life and the Passion of Christ*, a text that Roelof van den Broek (*Pseudo-Cyril of Jerusalem* On the Life and the Passion of Christ: A Coptic Apocryphon, VCSup 118 [Leiden: Brill, 2013], 69–70), dates to the early ninth century. And while Landau dates the Judas Thomas Episode to the third century based on similarities with the *Acts of Thomas*, Heal observes that the JTE contains vocabulary more often seen in fifth century texts (297, n. 10).

assumption that the Syriac text of *RevMagi* is a much expanded form of the version attested by the *OIM*.[36] Landau has rightly cast doubt on this assumption,[37] while Witakowski has argued that the treatment of the Holy Spirit as grammatically feminine in *RevMagi* makes a date in the fourth century more likely.[38] In all probability, the *Revelation of the Magi* was composed in the fourth or early fifth century, in which case the *TAS* would have been interpolated sometime between the fourth and eighth centuries. We can only guess when the testament itself was written, though sometime between the second and fourth centuries seems a reasonable assumption.[39]

As for the original language of the *Testament of Adam to Seth*, there is little reason to doubt that it too was written in Syriac.[40] There are certain wordplays that

---

[36] Monneret de Villard, *Le leggende orientali sui Magi evangelici*, 67–8.

[37] Landau, "Sages and the Star-Child," 167–70.

[38] Witakowski, "The Magi in Syriac Tradition," in George A. Kiraz (ed.), *Malphono w-Rabo d-Malphone: Studies in Honor of Sebastian P. Brock*, Gorgias Eastern Christianity Studies 3 (Piscataway, NJ: Gorgias, 2008), 814.

[39] If the *TAS* is a Christian work composed in Syriac, as seems to be the case, any date prior to the second century is excluded; and since most Jewish traditions appear to have entered Syriac literature before the end of the fourth century (thus Sebastian Brock, "Jewish Traditions in Syriac Sources," *JJS* 30 [1979]: 212–32), a date prior to the fifth century (or at least the sixth) seems most probable.

[40] It seems fairly certain that *RevMagi* was composed in Syriac, though Monneret de Villard had suggested that the author of the *Opus imperfectum* had access to a Greek translation of *RevMagi* (*Le leggende orientali sui Magi evangelici*, 67–8), a position argued more recently and vigorously by Landau in "Sages and the Star-Child," 137–41, 170–3; "The *Revelation of the Magi* in the *Chronicle of Zuqnin*," 195–6; "'One Drop of Salvation from the House of Majesty': Universal Revelation, Human Mission and Mythical Geography in the Syriac *Revelation of the Magi*," in Ellen B. Aitken and John M. Fossey (eds.), *The Levant: Crossroads of Late Antiquity*, McGill University Monographs in Classical Archaeology and History 22 (Leiden: Brill, 2014), 86; "The *Revelation of the Magi*: A Summary and Introduction," 21; "The Coming of the Star-Child: The Reception of the Revelation of the Magi in New Age Religious Thought and Ufology," *Gnosis* 1 (2016): 196–217, here 201. However, I would suggest that there is no need to posit a lost Greek *Vorlage* to account for the summary in the *OIM*. According to van Banning, the author of the *OIM* was a native Latin speaker with secondary competence in Greek, and had access to a wide variety of written *and oral* sources in Constantinople in the late fifth century (*Opus imperfectum*, v–vi). By this time Constantinople had become a multilingual city, where Greek and Latin as well as Syriac were spoken; see, e.g., Fergus Millar, "Linguistic Co-existence in Constantinople: Greek and Latin (and Syriac) in the Acts of the Synod of 536 C.E.," *JRS* 99 (2009): 92–103. Thus it seems equally likely that the author had heard an account of the tale in Greek or Latin while in Constantinople and later wrote the summary from memory. Finally, it should be noted that translations from Syriac into Greek were far less common at this time than renderings of Greek into Syriac; see Sebastian Brock, "Greek into Syriac and Syriac into Greek," in *Syriac Perspectives on Late Antiquity* (London: Variorum Reprints, 1984), 11–14.

appear to function only in Syriac,[41] such as the play on the Syriac verb ܦܠܓ found in 7.2. Adam tells Seth that his descendants will tell tales about his folly in the Garden of Eden, saying: "'Every kingdom that is *divided* (ܬܬܦܠܓ) against itself shall not stand.' This is fulfilled about me, for I was in *doubt* (ܐܬܦܠܓܬ) about the kingdom in which I stood." Thus there is a play on "dividing" and "doubting," whereby the kingdom of Mark 3:24 is taken to refer to Adam's dominion in paradise.

However, there are certain instances in the *TAS* where something seems to have been lost in translation. In 7.4, Adam says of Eve: "I even prophesied when I saw her and said, 'This time (ܙܒܢܐ) is bone and flesh from me.' Fittingly did I call her 'time' (ܙܒܢܐ), since she has become a stumbling block (ܬܘܩܠܬܐ) for me." This is, of course, a partial citation of Genesis 2:23, which according to the Peshitta also reads "This *time* (ܗܢܐ ܙܒܢܐ) is bone of my bones and flesh of my flesh." Yet there is no apparent connection between the words ܙܒܢܐ ("time") and ܬܘܩܠܬܐ ("stumbling block") in Syriac. The MT of this verse reads, "This *at last* (זאת הפעם) is bone of my bones and flesh of my flesh." In addition to the meaning "time, occurrence," the Hebrew פעם may also have the meaning of "foot" or "anvil,"[42] and thus the sense of "stumbling" is not too far removed. This may mean that *RevMagi* 7.4 is a midrash of Gen 2:23 originally written in Hebrew, which only later made its way into Syriac. As Brock has shown, Christian authors writing in Syriac were much more familiar than their Western counterparts with Rabbinic tradition and Aramaic translations and interpretations of the Jewish scriptures,[43] and thus it would not be surprising if a Hebrew midrash of this sort had been integrated into the *Testament of Adam to Seth*.

The Testament of Adam to Seth *among the Pseudepigrapha*

The *Testament of Adam to Seth* does not appear to correspond to any known Adam pseudepigraphon. There are, however, some points of contact with the more well-known *Testament of Adam* (*T. Adam*), particularly the prophecy section, in which Adam foretells the birth, passion, and death of Jesus (3.1-7).[44] Yet it is not the

---

[41] So also Landau, "The *Revelation of the Magi*: A Summary and Introduction," 21 n. 10.

[42] BDB, s.v. פעם; *HALOT*, s.v. פעם.

[43] Brock, "Jewish Traditions in Syriac Sources," 212–32.

[44] Stephen E. Robinson, *The Testament of Adam: An Examination of the Syriac and Greek Traditions*, SBLDS 52 (Chico, CA: Scholars Press, 1982); Robinson, "Testament of Adam: A New Translation and Introduction," in James H. Charlesworth (ed.), *The Old Testament Pseudepigrapha*, 2 vols., ABRL (Garden City, NY: Doubleday, 1983–1985), 1:989–95. The *Testament of Adam* is a composite document, comprised of three sections which in their final form date to about the third or fourth century CE. In addition to the *prophecy*, there is the *horarium*, in which Adam tells Seth about which part of creation worships God at which hour (1.1-2.12), and the *hierarchy* or *angelology*, in which Adam describes the different orders of heavenly beings (4.1-8). On the various recensions of *T. Adam*, see Robinson, *The Testament of Adam*, 45–52; Gerrit Reinink, "Das Problem des Ursprungs des Testamentes Adams," *OrChrAn* 197 (1972): 387–99.

prophecy itself that holds interest, but its conclusion. As Adam's prophecy draws to a close (3.5), Seth is identified as the one who wrote down the testament (3.6). Adam is buried in the east of paradise, carried off to his tomb by the angels and powers of heaven (3.6). We are then told that Seth and his children "sealed the testament and placed it in the *cave of treasures* along with the offerings which Adam had taken out of paradise, *gold and myrrh and frankincense*. And the *sons of kings, the magi*, will come and get them and bring them to the son of God, to Bethlehem of Judea, to the cave" (3.7).[45] The *Testament of Adam* thus clearly indicates that a testament of Adam recorded by Seth was placed in a Cave of Treasures associated with the Magi, which is precisely what we find in the *Revelation of the Magi*.

The contents of the book from which the Magi read are, however, quite different from what we see in the *Testament of Adam*. Most remarkably, *T. Adam* promises Adam's ultimate deification—Adam wanted to be "like God" (Gen 3:5), and a god he shall eventually be (3.2, 4). By contrast, the *TAS* keeps Adam firmly in his place. In falling victim to the serpent's promise, Adam simply did not understand that "the clay could not be like its potter, nor the servant like his master" (10.2).[46] While in *T. Adam* the Lord tells Adam that he and his progeny will be food for the serpent (3.3), in the *TAS* Adam is told that he will trample upon the serpent (8.5).[47] The *T. Adam* foretells the coming of the Noachian flood, after which 6,000 years shall pass (3.5); in the *TAS* there will be apostasies among the faithful (9.2-6).

Despite the differences in content between the *T. Adam* and the *TAS*, the latter still has features that clearly associate it with the testamentary genre.[48] Above all, the *Testament of Adam to Seth* is brimming with paraenesis.[49] All of Adam's ruminations on his time in paradise serve to encourage Seth to succeed where his father had failed. Adam's disappointment with himself for listening to Eve (7.3-8) as well as his failure to understand how good he had it in Eden (8.1-7) function as

---

[45] Trans. Robinson, "Testament of Adam," 1:994 (modified; italics mine). I have followed the versification found in Robinson's dissertation (*Testament of Adam*, 65, 101); in the *OTP* translation, 3.6-7 is 3.6.

[46] Isa 29:16; 45:9; 64:8; Jer 19:1-6; Matt 10:24-25; John 13:16; 15:20.

[47] Cp. Gen 3:15; Mark 16:18; Luke 10:19.

[48] The genre of the *Testament of Adam to Seth* is never specified by *RevMagi*, which speaks more generically of "writings" or "books" (Syr. ܟܬܒܐ; 2.5; 3.2–7; 4.1; 6.1; 10.8 [ܟܬܒܐ]). The references to the *TAS* in 6.1 and 10.8 seem to indicate that it was but one of several writings that could be found in the Cave of Treasures.

[49] For ethical paraenesis as well as apocalyptic forecasts as defining features of the testament genre, see Anitra Bingham Kolenkow, "The Literary Genre 'Testament,'" in Robert A. Kraft and George W. E. Nickelsburg (eds.), *Early Judaism and Its Modern Interpreters*, BMI 2 (Atlanta: Scholars Press, 1986), 266-7; on the function of midrash in testaments, see pp. 264–6. Eckhard von Nordheim in fact weights the genre more heavily toward ethical instruction ("Verhaltensanweisung"); see *Die Lehre der Alten*, vol. 1: *Das Testament als Literaturgattung im Judentum der Hellenistisch-Römischen Zeit* (ALGHJ 13; Leiden: Brill, 1980), 233.

a sober warning to his son: Do not listen to your mother's advice (8.8). Yet Adam is also confident that he too shall enjoy the resurrection (10.1-4) and assures Seth that the sins of the father will not be reckoned against the son (10.5-6); after all, God is merciful toward anyone who repents (10.7). Secondly, the *Testament of Adam to Seth* contains predictions for the future: Adam notifies Seth that some of his descendants will rebel at the end of time, blaspheming and worshipping idols (9.1-6). Finally, in addition to these testamentary features, designating the *TAS* as a "testament" also links it to the end of the prophecy section of the *Testament of Adam*, where Adam's testament is said to be kept in a Cave of Treasures connected with the Magi (3.7).[50]

While Adam's reflections on his fall from glory and his deception by Eve and the serpent are not paralleled in the *Testament of Adam*, traditions of Adam's regret and penitence are found throughout the various Adam writings, most notably the *Life of Adam and Eve* (*LAE*).[51] There too we see that Adam enjoyed a very lofty position within paradise—even the angels were to worship him in all his splendor (*LAE* 14.1-3). So too in the *Testament of Adam to Seth*, Adam enjoyed great "majesty" (ܪܒܘܬܐ) and "kingdom" (ܡܠܟܘܬܐ), a dominion from which the "Evil One" wished to be free (8.5).[52] But unlike the *LAE*, famous for its description of a luciferous angel that fell from glory (*LAE* 16.1-3), the *TAS* says little more than that a sneaky snake lost his feet (8.6). Yet while the snake is doomed to swallow dust, Adam is assured that he shall rise again from the dust (10.3). On the last day, the savior will descend into the abysmal darkness and bring light to his eyes once again, just as he did on the day of his creation (10.4). Finally, if Adam's encounter with the star (6.2-3) may be reckoned to the contents of the *Testament of Adam to Seth*, it would surely be one of its most striking features: The brilliant star that the Magi saw on their mountain in the distant East was the *same* star that appeared to Adam in Eden—Christ himself in luminous form. The light of the star here and

---

[50] For more on this tradition, see A. F. J. Klijn, *Seth in Jewish, Christian and Gnostic Literature*, NovTSup 46 (Leiden: Brill, 1977), 53–60.

[51] M. D. Johnson, "Life of Adam and Eve," in *The Old Testament Pseudepigrapha*, 2: 249–95. The text of the various versions may be found in Gary A. Anderson and Michael E. Stone, *A Synopsis of the Books of Adam and Eve*, EJL 17 (2nd rev. ed., Atlanta: Scholars Press, 1999). The date of the *LAE* as well as whether it is a Jewish or Christian composition are much debated questions; see the discussion in Michael E. Stone, *A History of the Literature of Adam and Eve*, EJL 3 (Atlanta: Scholars Press, 1992), 6–74. On Adam's penitence, see Gary A. Anderson, "The Penitence Narrative in the *Life of Adam and Eve*," in Gary Anderson, Michael Stone, and Johannes Tromp (eds.), *Literature on Adam and Eve: Collected Essays*, SVTP 15 (Leiden: Brill, 2000), 3–42.

[52] *RevMagi* 6.3; 7.2, 7; 8.1, 7. On the tradition that Adam enjoyed dominion and kingship in paradise (Gen 1:26-28), see Wis 9:1-4; 10.1-2; Sir 17:2-4; Ps 8:6; *Jub.* 2.14; *2 En.* 30.12; *4 Ezra* 6.53-54; *Cav. Tr.* 2.10-11, 17-25. See further John R. Levison, *Portraits of Adam in Early Judaism: From Sirach to 2 Baruch*, JSPSup 1 (Sheffield: JSOT Press, 1988).

elsewhere in *RevMagi* is in many ways reminiscent of the divine Shekinah and its luminosity in Rabbinic tradition,[53] again showing the extent to which Jewish traditions were received in Syriac sources.

Indeed, there are many potential parallels that could be explored in future studies of the *TAS*. In the present essay, I have had only the modest aim of proposing that the *TAS* deserves study as a composition in its own right, as a writing that originated independently of the *Revelation of the Magi*. Its existence as an independent composition is justified, I believe, by applying many of the same criteria that Landau deployed in his arguments regarding the Judas Thomas Episode (*RevMagi* 29-32). If the *TAS* is indeed a separate composition, it was likely composed in Syriac sometime between the second and fourth centuries, and integrated into *RevMagi* sometime between the fourth and eighth centuries, before the *Revelation of the Magi* was itself incorporated into the *Chronicle of Zuqnin*. As the question mark in the title of this study indicates, however, much work remains to be done in exploring the contents of the *Testament of Adam to Seth* and in determining what its origins and scope might have been. It is my hope that this brief study will stimulate further research on this fascinating yet poorly known text.

---

[53] *Gen. Rab.* 3.1-5; 19.7; *3 Enoch* 5:1-6, 12-13 (and P. Alexander, "3 (Hebrew Apocalypse of) Enoch," in *The Old Testament Pseudepigrapha*, 259–60.

Chapter 4

THE *SHEPHERD OF HERMAS*' APOCALYPTIC VISIONS AND ANGELIC INTERMEDIARIES IN AND IN LIGHT OF CLEMENT OF ALEXANDRIA

Christopher S. Atkins

The search for a historical Hermas has left some with the conclusion that the document is a pseudepigraphon;[1] nevertheless, it is rarely grouped together with Jewish and Christian pseudepigrapha. I will not dwell on questions of attribution and authorship in the present chapter primarily because the work makes no claim to having been authored by either a worthy of the Jewish scriptures or one of the apostles of Jesus. The claim to be the "shepherd," or pastor, of Hermas, even if fictitious, is quite modest.[2]

One of the most popular Christian texts before the fourth century and one of the most attested Christian texts among surviving manuscripts in Egypt through the fifth century,[3] the *Shepherd of Hermas* is often considered a puzzling text with

---

[1] See, e.g., P. Henne, "Hermas, un pseudonym," *StPatr* 26 (1993): 136–9.

[2] On the question of authorship, see Carolyn Osiek, *The Shepherd of Hermas: A Commentary*, Hermeneia (Minneapolis, MN: Fortress, 1999), 8–10; David Hellholm, "The Shepherd of Hermas," in Wilhelm Pratscher (ed.), *The Apostolic Fathers: An Introduction* (Waco, TX: Baylor University Press, 2010), 237–8.

[3] N. Gonis, "4705–4707. Hermas," in N. Gonis et al. (eds.), *The Oxyrhynchus Papyri*. Volume LXIX, Graeco-Roman Memoirs 89 (London: Egypt Exploration Society, 2005), 1–17; Malcolm Choat and Rachel Yuen-Collingridge, "The Egyptian Hermas: The Shepherd in Egypt before Constantine," in Thomas J. Kraus and Tobias Nicklas (eds.), *Early Christian Manuscripts: Examples of Applied Method and Approach*, TENTS 5 (Leiden: Brill, 2010) 191–212. C. H. Roberts, *Manuscript, Society and Belief in Early Christian Egypt* (London: Oxford University Press, 1979); Craig A. Evans, "A Preliminary Survey of Christian Literature Found in Oxyrhynchus," in Lee Martin McDonald and James H. Charlesworth (eds.), *"Non-Canonical" Religious Texts in Early Judaism and Early Christianity*, JCT 14 (London: T&T Clark, 2012), 26–51; Bart D. Ehrman, *The Apostolic Fathers*, vol. 2, LCL 25 (Cambridge, MA: Harvard University Press, 2003) 162. Eldon Jay Epp, "The Oxyrhynchus

a puzzling reception.⁴ Much of the puzzlement regarding *Hermas* results from its ultimate non-inclusion in enduring Christian canonical traditions despite its broad distribution and influence in antiquity. In attempt to move beyond the binaries of "canonical" and "noncanonical"—terms that often prejudice our analysis and interpretation—I will consider the reception of *Hermas* without recourse to its canonicity,⁵ focusing instead on the specifically revelatory nature of its early reception in Clement of Alexandria. I will devote excursive attention to its reception in Irenaeus and the Muratorian Fragment for comparative purposes.⁶

Through a close study of both Clement's use of *Hermas* and portions of *Hermas* in light of Clement's use of it, I derive two primary conclusions. First, I argue that Clement, in alluding to *Hermas* by reference to "the power," engages *Hermas* in a nuanced manner, deliberately drawing out elements already present in *Hermas*. Building on this, I secondly argue that it is plausible that Clement is to some degree indebted to *Hermas* for his use of intermediary figures, particularly "the power(s)." I support this claim by detailing the sophisticated and systematic contextual connections between the "power(s)" and the "first-created (angels)" in both *Hermas* and Clement.⁷ In arguing thus, I take Batovici's recent study—in which he argued that Clement considered *Hermas* authoritative based on its apocalyptic elements—as a point of departure. In deriving the two aforementioned conclusions, I aim to move beyond his study by detailing contextual connections that illuminate Clement's interaction with *Hermas*.

New Testament Papyri: 'Not Without Honor Except in Their Hometown'?"; in *Perspectives On New Testament Textual Criticism: Collected Essays, 1962-2004* (Leiden: Brill, 2005), 743–802, here 754; Osiek, *The Shepherd of Hermas*, 1; Dan Batovici, "A New Hermas Papyrus Fragment in Paris," *APF* 62 (2016): 20–36, here 21.

⁴ Eldon Jay Epp, "Issues in the Interrelation of New Testament Textual Criticism and Canon," in *Perspectives on New Testament Textual Criticism*, NovTSup 181 (Leiden: Brill, 2005), 595–640, here 609. See also Bogdan Gabriel Bucur, *Angelomorphic Pneumatology: Clement of Alexandria and Other Early Christian Witnesses* (Leiden: Brill, 2009), 113–14, 122. Robert J. Hauck, "The Great Fast: Christology in the Shepherd of Hermas," *AThR* 75 (1993): 187–99; M. C. Steenberg, "Irenaeus on Scripture, *Graphe*, and the Status of *Hermas*," *St. Vladimir's Theological Quarterly* 53 (2009): 29–66, here 59.

⁵ Similarly, see Dan Batovici, "Hermas in Clement of Alexandria," *StPatr* 66 (2013): 41–51, here 42.

⁶ I have decided to structure the chapter thus due to my conviction that close attention to individual receptions and lives of a text—the singularity of which can be misleading due to convoluted textual histories—ought to precede comparison. Even then, in comparing instances of a text's reception, one ought to give due attention not only to matters of provenance, but also to tradition-critical matters, paying closer attention to each individual author's intellectual influences.

⁷ On the interaction between pneumatology and christology in *Hermas* in connection with Clement of Alexandria, cf. Bogdan G. Bucur, "The Son of God and the Angelomorphic Holy Spirit: A Rereading of the Shepherd's Christology," *ZNW* 98 (2007): 120–42, here 138–42.

In light of these two contentions and in conversation with *Hermas'* reception by Irenaeus and in the Muratorian Fragment, I also conclude that such insights into the specifics of *Hermas'* authority are often missed because of the hegemony of the question of *Hermas'* canonicity. Nevertheless, the role of *Hermas* in scholarly literature on canon is voluminous,[8] and, given a recent review article addressing it,[9] there is no need to rehearse it here.

Hermas *in Clement of Alexandria*

In sharp contrast to Irenaeus Clement alludes to and quotes from all three sections of *Hermas*. Based on this evidence, some have concluded that *Hermas*

---

[8] Although scholarly attention to "canon" lacks a standard demarcated clearly enough from which to discern deviation, *Hermas* seems to represent an anomaly. For instance, while some present the apparent early authority of *Hermas* as evidence that canon formation does *not* antedate the fourth century, Metzger includes *Hermas* in his section entitled, "Books of Temporary and Local Canonicity." See Bruce M. Metzger, *The Canon of the New Testament: Its Origin, Development, and Significance* (New York: Clarendon Press and Oxford University Press, 1987), 188; Lee M. McDonald, "What Do We Mean by Canon? Ancient and Modern Questions," in James H. Charlesworth and Lee M. McDonald (eds.), *Jewish and Christian Scriptures: The Function of "Canonical" and "Non-Canonical" Religious Texts*, JCT 14 (New York: T&T Clark, 2010), 8–40, here 21. McDonald recognizes *Hermas* as a text that experienced "transient authority." Akin to Metzger, McDonald indicates (21–2) that *Hermas* appears to represent the elusive phenomenon of "decanonization," a phrase which he admittedly uses cautiously. Osiek writes, "There is no doubt that at some times and places, *Hermas* was considered both scripture, that is, inspired, and canonical, part of the rule of faith sanctioned for liturgical use." Osiek, *The Shepherd of Hermas*, 5. Gamble adds that the attention paid to *Hermas* was "appreciably earlier, more continuous, and more widespread than to many of the writings that were finally accepted in the canon." See Harry Gamble, "The New Testament Canon: Recent Research and the Status Quaestionis," in Lee Martin McDonald and James A. Sanders (eds.), *The Canon Debate: On the Origins and Formation of the Bible* (Peabody, MA: Hendrickson, 2004), 267–94, here 290. See also Gamble, *The New Testament Canon: Its Making and Meaning* (Philadelphia: Fortress Press, 1985), 70–1. Ehrman cites Codices Sinaiticus and Claromontanus (*The Apostolic Fathers*, 169), as well as Didymus the Blind, as witnesses to the canonical status attributed to *Hermas*. Bart D. Ehrman, "The New Testament Canon of Didymus the Blind," *VC* 37 (1983): 1–21, here 11–12. See also Choat and Yuen-Collingridge, "The Egyptian Hermas," 191.

[9] Dan Batovici, "The *Shepherd of Hermas* in Recent Scholarship on the Canon: A Review Article," *ASE* 34 (2017): 89–105; cf. David Nielsen, "The Place of the *Shepherd of Hermas* in the Canon Debate," in Lee Martin McDonald and James H. Charlesworth (eds.), *"Non-Canonical" Religious Texts in Early Judaism and Early Christianity*, JCT 14 (London: T&T Clark, 2012), 162–76.

was circulating as a unity by the end of the second century[10]; nevertheless, given *Hermas*' textual-history, there is no certainty that Clement possesses a unified text of *Hermas* as we now know it. Clement's references to *Hermas* are less frequent than the four gospels, yet similar in number to other texts eventually included in the New Testament.[11]

In beginning our analysis of Clement's use of *Hermas*, it will be helpful briefly to narrate Batovici's study.[12] Batovici attempts to account for Clement's view that *Hermas* is authoritative. In doing so, he argues that "[*Hermas*'] apocalyptic character, which Clement considers to be genuine," accounts for his "high esteem" for *Hermas*. More specifically, it is the way in which the "revealing agents … are presented" that convinces Batovici of this conclusion. (These "revealing agents" are "the powers," αἱ δυνάμεις.) Botavici presents his case based on Clement's understanding that *Hermas* constituted true revelation, that is, that the visions recorded were not mere literary invention.[13] He argues especially from Clement's use of ἡ δύναμις,[14] a category already fixed in Clement's thought, which he adopts (and adapts) from Philo.[15] Batovici, however, does not address the possibility that Clement finds support for the category of "power(s)" in *Hermas*. A closer analysis of the portions of *Hermas* to which Clement alludes provides evidence that Clement deliberately draws out visionary elements already in *Hermas*. This helps account for Clement's distinctive quotative frames and, more importantly, *Hermas*' specifically apocalyptic and visionary influence on Clement and his reference to angelic intermediaries. We will thus now consider two of Clement's allusions to *Hermas* and the ways in which he frames them.

---

[10] For example, Osiek, *The Shepherd of Hermas*, 4; cf. 8.

[11] James A. Brooks, "Clement of Alexandria as a Witness to the Development of the New Testament Canon," *SecCent* 9 (1992): 41–55, here 47; Carl P. Cosaert, *The Text of the Gospels in Clement of Alexandria*, NTGF 9 (Atlanta, GA: Society of Biblical Literature, 2008), 22.

[12] Batovici, "Hermas in Clement of Alexandria."

[13] Ibid. He writes (51): "In light of this, it becomes clear that, put bluntly, Clement believed Hermas' visions to be genuine. Not a literary genre, not the book of a venerable man, or gnostic or saint, but an account of a genuine revelation, where Hermas is technically a prophet."

[14] Ibid, Batovici writes (51): "Bucur too mentions Clement's two introductory remarks involving the powers who speak to Hermas, as examples for the use of δύναμιν within 'a venerable history in Jewish and Jewish-Christian angelology and demonology,' the context being that '[b]oth Philo and Clement know about 'power' as an angelic being,'" alluding to Bucur, *Angelomorphic Pneumatology*, 78 n. 17.

[15] David T. Runia, "Clement of Alexandria and the Philonic Doctrine of the Divine Power(s)," *VC* 58 (2004): 256–76. On Clement's use of Philo more broadly, see Annewies van Den Hoek, *Clement of Alexandria and His Use of Philo in the Stromateis: An Early Christian Reshaping of a Jewish Model*, VCSup 3 (Leiden: Brill, 1988). Also important here is van den Hoek, "The 'Catechetical' School of Early Christian Alexandria and Its Philonic

Strom. 1.81.1[16]

First is *Strom.* 1.181.1, which, alluding to *Hermas Vis.* 3.4.3 [12], reads, "Divinely, therefore, the power which spoke to Hermas according to a revelation said, 'The visions and the revelations are for the double-minded, who ponder in their hearts whether these are or are not.'"[17] In *Hermas*, this quotation appears in the context of the woman church addressing Hermas' questions regarding the identity of the figures associated with the building of the tower, particularly the six young men, who themselves are the "holy angels of God who were the first to be created."[18] It is worth noting that, in Clement's celestial hierarchy, the πρωτόκτιστοι occupy the most elevated position under the logos.[19]

Most relevant in Clement's allusion to *Hermas*, as noted by Batovici, is the way in which he introduces the quotation; he refers to the revealing agent, i.e., the woman church, as, "the power," ἡ δύναμις, and he says the power spoke "divinely," θείως. In the previous chapter, Clement identified "the true wisdom" as δύναμις θεία, "the

---

Heritage," HTR 90 (1997): 59–87. Cf. Arkadi Choufrine, *Gnosis, Theophany, Theosis: Studies in Clement of Alexandria's Appropriation of His Background*, Patristic Studies 5 (New York: Peter Lang, 2002), 165–7. On "the powers" in Philo, cf. Cristina Termini, *Le potenze di Dio: studio su dynamis in Filone di Alessandria* (Rome: Institutum patristicum Augustinianum, 2000).

[16] Translations are mine and based on Sources chrétiennes for the *Stromateis* (Stromate I, 30, 1951; Stromate II, 38, 1954; Stromate VI, 446, 1999) and the Loeb Classical Library version for *Hermas* (Ehrman 2003), unless otherwise noted.

[17] Θείως τοίνυν ἡ δύναμις ἡ τῷ Ἑρμᾷ κατὰ ἀποκάλυψιν λαλοῦσα « τὰ ὁράματα » φησὶ « καὶ τὰ ἀποκαλύμματα διὰ τοὺς διψύχους, τοὺς διαλογιζομένους ἐν ταῖς καρδίαις αὐτῶν, εἰ ἄρα ἔστι ταῦτα ἢ οὐκ ἔστιν». Batovici ("Hermas in Clement of Alexandria," 44) notes that, in Clement, "the 'double-minded' [διψύχους] are the Greeks, with their younger teaching."

[18] *Vis.* 3.4.1 [12] … οἱ ἅγιοι ἄγγελοι τοῦ θεοῦ οἱ πρῶτοι κτισθέντες.

[19] Bucur, *Angelomorphic Pneumatology*, 36. He also writes (xxii–xxiii): "Clement reworks early Jewish and Christian traditions about the seven first-created angels (πρωτόκτιστοι), providing a complex exegesis of specific biblical passages (Zech 4:10; Isa 11:2-3; Matt 18:10)." He later writes (39–40): "Clement's protoctists echo Jewish and Christian traditions about the sevenfold highest angelic company. Among Christian texts, for instance, Revelation mentions seven spirits/angels before the divine throne (Rev 1:4; 3:1; 4:5; 5:6; 8:2), and the Shepherd of Hermas knows of a group of seven consisting of the six 'first created ones' (πρῶτοικτισθέντες) who accompany the Son of God as their seventh (Herm. *Vis.* 3.4.1; Herm. *Sim.* 5.5.3). It is clear, however, that Clement subjects this apocalyptic material to the spiritualizing interpretation and the Logos-theology inherited from Philo. The protoctists are both 'angelic powers' and 'powers of the Logos' that mark the passing of divine unity into multiplicity, and, conversely, the reassembly of cosmic multiplicity into the unity of the Godhead."

power of God."[20] In the present chapter, Clement's focus is on the divine νόμος and the oneness of truth. After quoting from *Hermas*, he goes on to cite Prov 6:23, "'The good commandment, then, is a lamp,' according to the scripture, 'and νόμος a light for the path; for instruction reproves the paths of life.'"[21] The function of the allusion to *Hermas* thus appears to serve as a proof in Clement's argument that not only is God the source of all truth, but God's revelations are particularly for the purposes of instruction and reproof.

Strom. *2.3.5*

Second is *Strom.* 2.3.5, which reads: "For the power who appears said in a vision to Hermas, 'That which can be revealed to you will be revealed.'"[22] Clement here alludes to *Vis.* 3.13.4 [21], which, in *Hermas*, comes from the mouth of the woman church, telling Hermas that he has the full revelation and that he need not ask anything more about any revelation. The straightforward message functions similarly in Clement. Of note is Clement's repeated use of ἡ δύναμις in reference to the revealing agent, the woman church.[23]

Closer analysis of *Vis.* 3 in *Hermas* is due, as it will provide a plausible antecedent to Clement's understanding of "powers" and spiritual hierarchies and it will allow us to consider *Hermas*' role as an authoritative transmitter for Clement. The power(s) are not foreign to *Vision* 3 of *Hermas*, and further, they are closely connected to the πρωτόκτιστοι, as they are in Clement's thought. Studies by Runia and van den Hock on Clement's often-elusive manner of allusion and the means by which he includes and appropriates anterior material provide methodological support for what follows.[24]

---

[20] *Strom.* 1.178.1, noted by Batovici, "Hermas in Clement of Alexandria," 44. Cf. Bogdan Bucur, "Revisiting Christian Oeyen: 'The Other Clement' on Father, Son, and the Angelomorphic Spirit," *VC* 61 (2007): 381–413, here 388–90.

[21] *Strom.* 1.181.3. «λαμπτὴρ ἄρα ἐντολὴ ἀγαθή,» κατὰ τὴν γραφήν, «νόμος δὲ φῶς ὁδοῦ· ὁδοὺς γὰρ Βιότητος ἐλέγχει παιδεία.» Cf. Runia, "Clement of Alexandria," 264 n. 23.

[22] The full Greek text of *Strom.* 2.3.5 reads: Εἴ τις οὖν τοῦ ὁμοίου θεωερίτικος ἐν πολλοῖς τοῖς πιθανοῖς τε καὶ Ἑλληνικοῖς τὸ ἀληθὲς διαλεληθέναι ποθεῖ, καθάπερ ὑπὸ τοῖς μορμολυκείοις τὸ πρόσωπον τὸ ἀληθινόν, πολυπραγμονήσας θηράσεται. Φησὶ γὰρ ἐν τῷ ὁράματι τῷ Ἑρμᾷ ἡ δύναμις ἡ φανεῖσα· «ὃ ἐὰν ἐνδέχηταί σοι ἀποκαλυφθῆναι, ἀποκαλυφθήσεται».

[23] Another reference to the revealing agent as ἡ δύναμις can be found in *Strom.* 6.131.2 [15], noted by Batovici, "Hermas in Clement of Alexandria," 48–9.

[24] Runia, "Clement of Alexandria," 260; van den Hoek, *Clement of Alexandria*, 1.

Hermas Vis. *3.3.5 [11]*

In *Vis.* 3.3.5 [11], the woman church—after revealing that both the church (i.e., the tower) and the Christian have been founded upon the water(s)—says to Hermas, "The tower has been set on a foundation by the word of the almighty and glorious Name, and is strengthened by the unseen power of the Master."[25] Here the author of *Hermas*, by alluding to his earlier reference in *Vis.* 2 that the church is the "firstborn of creation,"[26] connects the baptismal water to the primeval waters. This, however, also echoes *Vis.* 1.3.4 [3], which contains a discourse on the "God of powers," ὁ θεὸς τῶν δυνάμεων, who created the world by his "invisible power," ἀορτάτῳ δυνάμει.[27] *Vision* 3 of *Hermas*—to which Clement alludes, utilizing ἡ δύναμις in reference to the revealing agent—not only contains references to the "power(s)," but also connects the "power(s)" to a protological vision of creation itself, as well as the church. The author does this by alluding to the previous two visions, wherein *Hermas* draws on traditional Jewish and Christian motifs of "powers," spiritual hierarchy, and angelic intermediaries.[28] All of this indicates that there is more than a mere lexical correspondence between *Hermas* and Clement. Further examples of δύναμις in *Vision* 3 can be found in 3.4.3 [12] and 3.8.5-8 [16]. We will consider these in reverse.

Hermas Vis. *3.8 [16]*

Hermas Vis. 3.8 [16] focuses on the seven women supporting the tower. The woman church herself brings these seven to Hermas' attention. After describing

---

[25] Translation from Michael W. Holmes, *The Apostolic Fathers*, Second Edition (Grand Rapids: Baker, 1989), 203. τεθεμελίωται δὲ ὁ πύργος τῷ ῥήματι τοῦ παντοκράτορος καὶ ἐνδόξου ὀνόματος, κρατεῖται δὲ ὑπὸ τῆς ἀοράτου δυνάμεως δεσπότου.

[26] *Vis.* 2.4.1 [8]: πάντων πρώτη ἐκτίσθη· διὰ τοῦτο πρεσβυτέρα, καὶ διὰ ταυτην ὁ κόσμος κατηρτίσθη. The referent in 2.4.1 is ἡ ἐκκλησία.

[27] *Vis.* 1.3.4 [3]: ἰδοὺ ὁ θεὸς τῶν δυνάμεων, ὁ ἀορτάτῳ δυνάμει καὶ κραταιᾷ καὶ τῇ μεγάλῃ συνέσει αὐτοῦ κτίσας τὸν κόσμον καὶ τῇ ἐνδόξῳ βουλῇ περιθεὶς τὴν εὐπρέπειαν τῇ κτίσει αὐτοῦ, καί τῷ ἰσχυρῷ ῥήματι πήξας τὸν οὐρανὸν καὶ θεμελιώσας τὴν γῆν ἐπὶ ὑδάτων καὶ τῇ ἰδίᾳ σοφίᾳ καὶ προνοίᾳ κτίσας τὴν ἁγίαν ἐκκλησιάν αὐτοῦ, ἥν καὶ ηὐλόγησεν. "Behold, the God of powers, who by [his] invisible power and might and great understanding created the world, and by his glorious plan clothed his creation with beauty, and by his strong word fixed the sky and founded the earth upon the waters, and by his own wisdom and foreknowledge, created his holy church, which he also blessed."

[28] See Jarl Fossum, "Jewish-Christian Christology and Jewish Mysticism," *VC* 37 (1983): 260–87, here 272–5; Charles Gieschen, "The Divine Name in Ante-Nicene Christology," *VC* 57 (2003): 115–58, here 152–3. On τὸ ὄνομα in *Hermas*, see also *Sim.* 9.12.8 [89] and 9.13 [90]. See also Runia, "Clement of Alexandria," 60.

two of the women—Faith and Self-Control—Hermas inquires by saying, "I desire to know, Lady, what power each of them has."[29] The woman goes on to explain that "the powers" follow one another and are controlled by one another; she says, "The works of [the powers] are pure and reverent and divine."[30] Of significance here is not only that *Hermas* contains a substantial discourse and sustained dialogue on "the powers," but also that what follows this dialogue is a consideration of "the times." Hermas proceeds to ask the woman church about "the times, [especially] if the end had already come."[31] The protological connection with "the powers" in *Vis.* 3.3 and *Vis.* 1.3 is here matched by an eschatological connection. Further, whereas Clement wrote that the power spoke "divinely" to Hermas, θείως, the woman church, in *Vis.* 3.8, whom Clement refers to as ἡ δύναμις, refers to "the powers" as having "divine" works, θεῖα. In light of the work of others on Clement's christological adaptation of Philo's notion of the "power(s),"[32] I consider it plausible that *Hermas*' nuanced ecclesial and cosmological interweaving of protology and eschatology, wherein the "power(s)" play a prominent role, would not have escaped Clement, especially given Clement's often-elusive manner of allusion to authoritative predecessors.

Hermas Vis. 3.4.3 [12]

The last portion of *Vision* 3 to consider is 3.4.3 [12]. In the immediate context of *Vis.* 3.4, the πρωτόκτιστοι are the primary focus.[33] After indicating the superiority

---

[29] *Vis.* 3.8.6: ἤθελον, φημί, γνῶμαι, κυρία, τίς τίνα δύναμιν ἔχει αυτῶν. Cf. *Sim.* 9.13, where it is revealed to Hermas that one must clothe oneself in the clothing of the virgins, who themselves are δυνάμεις τοῦ θεοῦ (9.13.2). This is in contrast to one who merely bears τὸ ὄνομα. 9.13a reads: τοὺς δὲ λίθους, οὓς εἶδες ἀποβεβλημένους, οὗτοι τὸ μὲν ὄνομα ἐφόρεσαν, τὸν δὲ ἱματισμὸν τῶν παρθένων οὐκ ἐνεδύσαντο. In 9.13.4, "their clothing" is identified as the "power" of the virgins.

[30] *Vis.* 3.8.7: ... τούτων οὖν τὰ ἔργα ἁγνὰ καὶ σεμνὰ καὶ θεῖά ἐστιν. *Vis.* 3.8.8, the following verse in *Hermas*, reads: ὅς ἂν οὖν δουλεύσῃ ταύταις καὶ ἰσχύσῃ κρατῆσαι τῶν ἔργων αὐτῶν, ἐν τῷ πύργῳ ἕξει τὴν κατοίκησιν μετὰ τῶν ἁγίων τοῦ θεοῦ. The powers, therefore, are to be "served."

[31] *Vis.* 3.8.9: ἐπηρώτων δὲ αὐτὴν περὶ τῶν καιρῶν, εἰ ἤδη συντέλειά ἐστιν. The eschatological question functions as a call to repentance in *Hermas*.

[32] Runia, "Clement of Alexandria, "276; van den Hoek, *Clement of Alexandria*, 129; Bucur, *Angelomorphic Pneumatology*, 30. Cf. Henny Fiskå Hägg, *Clement of Alexandria and the Beginnings of Christian Apophaticism*, OECS (Oxford: Oxford University Press, 2006), 232.

[33] οἱ ἅγιοι ἄγγελοι τοῦ θεοῦ οἱ πρῶτοι κτισθέντες. Cf. Everett Procter, *Christian Controversy in Alexandria: Clement's Polemic against the Basilideans and Valentinians* (New York: Peter Lang, 1995), 72–3, 84 n. 14.

of these "first-created angels," Hermas poses another inquiry: "Lady, I wish to know about the destination of the stones and their δύναμις, of what sort it is."³⁴ Translators and commentators, for the most part, avoid translating δύναμις as "power" here, typically opting for the gloss "meaning" instead.³⁵ Whether these commentators best capture the sense of the word in *Hermas* we ought not think Clement understood δύναμις as they did. The woman church identifies the first batch of stones with ecclesiastical offices; yet when she does, she qualifies her identification. They are not merely those who hold such offices; rather, they are the ones "who have lived according to the holiness of God, performing their duties as bishops, teachers, and deacons in a holy and honorable manner for the elect of God."³⁶

Returning to Clement of Alexandria, we see something exceptionally similar. Clement writes:

Such one is in reality a presbyter of the Church, and a true minister (deacon) of the will of God, if he do and teach what is the Lord's; not as being ordained by men, nor regarded righteous because a presbyter, but enrolled in the presbyterate because righteous. And although here upon earth he be not honored with the chief seat, he will sit down on the four-and-twenty thrones, judging the people, as John says in the Apocalypse.³⁷

Clement accorded authority to ecclesiastical hierarchy insofar as it modeled spiritual hierarchy. Further, Clement's allegorizing of ritual elements of the Jewish priestly temple cult—an interpretive move for which he is indebted to his Alexandrian predecessor, Philo—displays a similar tendency and interpretive methodology.³⁸

---

³⁴ *Vis.* 3.4.3 [12]: Κυρία, ἤθελον γνῶναι τῶν λίθων τὴν ἔξοδον καὶ τὴν δύναμιν αὐτῶν, ποταπή ἐστιν.

³⁵ Holmes (*Apostolic Fathers*, 203) translates: "Madam, I wish to know about the destination of the stones, and *what kind of meaning they have*" (my emphasis). Ehrman, too, uses "meaning" (202-3). Osiek's translation is substantially the same, using "import" (65). Cf. Joseph Barber Lightfoot and J. R. Harmer, *The Apostolic Fathers* (London: Macmillan, 1891), 413. Lightfoot uses "end" and "power" for ἔξεδον and δύναμις.

³⁶ *Vis.* 3.5.1 [13]: οὗτοί εἰσιν οἱ ἀπόστολοι καὶ ἐπίσκοποι καὶ διδάσκαλοι και διάκονοι οἱ πορευθέντες κατὰ τὴν σεμνότητα τοῦ θεοῦ καὶ ἐπισκοπήσαντες καὶ διδάξαντες καὶ διακονήσαντες ἁγνῶς καὶ σεμνῶς τοῖς ἐκλεκτοῖς τοῦ θεοῦ.

³⁷ *Strom.* 6.13.106, in Bucur, *Angelomorphic Pneumtalogy*, 49. Οὗτος πρεσβύτερός ἐστι τῷ ὄντι τῆς ἐκκλησίας καὶ διάκονος ἀληθὴς τῆς τοῦ θεοῦ βουλήσεως, ἐὰν ποιῇ καὶ διδάσκῃ τὰ τοῦ κυρίου, οὐχ ὑπ'ἀνθρώπων χειροτονούμενος οὐδ', ὅτι πρεσβύτερος, δίκαιος νομιζόμενος· κἂν ἐνταῦθα ἐπὶ γῆς πρωτοκαθεδρίᾳ μὴ τιμηθῇ, ἐν τοῖς εἴκοσι καὶ τέσσαρσι καθεδεῖται θρόνοις τὸν λαὸν κρίνων, ὥς φησιν ἐν τῇ ἀποκαλύψει Ἰωάννης.

³⁸ van den Hoek, *Clement of Alexandria*, 116-48; Runia, "Clement of Alexandria," 262-3.

We thus see that there is considerable and specific conceptual overlap between *Hermas* and Clement regarding the "power(s)" and spiritual hierarchy.

The immediate contexts of the passages from *Hermas* to which Clement alludes contain a conglomeration of prominent themes found in Clement's writings, most especially relating to Clement's spiritual universe—e.g., the πρωτόκτιστοι and the "power(s)"—inclining us to think that Clement's use of *Hermas* is plausibly more nuanced than often recognized. Clement's understanding of ecclesiastical hierarchy and authority as based on a paradigm of spiritual hierarchy and authority ought to inform our understanding of his engagement with *Hermas*, and thus *Hermas*'s reception, function, and (relative) authority in Clement. In *Hermas*, "the powers" interrelate with ecclesiastical offices, and in Clement, they are part of the spiritual hierarchy headed by the logos and the "first-created (angels)."

Final Remarks on Hermas's Function and Authority in Clement

It is important to remember that the first of Clement's allusions to *Hermas* that we noted—from *Strom.* 1.181.1—occurs in a context where Clement focuses on the nature of truth, wisdom, and νόμος.[39] Clement, however, in appealing to *Hermas*, rather than invoking the authority of an ecclesiastical office, refers to the power, the spiritual agent who reveals truth. Further, in light of the foregoing analysis of both Clement's allusions and the text of *Hermas*, it is plausible that Clement is to some degree indebted to *Hermas* for his use of the "power(s)," as demonstrated especially by the nuanced contextual connections between the "power(s)" and the "first-created (angels)" in both. This relationship, as should now be apparent, contributes to *Hermas*'s authority for Clement.

This conclusion further informs our understanding of the dynamics of *Hermas*'s authority for Clement. Apocalyptic elements play a role in contributing to the authority of *Hermas* for Clement, but not apocalyptic elements *qua* apocalyptic elements, for there is a specificity in matters of tradition-history and spiritual hierarchy, without which we can only surmise that Clement would have interacted with *Hermas* differently. For Clement, specifically visionary elements matter most, including angelic visionary intermediaries, particularly "power(s)."

The previous analysis of select allusions to *Hermas* from Clement of Alexandria's *Stromateis* confirms that *Hermas* is authoritative for Clement. When we shift the conversation away from "canonical" and "noncanonical"—binaries which often disallow both breadth and depth of analysis and obfuscate historical particularities anachronistically—to a discussion of function and thus relative authority, and further, when we pay attention to the various intellectual and interpretive traditions which converge in Clement's thought, manifesting themselves in his engagement with and reception of *Hermas*, we can account for *Hermas*' history of use and

---

[39] Cf. Choufrine, *Gnosis, Theophany, Theosis*, 170.

interpretation in a more detailed and nuanced way and thereby open up new paths in the study of *Hermas* itself.

There nevertheless remains the question of whether we have been forced to focus on *Hermas*' function because Clement does not make an assertive value judgment regarding *Hermas*. This, however, is indicative of the environment and state of the negotiation of *Hermas*' authority between Clement and his (perceived) audience, and those with whom his audience might dialogue. Brief excursive attention to Irenaeus and the Muratorian Fragment will shed light on this point, as they each disclose different dynamics of *Hermas*'s variegated reception. Our intention is to discern what accounts for the relative authority or non-authority of *Hermas* in each and to discern the presence or absence of tension within the negotiation of the authority of *Hermas* between each author (i.e., Irenaeus and the anonymous author of the Muratorian Fragment) and their audiences.

Excursus I: Hermas *in Irenaeus*

The majority of scholars consider *Hermas* an authoritative text for Irenaeus yet, as far as we know, Irenaeus only quoted from one verse of *Hermas*, *Mand.* 1.1. The most relevant quotation of *Mand.* 1.1 is found in *Adv. haer.* 4.20.2, where Irenaeus writes:

> Therefore scripture rightly says: "First of all, believe that God is one, who created and furnished all things, and made all things to exist from what did not, who contains all things but is himself alone uncontained."[40]

Of continued debate is the semantic value of ἡ γραφή.[41] Although one solves the semantic question, we can note that there is no evidence of a dispute *over the way*

---

[40] Adelin Rousseau et al. (eds.), *Irénée de Lyon, Contra les hérésies, Livre IV*, SC 100 (Paris: Cerf, 1965), 628–9: Καλῶς οὖν ἡ γραφὴ ἡ λέγουσα «Πρῶτον πάντων πίστευσον ὅτι εἷς ἐστὶν ὁ θεὸς ὁ τὰ πάντα κτίσας καὶ καταρτίσας, καὶ ποιήσας ἐκ τοῦ μὴ ὄντος εἰς τὸ εἶναι τὰ πάντα καὶ πάντα χωρῶν, μόνος δὲ ἀχώρητος ὤν».

[41] Those who consider *Hermas* "scripture" for Irenaeus include: Batovici, "Hermas' Authority in Irenaeus' Works: A Reassessment," 30; M. C. Steenberg, "Irenaeus on Scripture, Graphe, and The Status of Hermas," 65; idem, "Tracing the Irenaean Legacy," in Sara Parvis and Paul Foster (eds.), *Irenaeus: Life, Scripture, Legacy* (Minneapolis: Fortress, 2012), 199–211, here 202; Gamble, "The New Testament Canon," 289; Metzger, "Books of Temporary and Local Canonicity," 188; Osiek, *The Shepherd of Hermas*, 5; Michael Slusser, "The Heart of Irenaeus's Theology," in *Irenaeus: Life, Scripture, Legacy*, 133–9, esp. 134. Cf. C. E. Hill, "'The Writing which Says …' *The Shepherd* of Hermas in the Writings of Irenaeus," *StPatr* 65 (2013): 127–38. Hill takes ἡ γραφή as "the writing."

in which Irenaeus uses Hermas in the negotiation of *Hermas*'s authority between Irenaeus and his audience. In accounting for *Hermas*'s authority for Irenaeus, we can also have a reasonable degree of confidence that it was the theological outlook of (this particular portion of) *Hermas* that accounts for his high regard for it.

Of Irenaeus' introduction to *Hermas*—i.e., his initial reception of it and his (assumed) background knowledge regarding its provenance, production, and anterior receptions—we must be content to remain ignorant. Irenaeus' use of *Hermas* is thus both similar to and different than Clement's. The difference of most significance is that Irenaeus accords authority to *Hermas* on the basis of its consistency with the *regula fidei*.

Excursus II: Hermas *in the Muratorian Fragment*

Hermas appears at the fore of discussions of the Muratorian Fragment, for the anonymous author's treatment of *Hermas* in lines 73–80 contains the most pertinent internal evidence for considering the provenance of the fragment. Lines 73–80 read:

> (73) But Hermas wrote the *Shepherd* (74) very recently, in our times, in the city of Rome, (75) while bishop Pius, his brother, was occupying the [episcopal] chair (76) of the church of the city of Rome. (77) And therefore it ought indeed to be read; but (78) it cannot be read publicly to the people in the church either among (79) the prophets, whose number is complete, or among (80) the apostles, for it is after [their] time.[42]

Some propose a late-second-century date (e.g., Metzger, Ferguson),[43] arguing primarily from lines 74 to 76 and the use of *temporibus nostris* in conjunction with Pius's tenure (ca. 150), while others prefer a late-fourth-century date (e.g.,

---

[42] Translated by Metzger, *The Canon of the New Testament*, Appendix IV, 305–7. Hans Lietzmann, *Das Muratorische Fragment und die Monarchianischen Prologue zu den Evangelien*, Kleine Texte 1 (Bonn, 1902; 2nd ed., Berlin, 1933), 8–11: [73] … *pastorem uero* [74] *nuperrim e* temporibus nostris in urbe* [75] *roma herma conscripsit sedente cathe* [76] *tra urbis romae aeclesiae pio eps fratre* [77] *eius et ideo legi eum quidē oportet se pu* [78] *plicare uero in eclesia populo neque inter* [79] *profetas conpletum numero neqe inter* [80] *apostolos in finē temporum potest*.

[43] Metzger, *The Canon of the New Testament*, 188–94; Everett Ferguson, "Canon Muratori: Date and Provenance," *StPatr* 48 (1982): 677–83.

Hahneman, McDonald, Sundberg),[44] often arguing that the fragment is anomalous when situated in the second century, but more fitting in the context of the fourth century.

As it pertains to our two aims, it is clear on what grounds the fragment mandates the private reading of *Hermas* and rejects its public reading; it was written, as lines 74–76 read, "very recently, in our times, in the city of Rome, while bishop Pius, his brother, was occupying the chair," however one understands that. On the other hand, while the point ought not be overstated, the fragment plausibly preserves a relative degree of perceived tension in the negotiation of *Hermas*' authority between the author and his perceived audience(s). We can discern this in the way in which the author justifies his decision at length, as well as the way in which he not only permits but also mandates the private reading of *Hermas*.

Conclusion

Whereas Irenaeus accords a degree of authority to *Hermas* on the basis of its conformity to the *regula fidei*, and the anonymous author of the Muratorian Fragment accords a private authority to *Hermas* on the basis of the relatively late date of its composition—however one understands that—Clement accords a significant degree of authority to *Hermas* at least partially on the basis that it transmits revealed wisdom for the purpose of edification by means of visions imparted by divine "power(s)." Further, while the treatment of *Hermas* in the Muratorian Fragment plausibly preserves evidence of tension in the negotiation of *Hermas*'s authority, Clement's use of *Hermas* leaves no trace of any perceived dissension in the negotiation of *Hermas*'s authority between Clement and his perceived audience(s).

As demonstrated in the foregoing analysis, Clement of Alexandria's engagement with and reception of *Hermas* is marked by the confluence of interpretive traditions regarding angelic intermediary figures. As also demonstrated above, attention to *Hermas* itself provides good reason to think that Clement, in alluding to *Hermas* by reference to "the power," engages *Hermas* in a nuanced manner, deliberately drawing out elements already present in *Hermas*.

---

[44] Geoffrey Mark Hahneman, "The Muratorian Fragment and the Origins of the New Testament Canon," in Lee Martin McDonald and James A. Sanders (eds.), *The Canon Debate: On the Origins and Formation of the Bible* (Peabody, MA: Hendrickson, 2004), 405–39; Lee Martin McDonald, *The Biblical Canon: Its Origin, Transmission, and Authority* (rev. 3rd ed., Peabody, MA: Hendrickson, 2007), 368–78; Albert C. Sundberg Jr., "Canon Muratori: A Fourth-Century List," *HTR* 66 (1973): 1–41. See now Clare K. Rothschild, "The Muratorian Fragment as Roman Fake," *NovT* 60 (2018): 55–82, which appeared after I submitted my chapter to the editors for publication.

On a methodological level, this study rejects the wedding of *Hermas*'s reception-historical questions with questions of "canon" and "canonicity." Binary-driven approaches—including approaches motivated by canonical questions—often limit the scope of inquiry and disallow due attention to be given to the various particularities. Insights such as those offered in the present study are often missed because of the hegemony of the question of *Hermas*' canonicity. Reception, function, and authority are all dynamic categories; they are neither static nor fixed, and our methods of inquiry, as well as our aims, need to respect this dynamism, as I hope to have shown in the case of Hermas's δύναμις.

Part II

VIOLENCE AND POLEMIC IN THE PSEUDEPIGRAPHA

Chapter 5

VIOLENCE AND DIVINE FAVOR IN *LIBER ANTIQUITATUM BIBLICARUM*

Benjamin J. Lappenga

Modern readers often recoil at the apparent celebration of violent deeds in biblical texts. Concerning the story of Jephthah in Judges 11, for example, we might be horrified not simply by the element of human sacrifice but also by the lack of a clear condemnation of Jephthah in the biblical account. The silence of the narrator in Judges itself, the lauding of Jephthah for delivering Israel in 1 Sam 12:11,[1] Jephthah's place among the "heroes of faith" in Heb 11:32, and other early Christian interpretations that remember and exalt Jephthah but forget his daughter—all of these are deeply troubling.[2] How could the God who categorically opposes human sacrifice (Jer 19:5) allow such a thing? What influences on the biblical editors led them to allow Jephthah a pass?[3] Why does violence seem to be endemic to religion, even religions that celebrate *peace*, and whose texts are infused with impulses toward nonviolence?[4]

---

[1] As Phyllis Trible summarizes: "Challenged by armed Ephraimites, Jephthah leads the Gileadites to a resounding victory. The mighty warrior prevails uncensured; the violence that he perpetrated upon his only daughter stalks him not at all. In the end he dies a natural death and receives an epitaph fit for an exemplary judge (12:7). Moreover, his military victories enhance his name in the years to come. Specifically, the prophet Samuel proclaims to Israel that 'Yahweh sent Jephthah ... and delivered you out of the hand of your enemies' (1 Sam 12:11, RSV)" (*Texts of Terror: Literary-Feminist Readings of Biblical Narratives* [Philadelphia: Fortress, 1997], 107).

[2] For an example from Christian literature of later centuries, see Ephrem the Syrian, *Comm. Heb.* 226-27.

[3] Later Jewish legend suggests that Jephthah was punished by dismemberment (see Louis Ginzberg, *The Legends of the Jews*, vol. IV [Philadelphia: JPS, 1968], 43-7).

[4] As Trible comments regarding the forgotten daughter: "Thus has scripture violated the ancient story, and yet that story endures to this day for us to recover and appropriate" (*Texts of Terror*, 108).

The aim of this chapter is to show that the ancient author known as Pseudo-Philo *shares* our disquiet, and, importantly, offers an example of how *narrative retelling* may be used to address the relationship between divine favor and violent deeds. Four pairs of key figures will serve to illustrate Jephthah/Seila (*LAB* 39-40), Moses/Phinehas (*LAB* 12 and 47), Hannah/Peninnah (*LAB* 50-51), and Saul/David (*LAB* 56-65). At first glance, Pseudo-Philo's retellings seem to affirm that the prayers of key individuals for God's merciful action on behalf of the people are rendered efficacious by public acts of violent "zeal." If we attend carefully to a series of textual signals and narrative strategies throughout *Liber Antiquitatum Biblicarum*, however, we encounter a subtle but strong condemnation of the view that violent expressions of power are necessary to secure divine blessing. Sometimes taking its cues from the biblical text, but also certainly going beyond it, Pseudo-Philo's narrative "shapes" language (a concept I will address below) in order to challenge the implication that violent zeal can incur God's favor.

Before examining the narrative, it is necessary briefly to address the particular linguistic framework that informs my reading. I have argued at length elsewhere that the "zeal" word group (in Hebrew, Greek, and Latin) is best viewed as monosemic.[5] That is, if we employ a "monosemic bias" (a concept used by theorists working within a variety of linguistic frameworks),[6] all instances of the *zelo/zelus* word group are viewed *together*, rather than as distinct lexical inputs from separate domains ("zeal," "jealousy," "eagerness," etc.).[7]

From a relevance-theoretic linguistic perspective, we may speak of the strategic "shaping" of the terms *zelo* and *zelus* within Pseudo-Philo's text, where the meaning of the term *zelus*, and by extension the *concept* of "zeal," is constructed by the reader from an encyclopedia of mental items such as memories, images, and pieces of anecdotal information.[8] The text itself influences which mental items

---

[5] See Benjamin J. Lappenga, *Paul's Language of Ζῆλος: Monosemy and the Rhetoric of Identity and Practice*, BibInt 137 (Leiden: Brill, 2016). Ancient writers as diverse as Cicero, Plutarch, and the apostle Paul advance a variety of rhetorical aims by the repeated and strategic use of the terms קנאה/ζῆλος/*zelus*. These rhetorical strategies often go unnoticed when the word group is viewed as polysemic and therefore translated using different English words.

[6] See, e.g., Thorstein Fretheim, "In Defense of Monosemy," in Németh T. Enikö and Károly Bibok (eds.), *Pragmatics and the Flexibility of Word Meaning* (Amsterdam: Elsevier Science, 2001), 79–115; Gregory P. Fewster, *Creation Language in Romans 8: A Study in Monosemy*, LBS 8 (Leiden: Brill, 2013); and Charles Ruhl, *On Monosemy: A Study in Linguistic Semantics* (Albany: State University of New York, 1989).

[7] *LAB* survives only in Latin, but scholars generally agree that the Latin is a translation from the Greek, which is itself a translation from a Hebrew original; see especially Daniel J. Harrington, "The Original Language of Pseudo-Philo's *Liber Antiquitatum Biblicarum*," HTR 63 (1970): 503–14; and the discussion in Howard Jacobson, *A Commentary on Pseudo-Philo's Liber Antiquitatum Biblicarum*, AGJU 31 (Leiden: Brill, 1996), 215–24.

[8] See further Agustín Rayo, "A Plea for Semantic Localism," *Noûs* 47 (2013), 647–79.

are activated, with the result that a later occurrence of *zelo/zelus* recalls the earlier contexts in which *zelo/zelus* was used.⁹

As is evident from a wide range of texts in antiquity, it is the *object toward which zeal is directed* that determines whether zeal is to be evaluated positively or negatively. Pseudo-Philo sometimes refers to *zelo/zelus* positively (e.g., 9.6; 11.6), but also employs several *negative* examples of zealous action (e.g., 18.11). The text suggests, then, that zeal is a good thing only when rightly directed and rightly motivated, and God extends mercy in response to the right kind of zeal. The question implicit in the text is: what constitutes the right kind of zeal?

The process of engaging with this question may be unconscious for audiences close in time, culture, and language to the writing of the book, but modern readers must work to expose significant linguistic patterns in the narrative that are otherwise masked in translation. The benefits of such work can only be evaluated by the readings themselves, to which we now turn.

I. Jephthah (LAB 39–40) and Hannah (LAB 48–51): Preliminary Readings

At first glance, the figure of Jephthah is somewhat ambiguous in Pseudo-Philo's retelling, since, just like in Judges 11, Jephthah does in fact win victory over Israel's enemies (the Ammonites), and Jephthah serves as a judge for many years and is "buried with his fathers" (*LAB* 40.9). Thus it is not surprising that modern interpreters of Pseudo-Philo regularly speak of Jephthah as "the judge who has saved Israel,"[10] one who "seems to prove himself a good leader,"[11] and who "defends Israel successfully."[12]

Yet interpreters have also given attention to the ways in which Pseudo-Philo *changes* the biblical story, especially the way that the narrative elevates the role of Jephthah's daughter and works to exonerate God from complicity in the girl's horrific death. In *LAB* 39.11, God is "very angry" about Jephthah's vow (if mostly at the possibility that the offering could be a dog); the daughter dies willingly as a sacrifice for the people (40.3); God declares that she "is wise in contrast to her father and … all the wise men" (40.4); and, significantly, the girl is given a name (Seila, likely שאולה, which could mean "she who is requested/demanded"; 40.1).

---

⁹ The *zelus* word group occurs twenty times in *LAB*: 9.6; 11.6; 18.11; 20.5; 32.1, 2; 39.2; 44.7; 44.10; 45.6; 47.1 (two occurrences); 47.7; 50.5; 58.1; 59.4; 62.1, 11 (two occurrences); 64.8.

[10] George W. E. Nickelsburg, "Good and Bad Leaders in Pseudo-Philo's *Liber Antiquitatum Biblicarum*," in John J. Collins and George W. E. Nickelsburg (eds.), *Ideal Figures in Ancient Judaism: Profiles and Paradigms*, SBLSCS 12 (Chico: Scholars, 1980), 57.

[11] Frederick J. Murphy, *Pseudo-Philo: Rewriting the Bible* (New York: Oxford University Press, 1993), 164; cf. 238.

[12] Mary Therese DesCamp, *Metaphor and Ideology*: Liber Antiquitatum Biblicarum *and Literary Methods through a Cognitive Lens*, BibInt 87 (Leiden: Brill, 2007), 255.

These additions to the biblical account serve to de-emphasize Jephthah, yet on their own fall short of condemning Jephthah's legacy as a successful judge. Even if God is in some sense absolved, Jephthah's carelessness and violence have not prevented him from being hailed as a successful leader.

However, there exists an additional detail that interpreters have largely missed and mistranslated. On occasion, the text of *LAB* presents linguistic conundrums that impede interpretation, usually involving some uncertainty about the Latin. The quandary in 39.2, by contrast, is simply that the text as it stands does not seem to make sense. Since in Judg 11:2 Jephthah's brothers "drove him away" (ויגרשו), modern translators have tended to amend the text from the Latin "he envied his brothers" (*zelaret fratres suos*) to "his brothers envied him."[13] Yet in the Latin Jephthah is unexpectedly, yet clearly, designated as the figure who is characterized by "zeal."

If we turn our attention to a similar instance later in Pseudo-Philo's narrative, we begin to see just what such an assessment of Jephthah might be taken to indicate.[14] The Hannah episode in *LAB* follows the basic plot from 1 Samuel: Hannah prays silently for a child, is thought to be drunk by Eli, and eventually gives birth to the child, Samuel, who will deliver the Israelites. Regarding Pseudo-Philo's retelling, interpreters remain puzzled about at least two details in the passage. First, scholars are uncertain how to understand the present participle of *zelo* in Hannah's reference to Peninnah's daily taunts in 50.5 (*plus me zelans improperet mihi*). Peninnah might legitimately be seen as "eager" (Harrington), "jealous"/"envious" (Jacobson, Cazeaux), or "rivalrous" (Murphy).[15] Second, it is unclear why Pseudo-Philo repeats in 50.3 that Eli was appointed by "Phinehas the son of Eleazar the priest," since there is no mention of Phinehas in 1 Samuel, Phinehas has nothing to do with the Hannah story, and this information has just been reported in the previous chapter when Eli was first introduced (48.2).

---

[13] See, e.g., Jacobson, *Commentary*, 946–7.

[14] Portions of this section are adapted from my longer treatment in "'Speak, Hannah, and Do Not be Silent': Pseudo-Philo's Deconstruction of Violence in *Liber Antiquitatum Biblicarum* 50–1," *JSP* 25 (2015): 91–110.

[15] Harrington translates, "Peninnah will then be even more eager to taunt me" ("Pseudo-Philo: A New Translation and Introduction by D.J. Harrington," in James H. Charlesworth (ed.), *The Old Testament Pseudepigrapha Expansions of the "Old Testament" and Legends* [Garden City, NY: Doubleday, 1983], 364); Jacobson translates, "Peninnah in her envy of me will mock me more" (*Commentary*, 176); Jacques Cazeaux translates, "dans sa jalousie, Peninna me fera des remarques encore plus fielleuses" (*Pseudo-Philon: Les antiquités bibliques. I. Introduction et text critiques*, SC 229 [Paris: Éditions du Cerf, 1976], 305); and Frederick J. Murphy in his commentary speaks of Peninnah here as Hannah's "rival" (*Rewriting*, 190).

The Zeal of Phinehas in LAB 47

Taken together, however, these two details ("zeal" and Phinehas) are not in fact obscure or insignificant, because they recall a prominent motif from the preceding chapters. Through a clever use of flashback, the moment that defines the legendary zealot Phinehas is recounted in *LAB* 47, rather than in its expected place in *LAB* 18.14 (the account of the Israelites' fornication with the Midianite women).[16] In addition, despite the fact that six of the twenty total occurrences of *zelo/zelus* are clustered in *LAB* 44-47, translators have largely muted the motif of zeal in these chapters by failing consistently to translate the occurrences of *zelo/zelus*.

In chapter 44, Pseudo-Philo recounts the tale of Micah and his idols (Judg 17). God expresses anger at Israel for violating each of the ten commandments, saying, "And though I commanded them not to commit adultery, they have committed adultery with their zeal [*zelum suum mechati sunt*]" (44.7). The problem is not that the people have *zelus*, but that it is directed at the wrong object. Immediately following, God promises to punish not only Micah, but all the people who "sin against me," declaring that the "race of men will know that they were not zealous for me in the inventions they made" (44.10). In the next chapter, Pseudo-Philo records the horrific story of the Levite's concubine (cf. Judg 19). God expresses anger that the "foolish people" were not disturbed when Micah led them astray with the idols, but *were* stirred by what happened with the Levite's concubine. The assessment is clear: "And so, because they were not zealous then (*quia non sunt tunc zelati*), therefore he let their plan turn out badly and their heart be confused" (45.6).

These occurrences set the stage for the three instances of *zelo/zelus* in *LAB* 47. Phinehas is in a desperate predicament. The Israelites had taken Phinehas' advice to consult the priestly lots and had received assurance of victory (*LAB* 46.1; cf. Judg 20:28), but are routed by the Benjamites (*LAB* 46.3; cf. Judg 20:21, 25).[17] Tearing their clothes and placing ashes on their heads, the people pleadingly question God about God's deception (*LAB* 46.4). Will the people rise up against Phinehas? Will God finally answer their cries for help? Phinehas prays in *LAB* 47.1:

> For I remember in my youth when Zimri sinned in the days of Moses your servant, and I went in and was zealous with the zeal of my soul [*zelatus sum zelum anime mee*], and hoisted both up on my spear.

The point is reiterated with one final occurrence of *zelus* in *LAB* 47.7. In the form of an analogy, the "fable of the lion" reiterates the people's inaction and solidifies

---

[16] Some material in this section is adapted from *Paul's Language of* Ζῆλος, 92–106.

[17] In Judg 20, the Israelites are twice routed before consulting Phinehas, after which they are eventually victorious. Pseudo-Philo places Phinehas in a predicament by having him involved *before* the people are routed, which sets up Phinehas' pleading prayer in *LAB* 47.1-3.

the connection between rightly directed zeal and God's favorable response. The episode is also another example of the verbal link between the motif of zeal and the motif of "silence" (e.g., *LAB* 28.3; 51.6; 63.3-4). Just before we hear that God answers Phinehas' prayer at the conclusion of the fable, God sums up the central issue: "No one acted zealously [*zelavit*] but all of you were led astray … and you were silent like that evil lion" (*LAB* 47.7).

Given the way the *zelo/zelus* word group has been shaped by the narrative, and given the literary technique of omitting mention of this significant event in *LAB* 18.14, this short paraphrase is conspicuous. Unquestionably, Phinehas' act of godly zeal is rightly directed. Given the setup in 45.6 ("because [the people] were not zealous then … "), it seems clear that Phinehas' zeal is precisely the zeal that has been missing.

But here, two possibilities present themselves. On the one hand, it is difficult to avoid the implication that in practice zeal means *violence*. If Pseudo-Philo's readers are familiar with the biblical story of Num 25 (and *LAB* does seem to assume this), they would be aware that in the biblical account God adopts Phinehas's zeal *as his own* (בקנאו את־קנאתי בתוכם, "he was zealous with *my* zeal among them"; Num 25:11). Pseudo-Philo even reinforces the point by reworking the chronology of Moses' smashing of the tablets (Exod 32:19) in *LAB* 12.4-10 so that Moses' violent demonstration corresponds with that of Phinehas in *LAB* 47.[18] In other words, Phinehas' violent slaying of Zimri is a manifestation of the very zeal of God.

On the other hand, since the text is clear in these cases that it is the *prayer* of Phinehas (or Moses or others) that is efficacious, God's favorable answer in *LAB* 47.3 could be interpreted as a response only to Phinehas's *prayer* and not to his violent action. Phinehas boldly challenges God to answer his prayer. Pseudo-Philo records God's response:

> And the Lord, seeing that Phinehas had prayed earnestly in his sight, said to him, "I swear by myself, says the Lord: *if you had not then prayed*,[19] I would not have been mindful of you in what you said, nor would I have answered you today."

(*LAB* 47.3)

This, in fact, was the interpretation of Numbers 25 espoused by later writers, who seem troubled that Phinehas' own zealous initiative constitutes an act of

---

[18] For a detailed examination, see Lappenga, "Speak," 101–3.

[19] The editio princeps reads *iurassem*, thus indicating God as the one who "swore an oath," but all other manuscripts read *iurasses* ("you swore"). Most translators accept the reading of the editio princeps, but in light of the importance of the efficacy of prayer in the text, it is more likely that Phinehas is indeed the intended subject, and that *iurasses* is a corruption of *orasses* ("you prayed"). This same confusion occurs in Ovid, *Her.* 8.117 (*Per genus infelix iuro*[*oro*]; "By the unhappy line I *swear*"), so the emendation is not without precedent. The idea that God would credit Phinehas' *prayer* makes much more sense in the context than some unmentioned *oath* sworn by Phinehas or God. See further Jacobson, *Commentary*, 1049.

atonement (כפר) for the people (Num 25:13). The rabbis and targumic writers did praise Phinehas' zeal as a model for action (e.g., *Tg. Ps.-J.* to Num. 25:8: יזכון כהניא לתלת מתנן ... וצלי ... וחולף דאחד רומחא ["Because he grasped the spear ... and prayed ... the priests merit three gifts ... "]), but separated that action from its capacity to affect God's will (e.g., *Sifre Num.* 131: לכפר לא נאמר ["'To atone' is not said ... "]).[20] These writers seem to be reading Num 25 through the lens of the "softened" version of the episode recounted in Ps 106:28-31, which makes no mention of Phinehas' zeal:

> They joined themselves to the Baal of Peor ... they provoked [the Lord] by their deeds ... and Phinehas stood and *prayed* [פלל], and the plague was restrained—and it was reckoned to him as righteousness, from generation to generation forever.

So how do we adjudicate between these two options? For Pseudo-Philo's readers, is the zeal that moves God to action to be understood as violence, or prayer?

Hannah and Seila: Exemplars of Nonviolent Zeal

The occurrences of *zelo/zelus* in the Hannah and Jephthah episodes prompt Pseudo-Philo's readers to pursue an answer. Peninnah's "zealous" taunting (*zelans improperet* [50.5]) is a signal that the Hannah narrative will participate in the text's exploration of the nature of zealous human initiative. Peninnah's zeal is a foil, indicating that Hannah's commendable act of praying silently is itself an act of zeal. Although Hannah's zeal is positive like that of Moses and Phinehas, her zealous act is simultaneously unlike theirs. Whereas their acts are violent and lead to public acclaim (cf. 14.5; 47.3), Hannah's prayer is silent and opens her up to public ridicule (50.2). In an unexpected turn in the pattern established thus far in the narrative, Hannah's prayer is not only answered but is accepted as the accompanying act for the *people's* prayer (*populus oravit pro hoc*; *LAB* 51.2). Thus the ultimate deliverance of the people arrives not by the violent deeds of Moses and Phinehas, but by the silent zeal of Hannah.

Likewise, just as it is the prayer of Hannah that is acceptable to God, God says to Jephthah, "But I will surely free my people in this time, not because of [Jephthah] but because of the *prayer* that Israel *prayed*" (*LAB* 39.11). In addition,

---

[20] As David Bernat summarizes the range of interpretations in Midrashic passages, recensions of the Phinehas-miracle legend, and *Sifre Num.*: "In the Rabbinic and Targumic reconstruction of the narrative, Phinehas' act of violence is fully decoupled from the reversal of the plague. Thus the priest's zealotry is completely denuded of its power to affect God's will …. [O]n the other hand … [w]hen Phinehas stood and prayed, he protected his people from decimation by revealing the mercies of heaven" ("Phinehas' Intercessory Prayer: A Rabbinic and Targumic Reading of the Baal Peor Narrative," *JJS* 58 [2007]: 282).

Seila's willing submission to her death is a vicarious and zealous act, just as in the Hannah narrative. The Lord says, "And now let her life be given at his request, and her death will be *precious* (Lat.: *preciosa*/Heb.: יקרה) before me always, and she will go away and fall into the bosom of her mothers" (40.5). Seila, too, says, "If I did not offer myself willingly for sacrifice, I fear that my death would not be acceptable or I would lose my life in vain" (40.3). Thus Pseudo-Philo's telling of Seila's story represents an alternative to the pattern of violent zealous action, and anticipates the deconstruction of that pattern in the ensuing narratives involving Phinehas and then Hannah.

By attributing "zeal" to Jephthah, then, Pseudo-Philo has indicated at the beginning of the episode that Jephthah is a figure who will be characterized by violent zeal. Jephthah is a foil (like Penninah), and his violent zeal is lumped in with that of figures like Phinehas and Moses.[21] By this point in the narrative, and then especially after the cluster of occurrences in the Phinehas episodes, specific mental images associated with the term *zelo/zelus* have been activated. Thus readers are primed to see in the Hannah narrative in chapter 50 an alternative portrait of zealous action. Pseudo-Philo's presentation of Hannah's prayer challenges the implication in biblical passages such as Numbers 25 that public prayer accompanied by violent zeal is what prompts God's favorable response.

Saul and David (LAB 56-65)

Given that *LAB* (in)famously concludes without narrating David's full accession to power, we might expect a straightforward continuation of this deconstruction of violence in Pseudo-Philo's treatment of Saul, who "sought to smite [the Gibeonites] in his zeal [קנאה] for the people of Israel and Judah" (2 Sam 21:2). What we find, however, is something more ambiguous.

The figure of Saul is a more obvious foil for David in *LAB* than is even Penninah to Hannah or Jephthah to Seila. Pseudo-Philo leaves out portions of the biblical Saul's story that might lead to a sympathetic view of Saul, and Saul is viewed as

---

[21] This is further confirmed when we consider the extent to which Pseudo-Philo has cast Seila as the new/more complete Isaac. Pseudo-Philo does not relate the story of Isaac in its chronological order, but rather refers to it in three different places: at 18.5, in the midst of a divine speech to Balaam; at 32.2-4, at the beginning of Deborah's song; and at 40.2, as part of Seila's address to her father. In all three references, Pseudo-Philo emphasizes that Isaac was willing to die. Tellingly, even in the brief flashbacks to the Isaac story, Pseudo-Philo frames Isaac as one who engages in a vicarious act in contrast to the "zeal" or jealousy of *angels* in 32.1-2. The "jealous angels" motif is less familiar to us, but first-century Jewish readers would not miss the linguistic connection between such figures and the later representation of leaders and foils who embody violent zeal and jealous provocation. See the variations on the "jealous angels" tradition in *Jub.* 17.16; 18.12; *Gen. Rab.* 55.4; 56.4; *b. Sanh.* 89b; and Job 1:6-12.

bloodthirsty and violent. For example, in 1 Sam. 22:18, Doeg does the killing, but in *LAB* 63.2 it is Saul who kills Abimelech. In addition, in 63.3-4, there is a parallel to the "silence" of the people at the death of the Levite's concubine (chapter 45) in 47.4-8. God criticizes them for being upset at Saul's plans to kill Jonathan but remaining "silent" when 385 priests perish. There are also repeated references to Saul's *jealousy*, to which we will return in a moment (62.1, 11; 64.8).[22] All of this would seem to provide a rather straightforward indictment of Saul as a violent, bad leader, paving the way for David as the paragon of prayer and good leadership.

But this is not exactly what we find. Once again, at first glance the narrative seems to indicate that God's deliverance is secured because of David's deeds of violence. Immediately after being anointed by Samuel, David kills a lion and a bear that attack his flock, prefiguring his killing of Israel's enemies later:

> And while David was still speaking, behold, a fierce lion from the forest and a bear from the mountain seized the oxen of David. And David said, "Behold this will be a sign for me as a most striking beginning of my victory in battle, and I am going out after them and will rescue what has been snatched away and kill them." And David went out after them and took stones from the forest and killed them. And God said to him, "Behold with stones I have delivered up these beasts for you. Moreover this will be a sign for you, because with stones you will kill the enemy of my people later on [*lapidibus interficies post tempus inimicum populi mei*]."
>
> (*LAB* 59.5)

Even more troubling, unlike in 1 Samuel 17, in *LAB* 61.1, we are told that David has already killed 15,000 Midianites in battle even before facing Goliath. Even the Goliath episode itself in *LAB* seems to revel in the violent details (e.g., "And then David cut off his head; 61.8). Worst of all, David indicates that this killing is done at the bidding of God: "And when I killed Goliath *according to the word of the Most Powerful ...* " (62.4).

Given the clever and powerful subversion of patterns of violence we have considered in the Seila and Hannah episodes, what prevents Pseudo-Philo from reworking the story of David to leave out the slaying of Goliath or the other examples of David's violent triumphs? Perhaps the missed opportunity stems from Pseudo-Philo's efforts to portray David in the pattern of the invented ideal leader Cenaz (*LAB* 25-28).[23] Or perhaps Pseudo-Philo chooses to leave only subtle hints in the direction of nonviolence. For instance, there are a number of changes to the Goliath episode that distance David from the violent deed itself, not least by revealing that Goliath realizes his death is not due to David alone but to God's angel:

---

[22] David's anointing and song also mentions Cain's jealousy (*zelus* in 59.4) and murder of Abel.

[23] See, e.g., *LAB* 27.8-14, where Cenaz slaughters the Amorites and is lauded by the people.

And David said to him, "Before you die, open your eyes and see your slayer, who has killed you." And the Philistine looked and saw an angel and said, "Not you alone have killed me, but also the one who is present with you, he whose appearance is not like the appearance of a man."

(*LAB* 61.8)

The next sentence unfortunately (!) reads, "And then David cut off his head." Still, Saul does not even recognize David afterward because of David's association with the angel:

The angel of the Lord had changed David's appearance, and no one recognized him. When Saul saw David, he asked him who he was, and there was no one who recognized him.

(*LAB* 61.9)

So perhaps David's violence is not endorsed as the violent zeal that brings about God's favor, but it is understandable if we continue to be troubled by the overall portrayal of David's violence.

If we read more carefully, however, there is another angle from which we may catch a glimpse of the Pseudo-Philo of the Seila and Hannah episodes. The key is to recognize just who the enemy is from whom the Israelites need deliverance by God. Interestingly, it is not the Philistines in the Goliath episode, or any of the other typical enemies. In the case of David, the enemy that the Israelites need to be delivered from is actually *Saul*. This is made quite explicit in *LAB* 56.3: "I will send them a king who will destroy [the people], and he himself will be destroyed afterward."[24]

This provides a perfect opportunity for David to carry out the triumphant act of zealous violence. But David does not do so. Our first linguistic cue comes in *LAB* 58, where God instructs Samuel to remind Saul of the words Moses spoke about Amalek. Although it is masked in English translations, God refers to Moses as speaking "with my zeal":

"You [Saul] have been sent to destroy Amalek in order that the words that Moses my servant spoke may be fulfilled: 'I will destroy the name of Amalek from the earth,' which he spoke with my zeal [*sub zelo meo*]."

(*LAB* 58.1)

The narrative had already provided a strong link between Moses and Phinehas,[25] and here again Pseudo-Philo uses the term *zelus* to create a frame by which the

---

[24] See also *LAB* 63.3: "When 385 priests are killed, they are silent … And so behold … I will deliver them into the hands of their enemies, and they will fall wounded with their king."

[25] Cf. *LAB* 12.4-10 and 47.1-3; see further Lappenga, "Speak," 101–3.

actions of key figures are to be evaluated. In *LAB* 60.3, we are told that David *sustains*, rather than kills, Saul: "as long as David sang, the spirit spared Saul." Likewise, David's conversations with Jonathan center on Saul's "jealousy" (*zelus*) and David's work to protect Saul:

> And it would have been better, brother, if I had been slain in battle than that I should fall into the hands of your father. For in the battle my eyes were looking everywhere that I might protect him from his enemies.
>
> (*LAB* 62.8)

> Do not remember the hatred with which my father hates you in vain but my love with which I have loved you …. Do not remember the jealousy with which [Saul] was jealous of you so evilly [*zelum quo te zelavit male*] but the truth.
>
> (*LAB* 62.11)

Finally, in 64.2, the important element of *prayer*, rather than zeal, resurfaces in the description of Samuel's death: "Behold Samuel the prophet is dead, and who *prays* for Israel? And David, who fought on their behalf, is Saul's enemy" (*LAB* 64.2).

All of this sets up the very last line of the *Biblical Antiquities*, which I take to be the book's original ending.[26] After recounting Saul's despair at being routed by the Philistines, the narrative ends on a note of reconciliation:

> Saul said to his armor-bearer, "Take your sword and kill me before the Philistines come and abuse me." The armor-bearer was not willing to lay his hands on him. So he fell upon his own sword, but was not able to die. He looked behind him, saw a man running, and he called to him and said, "Take my spear and kill me; my soul is still in me." He came to kill him and Saul said to him, "Before you kill me, tell me who you are." He said to him, "I am Edabus, son of Agag, king of the Amalekites." And Saul said, "Behold now the words of Samuel have come to pass upon me, for he said, 'He who will be born of Agag will be a stumbling block for you.' Now go and tell David, 'I have killed your enemy.' And say to him, 'So says Saul: do not remember my hatred and my injustice.'"
>
> (*LAB* 65.2-5)

Here, I would suggest, we see that *God* has provided the deliverance, not through or in response to some violent action on the part of David. Quite the contrary: David

---

[26] See further Louis Feldman, in M. R. James, *Antiquities* (New York: KTAV, 1971 reprint), lxxvii; Perrot, *Pseudo Philon*, 2.21-22; and Murphy, *Rewriting*, 16–17.

has resisted harming Saul all along, and the narrative concludes by leaving justice and deliverance in God's hands. In light of the pattern we have considered in the wider narrative, this ending may be read as an invitation to take up a nonviolent approach to living.

Conclusion

The ending of *LAB* has been compared to the ending of the Gospel of Mark, where Mark's suspended ending leaves the reader uneasy and dissatisfied, with the result that readers are invited to complete the book and participate in forms of living that are imagined in the narrative.[27] Our readings show that Pseudo-Philo's retellings are indeed crafted to forego facile propositions in favor of invitations to close and careful readings that open the reader to new patterns of living. Jephthah seems to be a successful leader, but his characterization as a man of violent zeal shifts the spotlight toward Seila's sacrificial act. Hannah's silent prayer subjects her to public ridicule, but Peninnah's jealous taunting frames Hannah as a paragon of true zeal. Phinehas' violence appears to emulate God's zeal; yet, Pseudo-Philo's careful language deconstructs the notion of violent zeal by showing the efficacy of prayer. And finally, Saul's zealous "hatred and injustice" (*LAB* 65.5), and even David's own violent deeds in battle, are rejected in favor of a life characterized by protection, forgiveness, and sustenance.

Nevertheless, we may be inclined to think that a truly proper course for combatting the violence inherent in the text is to stop telling the stories of Jephthah, Phinehas, or even David altogether.[28] Yet as so often in the biblical narratives themselves, as well as in narrative and art in general, readers are *shaped* during the experience of reading. If we are willing to be formed by our encounter with the text, Pseudo-Philo's subversion of violent zeal is a welcome resource in our efforts to grapple with violent elements in religious texts and in modern life.

---

[27] See, e.g., Murphy, *Rewriting*, 17–18 and Morna Hooker's discussion of the way "[w]e long to complete the book—and that, of course, is precisely what Mark wants us to do!" (*Endings: Invitations to Discipleship* [London: SCM Press, 2003], 23).

[28] As Trible points out, in the biblical account forgetting is not an option: "The unnamed virgin child becomes a tradition in Israel because the women with whom she chose to spend her last days have not let her pass into oblivion" (*Texts of Terror*, 106–7).

Chapter 6

"CLEAR EYES, FULL HEARTS, CAN'T LOSE": THE RHETORIC OF VIOLENCE IN THE *ANIMAL APOCALYPSE*

John Garza

The *Animal Apocalypse* (*1 En.* 85-90) is a complex and multi-layered text that recasts Israel's history using animals as stand-ins for the different characters of that history.[1] One of the most prevalent and important motifs within this narrative menagerie is opened and closed eyes, where blindness is equated with spiritual darkness and absence of proper relationship with God, and sight is equated with rectitude and a righteous relationship with God.[2] The very context and framing of

---

[1] All references and quotations to the *An. Apoc.* are from George W. E. Nickelsburg and James C. VanderKam, *1 Enoch: The Hermeneia Translation* (Minneapolis: Fortress Press, 2012).

[2] Though a variety of proposals have been made, a consensus concerning the meaning of the sight and blindness motif in the *An. Apoc.* has not been established. Some scholars attempt to explain the motif by locating its first occurrence in the *An. Apoc* and then determining the closest biblical corollary. Patrick Tiller identifies *1 En.* 89:28 as the first occurrence of the motif and correlates it with Exod 15:25b-26 as the corresponding verse in the biblical text and suggests that seeing in the *An. Apoc* equals possessing God's law and obeying it. See Patrick A. Tiller, *A Commentary on the Animal Apocalypse of I Enoch* (Atlanta. Scholars Press, 1993), 292. George Nickelsburg also sees Exod. 15:25b-26 as the "revelatory event" to which the open and closed eyes motif refers. See George W. E. Nickelsburg, *1 Enoch 1: A Commentary on the Book of 1 Enoch, Chapters 1-36; 81-108* (Minneapolis: Fortress Press, 2001), 379. Daniel Olson suggests Exod 16:4-10 is the most appropriate "scriptural trigger" for the motif because it explains both the image and its meaning: Olson claims that the "seeing the glory of Yahweh" described in Exod. 16:7 makes sense as the trigger because the passages in the *An. Apoc.* that occur immediately before and after 89:28 refer to seeing the Lord of the sheep's face and appearance. Thus, having open eyes in the *An. Apoc.* means the ability to see the glory of God, and, for Olson, the force of locating the scriptural trigger here is that it removes any notions of obedience or disobedience from the metaphor as it now more appropriately symbolizes an experience of God rather than actions for or against God. See Daniel C. Olson, *A New Reading of*

the vision—a clear-eyed Enoch sees a dream in closed-eyed slumber and recounts it to a wide-eyed Methuselah—emphasizes the importance of proper seeing by positioning open eyes as spiritually ideal, as embodied by Enoch himself.[3] With Methuselah as their proxy, the audience is invited to see the truth of Enoch's vision, and, with "clear eyes" and "full hearts" illuminated and filled by the truth, is challenged to respond appropriately to the eschatological vision of the world set before them that ensures that they "can't lose" as they strive to make that vision a reality.[4] The type of response that the rhetoric of the *An. Apoc.* is attempting to invoke is a violent one, and those with the eyes to see the necessity of violence are supposed to understand both when and how to use it. In what follows, I suggest

---

the Animal Apocalypse of 1 Enoch: "All Nations Shall be Blessed," VTP 24 (Leiden: Brill, 2013), 66–75. James VanderKam emphasizes the broader sense of seeing as an experience of God and suggests a move away from determining a specific corollary in Exodus toward the tradition of Gen 32:24-32 where Jacob sees God "face-to-face" after wrestling through the night with the unknown figure who renames him "Israel." For VanderKam, "the image of sight/blindness to express Israel's relation to the deity also arose from a well-attested etymology of the name *Israel* as 'one who sees God,'" and thus, to have open eyes in relation to God is to be in right relationship to God, characterized by covenantal obedience, while to have closed eyes in relation to God is to be absent that relationship and to be disobedient. See James C. VanderKam, "Open and Closed Eyes in the Animal Apocalypse (1 Enoch 85-90)," in Hindy Najman and Judith Newman (eds.), *The Idea of Biblical Interpretation: Essays in Honor of James L. Kugel*, JSJSup 83 (Leiden: Brill, 2004), 279–92, here 287, 292.

[3] VanderKam notes, "Enoch introduces the vision report to his son Methuselah with the words 'after this I saw another dream' (85:1; cf. v. 3), and the author sprinkles other such notices throughout the text so that the reader is regularly reminded that the text is an account of a visual experience (e.g., 85:4, 5, 7, 9; 86:1, 2, 3, 4; 87:1, 2, 4; 88:1, 3; 89:2, 3, 4, 5, 6, 7, 16, 19, 21, 27, etc.)." VanderKam, "Open and Closed Eyes," 280–1. Portier-Young connects this even more directly in that the repetitive "use of sight language to characterize the lambs thus emphasizes not only their obedience to God's law, but also their status as heirs to the Enochic visionary tradition. This language also points to apprehension of those visions, including those contained in the Book of Dreams itself, as a precondition for right action in the hour of crisis." Anathea E. Portier-Young, *Apocalypse against Empire: Theologies of Resistance in Early Judaism* (Grand Rapids: Eerdmans, 2011), 367–8. The text's framing and the repetitive reminders of it being Enoch's vision ("I saw … ") work to implicate the audience itself into the text, with the clear moral imperative that they too ought to be like the sheep in 90:6 who, in having opened eyes, act out a proper relationship to God.

[4] Since the original setting for this chapter was the 2016 Society of Biblical Literature Annual Meeting in San Antonio, Texas, a title for this chapter that paid homage to a foundational element of Texas' (my own home-state) religious and cultural experience seemed appropriate. The phrase, "Clear eyes, full hearts, can't lose," comes from the 2006–11 TV series, *Friday Night Lights*, itself an adaptation of a film by the same name, with both being an adaptation of a book by H. G. Bissinger entitled, *Friday Night Lights: A Town, A Team, A Dream*. Coach Taylor, the team patriarch and visionary, regularly uses the phrase as a mantra and rallying cry for the team, particularly when it looks like all is lost.

that the open and closed eyes motif in the *An. Apoc.* does more than just sanction the use of violence by correlating open eyes with obedience and the successful overthrow of oppression. The text also deploys the open and closed eyes motif to critique an earlier epoch's dependence upon God's deliverance while lauding a later (and contemporaneous) epoch's use of violence. I take as my starting point the productive engagement concerning violence in the *An. Apoc.* between Anathea Portier-Young and Daniel Assefa. The subsequent exegesis that I offer will attempt to reconcile their differences by demonstrating that the source of their disagreement is in fact a feature of the text: the open and closed eyes motif is used to emphasize and validate the warrior-like Joshua tradition over and against the more prophetic and passive tradition that Moses and the Exodus represent, thereby making an argument against the quality and depth of that ideology's spiritual engagement with God, and critiquing the attending impotence of its myopia.

The Function of Violence in the Animal Apocalypse

In *Apocalypse against Empire*, Anathea Portier-Young explores the motif of sight and blindness using James VanderKam's understanding of the motif as demonstrating what constitutes right relationship with God. For Portier-Young, "sight symbolizes a knowledge of and attention to God's will that leads to obedience, knowledge of God's creation, and the ability to see things as they are and know what lies in store."[5] In a sense, Enoch's telling of the vision itself has the power to bring into reality the very sightedness that it is describing, with the result being that the "visual perception of God's holiness and glory in the Animal Apocalypse evokes confidence in the sovereign power and plan of God, even in the face of destructive and oppressive temporal powers."[6] The rhetorical effect of this is that the narrative of the *An. Apoc.* invites its audience to see the same vision as Enoch, and thus identify with the sheep in 90:6 who have begun to truly see and obey. As Portier-Young puts it, this rhetorical device "further emphasizes the importance of their knowledge and understanding of the Enochic revelations for the work that they perform in the end time, for their own salvation and that of their fellow Jews."[7] What remains to be seen—and what Portier-Young further illuminates—is the precise shape and nature of that obedience.

In conjunction with her exploration of sight and blindness in the *An. Apoc.*, Portier-Young offers an explicit rebuttal to Daniel Assefa's assertion that the text was, in its original version, nonviolent.[8] While noting Assefa's contention that the

---

[5] Portier-Young, *Apocalypse against Empire*, 366.
[6] Ibid., 366.
[7] Ibid., 367.
[8] See her discussion and point-by-point rebuttal in ibid., 349–52. For Assefa's work, see Daniel Assefa, *L'Apocalypse des animaux (1 Hen 85-90): une propogande militaire? Approches narrative, historico-critique, perspectives théologiques*, JSJSup 120 (Leiden: Brill, 2007), esp. 190–236.

An. Apoc. opposes blindness and not political power, she subsequently contends that this very opposition against blindness and focus on inculcating sight, over and against the pacifying blindness desired by the empire, is "an act of resistance, and is not inconsistent with other forms of opposition to the empire, be they nonviolent or violent."[9] Because obedience, construed as sight in the *An. Apoc.*, occurs within an imperialistic and oppressive context that requires blindness in order to maintain control, the very act of "seeing" is subversive and anti-imperialistic. Whereas here she seems to suggest that seeing itself is the anti-imperial act, in her subsequent exegesis of the text she concludes that "seeing" also leads to a certain type of action "not inconsistent with other forms of opposition to the empire, be they nonviolent or violent."[10] The rhetorical force of the *An. Apoc.* is thus clear: the success of the sheep in the text is meant to model for the audience the appropriate form of militant resistance against oppression.

As Portier-Young traces the motif of sight and blindness in the *An. Apoc.*, she emphasizes the shift in the text that conjoins clear-eyed vision with correct action—in other words, obedient resistance that uses violence both to maintain and to instantiate open eyes. The sheep first begin to "open their eyes" in *1 En.* 89:28, after the narration of the Exodus event. This marks the beginning of movement between blindness and vision, mirroring the biblical account in Exodus. Sheep blindness occurs first in the episode of the golden calf, and that blindness continues through the period of the Judges (89:39-45), the Davidic and Solomonic reigns (89:46-50), the apostasy of the two kingdoms (89:51-58), and the commissioning and rule of the seventy shepherds (89:59–90:6). At this point in the text, Portier-Young notes that the description of the lambs who open their eyes and begin to see in 90:6 echoes the description of Enoch that introduces the Enochic corpus in *1 En.* 1:2.[11] This identifies the lambs as the rightful recipients of Enoch's vision and also valorizes their actions as appropriate for the context. Portier-Young notes that these lambs who see are supposed to serve a prophetic function (90:7), albeit one that ultimately fails.[12] As a result of the failure of this prophetic function, the lambs must grow horns, or take up arms, as a means of overthrowing their oppressors. Within this context, a sheep (whom she identifies as Judas Maccabeus) sprouts a great horn, is persecuted, cries out for help, and receives help from God.

---

[9] Portier-Young, *Apocalypse against Empire*, 350.

[10] Ibid.

[11] Ibid., 356.

[12] Concerning the prophetic function of these lambs, Portier-Young suggest, "Like the prophets who followed Elijah, and like Moses who preceded them, they testify to the will of God and exhort the people to return to covenant obedience. Moses also models the merging of prophetic and militant roles to achieve religious reform." Ibid., 371. Her use of "militant" here deserves some nuance: Moses's militancy is only inwardly focused for religious reform, and thus, though he is militant, it is important to note that he is not militant in the same way that Joshua is in exercising violence outwardly; he does not use it to start a revolution but to quell idolatry and apostasy.

Significant here is the giving of a large sword to the sheep, who then go "out against all the wild beasts to kill them, and all the beasts and the birds of heaven fled before them" (90:19). For Portier-Young, "the theophanies that follow Judas's cry draw on divine warrior traditions that exhibit a synergistic understanding of warfare, in which neither God nor God's people fight alone, but both enter the fray together."[13] She concludes that this synergistic understanding is an intentional echo of Joshua's role as a military leader and that, "by highlighting similarities between the battles led by Judas and Joshua, the writer underscores the necessity of covenant fidelity in the Judean struggle against the program of Antiochus."[14] Thus, to have one's eyes opened, to be faithful to the covenant, also entails violent action against those powers that would seek to perpetuate blindness.

The post-Noachic and Exodus portions of the *An. Apoc.*, wherein God, as the "Lord of the sheep," acts on behalf of the sheep, seem to support Assefa's assertion that the text was originally nonviolent, or at the very least, that violence is not a legitimate resource for combatting blindness.[15] Portier-Young's reading of the *An. Apoc.*, however, and her conclusion that, in the end, the text sanctions militancy as a means of resistance against oppression are also convincing.[16] As opposite extremes, it seems that both readings cannot stand together. I contend, however, that this productive disagreement between Portier-Young and Assefa reveals more than just a tension in the scholarship on the *An. Apoc.*; it also reveals a tension within the text itself. Whereas the initial narration of the text focuses on God's overriding power to deliver the Israelites from their oppression and blindness, the narrative ultimately envisions a cooperative model whereby those with opened eyes see and perceive the necessity of joining with Yahweh in their own deliverance through the use of violence against their oppressors. The text adeptly uses the motif of open and closed eyes to symbolize degrees of obedience throughout Israel's history while simultaneously critiquing earlier traditions that emphasized the role of Yahweh as the warrior/deliverer. In doing so, the *An. Apoc.* encourages the contemporary audience, as sheep with open eyes who see the necessity of participating in their own deliverance from outside oppressors, to use violent

---

[13] Ibid., 377.

[14] Ibid., 379

[15] In the text's review of the Primeval History, Enoch watches as a sword is given to the elephants and camels and asses (the Watchers) who then begin to strike one another (88:1-3). While this is certainly an event of violence in the text, and it is tempting to relate the giving of a sword here to the giving of a sword in 90:19, there are four reasons I think it does not apply to divinely sanctioned violence or to the open and closed eyes motif: (1) it happens well before the open and closed eyes motif begins in 89:28; (2) it is not God who gives them the sword but an angel; (3) God, in fact, does not even appear as a character within the narration until 89:15, when the sheep being oppressed by the wolves begin to make complaint to their Lord; and (4) there is no covenant here and thus nothing to which sight and blindness, or proper action, can be correlated.

[16] Ibid., 352.

resistance against the empire, together with Yahweh, as a means of ushering in the eschatological age when all eyes will be opened (90:35). A brief exegesis of the salient texts will help illuminate this trajectory as it occurs in the text.

Exegesis: "Clear Eyes, Full Hearts ..."

Beginning with its retelling of the story of the Exodus, the text highlights the role of the Lord of the Sheep in delivering the sheep from the wolves. The only action the sheep take upon themselves is "groaning and crying out and petitioning their Lord with all their might" (89:15). This lament prompts the Lord of the sheep to begin the exodus from Egypt via the "diplomatic" intervention of Moses and Aaron. The Lord of the sheep sees and hears the sheep, descends down to them, and commissions Moses and Aaron to petition the wolves. The text, however, then explicitly references the sole agency of the Lord of the sheep in the plagues: "Their Lord came to the sheep and began to strike the wolves, and the wolves began to lament" (89:20). Enoch then watches as the sheep go out from among the wolves, who then, with blinded eyes, go after the sheep with all their might (89:21). The text then notes, "And the Lord of the sheep went with them, leading them, and all his sheep followed him. And his face was dazzling and glorious and fearful to look at" (89:22). This note about the Lord of the sheep's face being dazzling, glorious, and fearful to behold is interesting in that it is unclear who exactly is seeing the Lord's face. Are the sheep who are being led out from among the wolves able to see it? A better option might be that it is a narrative aside spoken by Enoch as part of his telling of the vision. As such, it further reinforces the framing of the vision as well as the invitation to the audience to be like Enoch who can behold such glory with clear and open eyes. The Lord of the sheep then leads them through the "swamp of water" and, in doing so, "stood between them and the wolves" who pursued them (89:24). The ending of the story is well known: the Lord of the sheep delivers the sheep as the wolves drown. Other than crying out in lament, the sheep as a whole do nothing, and the role of Moses and Aaron is strictly diplomatic; God is here the primary agent of their deliverance.

After leaving Egypt and heading into the wilderness, the sheep "began to open their eyes and see" (89:28), ultimately seeing the Lord of the sheep and becoming afraid (89:30-31). Echoing his aside in 89:22, Enoch also says that he "saw the Lord of the sheep who stood before them, and his appearance was majestic and fearful and mighty," but then also includes the sheep, that "saw him and were afraid before him" (89:30). Here, the clear-eyed vision of Enoch is equated with the clear-eyed vision of the sheep, demonstrating their similar standing before the Lord of the sheep. This Sinai experience is an initial high point of Israel's right relationship with the Lord of the sheep and, as the first occurrence of the open eyes motif, illustrates well the correlation between open eyes and covenantal faithfulness. The mountaintop experience, however, soon descends into the valley: as the sheep wait at Sinai, they become blinded—in other words, idolatrous—which enrages the Lord of the sheep who then sends Moses back down to deal with their apostasy by slaughtering those sheep who had become idolatrous.

As the text narrates the death of Moses and entry into the Promised land through Joshua's leadership, it describes the state of affairs quite interestingly: "And I saw the sheep until they were entering a good place and a pleasant and glorious land. And I saw those sheep until they were satisfied, and that house was in their midst in the pleasant land" (89:40). This passage both echoes the sheep's experience of the Lord at Sinai while also foreshadowing the right relationship and satiation found in the eschatological age of 90:35-36. The description of the sheep's experience here is perhaps even more important—and paradigmatic—than the description of their experience at Sinai in that it describes the presence of the Lord of the sheep's house in combination with the sheep being in the land and in right relationship with Lord of the sheep.[17] The sheep quickly begin a cycle of vacillating between open eyes and blinded eyes within the period of the Judges (89:41-45), the Davidic and Solomonic reigns (89:46-50), and the apostasy of the two kingdoms (89:51-58). During this time period, various rams arise to protect the sheep from the foxes, wild boars, dogs, and beasts that try to devour the sheep. The text here clearly sanctions the use of violence as a means of protection, but this violence does not occur within a context of outright imperial oppression, nor does it occur with the assistance of or in conjunction with God's actions as a divine warrior fighting on behalf of Israel. The various rams act to protect the sheep from outside nations as the overseers of the sheep.

The sheep continue on in their blindness, leading the Lord of the sheep to abandon them "into the hands of all the beasts as fodder" (89:58). Noteworthy here is Enoch's response as he sees this happening: "And I began to cry out with all my might and to call to the Lord of the sheep and to show him concerning the sheep" (89:57). Enoch echoes the lament of 89:15, with the expectation that, just as in the days of the Exodus, the Lord of the sheep will deliver the sheep from oppression. Enoch's intercession, however, falls on deaf ears, as the Lord of the

---

[17] As Tiller notes of this passage, "the crossing of the Jordan River is mentioned almost in passing and the entrance and occupation of Canaan is treated as if there were no difficulties involved ... This is all in sharp contrast to the detailed treatment of Genesis and Exodus. Apparently, the author is not very interested in Leviticus through Judges." Tiller, *A Commentary*, 299. The narrative certainly does move through this section of Israel's history rather quickly, and one would perhaps expect to see Joshua play a much more prominent role here if, as I am suggesting, the text is emphasizing a Joshua motif over and against an Exodus motif. I think, however, that the text, in emphasizing Israel's spiritual state of affairs here, foreshadows the Eschatological age, allowing the reader (or hearer) to connect the dots between the two as the narrative progresses. Likewise, if it were accepted that, to a certain degree, the community receiving this vision *already* shares a belief in the efficacy of the Joshua motif over and against the Exodus motif, an overly elaborate emphasis on Joshua here would have been unnecessary. Finally, to describe this portion of Israel's history in such a way serves an ideological function for the audience: just as Joshua's campaign into the Promised Land proved overwhelmingly effective in abolishing the idolatry and apostasy of Israel's enemies, such that it barely warrants mention, so too will the fight against our own idolatrous oppression.

sheep "was silent, though he saw (it)" (89:58).[18] In addition to signaling the Lord of the sheep's anger at the Israelites, the text also hints at the necessity of more than just lament for deliverance.[19] Whereas God was before intimately involved in the affairs of the sheep and actively intervening on their behalf, God has now abandoned them on account of their idolatry and blindness; God's silence here functions as an imperative. The blindness of the sheep continues throughout the period of the seventy shepherds and the return from Babylon (89:74). Even after the return, the text notes that "the eyes of the sheep were blind, and they did not see, and their shepherds likewise … And the Lord of the sheep remained silent until all the sheep were scattered over the field and were mixed with them, and they did not save them from the hand of the beasts" (89:74-75).

In the midst of ongoing persecution, the text then recounts that these scattered and dispersed sheep who are being attacked by all the birds of heaven "cried out because their flesh was being devoured" (90:3). Echoing his earlier laments in 89:57 and 68, Enoch laments again, though to no avail.[20] Then, moving into the first layer of tradition found in 90:6, "lambs were born of those white sheep, and they began to open their eyes and to see and to cry out to the sheep."[21] But the

---

[18] Enoch laments again in 89:69: "And more than was prescribed for them each of them was killing and destroying, and I began to weep and lament because of those sheep." Olson reads God's silence to mean "that laments and petitions directed toward heaven are effective in moving God's hand unless he has set a timetable in place that does not allow it, in which case not even a figure as exalted as Enoch can persuade him to intervene." Olson, *A New Reading*, 171. While this reading is consistent with Olson's overall project and reading of the motifs in the *An. Apoc.*, it seems less consistent with the narrative of the text. As I am arguing, the shape of the narrative and how it figures lament beginning in the Exodus and continuing through the Eschatological age suggest that, though lament was sufficient in a former time, the Lord of the sheep now requires more than just lament in order to act.

[19] Nickelsburg notes that the shift to the Enochic perspective in this section demonstrates that "God has adopted a new modus operandi by distancing himself from the flock." Nickelsburg, *A Commentary*, 390.

[20] Nickelsburg notes that "different from 89:57 [and 68], where he cries out with all his might and formally functions as an intercessor, here he can only lament over the shepherds' malfeasance of office. As the continuation of the narrative indicates, the lament is ineffectual." Ibid., 395–6.

[21] As Portier-Young notes, the wording here is identical, with only a slight variation in word order, to the wording in 89:28, the first instance of the open eyes motif in the Animal Apocalypse. Portier-Young, *Apocalypse against Empire*, 365. Concerning the two different layers of tradition, Nickelsburg notes, "Specifically, vv 6–9a begin with reference to the many lambs and their horns. Then in vv 9b.10 we hear of one sheep and his horn. Verse 11 returns to the many, who are devoured by the birds, and to the cry of the rams. Without transition or indication of antecedent, v 12 takes up the earlier reference to the one sheep and 'its' horn and continues that series of events through v 16." Nickelsburg, *A Commentary*, 396. He also includes a helpful table with the two sections in parallel on p. 397.

sheep pay no attention to the lambs because "they were extremely deaf, and their eyes were extremely and excessively blinded" (90:7). Subsequently, in 90:9a, Enoch watches as "horns came out on those lambs" while they continue to be persecuted. This passage, where the lambs with open eyes cry out, echoes the previous account of the Exodus, creating an expectation of deliverance: perhaps now the Lord of the sheep will finally make a grand entrance. This time, though, unlike in the previous account of the Exodus, God seemingly does not hear the lambs in their persecution. At the same time they are crying out to God, the lambs are also lodging a critique against the sheep who were crying out—the ones imitating the previous understanding of God's deliverance—and in doing so make room for a new, more cooperative understanding of how that deliverance occurs. In other words, the older generation of sheep—whose eyes are closed—assume that crying out and lamenting to God will help. The new generation of lambs—who, now having grown horns, "began to open their eyes and to see"—cry out to the older generation for help, yet nothing occurs. Then, in 90:11, the sheep become silent, while the rams, whose horns represent the taking up of arms, lament and cry out with open eyes.

It is here, once open eyes, the willingness to take up arms, and lament are combined, that the Lord of the sheep reappears: "And I saw until the Lord of the sheep came to them and took in his hand the staff of his wrath and struck the earth, and the earth was split, and all the beasts and all the birds of heaven fell (away) from among those sheep and sank in the earth and it covered them" (90:18). Finally, the text recounts that "a large sword was given to those sheep, and the sheep went out against all the wild beasts to kill them, and all the beasts and the birds of heaven fled before them" (90:19). At this point, the text has moved from emphasizing deliverance provided by God to emphasizing that deliverance occurs through militant resistance together with God's power and sanction.

The critique is even more apparent in the second level of tradition found in 90:9b-10, 12-16.[22] In this section, Enoch watches as a great horn sprouts on one of the sheep—Judas Maccabeus—who then looks on the other sheep that then have their eyes opened (90:9b-10). The eagles and kites and vultures then attempt to smash the horn of that ram, making war against it. The ram then cries out that "its help might come" (90:13, 16). Again in this layer, "open eyes," militant activity, and lament are conjoined. The result becomes clear in 90:15: "And I saw until the Lord

---

[22] Nickelsburg helpfully sums up the events of the two traditions: "The elements occur in the same order. Each begins with a new event: lambs are born; a horn sprouts. The lambs open their eyes; the horn see that they are opened. The lambs cry, but the sheep do not listen. The horn cries, and the sheep run to it. The ravens devour and cast down the lambs' horns; the ravens struggle and attempt to destroy the horn. All the birds enter the conflict. The seer looks and sees the heavenly scribe involved in the same activity. He looks again and sees the Lord of the sheep acting in wrath and all the opponents disappearing in the earth or in darkness. There is a final sortie with a plurality of opponents." Ibid., 397.

of the sheep came upon them in wrath, and all that saw him fled and all fell into darkness before him."

The singular ram with the horn, Judas Maccabeus, does not follow the model of Moses; instead, Judas follows the militant role of Moses's successor, Joshua. As noted earlier, Portier-Young suggests the intervention of the Lord of the sheep follows a synergistic understanding of warfare where God and God's people fight together. In pointing to Josh. 10 as a parallel for *1 En.* 90:9-19, she demonstrates that the ram, Judas, more closely approximates Joshua than the sheep mentioned earlier in the narrative which represents Moses. The latter is a figure who assists God in bringing about the deliverance of the Israelites, but God is the primary agent and actor in that deliverance. The former assists God in effecting the deliverance of his people by taking up arms, together with God, both acting as agents with the ultimate goal of the Promised Land/Eschatological age in mind. As Portier-Young sums it up, the *An. Apoc.* "imagined that like Joshua, Judas would bring Judeans to covenant fidelity, that they might reject the religion now practiced by the people who lived in their midst, follow the law of Moses, and worship the Lord in the pleasant land."[23] What my exegesis has surfaced, in addition to what Portier-Young claims, is that, in combining obedience, lament, *and* a cooperative model of violent action, the *An. Apoc.* also critiques as ineffectual the early Mosaic tradition of deliverance.[24]

Conclusion: " ... Can't Lose"

This short exegesis of the *An. Apoc.* reveals a unique rhetorical trajectory within the text, especially given that the Exodus motif played such a primary role in the rhetoric and tradition of Israel. It is clear that the *An. Apoc.* intentionally chooses to emphasize a different motif, and indeed, one less reliant on the provision and deliverance of Yahweh.[25] Even more clearly, the text demonstrates that the deliverance referred to within the Exodus motif is ultimately not sufficient for

---

[23] Portier-Young, *Apocalypse against Empire*, 378–9.

[24] The combination of obedience, lament, and a cooperative model of violent action might also explain why the lament of Enoch, though he is the paradigmatic seer of this vision, is ineffectual: he is not a militant figure, and thus only combines obedience and lament.

[25] Nickelsburg, following Tiller, draws a correlation between God's descent in the Exodus account and God's descent in the final judgment of 90:18, noting that it "thus depict[s] the exodus as a prefiguration of the final judgment." Nickelsburg, *A Commentary*, 379. In fact, as I have shown, the circumstances that prompt God's descent in the Exodus fail to continue to do so throughout Israel's history, and the circumstances that finally prompt God's descent for the final judgment are markedly different from those described in the Exodus. Likewise, the valuation of these circumstances over and against the failure of the Exodus motif to perdure instantiates a critique of that motif.

maintaining clear-eyed vision: there is no eschatological age ushered after the exodus from Egypt, just a brief moment of clarity at Sinai, and then more blindness. Instead, the text valorizes the Joshua motif—one that necessitates violent action as a result of vision—as that which finally brings about the eschatological reality wherein the eyes of all are opened (90:35).[26] The emphasis and ultimate success of the Joshua motif over and against the exodus motif, in conjunction with the critique leveled at previous epochs of history via the open and closed eyes motif, suggest that to have open eyes—to be in right relationship with God—also means to engage in violent action together with God.

To sum up, in tracing the deployment of the blindness/sight motif in the *Animal Apocalypse*, I have demonstrated how it specifically uses the interplay between sight and blindness to create an expectation of deliverance that, though initially fulfilled in the Exodus portion of the retelling when the sheep groan and cry out, only gets fulfilled in the exilic portion of the story when the ram with the horn, representing Judas Maccabeus, cries out for help, which results in the giving of a large sword to the sheep. This emphasis on the Joshua-like character of Judas and his use of violence reflects a critique of a more passive Exodus ideology and challenges the then contemporary audience to associate with a specific epoch and specific characters so that they will prove themselves to be different from those sheep who so often failed to maintain clear-eyed obedience before them. Instead, they will be like those sheep that cried out with open eyes, became rams, and whose sight proved effective in overthrowing their oppression through violent, and divinely sanctioned means.

---

[26] Recalling the idyllic description of Israel's success under Joshua's leadership in 89:40, Portier-Young notes that 90:35 "prefigures the ideal age that would follow the final defeat of Israel's enemies … Yet the writer also portrays this ideal future in terms that far outstrip the glories of the past." Portier-Young, *Apocalypse against Empire*, 379.

Chapter 7

THE POWER OF POLEMICS: JEWISH SLANDER AGAINST SAMARITANS IN LATE SECOND TEMPLE PERIOD LITERATURE

Tim Wardle

Introduction

The ancient world, much like the modern one, had political borders that separated empires, countries, fiefdoms, and the like. In some locations, say the Great Wall of China or Hadrian's Wall in Britain, borders were well-marked and maintained. These walls clearly demarcated when and where a traveler was crossing a known and defined boundary and moving into new territory. But in other locations borders were ill-defined and/or shifted often. In these spaces, it was not always easy to know where one stood vis-à-vis the boundaries and at what point one had crossed from one territory to another. The subject of this chapter is about borders, but borders of a different kind. In the ancient world—again, much like the modern world—rhetorical borders separated one group of people from another. These rhetorical borders could be fixed, but more often than not they experienced a remarkable degree of fluidity, depending on, for example, time, location, and personal disposition. And these rhetorical boundaries had to be vigilantly maintained. Exactly who was responsible for the construction and maintenance of these borders likely also fluctuated, with the literary elites certainly playing important roles. This, at least, is the case with Jews and Samaritans in the late Second Temple period.[1]

By the second century BCE, the sometimes parallel, sometimes interweaving, history connecting Jews and Samaritans was in the process of

---

[1] I would like to thank Evan Talbert and Rebecca Lankford, two of my students, for reading a draft of this chapter. Their keen eye and astute comments sharpened several of my arguments.

unraveling.² On the one hand, both groups were Yahwist, lived in the geographical footprint of ancient Israel, held the books of Moses as authoritative, practiced circumcision, observed the Sabbath, and had a shared longevity of living as near neighbors.³ They both were, or claimed to be, descendants of the nation of Israel. On the other hand, Jews and Samaritans had also developed a history of mistrust, disagreement, and animosity. Military intervention is part of this narrative, as are rival temples, textual emendations, shifting alliances, and slanderous accusations. Moreover, both held legitimate and competing claims to be the true tradents of Israelite identity. In what follows, I will outline the contours of the complex relationship that existed between Jews and Samaritans in the late centuries BCE

---

² Recent years have seen a growing number of important studies investigating Samaritan origins and Samaritan-Jew relations. For example, see Jonathan Bourgel, "The Destruction of the Samaritan Temple by John Hyrcanus: A Reconsideration," *JBL* 135 (2016): 505–23; Edmond L. Gallagher, "Is the Samaritan Pentateuch a Sectarian Text?" *ZAW* 127 (2015): 96–107; Gary Knoppers, *Jews and Samaritans: The Origins and History of Their Early Relations* (New York: Oxford University Press, 2013); Stefan Schorch, "The Construction of Samari(t) an Identity from the Inside and from the Outside," in Rainer Albertz and Jakob Wöhrle (eds.), *Between Cooperation and Hostility: Multiple Identities in Ancient Judaism* (Gottingen: Vandenhoeck & Ruprecht, 2013), 135–49; Jan Dušek, *Aramaic and Hebrew Inscriptions from Mt. Gerizim and Samaria between Antiochus III and Antiochus IV Epiphanes*, CHANE 54 (Leiden: Brill, 2012); Reinhard Pummer, *The Samaritans in Flavius Josephus*, TSAJ 129 (Tübingen: Mohr Siebeck, 2009); Magnar Kartveit, *The Origins of the Samaritans*, VTSup 128 (Leiden: Brill, 2009); Yitzhak Magen, *Mount Gerizim Excavations Volume 2: A Temple City* (Jerusalem: Israel Antiquities Authority, 2008); A Schenker, "Le Seigneur choisira-t-il le lieu de son nom ou l'a-t-il choisi? L'apport de la Bible grecque ancienne à l'histoire du texte samaritain et massorétique," in Anssi Voitila and Jutta Jokiranta (eds.), *Scripture in Transition* (Leiden: Brill, 2008), 339–51; Yitzak Magen, Haggai Misgav, and Levana Tsfania, *Mount Gerizim Excavations Volume 1: The Aramaic, Hebrew, and Samaritan Inscriptions* (Jerusalem: Israel Antiquities Authority, 2004); Yitzhak Magen, "The Dating of the First Phase of the Samaritan Temple on Mount Gerizim in Light of the Archaeological Evidence," in Oded Lipschits, Gary N. Knoppers, and Rainer Albertz (eds.) *Judah and the Judeans in the Fourth Century BCE* (Winona Lake, IN: Eisenbrauns, 2007), 157–211; Bob Becking, "Do the Earliest Samaritan Inscriptions Already Indicate a Parting of the Ways?" in Oded Lipschits, Gary N. Knoppers, and Rainer Albertz (eds.), *Judah and the Judeans in the Fourth Century BCE* (Winona Lake, IN: Eisenbrauns, 2007), 213–22; Ingrid Hjelm, *The Samaritans and Early Judaism: A Literary Analysis*, JSOTSup 303 (Sheffield: Sheffield Academic Press, 2000); Seth Schwartz, "John Hyrcanus I's Destruction of the Gerizim Temple and Judaean-Samaritan Relations," *Jewish History* 7 (1993): 9–25.

³ See Knoppers, *Samaritans and Jews*, 2–3, 217–18; R. J. Coggins, *Samaritans and Jews: The Origins of Samaritanism Reconsidered* (Atlanta: John Knox, 1975), 8–9; Francis Schmidt, *How the Temple Thinks: Identity and Social Cohesion in Ancient Judaism*, trans. J. Edward Crowley (Sheffield: Sheffield Academic Press, 2001), 120.

and early centuries CE, discuss the creation of Jewish rhetoric used to "foreignize" the Samaritans, and explore the effect that this rhetoric had in the Hasmonean era and beyond.

Definitions

Any discussion of race and ethnicity, both in the ancient world and in our own, requires some methodological discussions and/or distinctions. In this case, I need to say something, at least at a cursory level, regarding (1) sources and (2) terminology.

First, our sources for this time period are uneven. All of the extant sources that speak of Jews and Samaritans between the years 400 BCE and 400 CE are Jewish, and most of these sources evidence varying degrees of hostility toward the Samaritans.[4] This means that during the Second Temple period and for a few centuries thereafter, we hear only one side of what was assuredly a heated and multidimensional debate over issues of identity.

Second, the terms "Jew" and "Samaritan" are fraught with difficulty. In the mid-to-late Second Temple period, the term "Jew" carried a combination of geographic, ethnic, and religious connotations.[5] While the Hebrew יהודי and Greek Ἰουδαίοις originally referred to a person who lived in the territory of Judah or who was a member of the tribe of Judah, at a certain point in time (exactly when is debated) the term came to be used in an ethnic and religious sense irrespective of geographical considerations. This fluidity makes precise use of the term difficult. The term "Samaritan" is similarly difficult to define.[6] As scholars have increasingly noted, the most appropriate term for the descendants of the region of Samaria who were affected by the fall of the northern kingdom of Israel is the term "Samarian," not "Samaritan."[7] However, the construction of a temple distinct from the one in Jerusalem but still dedicated to the worship of the God of Israel, and the accompanying Samarian allegiance to this temple on Mount Gerizim and its cult, added a distinct religious aspect to Samarian identity and seems to have paved the

---

[4] The earliest Samaritan sources date to the Byzantine period.

[5] Shaye J. D. Cohen, "*Ioudaios, Iudaeus*, Judaean, Jew," in *The Beginnings of Jewishness* (Berkeley: University of California Press, 1999), 69–106.

[6] Pummer, *The Samaritans in Flavius Josephus*, 4–7; Coggins, *Samaritans and Jews*, 8–9; cf. Rita Egger, "Josephus Flavius and the Samaritans," in Abraham Tal and Moshe Florentin (eds.), *Proceedings of the First International Conference of the Société d'études Samaritaines; Tel-Aviv, April 11–13, 1988* (Tel Aviv: Chaim Rosenberg School for Jewish Studies, 1991), 109–14.

[7] Most recently, see Knoppers, *Jews and Samaritans*, 14–17. Knoppers largely eschews the terminology of Jews and Samaritans, and instead employs the terms "Yahwistic Samarians" and "Yahwistic Judeans," in order to emphasize the long period of continuity between these two groups.

way for a new "Samaritan" identity. While a precise date for the transition from Samarian to Samaritan identity is unclear (and likely very uneven), what is clear is that various Jewish sources from the second century BCE onward begin to speak of "Samaritans" as a distinct entity. To add further complexity, later Samaritan sources eschew the terms "Samarian" and "Samaritan" altogether, preferring instead to call themselves the "keepers" or "guardians" (שמרים)—a terminological choice which suggests an understanding of themselves as the true possessors of the Mosaic law.[8]

This discussion of terminology alerts us to the fact that group identity, in our world as much as theirs, is constantly evolving, both in terms of what a community says about itself and what outsiders have to say about them. The ways in which one side (the Jews) constructed rhetorical boundaries in order to differentiate themselves from a second group (the Samaritans) are the subject of the remainder of this chapter. As I am principally concerned with events and literature stemming from the early second century BCE, I will, for the sake of convenience, most often employ the terms "Jews" and "Samaritans," for by the year 200 BCE these terms begin to have real meaning. I recognize, however, that this nomenclature is debatable and in some senses begs the question, as the very intent of the terminology was to create distance and differentiation between two groups that were remarkably similar.

History of Conflict

In order to better situate how and why the rhetorical boundaries came to be, we first must engage with the historical and political realities that gave meaning to the rhetoric.

The "parting of the ways" between Jews and Samaritans took place over the space of many centuries. Following the reign of Solomon in the late tenth century BCE, the united kingdom of David and Solomon gave way to two separate kingdoms. The Northern Kingdom, or the Kingdom of Israel, was composed of ten of the twelve Israelite tribes and had its capital in Samaria. The Southern Kingdom, or the Kingdom of Judah, had its capital in Jerusalem and was made up of the remaining two tribes. Though politically separate, these two kingdoms held much in common, such as a shared history, cultural and religious practices, genealogical lines, and the like. The Assyrian invasion, however, altered this situation.

2 Kings 17 narrates the fall of the Northern Kingdom of Israel to the Assyrians in 721 BCE. Its description of these events assumes that this defeat was total, and that the ten northern tribes ceased to exist as viable entities from this point forward. 2 Kgs 17:18 and 17:23 summarily conclude: "therefore the Lord was very

---

[8] Coggins, *Samaritans and Jews*, 8–12; V. J. Samkutty, *The Samaritan Mission in Acts*, LNTS 328 (London: T&T Clark, 2006), 59; Pummer, *The Samaritans in Flavius Josephus*, 4–7.

angry with Israel and removed them from his sight; none was left but the tribe of Judah alone," and "the Lord removed Israel out of his sight …. So Israel was exiled from their own land to Assyria until this day." In place of the former inhabitants of the Northern Kingdom, 2 Kgs 17 relates how peoples from Babylon, Cuthah, Avva, Hamath, and Sepharvaim were settled in the land formerly occupied by the Kingdom of Israel, and that these new inhabitants refused, at least initially, to worship YHWH, chose instead to worship their own gods (2 Kgs 17:25, 29-34), and eventually developed syncretistic forms of worship (2 Kgs 17:41). This account of "Samaritan origins" in 2 Kgs 17 proved to be a foundational narrative for many later Jews (especially for Josephus and the rabbis), with the result that the former inhabitants of the Northern Kingdom are portrayed in many Jewish documents as being at a considerable remove—ethnically, historically, and religiously—from the Jews of Judea and Galilee.

That the narrative in 2 Kgs 17 is tendentious is widely agreed: other sections of the Hebrew Bible report continuing interactions between the inhabitants of Samaria and Judea (e.g., Jer 41:4-8); archaeological surveys of the region of Samaria reveal that the Assyrian invasion did not disrupt the population anywhere near the degree suggested by 2 Kgs 17;[9] and a few Second Temple texts tacitly acknowledge a kinship between Jews and Samarians. For example, our earliest witness to a continuing close relationship between these two communities comes from the Elephantine correspondence (ca. 400 BCE). In these letters, the Jews at Elephantine wrote to Bigvai, the governor of Judah; to Johanan, the high priest in Jerusalem; and to Delaiah and Shelemiah, the sons of Sanballat, governor of Samaria.[10] The joint reply from Bigvai and Delaiah, the political leaders of Judah and Samaria, suggests close political ties between these two communities.[11] Further evidence for a continuing close relationship between Jews and Samaritans may be seen in 2 Maccabees 5:22-23, a Jewish text from the second century BCE which includes the Samaritans in its description of "our people/race" (τὸ γένος).[12]

---

[9] See Knoppers, *Jews and Samaritans*, 18–44; Timothy Wardle, *The Jerusalem Temple and Early Christian Identity*, WUNT 2.291 (Tübingen: Mohr Siebeck, 2010), 100–2.

[10] See papyri 30–34 in A. E. Cowley, *Aramaic Papyri of the Fifth Century BCE* (Oxford: Clarendon, 1923), 108–29.

[11] Alan D. Crown, "Another Look at Samaritan Origins," in *Essays in Honour of G. D. Sexdenier: New Samaritan Studies of the Société d'études Samaritaines III & IV* (Sydney: Mandelbaum, 1995), 149; James C. VanderKam, *From Joshua to Caiaphas: High Priests after the Exile* (Minneapolis: Fortress, 2004), 58.

[12] Jonathan Goldstein, *2 Maccabees: A New Translation with Introduction and Commentary*, AB 41A (Garden City: Doubleday, 1983), 261; cf. Schmidt, *How the Temple Thinks*, 129; József Zsengellér, "Maccabees and Temple Propaganda," in *The Books of the Maccabees: History, Theology, Ideology: Papers of the Second International Conference on the Deuterocanonical Books, Pápa, Hungary, 9–June 11, 2005* (Leiden: Brill, 2007), 186–7. Compare *4 Baruch* 8:1–12, which places the origins of the Samaritans in the exilic return from Babylon and highlights their relationship with Israel.

Although Josephus is generally hostile toward the Samaritans,[13] he also speaks on multiple occasions of considerable levels of rapport between Jews and Samaritans. One example will suffice. *Antiquities* 9.291 relates that when the Samaritans see the Jews prospering, they call themselves their kinsmen (συγγενεῖς), claiming a common origin due to their claimed descent from Joseph. Conversely, the Samaritans repudiated this claim to kinship (συγγενεῖς) during the persecutions of Antiochus Epiphanes, and even tried to hide the fact that they worshiped "the most High God" in their temple (*Ant.* 12.257). Thus Josephus acknowledges that the Samaritans recognized a common ancestry with the Jews, alternately claiming kinship and repudiating it.

Each of these examples points to a real, though sometimes strained, bond between Samaritans and Jews.

The Samaritan Temple on Mount Gerizim and the Rise of the Hasmoneans

During this same time period, however, a slowly widening rift developed between Jews and Samaritans. Ancient (Josephus, *Ant.* 11.302-347) and modern scholars alike agree that the construction of the Samaritan temple on Mount Gerizim in the early Second Temple period had a significant effect on both the rise of Samaritans as a distinct group vis-à-vis Jews and the deterioration in the relationship between these two peoples.[14] This temple on Mount Gerizim had much to commend it—a proper priesthood, an ancient and sacred site, and a parallel worship of the God of Israel. Yet it was also perceived as a distinct rival to the Jewish Temple to the God of Israel in Jerusalem. The religious competition surrounding these two Yahwistic temples brought into sharp relief the simmering tensions between those loyal to Gerizim and those loyal to Jerusalem. For the first few centuries of the existence of both temples (roughly the fifth through the third centuries BCE) the Samaritans were the more politically powerful of the two groups.[15] This power dynamic remained tilted in favor of the Samaritans through the early second century BCE, a time the Seleucids elevated Samaria at the expense of Judea and when the city and temple on Mount Gerizim reached its greatest extent.[16]

---

[13] For example, see Sean Freyne, "Behind the Names: Galileans, Samaritans, Ioudaioi," in *Galilee and Gospel* (Leiden: Brill, 2002), 121; cf. Louis H. Feldman, "Josephus' Attitude Toward the Samaritans: A Study in Ambivalence," in *Jewish Sects, Religious Movements, and Political Parties: Proceedings of the Third Annual Symposium of the Philip M. and Ethel Klutznick Chair in Jewish Civilization held on Sunday–Monday, October 14–15, 1990* (Omaha: Creighton University Press, 1992), 34–9.

[14] Magen, *Mount Gerizim Excavations vol. 2*, 167–80; Knoppers, *Jews and Samaritans*; Wardle, *Jerusalem Temple*, 110–14.

[15] See Knoppers, *Jews and Samaritans*, 169–73.

[16] Dušek, *Aramaic and Hebrew Inscriptions*, 70–3; Magen, *Mount Gerizim Excavations vol. 2*, 176; cf. *Ant.* 12.154-224. Antiochus III does not seem to have distinguished between Samaritans and Jews. The same rights given to the Jews in Jerusalem were also granted to the Samaritans and Mt. Gerizim.

The emergence of the Hasmoneans in the middle of the second century BCE altered this arrangement for Samaria and Judea.[17] In the decades following their emancipation of Jerusalem from Seleucid control, the Hasmoneans consolidated their rule and began to enlarge their territory at the expense of those living in Samaria, Idumea, Galilee, Gilead, Perea, and Moab.[18] During this time they also gained a number of concessions from the Seleucids. For example, in 152 BCE, Alexander Balas granted Jonathan, the Hasmonean ruler, the title of high priest (1 Macc 10:17-21; Josephus, *Ant.* 13.45), and several years later three Samarian tracts of land—Aphairema (Ephraim), Lydda (Lod), and Ramathaim—were also given to Jonathan (1 Macc 11:34-36; cf. 10:30, 38).[19] Along with these territories, tax exemptions were granted to all who would sacrifice in the Jerusalem temple, a privilege not given to those sacrificing at the Samaritan temple on Mount Gerizim (1 Macc 11:34).[20] In short, the Seleucids began to privilege the Hasmoneans over against the Samaritans, granting the emerging Jewish leadership important titles, territory, and tax exemptions for those who would bring their religious sacrifices to the Hasmonean capital in Jerusalem.

Taken together, by the mid-to-late second century BCE, the political tide had clearly turned in favor of the Hasmoneans, and two temples in such close proximity proved to be one too many. In 111-110 BCE, the Hasmonean John Hyrcanus marched northward and destroyed the Samaritan temple (*Ant.* 13.254-256, 275-279; *J.W.* 1.63).[21] Soon thereafter, he destroyed the city of Samaria and took control of the entire region of Samaria (*Ant.* 13.275-281; *J.W.* 1.64-65).[22]

The destruction of this temple served to harden the lines separating Jews and Samaritans; Josephus and the New Testament provide continuing evidence of a relatively high level of mistrust and suspicion between Jews and Samaritans in the first century CE (John 4:9, 20; *Ant.* 18.29-30; 20.118),[23] and rabbinical sources

---

[17] Knoppers, *Jews and Samaritans*, 170-5; Dušek, *Aramaic and Hebrew Inscriptions*, 73-4.

[18] Knoppers, *Jews and Samaritans*, 172; Menachem Mor, "The Samaritans in Transition from the Persian to the Greek Period," in L. L. Grabbe and O. Lipschits (eds.), *Judah between East and West: The Transition from Persian to Greek Rule (ca. 400–200 BCE)* LSTS 90 (London: T&T Clark, 2011), 191–8.

[19] Knoppers, *Jews and Samaritans*, 172; Seth Schwartz, "The 'Judaism' of Samaria and Galilee in Josephus's Version of the Letter of Demetrius I to Jonathan (*Antiquities* 13:48–57)," *HTR* 82 (1989): 377–91.

[20] Goldstein, *2 Maccabees*, 433.

[21] For a recent discussion of Hyrcanus' actions, see Bourgel, "The Destruction of the Samaritan Temple," 505–23.

[22] Knoppers, *Jews and Samaritans*, 173; Magen, *Mount Gerizim Excavations vol. 2*, 170–1.

[23] Discrepancies exist between the accounts in *Antiquities* (20.120-121, 125) and *Jewish War* (2.232-240) as to the exact details of this antagonism. Cf. Martin Goodman, *The Ruling Class of Judaea: The Origins of the Jewish Revolt against Rome A.D. 66–70* (Cambridge: Cambridge University Press, 1987), 49.

describe continuing animosity extending well into the Roman and Byzantine periods.²⁴ Long after the Samaritan temple was gone, allegiance to Gerizim or Jerusalem continued to divide Jews and Samaritans.

Rhetorical Borders and Authoritative Texts

Increasing antagonism between Jews and Samaritans may be seen in a number of texts dating to the second century BCE and onward. In part of their efforts to differentiate themselves from, and to gain a competitive advantage over, the other group, both Jews and Samaritans fought "biblically." To be sure, there was no "bible" as we know it today, but certain texts—especially the Torah—were increasingly seen by both Jews and Samaritans as having a certain level of authority, and both sides, subtly, but surely, emended these texts to suit their own theological and political agendas. Of particular import in this game of textual emendation was the "correct" location for the God of Israel's temple, and whether Jerusalem or Mount Gerizim was, in Deuteronomic language, the "place that the Lord would cause his name to dwell."²⁵

In a similar fashion, beginning in the early second century BCE, a number of Jewish texts begin to castigate the Samaritans and define them as outside the bounds of Israel's inheritance, labeling them as "Cutheans," "Sidonians," "Shechemites," and the "foolish people in Shechem." It is in these descriptions that we begin to see rhetorical "othering" or "foreignization" taking place.²⁶ To be sure, this "othering" was not done wholesale. Some Jewish texts, like the ones mentioned above, do acknowledge or assert similarities between Jews and Samaritans in the late centuries BCE and early centuries CE. Nevertheless, a sharp uptick in the "foreignization" of Samaritans begins to occur in the early second century BCE—a time when the Samaritans were the more politically ascendant of the two groups—and this marginalization was to intensify throughout this and ensuing centuries. While the terms "Cutheans," "Sidonians," Shechemites," and "the fools in Shechem" might appear a rather innocuous way of saying "you are not us," each of these terms has roots in the authoritative texts that Jews and Samaritans shared in common, and Jews used this biblical language to strongly differentiate themselves from

---

²⁴ See Schiffman, "The Samaritans in Tannaitic Halakhah," *JQR* 75 (1985): 323–50. Knoppers (*Jews and Samaritans*, 174–6) stresses, however, that even in the first century CE, cooperation between these two groups continued unabated, and that scholars have assumed too much when suggesting a strong separation between Jews (or Yahwistic Judeans) and Samaritans (or Yahwistic Samarians).

²⁵ For a recent discussion of these textual emendations, see Knoppers, *Jews and Samaritans*, 178–216; Dušek, *Aramaic and Hebrew Inscriptions*, 85–96.

²⁶ See Elizabeth Schüssler Fiorenza, *Rhetoric and Ethic: The Politics of Biblical Studies* (Minneapolis: Fortress, 1999), 180–7.

Samaritans.²⁷ In so doing, some Jews were able to validate Samaritan associations with "Cutheans," "Sidonians," Shechemites," and "the fools in Shechem" precisely because they were able to anchor these connections in the biblical text. To put the matter differently, these "biblical" terms were a form of ancient slander that disparaged the Samaritans and carried a punch that more "secular" terminology could not. After briefly surveying some of the terminology used primarily by Josephus in the first century CE to describe the Samaritans, we will work our way backward to the first and second centuries BCE to see how some of this polemical "othering" of the Samaritans began.

First, in describing the Samaritans as "Cutheans," Josephus relied on 2 Kings 17 for his understanding of Samaritan origins (*Ant.* 9.288-290; 10.184; 11.19-20, 88, 302; 13.256; cf. 12.257). In *Antiquities* 9.288-290, Josephus portrays the Samaritans as idolatrous non-Jews who originated in Cuthah, a Mesopotamian city, and who were brought to Samaria by the Assyrians. Similarly, when Josephus describes the destruction of the Samaritan temple, he states that Hyrcanus captured "Shechem and Gerizim and the Cuthaean nation, which lives near the temple built after the model of the sanctuary at Jerusalem" (*Ant.* 13.255-256). This equation of Samaritans with Cutheans appears in numerous Josephan passages, each serving to emphasize the foreignness of the people who revered Mount Gerizim (e.g., *Ant.* 10.184; 11.19-20, 88, 302). For him, the term "Cuthean" was primarily an ethnic and religious one, making the Samaritans descendants of uncircumcised immigrants who engage in syncretistic forms of worship.²⁸ The term "Cutheans" also seems to have been a preferred term for the Samaritan people in later rabbinic descriptions (e.g., *b. Hullin* 6a; *b. Yoma* 69a; the tractate *Kutim*).

A second term that Josephus uses to describe and denigrate those living in the region of Samaria is "Sidonians" (*Ant.* 11.340-345; 12.257-264). In *Antiquities* 11.344, Josephus discusses the rival bids extended by Jews and Samaritans in order to curry favor with Alexander the Great for their particular temples, and he remarks that the Samaritans "said that they were Hebrews but were called the Sidonians of Shechem." In this conversation, Alexander pushes them by asking if they are "Jews," to which they reply that they are not.²⁹ Alexander then concludes that he had given certain privileges to the Jews but not to them, and Josephus summarizes this event by negating any links between the Jews and these Sidonians. Exactly why Josephus here prefers the term "Sidonian" is unclear from the text. On the one hand, it may be that Josephus refers to a colony of Sidonians that was living

---

²⁷ For some discussion of how discourse serves to create political communities, see Sean O'Rourke and Mary Stuckey, "Civility, Democracy, and National Politics," *Rhetoric and Public Affairs* 17 (2014): 711–36. For a discussion of how rhetoric gains greater force when anchored in a textual tradition, see James Darsey, *The Prophetic Tradition and Radical Rhetoric in America* (New York: New York University Press, 1997), 5–6, 15–34.

²⁸ Samkutty, *Samaritan Mission*, 63–4.

²⁹ This, of course, makes perfect sense. If "Jews" are understood as "Judeans," then the Samaritans were definitely not Jews.

in Shechem just as at Marisa, and it was these particular people who were engaged in petitioning Alexander.[30] On the other hand, Josephus uses the terms Sidonians and Samaritans interchangeably, and there is little reason for the Sidonians to have revered the temple on Mount Gerizim if they were not, in fact, Samaritans. In either case, Josephus seems to use the term "Sidonians" in a pejorative manner, emphasizing the foreign and idolatrous nature of the Samaritans. Moreover, as with the term "Cuthean," Josephus seems again to be engaging in biblical polemic. In Isaiah 23:2-4, the prophet denounces Sidon as being bereft of inhabitants, with the result that the Sidonians are not even a people (cf. Sir. 50:25).[31] In using the terms Sidonian and Samaritan interchangeably, Josephus biblically equates the Samaritans with a nation that had no claim to being descendants of the nation of Israel and thus totally foreign to the Jews and the God of Israel.

While the above terms are found almost exclusively in Josephus and the later rabbis, a third and earlier term for the Samaritans is found in a broad range of second- and first-century BCE texts. The term "Shechemites," and the similar description of the Samaritans as the "foolish people in Shechem," may be the most pernicious designation for the Samaritans in these early centuries. More than just a condescending way of speaking (e.g., those "fools" who live in the city of Shechem), the term "Shechemites" was almost assuredly polemical in nature, for Shechem was the name of the man who, in Genesis 34, seduced and raped Dinah, one of the daughters of Jacob. As a result, this labeling of the Samaritans as Shechemites did more than affirm their foreignness; it also likely called to mind the outrage committed by the house of Shechem against the house of Jacob. In rhetorically linking the Samaritans to the Shechemites, the Samaritans became descendants of a man who had preyed upon Jacob's family in the past and made them into an enemy that needed to be dealt with.

That some Jews in the Second Temple period connected the Samaritans with the Shechemites is overwhelmingly likely, and the connections that were made are fairly diverse. One claim common to many texts dated from the second century BCE through the first century CE is that the Shechemites are either uncircumcised or Gentiles (Theod., *On the Jews* 7-8; *T. Levi* 5:3-4; 6:6-8; 7:3; *Jub.* 30:12-13; Jdt 5:16; 9:2; Josephus, *Ant.* 1.337-340; cf. 11.342-347; Philo, *Migration* 224; *Names* 193-195,

---

[30] Dušek, *Aramaic and Hebrew Inscriptions*, 101–4; Rita Egger, *Josephus Flavius und die Samaritaner: Eine Terminologische Untersuchung zur Identitätsklärung der Samaritaner* (Göttingen: Vandenhoeck & Ruprecht, 1986), 251–83; Reinhard Pummer, "Genesis 34 in Jewish Writings of the Hellenistic and Roman Periods," *HTR* 75 (1982): 184–5; M. Delcor, "Vom Sichem der hellenistischen Epoche zum Sychar des Neuen Testaments," *ZDPV* 78 (1962): 35–8.

[31] See Thomas Fischer and Udo Rütersworden, "Aufruf zur Volksklage in Kanaan (Jesaja 23)," *WO* 13 (1982): 45–8; Coggins, "The Samaritans in Josephus," in Louis H. Feldman and Gohei Hata (eds.), *Josephus, Judaism, and Christianity* (Detroit: Wayne State University Press, 1987), 266.

199-200; *LAB* 8.7).³² While it is true that the ancient inhabitants of Shechem were uncircumcised, this was not necessarily true of Samaritans living in the second century BCE. But none of these texts make any effort to distinguish between the ancient Shechemites and second/first century Samaritans, who, as part of larger "Israel," would have been much more closely related to Second Temple Jews than not. By labeling the Samaritans as uncircumcised or Gentiles, these texts name the Samaritans as foreigners who have no part in Israel's heritage.

Not only do these texts draw distinctions between Jews and Samaritans, but they also condone violent actions against them. In Genesis 34, Dinah's brothers act treacherously against Shechem and the other men of the city by slaughtering them as they recovered from their circumcisions suggested to them by Jacob's sons. While the biblical text is ambivalent on whether this violence was necessary, Jewish texts from the second century were not. Indeed, this violence against the Shechemites is either highlighted as a positive or specifically ordained by God (*T. Levi* 5:3-4, 6:8; *Jub.* 30:18; Jdt 5:16; 9:2; Theod, *On the Jews* 7-8). Beyond the standard charge of revenge against the Shechemites (*Ar. Lev. Doc.* 2:1; 12:6; *Jos. Asen.* 23:14-15; *LAB* 8.7), several other rationales for violence against the Samaritans are also given.

First, in some texts, violence against the Shechemites is condoned on account of not only their sexual misconduct, but also their xenophobia. *Testament of Levi* 6:9-10 and Theodotus (*On the Jews* 7) highlight the inhospitable nature of the inhabitants of Shechem, above and beyond Shechem's actions against Dinah (cf. Jdt 9:1-4). As such, the sins of the Shechemites are equated with the sins of the Sodomites and are seen as justification for their deaths.³³

Second, the guilt for the rape of Dinah rests not just on Shechem, the perpetrator, but on all of the men who lived in the city with him. For example, *Testament of Levi* 7:1-3 claims that "they"—all the male inhabitants of Shechem—had committed an outrage in Israel by defiling Dinah. This collective guilt is seen also in Jdt (9:1-4) and *Jubilees* (30:3, 12).

Third, Judith and the *Testament of Levi* number the Shechemites among the Canaanites, and thus not only as people who were inhospitable or collectively guilty, but also as foreigners who have no part in the land whatsoever (Judith 5:16 and *T. Levi* 7:1). In *Testament of Levi* 7:1 the Shechemites are nearly synonymous

---

³² For an argument in favor of connecting the Shechemites in these extra-biblical sources with the Samaritans, see John J. Collins, "The Epic of Theodotus and the Hellenism of the Hasmoneans," *HTR* 73 (1980): 91–104. For an argument against this identification, see Pummer, "Genesis 34 in Jewish Writings of the Hellenistic and Roman Periods," 177–88. Pummer's cautions are important, but Collins seems correct in noting that the consistent denial of Shechemite circumcision in many third- and second-century texts occurs precisely in this period of increasing tension between Jews and Samaritans.

³³ Howard Jacobson, "Theodotus, 'On the Jews,'" in Louis H. Feldman, James L. Kugel, and Lawrence H. Schiffman (eds.), *Outside the Bible: Ancient Jewish Writings Related to Scripture* (Philadelphia: Jewish Publication Society, 2013), 1.724.

with the Canaanites; and in Judith the Shechemites are listed among the nations who were to be driven out of the land of Canaan by the Israelites on God's command (e.g., Exod 3:8, 17; Deut 7:1; Ezra 9:2). Though none of the biblical lists name the Shechemites among these nations, Judith does—listing the Shechemites alongside the Canaanites, Perizzites, Jebusites, and Gergesites (Jdt 5:16). As such, the Samaritans are understood to be outsiders to the worship of the God of Israel and deserving of the fate that awaited the Canaanites when Joshua entered Canaan.

As mentioned above, this divinely sanctioned violence directed toward the Shechemites is almost always connected to Genesis 34 and the revenge taken on the Shechemites by Levi and Simeon. But as James Kugel and others have pointed out, another line of evidence connects the Samaritans to Gen. 34 and has much to do with a fourth polemical phrase used against the Samaritans—that they are the "foolish people in Shechem."

This description of the Samaritans as "fools" or the "foolish people in Shechem" is found in several second and first-century BCE texts, and likely originated, in part, from a particular reading of Deuteronomy 32:21. This verse reads:

I will make them (Israel) jealous with what is no people (לא עם), and provoke them with a foolish nation. (גוי נבל)

Two particular phrases here are of note. First, this "no people" or לא עם was read in Second Temple times as related to those living in Shechem and Samaria, for these inhabitants were commonly understood to have a mixed lineage due to their mingling with other races.[34] This identification is clearly seen in the early-second-century text of Ben Sira (Sir. 50:25-26 [ms B]), where Ben Sira states:

Two nations my soul detests, and the third is not even a people (איננו עם): Those who live in Seir, and the Philistines, and the foolish people that live in Shechem. (וגוי נבל הדר בשכם)

According to Ben Sira, the people who live in Shechem—the Samaritans—are not even a people (לא עם). Not only does Ben Sira use the language of Deut 32:21 in his description of the Samaritans as "not a people," but he also appropriates the Deut 32:21 language of גוי נבל (foolish nation) and applies this same term to those who live in Shechem. For Ben Sira, the modern inhabitants of Shechem are the "no people" and "foolish nation" of Deut 32.

---

[34] James L. Kugel, *Traditions of The Bible* (Cambridge: Harvard University Press, 1998), 423–35; Magnar Kartveit, "Who Are the Fools in 4QNarrative and Poetic Composition[a-c]," in Anders Klostergaard Petersen (ed.), *Northern Lights on the Dead Sea Scrolls* (Leiden: Brill, 2009), 132.

This identification of Shechem as a foolish nation or people is seen in other texts dated to the second century BCE as well.[35] For example, 4Q372 uses polemical language to denigrate the Samaritans.[36] In this scroll, Joseph (commonly understood as a reference to the Samaritans) has been sent into exile, and Joseph's high place is mentioned in negative terms. Lines 11–14 of 4Q372 state:

> [and fools were dwelling in the land (ונבלים ישבים)][37] and making for themselves a high place upon a high mountain [i.e., the Samaritan temple on Mount Gerizim] to provoke Israel to jealousy ….and they acted terribly with the words of their mouth to revile against the tent of Zion … [and all] words of deceit they spoke to provoke Levi and Judah and Benjamin with their words. In all this, Joseph [was delivered] into the hands of foreigners.

This reference to the "fools" who made for themselves "a high place upon a high mountain to provoke Israel to jealousy" seems a clear allusion to the Samaritans, especially in light of the similar language seen in Ben Sira. Another text, the *Testament of Levi*, also labels the Samaritans as "fools," stating that Shechem will be called the "city of fools" because they committed a great "outrage" or "folly" in Israel by defiling Dinah (7:2-3).[38]

---

[35] James Kugel, "Testament of the Twelve Patriarchs," in Louis H. Feldman, James L. Kugel, and Lawrence H. Schiffman (eds.), *Outside the Bible: Ancient Jewish Writings Related to Scripture* (Philadelphia: Jewish Publication Society, 2013), 2:1733; Matthew Goff, "The Foolish Nation That Dwells in Shechem: Ben Sira on Shechem and the Other Peoples in Palestine," in Daniel C. Harlow, Karina Martin Hogan, Matthew Goff, and Joel S. Kaminsky (eds.), *The "Other" in Second Temple Judaism: Essays in Honor of John J. Collins* (Grand Rapids: Eerdmans, 2011), 173–88; cf. Collins, "Epic of Theodotus," 98; Hans Gerhard Kippenberg, *Garizim und Synagoge: Traditionsgeschichtliche Untersuchungen zur samaritanischen Religion der aramäischen Periode* (Berlin: de Gruyter, 1971), 90; Kartveit, "Who Are the Fools," 119–33.

[36] Eileen Schuller, "4Q372 1: A Text about Joseph," *RevQ* 14 (1990): 349–76, esp. 371–6; Hanan Eshel, "The Prayer of Joseph, a Papyrus from Masada and the Samaritan Temple on ΑΡΓΑΡΙΖΙΝ," *Zion* 56 (1991): 125–36; Esther Chazon with Yonatan Miller, "'At the Crossroads': Anti-Samaritan Polemic in a Qumran Text about Joseph," in Daniel C. Harlow, Karina Martin Hogan, Matthew Goff, and Joel S. Kaminsky (eds.), *The "Other" in Second Temple Judaism: Essays in Honor of John J. Collins* (Grand Rapids: Eerdmans, 2011), 381–7. Others have questioned whether this text is explicitly anti-Samaritan. See Robert A. Kugler, "Joseph at Qumran," in James V. VanderKam, Peter W. Flint, and Emanuel Tov (eds.), *Studies in the Hebrew Bible, Qumran, and the Septuagint presented to Eugene Ulrich* (Boston: Brill, 2006): 261–78; Matthew Thiessen, "4Q372 1 and the Continuation of Joseph's Exile," *DSD* 15 (2008): 380–95.

[37] The phrase "fools were dwelling in the land" is taken from 4Q371 and fills a lacuna in 4Q372.

[38] Cf. Philo, *De Mutatione Nominum*, 193–5, 199–200. Here Shechem is the son of folly (193) and those in Shechem are called "the fools who attempt to seduce her" (195).

Taken together, Ben Sira's denouncement of the "foolish people" who live in Shechem (וגוי נבל הדר בשכם) and 4Q372's description of the Samaritans as the "fools" living in the land (ונבלים ישבים) are linked by the Hebrew term נבל, which is often translated as "fool." Strikingly, Gen 34:7 describes the rape of Dinah with the term נבלה, often translated as an "outrage." These two words, נבל and נבלה, are semantically related, and the Testament of Levi highlights this connection by stating that having committed this נבלה (outrage), the city of Shechem will be known from this day forward as the city of נבלים (fools). By connecting the words "fool" (נבל) and "outrage" (נבלה), the Testament of Levi more explicitly states what is implied in Ben Sira and 4Q372: that the "fools" in Shechem are descendants of the Shechem who committed a heinous act against Dinah. Though this may push the evidence too far, it is tempting to think about ancient Jews using the term "fools" in such a way as to connote "sexual predators" or "violent opportunists."

If these texts contain some semblance of the common understanding of the Samaritans in the late Second Temple period—that they were descendants of Shechem, uncircumcised Gentiles, and deserving of God's punishment—then we may have further insight into the decision by the Hasmonean ruler John Hyrcanus to destroy Shechem and the temple on Gerizim. Namely, the "biblical" anti-Samaritan rhetoric that began in the early second century BCE when the Samaritans were politically more ascendant was to bear deadly fruit at the close of the second century when the political tables had turned, for John Hyrcanus marched northward and conquered the region of Samaria. A century of "foreignization" of the Samaritans resulted in violence and destruction.

One final intriguing—and quite speculative—possibility. Jubilees is among the texts that detail violent behavior against the Shechemites. It condones this behavior on the grounds that it was righteous of Levi and Simeon to avenge their sister Dinah against the uncircumcised Shechemites. But in Jubilees we see a different result arising from this violence, for Levi is chosen for the priesthood *precisely because of his slaughter of the Shechemites*. It is tantalizing to consider the possibility that John Hyrcanus internalized this interpretative tradition and may have seen it as an additional rationale for his decision to destroy Samaria and the Samaritan temple: just as Levi's priesthood was granted to him because of his slaughter of the Shechemites, so also Hyrcanus' rationale for fighting the modern-day Shechemites—the Samaritans—may have been to confirm his own priesthood. This is all speculative, to be sure. But it is an intriguing rationale as to why Hyrcanus decided to conquer Samaria and destroy the Gerizim temple, for ridding Samaria of the primary rival temple to the one in Jerusalem may well have served to consolidate his own claim as high priest.

Conclusions

Rhetoric creates boundaries no less real than political borders. In naming the Samaritans as Cutheans, Sidonians, Shechemites and the "foolish people" of Shechem, Jewish authors began to create relational and social distance between

Jews and Samaritans. Exactly how long anti-Samaritan sentiments had been percolating is difficult to ascertain definitively, but the period in which we first see this rhetoric developing—the early second century BCE—is a time in which the Jews were in a politically weak position vis-à-vis the Samaritans. *None of this rhetoric could be acted upon politically.* But the rise of the nationalistic Hasmoneans in the middle of the second century changed this equation. Now this Jewish "foreignization" of Samaritans, as seen in a variety of second-century BCE texts, could and did begin to take on more concrete forms. The rhetoric of "otherness" had created a reality of "otherness." That this Jewish rhetoric had biblical undertones doubtless strengthened the distancing, as those Jews predisposed toward this act of othering could claim divine sanction for their views and activities. Indeed, in the nationalistic Hasmonean era, texts such as Genesis 34, Deuteronomy 32, 2 Kings 17, and Isaiah 23 were likely wielded as weapons and surely contributed to a hardening of attitudes toward Samaritans both before and after the destruction of the temple on Mount Gerizim. The destruction of the Samaritan temple meant that the political borders between Jews and Samaritans had been altered. But so had the rhetorical boundaries. Labeling the Samaritans as Cutheans, Sidonians, Shechemites and fools served first to create, and then later reinforce, the political realities of separateness between Jews and Samaritans in the late Second Temple period and beyond.

Chapter 8

ESCHATOLOGICAL EXPECTATION AND REVOLUTIONARY VIOLENCE: ISRAEL'S PAST AS INDICATIVE OF ITS FUTURE IN 1QM AND JOSEPHUS' *JEWISH WAR*

Jesse P. Nickel

Within the diversity of Second Temple Judaism, a central component of eschatological expectation is widely attested: the certainty that at some point in the future there would be a turn of the ages, when the creator God would act in power to destroy evil, redeem his people, and restore his creation. Both Josephus, in the *Jewish War* 5.379-390, and the *Yaḥad*, the sectarian Jewish community that dwelt at Qumran, in 1QM XI, 1-18, use examples from Israel's history to make a statement about the nature and role of violence in these expected eschatological events.[1] 1QM proclaims that the righteous "sons of light" shall go forth in confidence that, as demonstrated by previous events and foretold by the prophets, the battle belongs to God, who will achieve eschatological victory over evil through the willing participation of his faithful people. In contrast, Josephus' reading of biblical history causes him to argue that Israel has *never* found success by taking up arms. For Josephus, Israel's past supports an argument *against* taking up arms; for the *Yaḥad*, it instills the expectation of and hope for success *through* faithful war.

After outlining the content of these passages from the *War* and 1QM, each will be situated in the context of the overall place and function of violence within the text to which it belongs. Although the two might at first glance seem unrelated to one another—the one an apocalyptic description of an eschatological battle in both the earthly and heavenly realms, the other an ostensibly historical account of the author's own rhetorical appeal to his besieged contemporaries—this chapter will demonstrate that the violent revolutionaries who Josephus sees as responsible for the uprising against Rome were motivated by an eschatological outlook similar to that described in 1QM. Undergirding this particular set of expectations for the future was a particular "reading" of Israel's history—one which saw in

[1] The decision to refer to the sectarian Qumran group associated with the DSS as the "*Yaḥad*" is based on the use of אנשי היחד in 1QS V, 1 and elsewhere.

paradigmatic moments of past deliverance a necessary element of synergism. While the ultimate agent of the punishment and destruction of the enemies of God and his people was affirmed to be God himself, this took place only through the obedient participation of the faithful—God's people who, in righteous zeal, would themselves take up the sword. Josephus, aware of the central and formative role that this reading of their shared past exerted upon the eschatological outlook of his seditious contemporaries, and the profound way that this eschatology motivated them to violently rebel against the power of the Roman empire, offers in his speech an alternative perspective upon Israelite history. In so doing, Josephus implies that eschatological deliverance would come *not* to those who recklessly took up the sword, but to those who, acknowledging God's sovereign control of all history, would faithfully and piously wait on God's own action.

Eschatological Violence in the Dead Sea Scrolls

1QM XI, 1–18: לכה המלחמה

At the heart of the description of the eschatological conflict found in 1QM, columns X–XIV contain a series of prayers and liturgies associated with its different stages. Much of the theological foundation of this war is here presented. Although it is difficult to determine the ordering of events with certainty, scholars have suggested that the material found in column XI was part of a priestly liturgical exhortation, intended to be read prior to the "sons of light" entering the final battle.[2]

This exhortation begins in column X.[3] First, X, 1-2 alludes to Deuteronomy 7:21-22, calling those in the camps to remain holy, for God is in their midst.[4] The listeners are then twice reminded of the words of Moses: first, from Deuteronomy 20:2-5, calling Israel not to be afraid, for God fights for them and will deliver them (X, 2-5); second, from Numbers 10:9, proclaiming that when Israel blows the trumpets of war against the oppressor in the land, they shall be remembered before God and

---

[2] For example, Bilha Nitzan, *Qumran Prayer and Religious Poetry*, trans. Jonathan Chipman, STDJ 12 (Leiden: Brill, 1994), 97, refers to 1QM X–XII as the "Prayer for the Appointed Time of War."

[3] For analysis of the use of the HB in 1QM, see Dean O. Wenthe, "The Use of the Hebrew Scriptures in 1QM," *DSD* 5 (1998): 290–319; cf. Moshe J. Bernstein, "Scriptures: Quotation and Use," in Lawrence H. Schiffman and James VanderKam (eds.), *Encyclopedia of the Dead Sea Scrolls* (New York: Oxford University Press, 2000), 839–72; and Michael Fishbane, "Use, Authority and Interpretation of Mikra At Qumran," in Martin J. Mulder and Harry Sysling (eds.), *Mikra: Texts, Translation, Reading and Interpretation of the Hebrew Bible in Ancient Judaism and Early Christianity*, CRINT 2.1 (Assen: Van Gorcum, 1988), 339–77.

[4] Andrew Chester, "Citing the Old Testament," in D. A. Carson and H. G. M. Williamson (eds.), *It Is Written: Scripture Citing Scripture. Essays in Honour of Barnabas Lindars* (Cambridge: Cambridge University Press, 1988), 145–6, argues that this opening citation is composite, formed from Deut 7:21 and 6:19 or 23:15.

delivered from their enemies (X, 6-8).⁵ A predominant theme of the exhortation is thus immediately apparent: the God of Israel, who does great works, displays mighty strength, and to whom none is comparable (X, 8-9; cf. XIII, 13-14; XIV, 4-15), fights *with* the "sons of light"; therefore, they need not fear.

The theme continues to be developed in column XI, through several references to moments of salvation in Israel's past:

1QM	HB	Event
XI, 1-2	1 Sam 17	David's defeat of Goliath
XI, 2-3	(e.g.) 1 Sam 23:1-5; 2 Sam 5:17-25; 8:1-14	David's defeats of the Philistines
XI, 3-4	1 and 2 Kgs	Victories during the monarchy
XI, 9-10	Exod 15:4; cf. 14:1-31	Exodus: deliverance at the Red Sea
XI, 11-12⁶	Isa 31:8; cf. 2 Kgs 18:13–19:37	Deliverance from the siege of Sennacherib

These examples from Israel's past alternate with the repeated refrain, "the battle is yours!" (לכה המלחמה, XI, 1, 2, 4).⁷ Again and again, God's agency is made clear—"you delivered ... you saved us many times ... thanks to your mercy ... by your great strength and by your mighty deeds" (XI, 2–5)—and the glory for the victory is given to him. Because of God's mighty deeds on Israel's behalf in the past, the "sons of light" may depend upon divine salvation in the future (cf. VI, 5-6; VII, 6-7; XII, 7-9; XIII, 14; XIX, 1).⁸ King David, who "trusted in [God's] powerful name and not in sword or spear" (XI, 2), exemplifies this mindset; his

---

⁵ Cf. 1QM XV, 8–9; Joseph A. Fitzmyer, "The Use of Explicit Old Testament Quotations in Qumran Literature and in the New Testament," *NTS* 7 (1960): 297–333 (328).

⁶ Yigael Yadin, *The Scroll of the War of the Sons of Light against the Sons of Darkness*, trans. Batya Rabin and Chaim Rabin (Oxford: Oxford University Press, 1962), 212, 312, 348–9, argues that the citation of Isa. 31:8 in 1QM XI, 11-12 should be read as a reference to the siege of Jerusalem by Sennacherib; Jean Duhaime, *The War Texts: 1QM and Related Manuscripts* (London: T&T Clark, 2004), 109, however, disagrees, calling reference to this story in 1QM XI "unlikely."

⁷ Yadin, *The Scroll*, 309, notes that this phrase echoes most closely 1 Sam 17:47 ([המלחמה ליהוה כי] ונתן אתכם בידנו); cf. 1 Chr 5:22; 2 Chr 20:15. Translations of the DSS are those of Florentino García Martínez and Eibert J. C. Tigchelaar, eds. *The Dead Sea Scrolls: Study Edition*, 2 vols. (Leiden: Brill, 1997).

⁸ Duhaime, *The War Texts*, 114; cf. Loren L. Johns, "Identity and Resistance: The Varieties of Competing Models in Early Judaism," in Michael Thomas Davis and Brent A. Strawn (eds.), *Qumran Studies: New Approaches, New Questions* (Grand Rapids: Eerdmans, 2007), 267 n. 35. Russell Gmirkin, "Historical Allusions in the War Scroll," *DSD* 5 (1998): 180–5, claims that this use of chronological resonances of the past in the present is a "common literary device" (180) of Jewish eschatological literature.

defeat of Goliath epitomizes a victory won not on the basis of human strength, but through divine favor.[9]

The focus then switches to two prophetic proclamations that, taken together, emphasize the particularly synergistic nature of this anticipated victory.[10] The citation of Isaiah 31:8 (XI, 11-12) continues the emphasis on God's role by making it clear that the future war will not be won by human effort: "Ashur will fall by the sword of *not a man*, the sword of *not a human being* will devour it" (XI, 11-12).[11] However, preceding this declaration, Numbers 24:17-19 is cited (XI, 5-7), in such a form as to culminate with the proclamation that "Israel will perform feats" (וישראל עשה חיל, XI, 7), thereby emphasizing the *human* role in the fulfillment of God's promise to defeat the enemy.[12] Through his "anointed ones," God has informed his people that in "the ti[mes of] the wars of your hands" "the poor, those you saved" would "fell the hordes of Belial" (XI, 7-9). Alluding to Zechariah 12:6, the text declares that wickedness will be consumed when God will "set aflame, like a torch of fire in straw" the "stricken of spirit" (XI, 10). Divine and human activity are thus combined (XI, 13-14; cf. XIII, 14; XIV, 4-15). Though the responsibility for the victory belongs to God, it is envisioned as taking place *through* his faithful people.

Bringing together historical antecedents of past salvation with prophetic declarations of future victory, 1QM XI thus exhorts the "sons of light" to a particular vision of the eschatological victory.[13] They are assured that God is in their midst, has promised to fight on their behalf, and will deliver them from their enemies (X, 1-8); reminded of the many times God has acted in fulfillment of these promises in the past (XI, 1-4, 9-12); and persuaded that God will accomplish even greater victories in the future, through the faithful participation of his true people.[14] The community of this text is thus exhorted to inaugurate and prosecute

---

[9] Jean Duhaime, "War Scroll," in James H. Charlesworth (ed.), *Damascus Document, War Scroll, and Related Documents*, vol. 2 of *The Dead Sea Scrolls: Hebrew, Aramaic, and Greek Texts with English Translations* (Louisville: Westminster John Knox, 1995), 86–7; Annette Steudel, "The Eternal Reign of the People of God—Collective Expectations in Qumran Texts (4Q246 and 1QM)," *RevQ* 17 (1996): 522.

[10] On the application of prophetic passages to future events in the DSS, see Fishbane, "Use, Authority"; cf. Brian Schultz, *Conquering the World: The War Scroll (1QM) Reconsidered*, STDJ 76 (Leiden: Brill, 2009), 274; Geza Vermes, "Biblical Proof-Texts in Qumran Literature," *JSS* 34 (1989): 493–508 (496).

[11] Cf. the stone cut out "not by human hands," in Dan 2:34, 45.

[12] On the distinctions between Num 24:17-19 here and in the MT, and their significance, see Fitzmyer, "The Use of Explicit," 323–4; Schultz, *Conquering*, 274; Steudel, "The Eternal Reign," 523; and Wenthe, "Hebrew Scriptures," 308.

[13] For further discussion of the combination of historical antecedent with prophetic expectation in 1QM, see Duhaime, "War Scroll," 88; cf. Chester, "Citing," 164.

[14] Fishbane, "Use, Authority," 338, notes the typological transference of אשור in 1QM as a "cipher for contemporary enemies of the covenanteers," part of their belief that these texts were divinely intended from the beginning to refer to their own day. This confidence that future events are preordained and in God's hands reflects Josephus' description of the beliefs of the Essenes (*Ant.* 13.172; 18.18); see David M. Rhoads, *Israel in Revolution: 6-74 C.E. A Political History Based on the Writings of Josephus* (Philadelphia: Fortress, 1976), 44.

the events of the eschatological war in full assurance of victory, trusting that they will be fighting God's battle as his "sons of light."

1QM XI, therefore, expresses the Yaḥad's confidence that God will "fight with them from heaven" (17-19), and their belief that God's eschatological victory would come about *through* the willing participation of his people, who act in faith that is rooted in their knowledge of God's actions in the past. This synergistic balance, which requires God's faithful people *both* to depend on him for evil's ultimate defeat *and* to participate in the conflict themselves, is a central characteristic of the eschatological violence of 1QM.

The Agents of Eschatological Violence in 1QM

The Violence of the Eschatological Culmination

Although depictions of violence appear elsewhere in eschatological contexts in the scrolls from Qumran, this subject matter is focused on most directly and at greatest length in 1QM.[15] Documenting the eschatological conflict of the archangel Michael, the heavenly armies, and the human "sons of light," against the forces of evil, led by Belial, and the human "sons of darkness," the *War Scroll* makes it clear that the *Yaḥad*, believing itself to be the truly righteous community of God (the "sons of light"), expected to participate in a climactic battle against their foes in the eschatological culmination.[16]

The abundant violence of this large-scale conflict, involving both heavenly and earthly participants, is beyond dispute. 1QM depicts the eschatological victory of God and his people in clearly militaristic terms: it will involve "savage destruction before the God of Israel, for this will be the day determined by him since ancient times for the war of extermination against the sons of darkness" (I, 9-10). The armies of the "sons of light" will "shed the blood" of the wicked (VI, 17), and God

---

[15] Examples of other depictions of violence in eschatological DSS texts include: CD VII, 19-21; 1QS III, 13–IV, 26 (cf. 4QSapiential Work A); 1QH XI, 19-36; XIV, 29-30; 1Q28b, V, 24-25, 27 (cf. 4Q285 frag. 6); and 4Q161 frags. 8-10; 4Q171 II, 14-15, 18-19; 4Q174 I, 18-19; 4Q426, 4Q471a, 4Q562. For lists and discussions of such texts, see Philip S. Alexander, "The Evil Empire: The Qumran Eschatological War Cycle and the Origins of Jewish Opposition to Rome," in Shalom M. Paul, et al. (eds.), *Emanuel: Studies in Hebrew Bible Septuagint and Dead Sea Scrolls in Honor of Emanuel Tov*, VTSup 94 (Leiden: Brill, 2003), 19–20; John J. Collins, *Apocalypticism in the Dead Sea Scrolls* (London: Routledge, 1997), 91; and Albert L. A. Hogeterp, *Expectations of the End: A Comparative Tradition-Historical Study of Eschatological, Apocalyptic and Messianic Ideas in the Dead Sea Scrolls and the New Testament*, STDJ 83 (Leiden: Brill, 2009), 374.

[16] Although the majority of scholars agree that 1QM portrays the climactic eschatological conflict, some urge caution about too quickly assuming this to be the case; see, e.g., Hogeterp, *Expectations*, 372.

is implored to "place your hand on the neck of your enemies and your foot on the piles of slain! Strike the peoples, your foes, and may your sword consume guilty flesh!" (XII, 11-12; cf. XIX, 3-4). The *War Scroll* thus describes the forthcoming destruction of Belial and the "sons of darkness" in graphically violent language.[17]

The Synergistic Nature of the Eschatological Victory

The *primary* agent of the eschatological victory depicted in 1QM is God himself: the standards carried by the "sons of light" declare that both the war (מלחמה אל, IV, 12) and the victory (נצה אל, IV, 13) belong ultimately to God.[18] The conflict between the opposing human and heavenly forces is only decided with God's intervention (I, 14-15).[19] The *Yaḥad* thus confidently expected God's decisive assistance.

In conjunction with its emphasis on divine agency, however, 1QM considers the participation of the people of God in the eschatological conflict to be of near-equivalent significance. This is evident from its opening lines: "The first attack *by the sons of light* will be launched against the lot of the sons of darkness, against the army of Belial" (I, 1; cf. I, 2). The column goes on to describe a series of terrible clashes between these two forces (I, 10-13), before God himself decisively intervenes (I, 14-16). The *War Scroll* thus describes the violent eschatological judgment upon and destruction of the enemies of God and his people as an event in which the "sons of light" will play an active, militaristic role. The *Yaḥad* must be ready to commit itself to engage in eschatological battle at the time determined by God.[20] In this way, "the rule of the Kittim" would "come to an end," and wickedness be defeated (I, 6); the "exalted greatness" of God would "shine for all the et[ernal] times, for peace, blessing, glory and joy" (I, 8-9); and "Israel [will] reign for ever" (XIX, 8).[21] This sectarian text thus gives voice to the expectation that the "sons of light" would participate alongside God in eschatological violence, thereby demonstrating their identity as the true eschatological community of God's people.[22]

---

[17] For further examples, see III, 8; VIII, 8-9, 16-18; IX, 1-2; XVI, 7, 9; XVII, 12-13.

[18] John J. Collins, "The Expectation of the End in the Dead Sea Scrolls," in Craig A. Evans and Peter W. Flint (eds.), *Eschatology, Messianism, and the Dead Sea Scrolls* (Grand Rapids: Eerdmans, 1997), 87.

[19] Cf. XV, 13-14; XVIII, 1.

[20] This motif is attested elsewhere in the DSS, e.g.: 1QpHab V, 4: "in the hand of his chosen ones God will place the judgment over all his peoples"; cf. 1QS VIII, 6-7, 10; IX, 23; 1QH VI, 29-30; XIV, 29-32; 1QpHab V, 3. See Duhaime, *The War Texts*, 41; Gordon Zerbe, *Non-retaliation in Early Jewish and New Testament Texts: Ethical Themes in Social Contexts*, JSPSup 13 (Sheffield: JSOT, 1993), 122.

[21] Cf. 1QM XII, 16; XVII, 7-8; 4Q246 II, 4, 5-9. Steudel, "The Eternal Reign," 517; see further 517–24.

[22] This point is emphasized particularly effectively by Alexander, "The Evil Empire," 28–9. On the identity of the *Yaḥad* as the "remnant" of Israel, especially as this concept is represented in CD, see Philip R. Davies, "Eschatology at Qumran," *JBL* 104 (1985): 39–55; Alex Jassen, "The Dead Sea Scrolls and Violence: Sectarian Formation and Eschatological Imagination," *BibInt* 17 (2009): 20–1, 38–9.

1QM XI, 1–18 as Representative of the Scrolls

Therefore, the biblically-rooted exhortation found in 1QM XI, 1-18 can be seen to reflect this significant, carefully balanced component of the *Yaḥad*'s eschatological expectations. *Only* because of God's intervention will the "sons of light" be victorious in the war against Belial and the sons of darkness—as the refrain states, לכה המלחמה. At the same time, however, the importance of the faithful, obedient, and *eager* participation of the *Yaḥad* itself is emphasized. Since it is *through his righteous elect* that God will defeat and destroy evil, the active involvement of the *Yaḥad* will mark them out as "true Israel" in a moment of glorious vindication. On that day, their confidence in God's deliverance would be rooted in their identity.[23] They would take courage from God's promises to fight in their midst, having been reminded of the many times God had delivered those who trusted him, defeating his enemies by the hand of his servants.

Josephus' Response to (Eschatologically Motivated) Revolutionary Violence

Jewish War 5.362-419: οὐκ ἔστιν ὅ τι κατώρθωσαν οἱ πατέρες ἡμῶν τοῖς ὅπλοις

In book five of the *War*, Flavius Josephus delivers a lengthy speech to the Jewish rebels under siege in Jerusalem. In this speech, Josephus is determined to convince his rebellious countrymen to lay down their weapons in surrender (5.416).[24] To this end, he makes two interconnected arguments. First, God, who is in control of history, has placed τύχη on the side of the Romans (5.367; cf. 2.390; 3.6; 4.622; 5.412; 6.38); therefore, the rebellious Jews are fighting not only against Rome, but also against God himself (5.378).[25] Second, God is well able to defeat Israel's enemies and deliver his people when it is his will to do so. If God so desired, Rome would have been dispatched long ago; yet, God has *not* intervened on the Jews'

---

[23] See Nitzan, *Qumran Prayer*, 301, and Lawrence H. Schiffman, "The Concept of Restoration in the Dead Sea Scrolls," in James M. Scott (ed.), *Restoration: Old Testament, Jewish, and Christian Perspectives*, JSJSup 72 (Leiden: Brill, 2001), 212, 220; cf. Wenthe, "Hebrew Scriptures," 310.

[24] Cf. the other moments at which Josephus, acting as a mediator between his countrymen and the Romans, appeals to the Jews to surrender—all in vain: 5.114, 261, 325-326, 541; 6.94, 118, 129, 365. See Per Bilde, *Flavius Josephus Between Jerusalem and Rome: His Life, His Works, and Their Importance* (Sheffield: Sheffield Academic, 1988), 55; Julia Walker, "'God Is with Italy Now': Pro-Roman Jews and the Jewish Revolt," in Benedikt Eckhardt (ed.), *Jewish Identity and Politics between the Maccabees and Bar Kokhba: Groups, Normativity and Rituals*, JSJSup 155 (Leiden: Brill, 2012), 181–3.

[25] Jonathan J. Price, "The Provincial Historian in Rome," in Joseph Sievers and Gaia Lembi (eds.), *Josephus and Jewish History in Flavian Rome and Beyond*, JSJSup 104 (Leiden: Brill, 2005), 117.

behalf (5.407-408).[26] Nor should they expect him to do so in the future, since they have defiled the Holy Temple through their impiety and internecine strife (5.402-403, 413; cf. 2.449-457; 6.108-110, 249-251).

Josephus begins his speech with a catalogue of Rome's praiseworthy attributes, reiterating the besieged rebels' hopeless situation (5.362-374). This tactic quickly fails, so Josephus decides to appeal to "reminiscences of their nation's history" (5.375). He launches into the pivotal section of the speech (5.376-390) with a series of questions (5.376-377):

> Unmindful of your own true allies, would you make war on the Romans with arms and might of hand? *What other foe have we conquered thus, and when did God who created, fail to avenge, the Jews, if they were wronged?* Will you not turn your eyes and mark what place is that whence you issue to battle and reflect how mighty an Ally you have outraged? (5.376-377)[27]

Josephus then proceeds to give five examples from the history of Israel in which God delivered his people *without* their taking up arms:

War	HB	Event
5.379-381	Gen 12:10-20; cf. 14:13-16	Sarah abducted by Pharaoh
5.382-383	Exod 1-14; cf. Deut 26:5	The exodus from slavery in Egypt
5.384-385	1 Sam 4:1–7:1	Philistines take the Ark of the Covenant
5.387-388	2 Kgs 19:35-36 (18:13–19:37)	Deliverance from the siege of Sennacherib
5.389	Ezra 1:1-8	Return from exile in Babylon

This leads Josephus to conclude, "there is *no instance* of our forefathers having triumphed by arms or failed of success without them when they committed their cause to God" (5.390). The history of Israel proves that when the Jews commit themselves in trust to God—to his fighting battles on their behalf (5.386)—they are delivered: "if they sat still they conquered … if they fought they were invariably defeated" (5.390-391).

---

[26] Jan Willem van Henten, "Commonplaces in Herod's Commander Speech in Josephus' *A. J.* 15.127-146," in Joseph Sievers and Gaia Lembi (eds.), *Josephus and Jewish History in Flavian Rome and Beyond*, JSJSup 104 (Leiden: Brill, 2005), 204 n. 81, observes that God's support is repeatedly portrayed as essential in the speeches found in the *War*: see 2.388-391; 3.484; 4.190-191; 7.318-319, 327-332, 358-359; cf. Pere Villalba i Varneda, *The Historical Method of Flavius Josephus* (Leiden: Brill, 1986), 99. Harold W. Attridge, *The Interpretation of Biblical History in the Antiquities Judaicae of Flavius Josephus* (Missoula: Scholars Press, 1976), 149–50, argues that this belief—"that God, as the ally … of his people, would intervene to save those faithful to him"—is central to the theology of the rebels, as this is portrayed by Josephus; cf. Price, "The Provincial Historian," 114.

[27] All quotations of Josephus' works are from the LCL translations.

Josephus' presentation of Israelite history is obviously selective; he himself cannot but have been aware that the story is more complicated than he makes it out to be.[28] Although each event mentioned in 5.379-389 is indeed an example of God's deliverance without resort to armed resistance, numerous other cases could be brought forth to make the opposite case. Yet Josephus, ignoring evidence to the contrary, selects these five episodes in order ostensibly to demonstrate to his besieged Jewish listeners (and, thereby, to his Roman readers) that a truly faithful Israelite should not put his hope in success through armed conflict, for God's deliverance of his people has *never* come about through such means.[29] In order to appreciate the significance of this speech to the case being set forth in this paper, we must first briefly discuss Josephus' perspective upon Jewish revolutionary violence, insofar as this can be discerned from his writings.

Violence and Eschatology in the Writings of Josephus

Josephus' Description of Revolutionary Judaism

Josephus lays a great deal of the responsibility for the war's disastrous outcome at the feet of several groups, including οἱ ζηλωταί, οἱ σικάριοι, and οἱ λῃσταί, as well as the followers of certain individual leaders, including John of Gischala and Simon bar Giora.[30] Although the competing ambitions and differing ideals of these groups

---

[28] Scholars have noted not only the selectivity of this list, but also the ways in which the stories Josephus *did* decide to include have, to varying extents, been reshaped, the better to support his appeal to his audience; see, e.g., Seth Schwartz, *Josephus and Judaean Politics* (Leiden: Brill, 1990), 28; Steve Mason, *Judean War 2*, vol. 1b of *Flavius Josephus: Translation and Commentary* (ed. Steve Mason; Leiden: Brill, 2008), 267; "Being Earnest, Being Playful: Speech and Speeches in Josephus and Acts," *Sapientia Logos* 3 (2011): 51–2; and Paul Spilsbury, "Reading the Bible in Rome: Josephus and the Constraints of Empire," in Joseph Sievers and Gaia Lembi (eds.), *Josephus and Jewish History in Flavian Rome and Beyond*, JSJSup 104 (Leiden: Brill, 2005), 213.

[29] This raises the very complicated question of Josephus' intended audience. Assuming that Josephus composed this speech to serve a rhetorical purpose, who was he trying to convince? This question has been the subject of extensive discussion; see, e.g., John M. G. Barclay, "The Empire Writes Back: Josephan Rhetoric in Flavian Rome," in Jonathan Edmondson, Steve Mason, and James Rives (eds.), *Flavius Josephus and Flavian Rome* (Oxford: Oxford University Press, 2005), 315–32; Steve Mason, "Of Audience and Meaning: Reading Josephus' *Bellum Judaicum* in the Context of a Flavian Audience," in Joseph Sievers and Gaia Lembi (eds.), *Josephus and Jewish History in Flavian Rome and Beyond*, JSJSup 104 (Leiden: Brill, 2005), 71–100.

[30] The question of the unity or disunity of these various groups, as well as an overview of their distinctive features, has also been extensively discussed. For overview and bibliography, see James S. McLaren, "Resistance Movements," in John J. Collins and Daniel C. Harlow (eds.), *The Eerdmans Dictionary of Early Judaism* (Grand Rapids: Eerdmans, 2010), 1135–40.

often resulted in conflict between them, they were united by their willingness to take up the sword against their Roman oppressors and all who supported them.³¹ Josephus' polemical opinion of these revolutionaries is marked by deep animosity and hostility: they were a dissolute group of false Jews, "the dregs of society and the bastard scum of the nation" (5.443;³² 442-445), driven to pursue independence from Rome by impiety and greed.³³ Josephus thus places the entire blame for the conflict on these στασιάζοι, who acted as τύραννοι in compelling the unwilling Jewish populace to join them.³⁴ The atrocities they committed—most notably, their transgression of the Law (2.517-518) and defilement of the temple (4.157, 323; 5.402, 412)—brought God's punishment upon the whole nation.³⁵

Of particular significance to the present study is Josephus' suggestion that a genealogical (and possibly ideological) connection existed between the revolutionary groups active in the 60s CE and a movement which began several decades earlier. Shortly after Judea had come under direct provincial Roman control in 6 CE, the Governor Quirinius instituted a census. In response, a group of Jews, under the leadership of Judas the Galilean and Saddok the Pharisee, revolted. Josephus famously describes the movement that resulted as the so-called fourth philosophy of Judaism (*Ant.* 18.9-10, 23; cf. *War* 2.118).³⁶

---

³¹ Mason, "Of Audience," 97, notes that Josephus' account of the war portrays it as much as a Judean civil war as a unified conflict against Rome; cf. Jonathan J. Price, "Revolt, First Jewish," in John J. Collins and Daniel C. Harlow (eds.), *The Eerdmans Dictionary of Early Judaism* (Grand Rapids: Eerdmans, 2010), 1146-47; Walker, "God Is With Italy Now," 184.

³² Josephus is here referring specifically to Simon bar Giora and John of Gischala.

³³ Martin Hengel, *The Zealots: Investigations into the Jewish Freedom Movement in the Period From Herod I Until 70 A.D.*, trans. David Smith (Edinburgh: T&T Clark, 1989), 16; see further 183-6; Per Bilde, "Josephus and the Bandits," *JSJ* 10 (1979): 189–202.

³⁴ Στασιάζοι, see *War* 1.27; 2.266, 274, 324, 422; 4.362; 5.30, 33; τύραννοι, see *War* 1.10-11; 2.84, 88, 208; 5.5, 11, 439; 6.98, 129, 143, and frequently elsewhere.

³⁵ Although these various groups undoubtedly played an important role in both the initiation of the uprising and its continuation, it seems highly unlikely that Josephus is correct in attributing the entire responsibility for the revolt to such individuals. Martin Goodman, *The Ruling Class of Judaea: The Origins of the Jewish Revolt against Rome, A.D. 66-70* (Cambridge: Cambridge University Press, 1987), offers one example of an alternative thesis, claiming that the primary responsibility for the war belonged not to various revolutionary groups, but to the priestly aristocracy—the Jewish social stratum to which Josephus himself belonged.

³⁶ See Matthew Black, "Judas of Galilee and Josephus's 'Fourth Philosophy,'" in Otto Betz, Klaus Haacker, and Martin Hengel (eds.), *Josephus-Studien: Untersuchungen zu Josephus, dem Antiken Judentum und dem Neuen Testament: Otto Michel zum 70sten Geburstag Gewidmet* (Göttingen: Vandenhoeck & Ruprecht, 1974), 45–54; James S. McLaren, "Constructing Judaean History in the Diaspora: Josephus's Accounts of Judas," in John M. G. Barclay (ed.), *Negotiating Diaspora: Jewish Strategies in the Roman Empire* (London: Clark, 2004), 90–108.

Two fundamental ideals set this "fourth philosophy" apart from the rest of Judaism: (i) the belief that "God alone is their leader and master" and (ii) "a passion for liberty that is almost unconquerable" (18.23). Each resonates with eschatological overtones. First, the belief that God alone was ἡγεμών and δεσπότης resonates with biblical portrayals of God's kingship, and expectations that God's reign would be manifested anew in the eschatological age.[37] The hope that God would one day rule over Israel, and that a pagan king—whether the Roman emperor or his local representatives—would not, was one with which most Second Temple Jews would have identified. What set those who belonged to the "fourth philosophy" apart, however, was their willingness to kill or be killed for the cause of its realization (18.24).[38]

The second ideal, the "difficult to conquer love of freedom" (δυσνίκητος ... τοῦ ἐλευθέρου ἔρως), can be better understood by examining the significance of ἐλευθερία elsewhere in Josephus' works.[39] Ἐλευθερία was connected to the ability of the Jewish people to worship God properly, that is, to live according to the laws and customs of their fathers (12.303). As such, it was the key concept for which the Maccabees fought and died (13.198),[40] and was identified by Herod Agrippa II as the main reason the Jews revolted against Rome (*War* 2.346).[41] However, Josephus makes clear his own belief that ἐλευθερία is entirely under God's control, to be dispersed to those who deserve it (5.365, 389, 396, 406). The prophet Samuel therefore encourages the Israelites "not to be content to yearn for ἐλευθερία," but to "do also the deeds whereby ye may attain it" (*Ant.* 6.20), which are given as the following:

> Be ye righteous and, casting out wickedness from your souls and purging them, turn with all your hearts to the Deity and persevere in honouring Him. Do ye

---

[37] See N. T. Wright, *The New Testament and the People of God* (Minneapolis: Fortress, 1992), 302–7.

[38] See *War* 7.254-255; William Horbury, *Jewish War under Trajan and Hadrian* (New York: Cambridge University Press, 2014), 327 n. 170.

[39] On ἐλευθερία in Josephus, see Daniel R. Schwartz, "Rome and the Jews: Josephus on 'Freedom' and 'Autonomy,'" in Alan K. Bowman et al. (eds.), *Representations of Empire: Rome and the Mediterranean World* (Oxford: Oxford University Press, 2002), 65–81; cf. Hengel, *The Zealots*, 110–15. On the significance of ἐλευθερία to the revolt and the revolutionaries more broadly, see Horbury, *Jewish War*, 136–42, 146–9.

[40] Louis H. Feldman, "Josephus' Portrayal of the Hasmoneans Compared with 1 Maccabees," in Fausto Parente and Joseph Sievers (eds.), *Josephus and the History of the Greco-Roman Period: Essays in Memory of Morton Smith*, StPB 41 (Leiden: Brill, 1994), 62.

[41] Cf. Josephus, *Ant.* 14.77; *War* 3.480; 4.177; 7.323-336, 341-388. See James S. McLaren, "Going to War against Rome: The Motivation of the Jewish Rebels," in Mladen Popović (ed.), *The Jewish Revolt against Rome: Interdisciplinary Perspectives*, JSJSup 154 (Leiden: Brill, 2011), 138; "Theocracy, Temple and Tax: Ingredients for the Jewish-Roman War of 66-70 CE" (paper presented at the Annual Meeting of the SBL, San Antonio, TX, 2004), 21–2; cf. Schwartz, "Rome and the Jews," 72.

but so and there will come prosperity, deliverance from bondage and victory over your foes, blessings which are to be won neither by arms nor by personal prowess nor by a host of combatants; for it is not for these that God promises to bestow these blessings, but for lives of virtue and righteousness. (*Ant.* 6.21)

The blessings associated here with ἐλευθερία (ἥξει τὰ ἀγαθά, δουλείας ἀπαλλαγὴ καὶ νίκη πολεμίων) are frequently attested elements of Jewish eschatological hope. Intriguingly, Josephus is clear that these will *not* be gained by warfare (ἃ λαβεῖν οὔθ᾽ ὅπλοις οὔτε σωμάτων ἀλκαῖς οὔτε πλήθει συμμάχων δυνατόν ἐστιν), but by ἀγαθοὺς εἶναι καὶ δικαίους. Therefore, the combined emphasis on ἐλευθερία and God's kingship in Josephus' description of the identifying beliefs of those who belonged to the "fourth philosophy" strongly suggests that eschatology played a primary role in motivating their actions.

At this stage of our discussion, two critical points must be acknowledged. First, there is a wide range of scholarly opinion regarding the plausibility of drawing connections (ideological, hereditary/dynastic, or organizational) between the "fourth philosophy" and Jewish revolutionary groups active in the mid-first century CE.[42] Nevertheless, it seems clear that Josephus himself intends his audience to see the lasting influence of Judas and Saddok at work in more recent events, given his own explanatory statement: "My reason for giving this brief account [of the origins of the fourth philosophy] is chiefly that *the zeal which Judas and Saddok inspired in the younger element meant the ruin of our cause*" (18.10).

Second, Josephus' characterization of the revolutionary groups who participated in the Jewish-Roman War must be read with critical awareness of how his own perspective—shaped by his personal background, present agenda, and the revolt's catastrophic results—was at work.[43] However, despite the polemical tone with which he describes these individuals, certain elements suggest that they were motivated not solely by greed and lawlessness, but also by the desire—shared with their Maccabean forefathers, whose "zeal" they sought to emulate[44]—to inaugurate God's promised eschatological deliverance of his faithful people.[45]

---

[42] For a summary of this debate, see McLaren, "Resistance Movements," 1137. Some have argued that the "fourth philosophy" developed into a distinct, carefully-organized resistance movement (e.g., Hengel, *The Zealots*, 5); others have denied any suggestion of (an) "official" resistance movement(s) within Judaism (e.g., Richard A. Horsley, "Josephus and the Bandits," *JSJ* 10 [1979]: 37-63; "The Zealots: Their Origin, Relationships and Importance in the Jewish Revolt," *NovT* 28 [1986]: 159-92). At the very least, Josephus seems to suggest direct connections between the "fourth philosophy" and the σικάριοι through Eleazar ben Ya'ir (*War* 2.252-253; also 2.447); see McLaren, "Resistance Movements," 1137; cf. Price, "Revolt," 1146.

[43] McLaren, "Going to War," 151.

[44] On ζῆλος at work among the revolutionary Jews, see *War* 2.230; 3.9; 5.21, 100; 6.79; 7.270, 389; on the centrality of "zeal" to first-century Jewish revolutionary movements, see Hengel, *The Zealots*, 146–228.

[45] The particular significance of "religious" motivation for the Jewish revolutionaries is emphasized by Cecil Roth, "The Zealots in the War of 66-73," *JSS* 4 (1959): 332–55.

As Schreiber notes, given Josephus' apologetically-driven desire to disassociate these impious revolutionaries from the true identity of Judaism, the fact that "eine religiöse Motivation der Aufständlischen" still comes through—even if only "in Andeutungen"—makes such hints appear "umso bezeichnender."[46]

Josephus on the Jewish Motivations for Revolt

That being said, Josephus makes few direct comments about the reasons for the outbreak of large-scale revolt in 66 CE.[47] Most of the factors to which he does refer are economic or political, and associated with a certain level of ineptitude, brutality, and cultural insensitivity displayed by the Roman leadership.[48] James McLaren has discussed such factors at length, arguing against the assumption that the rebellion's outbreak was somehow inevitable, noting the significance of the Jewish decision to revolt at *this point* (and not earlier), and emphasizing that this was a definitive choice, made with the intention of attaining freedom from Roman rule.[49] He declares that we need not suggest "distinctive factors, such as extremist ideologies or radical aspirations or hopes of divine assistance" in order to explain the beginning of the revolt.[50]

Notwithstanding McLaren's claims, when set alongside the description of the "fourth philosophy" analyzed above, some key passages from Josephus' account seem to suggest that Jewish eschatological expectations were, in fact, central to the outbreak of violence in 66 CE. Of particular relevance is Josephus' statement that:

> What *more than all else incited* [*the Jews*] *to the war* was an ambiguous oracle (χρησμὸς ἀμφίβολος), likewise found in their sacred scriptures, to the effect that

---

[46] Stefan Schreiber, "Am Rande des Krieges: Gewalt und Gewaltverzicht bei Jesus von Nazaret," *BN* 145 (2010): 94.

[47] Steve Mason, "Why Did Judaeans Go to War with Rome in 66–67 CE? Realist-Regional Perspectives," in Peter J. Tomson and Joshua Schwartz (eds.), *Jews and Christians in the First and Second Centuries: How to Write Their History*, CRINT 13 (Leiden: Brill, 2014), 126–206; cf. Rhoads, *Israel in Revolution*, 167–70.

[48] *War* 2.223-231, 289-308; cf. *Ant.* 18.25. On the ineptitude of Roman leadership in this period, see McLaren, "Going to War"; cf. Martin Goodman, "The First Jewish Revolt: Social Conflict and the Problem of Debt," *JJS* 33 (1982): 417–27. On the economic causes of the revolt, see Shimon Applebaum, "Josephus and the Economic Causes of the Jewish War," in Louis H. Feldman and Gohei Hata (eds.), *Josephus, the Bible, and History* (Detroit: Wayne State University Press, 1989), 237–64.

[49] McLaren, "Theocracy, Temple," 5–6; "Going to War," 135–7, 150.

[50] McLaren, "Going to War," 153. McLaren argues that it was in Josephus' interests to explain the conflict with such "convenient" alternatives (151). Against this position, Anthony J. Tomasino, "Oracles of Insurrection: The Prophetic Catalyst of the Great Revolt," *JJS* 59 (2008): 87, argues that it would have been in Josephus' interests to *downplay* religious ideological factors.

at that time one from their country would become ruler of the world. This they understood to mean someone of their own race, and many of their wise men went astray in their interpretation of it. (*War* 6.312-313a)[51]

Josephus here claims that a prophetic passage from the Jewish scriptures (the χρησμὸς ἀμφίβολος) was the *primary* factor leading to violent revolution against Rome. In other words, Josephus refers to a biblically-shaped expectation that a worldwide kingdom, ruled from Israel, would soon be inaugurated. This is undoubtedly eschatological. What is more, Josephus identifies this belief as the *foremost motivation* (τὸ δ' ἐπᾶραν αὐτοὺς μάλιστα πρὸς τὸν πόλεμον) for the revolt.[52]

There has been much discussion about the referent of the χρησμὸς ἀμφίβολος, with several options receiving scholarly support.[53] Tomasino has put forward a compelling argument for its primary identification as Daniel 9:24-27.[54] The Danielic prophecy of the seventy weeks is a likely candidate for several reasons: it anticipated deliverance following a period of great desolation, its eschatological interpretation is attested elsewhere, and it emphasizes chronology.[55] Moreover, Tomasino notes that Daniel had been regarded as a useful text "for inspiring messianic speculation and revolutionary fervour" since ancient times.[56]

Whatever the precise source of the χρησμὸς ἀμφίβολος, its significance to the present study is beyond doubt: it provides clear evidence that eschatological expectations played an important motivational role in the outbreak of revolt. This is further demonstrated by Josephus' repeated references to prophetic or messianic figures who took their followers out into the wilderness, claiming "that they would show them unmistakable marvels and signs that would be wrought

---

[51] Both Tacitus (*Hist.* 5.13) and Suetonius (*Vesp.* 4.5) mention a similar prophecy in their report of these events; see Lester L. Grabbe, "Eschatology in Philo and Josephus," in A. J. Avery-Peck and J. Neusner (eds.), *Death, Life-after-death, Resurrection and the World-to-come in the Judaisms of Antiquity*, vol. 4 of *Judaism in Late Antiquity*, HdO I/49 (Leiden: Brill, 2000), 177–81.

[52] See Valentin Nikiprowetzky, "Josephus and the Revolutionary Parties," in Louis H. Feldman and Gohei Hata (eds.), and Angela Armstrong (trans.), *Josephus, the Bible, and History* (Detroit: Wayne State University Press, 1988), 220.

[53] These include: Isa 10:33-34; Num 24:17; Dan 7; and the *Sibylline Oracles*; see Tomasino, "Oracles," 92–4.

[54] Tomasino, "Oracles," 96–7; cf. Wright, *The New Testament*, 312–14. For discussion of the interpretation of Dan 9:24-27 both before and after the revolt, see Tomasino, "Oracles," 97–104; cf. Horbury, *Jewish War*, 286–7 n. 32.

[55] See Tomasino, "Oracles," 95–102, for discussion, with thorough references.

[56] Tomasino, "Oracles," 95; see further "Daniel and the Revolutionaries: The Use of Daniel Tradition by Jewish Resistance Movements of Late Second-Temple Palestine" (PhD Dissertation; Chicago: University of Chicago, 1995).

in harmony with God's design" (*Ant.* 20.168).[57] Josephus—not surprisingly—has nothing but contempt for this group of "impostors and deceivers," "false prophets," "villains" and "charlatans," who, "under the pretence of divine inspiration fostering revolutionary changes ... persuaded the multitude to act like madmen."[58] For the most part, these groups do not appear to have intended to take up arms, but instead expected σημεῖα ἐλευθερίας (*War* 2.259) to herald the beginning of Rome's downfall. However, there is one noteworthy point at which Josephus describes some of these figures joining forces with the revolutionaries:

> The impostors (γόητες) and brigands (λῃστρικοί), banding together, incited numbers to revolt, exhorting them to assert their independence (πρὸς ἐλευθερίαν παρεκρότουν), and threatening to kill any who submitted to Roman domination and forcibly to suppress those who voluntarily accepted servitude. (*War* 2.264)[59]

This passage explicitly brings together pseudo-prophetic figures and revolutionaries, uniting them in their shared desire that Jewish ἐλευθερία would be attained through violence.

From all this, it appears that during the initial period of the Jewish-Roman War, much of the subject populace expected that the God-ordained moment of their deliverance had come. The benefit of hindsight, coupled with his own apologetic intentions, led Josephus to portray this aspect of the revolt in a negative light. Nevertheless, Josephus' emphasis on the distinctive features of the "fourth philosophy" and its enduring significance, the motivational role played by the "ambiguous oracle," and the prevalence of prophetic/messianic movements together make it clear that eschatological expectations, rooted in Scripture, were closely associated with the violent revolutionary activity of many of his contemporaries.

---

[57] For further on such figures, see Paul W. Barnett, "The Jewish Sign Prophets—AD 40-70: Their Intentions and Origin," *NTS* 27 (1981): 679–97; Rebecca Gray, *Prophetic Figures in Late Second Temple Jewish Palestine: The Evidence From Josephus* (New York: Oxford University Press, 1993), 112–44; Richard A. Horsley and John S. Hanson, *Bandits, Prophets and Messiahs: Popular Movements at the Time of Jesus* (Edinburgh: T&T Clark, 1985), 135–89; on their significance, Horbury, *Jewish War*, 147–8.

[58] In order, the quotations are from *Ant.* 20.167; *War* 2.261, 258, 261, 264 (cf. *Ant.* 20.97), 259. See further *War* 2.258-265; 6.286-288; *Ant.* 20.97-99, 167-172.

[59] See Tomasino, "Oracles," 87. Josephus also notes how, during the siege of Jerusalem, the revolutionary leaders used these prophetic figures to prevent the populace from deserting, by convincing them to await God's coming deliverance (*War* 6.286). See Tomasino, "Oracles," 105–6; cf. Warren J. Heard and Kazuhiko Yamazaki-Ransom, "Revolutionary Movements," in Joel B. Green (ed.), *Dictionary of Jesus and the Gospels*, Second Edition (Downers Grove: IVP Academic, 2013), 789–99, here 793.

Jewish War 5.379-390 as Representative of Josephus' Perspective on Jewish Attempts to Achieve Freedom through Violence

It is directly in connection with these prominent elements of Josephus' work—his portrayal of the Jewish revolt against Rome, the revolutionary groups he deems responsible for it, and their eschatological motivations—that we must understand his quasi-historical survey of biblical material in 5.379-390, for it was precisely such individuals to whom his speech was originally directed. Josephus himself had previously believed, and acted on the belief, that violent revolutionary action was appropriate for a faithful Jew.[60] However, by the time he wrote the *War*, Josephus had embraced a different view, whether for ideological or pragmatic reasons (or both). Aware of the formative role that Israel's history played in shaping Jewish expectations of God's forthcoming deliverance, he constructed this outline of Israel's past—though perfectly aware that it was selective, and not fully representative of the history of Israel—in order to convince his audience likewise.

A crucial component of this speech is Josephus' suggestion—implicit, but nevertheless present—that Rome is *not* eternal.[61] This results from what Jonathan Price calls Josephus' "teleological view of history," which places the Jews, "who are 'beloved of God' (θεοφιλεῖς, 5.381) at the centre."[62] Though τύχη might *presently* rest with the Romans, though God νῦν ἐπὶ τῆς Ἰταλίας εἶναι (5.367), this would *not* be forever. Josephus eagerly looks forward to the day when God would restore Israel to a position of self-ruled power, "when the 'rod of empire' would rest over Judaea instead of over Rome."[63] Crucially, however, Josephus believes that it is *not* the responsibility of God's faithful people either to inaugurate this day or to effect this transformation. The wise, trusting in God's providence, should not themselves try to engineer change—this is the prerogative of God alone. Rather, since (in the fullness of time) redemption is a certainty, faithful Israel is called to wait—peacefully and piously—on God's timing. Though God's plan involves the *eventual* establishment of Jerusalem as the place from which his rule would go forth through his people Israel, Josephus believes that their *present* subjugation to the power of Rome is also God's intention.[64] As had happened many times before,

---

[60] Josephus provides autobiographical accounts of his own military activity in *War* 1–3 and *The Life*. See Giorgio Jossa, "Josephus' Action in Galilee during the Jewish War," in Fausto Parente and Joseph Sievers (eds.), *Josephus and the History of the Greco-Roman Period: Essays in Memory of Morton Smith*, StPB 41 (Leiden: Brill, 1994), 265–78.

[61] Mason, "Josephus, Daniel," 176–7; on Josephus' subtle yet persistent emphasis on the temporary nature of Rome's rule, see Bilde, *Flavius Josephus*, 77, 148, 186–7.

[62] Price, "The Provincial Historian," 116; cf. Otto Kaiser, "'Our Forefathers Never Triumphed By Arms ...': The Interpretation of Biblical History in the Addresses of Flavius Josephus to the Besieged Jerusalemites in Bell. Jud. V. 356-426," in Núria Calduch-Benages and Jan Liesen (eds.), *History and Identity: How Israel's Later Authors Viewed Its Earlier History*, DCLY 2006 (Berlin: de Gruyter, 2006), 253.

[63] Spilsbury, "Reading the Bible," 226.

[64] Mason, "Josephus, Daniel," 181, 190.

God was using a foreign nation to punish the iniquity of his people—this time, as a result of the impiety of the ἄνομοι revolutionaries (5.395).[65]

Therefore, the passionate hostility which Josephus bears toward those he deems responsible for the revolt against Rome (and its resultant devastation) is rooted in his conviction that violence oriented toward overcoming power structures put in place by God is not only doomed to failure: as an act of rebellion against the divine will, it is itself *profane* (5.377, 378, 412). Those who oppose the Romans are in effect refusing to accept the punishment they deserve for their iniquity (*Ant*. 18.7-9). As Steve Mason observes, they are like the "violent ones" (בני פריץ) of Daniel 11:14, those who attempt to force the inauguration of God's kingdom ahead of the divine schedule.[66] In contrast, Josephus emphasizes that God's help had come to his people who endured their fate in faith and trust (*War* 1.377-392), and this deliverance came without the need for their violent participation.[67] "Though they might have delivered themselves by resort to arms and violence," God brought the Israelites out of slavery in Egypt "without bloodshed, without risk" (ἀναιμάκτους ἀκινδύνους, 5.382, 383). When it was according to God's will, the enemies of Israel were defeated *without* resort to arms (5.379-389); when they made their own decision to fight they were "invariably defeated" (5.390).[68]

Josephus' words in *War* 5.379-389 thus represent a response to those of his Jewish contemporaries whose desire for freedom from Rome had led to their disastrous and hopeless present situation under siege in Jerusalem. More significantly for our purposes, however, is the fact that insofar as that desire was rooted in a particular understanding and expression of the Jewish eschatological hope, Josephus' words represent a response to such motivations for violent revolution. Josephus believes that the *only* way the Jewish people will survive is by laying down their arms and trusting God for their future. Enlisting his rhetorical abilities in service of this point, Josephus draws out the lessons of the past in making an exhortation in the present.[69] To be a faithful Israelite was not to take up the sword against Rome, but to submit to those God had raised up over them, trusting that God would, out of his own faithfulness and in his own timing, one day himself act to deliver his people.

---

[65] Cf. 5.391-398, 6.110; see James S. McLaren, "Delving into the Dark Side: Josephus' Foresight as Hindsight," in Zuleika Rodgers (ed.), *Making History: Josephus and Historical Method* (Leiden: Brill, 2007), 59; cf. H. Lindner, *Die Geschichtsauffassung Des Flavius Josephus Im Belud Judaicum: Gleichzeitig Ein Beitrag Zur Quellenfrage* (Leiden: Brill, 1972), 33 n. 2.

[66] Mason, "Josephus, Daniel," 183–4.

[67] Walker, "God Is With Italy Now," 182.

[68] Mason, "Josephus, Daniel," 181; cf. Spilsbury, "Reading the Bible," 213–14.

[69] Bilde, *Flavius Josephus*, 76, and Price, "The Provincial Historian," 114, both observe that, although the rhetoric may have failed before the walls of Jerusalem, Josephus was *still* trying to convince his Jewish readers of his view, in order to prevent a repetition of the catastrophe of 70 CE.

Conclusion

Josephus' speech can thus be understood as an attempt directly to counter certain claims regarding the role of God's people in the eschatological culmination, claims that were founded on a particular reading of Israel's past. The Yaḥad's understanding of Israel's history and prophetic witness led them to expect that they themselves would be the instruments of God's violent judgment upon the wicked. Though declaring that the war ultimately belonged to God, the *War Scroll* clearly affirms that God's victory would be effected by the righteous who themselves, in faith, would take up the sword. By demonstrating the eschatologically-determined motivations lying behind much of the revolutionary activity recorded by Josephus, this chapter has suggested that 1QM can thus be seen to represent a literary embodiment of the eschatological perspective held by many of the Jews who took up the sword against Rome in 66 CE.

For Josephus, in contrast, the active role remains entirely with God. The obedience of the faithful is not expressed in their willingness to fight and die, but in "commit[ting] themselves to God" (5.382). Providing examples from Israel's past to support his claim, Josephus declares that those who lift up their hands to God, "at rest from arms" (5.388), would be delivered. Josephus does not dismiss Jewish longing for ἐλευθερία, nor deny its significance, but emphasizes the need to attain it by the proper methods (*Ant.* 6.20-21). Rather than resorting to violence out of righteous zeal, "the duty of the occupants of holy ground" is "to leave everything to the arbitrament of God and to scorn the aid of human hands" (*War* 5.400). Those who choose otherwise, taking the route of violent zeal, are without hope—indeed, it was the embrace of just such a perspective that resulted in the horror of the conditions in Jerusalem under Roman siege, and the terrible consequences of the rebellion's inevitable conclusion.

Thus, in his speech outside the walls of Jerusalem, Josephus offers an alternative interpretation of the events of Israel's past to that presented in the *War Scroll*, in order to make an alternative claim about what it means for faithful Israel to hope and trust in God's deliverance. Emphasizing God's control of history, Josephus argues that it is not taking up the sword in righteous zeal that identifies God's people; rather, true Israel is characterized by its faithful trust that God himself would act, in God's own timing, to fulfill his promises.

Chapter 9

THE FIERY ORIGINS OF GEHENNA IN ISAIAH, ENOCH, JESUS, AND BEYOND

Craig A. Evans

The concept of a fiery Gehenna as a place of eschatological judgment was entertained by many Jews, including Jesus of Nazareth, at the turn of the era. How and when the "Valley of Hinnom" (גיא הנם), south of Jerusalem and notorious for its history of human sacrifice, emerged as the face of hell is uncertain.[1] The grim history of the place is alluded to in Hebrew Scripture of the fifth and sixth centuries BCE. According to Jeremiah the prophet, God complains that the people of Judah "have built the high place of Topheth, which is in the valley of Ben Hinnom, to burn their sons and their daughters in the fire" (Jer 7:31; cf. 19:2-6; 32:35). Ahaz, king of Judah, is sharply criticized, because "he burned incense in the valley of Ben Hinnom, and burned his sons as an offering" (2 Chr 28:3; not in 2 Kgs 16:3). The same is said of Manasseh, who is said to have "burned his sons as an offering in the valley of Ben Hinnom" (2 Chr 33:6; not in 2 Kgs 21:6, but see 23:10). The Chronicler has enhanced the wickedness of kings Ahaz and Manasseh. Why the Valley of Hinnom is referred to as the "valley of Ben Hinnom," or, literally, the "valley of the son of Hinnom [גֵּי בֶן־הִנֹּם]" is unknown. The precise purpose of "passing through the fire" (as in 2 Kings) or "he burned with fire" in the Valley of Ben Hinnom (as in 2 Chronicles) is uncertain, but it may have had to do with divination (cf. Deut 18:10). It is not clear that child sacrifice was in view in the relevant passages in 2 Kings, but that appears to be the meaning in 2 Chronicles[2] and Jeremiah (esp. 19:5-6).[3]

---

[1] See the old but still very useful study by J. A. Montgomery, "The Holy City and Gehenna," *JBL* 27 (1908): 24–47. For more recent treatments, see L. R. Bailey, "Gehenna: The Topography of Hell," *BA* 49 (1986): 187–91; D. F. Watson, "Gehenna," *ABD* 2: 926-8. Bailey (188–89) and others rightly call into question the tradition that Hinnom was a garbage dump.

[2] S. Japhet, *I & II Chronicles*, OTL (Louisville: Westminster John Knox, 1993), 898.

[3] J. R. Lundbom, *Jeremiah 1-20: A New Translation with Introduction and Commentary*, AB 21A (New York: Doubleday, 1999), 496–8, 838–40.

It is possible that the actual location of the Valley of Hinnom was understood as the entrance into the realm of the god Molech (or Moloch).[4] It is out of this ancient practice and the severe criticism of it by Israel's prophets that the tradition of Gehenna as a place of fiery torment had its beginning. (In later Greco-Roman times, various caverns, some of them smoldering from volcanic fumes, were identified as openings to the underworld of Hades or Pluto.[5])

Early Traditions of Gehenna

The Judeo-Christian tradition of Gehenna begins with the "Valley of Hinnom" references that have already been mentioned, but it is the strange concluding verse in the book of Isaiah that decisively moves the tradition in an eschatological direction. The verse is strange, not simply because of its contents, but because of its location: it appears after several sublime oracles of restoration for Zion, such as: "Rejoice with Jerusalem, and be glad for her, all you who love her," the prophet enjoins (Isa 66:10). "Behold, I will extend prosperity to her like a river," the Lord promises, "and the wealth of nations … " (v. 12). "Those who sanctify and purify themselves" will enter the garden (v. 17). The Lord will gather all peoples to Zion, that they might see his glory (vv. 18-21). The Lord will make a new heaven and a new earth; Zion's descendants will remain with God; and "all flesh shall come to worship before me, says the Lord" (vv. 22-23). This last verse no doubt reminded ancient readers of the beginning of chapter 40, where the prophet comforts the people of Israel and promises that the "glory of the Lord shall be revealed, (and) all flesh shall see it together" (40:5). One would have expected the book of Isaiah to end with v. 23. But no, it ends with v. 24:

> And they shall go forth and look on the dead bodies of the men that have rebelled against me; for their worm shall not die, their fire shall not be quenched, and they shall be an abhorrence to all flesh.

Many interpreters have expressed dismay over the presence of this verse. In Jewish liturgy (i.e., the Sabbath *haphtarah*) v. 23 is repeated after v. 24,[6] so that the reading from Isaiah ends on a more positive note. No commentator has expressed more disappointment with Isaiah's conclusion than Bernhard Duhm, whose engaging discussion of v. 24 will give us much to discuss below. But as

---

[4] Montgomery, "The Holy City and Gehenna," 35–40. See also G. C. Heider, "Molech," in *ABD* 4: 895–8; idem, "Molech," in *DDD*, 581–5.

[5] For a description of the Plutonium at Hierapolis, see Strabo, *Geographica* 13.4.14; cf. 5.4.5.

[6] I. W. Slotki, *Isaiah*, Soncino Books of the Bible (London: Soncino Press, 1949), 326.

for his disappointment with this verse, this is what he says: "It is sad that a book that contains the most wonderful, sublime, most important, and most pious material in the whole of the Old Testament now closes with such a demonic dissonance."[7]

It is speculated that Isa 66:24 reflects or is perhaps a reworking of either Isa 50:11, or 66:15-16, or both. At 50:11 the prophet warns: "Behold, all you who kindle a fire, who set brands alight! Walk by the light of your fire, and by the brands which you have kindled! This shall you have from my hand: you shall lie down in torment." The threat of reciprocity, the reference to fire, and the reference to lying down "in torment" (מַעֲצֵבָה / ἐν λύπῃ) could have contributed to the baleful imagery of 66:24. That Isa 50:11 caught the interest of later Jewish interpreters is witnessed by the Targum, which paraphrases the text to read: "Behold, all you who kindle a fire, *who grasp a sword*! Go, *fall* in the fire *which you kindled* and on the *sword which you grasped*!" (with italics indicating departures from the Hebrew).[8] That Jesus himself in Matt 26:52 ("all who take the sword will perish by the sword") appears to echo the Aramaic paraphrase suggests that the eschatological interpretation of the passage was in circulation no later than the beginning of the first century CE.

At 66:15-16, where we again find fire and sword together, the prophet declares: "For behold, the Lord will come in fire, and his chariots like the stormwind, to render his anger in fury, and his rebuke with flames of fire.[16] For by fire will the Lord execute judgment, and by his sword, upon all flesh; and those slain by the Lord shall be many." In v. 17 the prophet promises that those who eat swine's flesh and practice other abominations "will come to an end together, says the Lord." It is

---

[7] B. Duhm, *Das Buch Jesaia*, HKAT III/1 (Göttingen: Vandenhoeck & Ruprecht, 1892), 458: *Es ist traurig, dass ein Buch, das mit das Herrlichste, Erhabenste, Bedeutendste und Frömmste im ganzen A. T. enhält, jetzt mit einem solchen dämonischen Missklang schliesst.* I am intentionally making use of Duhm's first edition, rather than the fourth edition (1922), which is the edition that commentators usually cite. Duhm's *dämonischen Missklang* (which is also what is said in the fourth edition) could also be translated "fiendish discordancy."

[8] The translation is by B. D. Chilton, *The Isaiah Targum*, ArBib 11 (Wilmington, DE: Michael Glazier, 1987), 99. Chilton also remarks on the parallel with Jesus's saying in Matthew and the probability that the targumic reading is early. Chilton believes the exegetical framework of the Isaiah Targum fits best the period between the two great Jewish rebellions of 66–70 CE and 132–135 CE. See B. D. Chilton, *The Glory of Israel: The Theology and Provenience of the Isaiah Targum*, JSOTSup 23 (Sheffield: JSOT Press, 1982). The Aramaic paraphrase of Isa 50:11 is probably earlier (and Chilton allows for earlier, as well as later traditions in the Targum), not only because of the evident coherence with an utterance of Jesus, but because the addition of *sword* may be a reflection of the several armed rebellions that plagued Judea in the aftermath of Herod's death and direct Roman rule. The dominical utterance coheres well with such a social setting.

possible that Isa 66:15-17 with its reference to fire and the slaying of many, perhaps read in the light of the threats of 50:11, inspired the graphic and crude v. 24.[9]

So when was Isa 66:24 added to the Isaianic collection? In his groundbreaking 1892 commentary on Isaiah, Duhm describes chapters 56-66 as a "third source" that is not as old as the material that makes up chapters 40-55, a section that had become known in nineteenth-century scholarship as Deutero-Isaiah. This third source, which Duhm suggested calling Trito-Isaiah, originally comprised two halves, chapters 56-60 and 61-66, which were ordered and added to the Isaianic collection by the scribe who edited chapters 40-55.[10] However, Duhm was not sure what to make of Isa 66:24. He thinks the author of this curious verse thought of the place of fire as *Ge Hinnom*, the Valley of Hinnom, described in *1 Enoch* 27, the precursor of what in Judeo-Christian eschatology would become hell, the place of everlasting judgment. Duhm believes that the author of this verse understood that the rotting, burning corpses of the wicked dead are never wholly consumed, which is part of the concept of hell. Duhm also draws attention to Dan 12:2, which will be discussed in a moment, then concludes his commentary, as well as his discussion of v. 24, on a note of sadness, as we have seen, that such a horrid image appears at the end of what is otherwise sublime and wonderful material.[11]

Duhm dates Isaiah 56-66 to the time of Ezra and Nehemiah, which later commentators have followed.[12] Duhm does not argue for a specific date for Isa 66:24, but two or three of his observations I think potentially help us date this verse. He calls our attention to Dan 12:2, where the angel tells Daniel that "many of those who sleep in the dust of the earth shall awake, some to everlasting life, and some to shame and everlasting contempt [דראון / αἰσχύνην]" and rightly notes

---

[9] Duhm (*Das Buch Jesaia*, 458) doubts the two fires of Isa 66:16 and 66:24 could be combined by a Jewish writer, for surely it would constitute a "blasphemy." I disagree. I doubt an ancient Jewish scribe would make such a fine distinction. There is no reason that the expressions "flames of fire" and "by fire ... execute judgment" in 66:15-16 could not, in the apocalyptic imagination of a pious scribe, be seen as linked to the fires of final judgment described in 66:24. The unquenchable fire of v. 24 expands upon and clarifies what is meant in v. 16, when we are told there that the Lord will execute judgment "by fire."

[10] Duhm, *Das Buch Jesaia*, xiii–xiv.

[11] Duhm, *Das Buch Jesaia*, 458. I have summed up the most salient points of Duhm's comments on Isa 66:24.

[12] For examples, see C. Westermann, *Isaiah 40-66*, OTL (London: SCM Press; Philadelphia: Westminster, 1969), 295–6; J. Blenkinsopp, *Isaiah 56-66: A New Translation with Introduction and Commentary*, AB 19B (New York: Doubleday, 2003), 52–60, esp. 54. Blenkinsopp dates the whole of Isaiah 56-66 to the middle of the fifth century BCE, perhaps a bit earlier. Westermann places the chapters "between 537 and 455" BCE. For a helpful overview of how Trito-Isaiah relates to Deutero-Isaiah (with emphasis on intertextuality), see B. S. Childs, *Isaiah: A Commentary*, OTL (Louisville: John Knox Press, 2001), 440–9.

that *dir'ōn* may echo Isa 66:24, where the cognate *dērā'ōn* occurs: "They shall be an abhorrence [דֵּרָאוֹן] to all flesh." These are the only occurrences of דרא in the Hebrew scriptures. It is probable that Dan 12:2 and Isa 66:24, in speaking of abhorrence/contempt, are describing the same eschatological scenario in which the wicked are judged. Although no fire is mentioned in Dan 12:2, it is mentioned in Dan 7:11, where Daniel says, "And as I looked, the beast was slain, and its body destroyed and given over to be burned with fire." The fire that will burn the beast's body is the fire of judgment.

Duhm also calls our attention to *1 Enoch* 27.[13] As we shall see below, *1 Enoch* 27 is describing Gehenna, to be sure, but a closer parallel, both in language and in chronology, is *1 Enoch* 90:24-27, which speaks of a fiery abyss located to the south of the city of Jerusalem. And finally, Duhm rightly suspects that Isa 66:24 is describing Gehenna, or the Valley of Hinnom, which is mentioned in old scriptures, as we have seen. It is, of course, the geographical setting that comes to be understood as the place of fiery Gehenna. At many points Duhm has put us on the right track. A review of the pertinent post-biblical texts and traditions will, I think, bear this out.

Early Expressions and Interpretations of Gehenna

One of the earliest post-biblical traditions to make reference to Gehenna, though not by this name, is found in *1 Enoch* 10, a passage from one of the oldest sources of the Enochic materials. It is believed that chapter 10, part of the so-called Book of the Watchers (*1 Enoch* 1-36), attested in old Aramaic fragments at Qumran,[14] probably dates to the third century BCE. The relevant part reads as follows (according to the Greek):[15]

> [13] Then they will be led away to the abyss of fire [τὸ χάος τοῦ πυρός], and to the torture, and to the prison where they will be confined forever. [14] And whoever

---

[13] Followed, among others, by Westermann, *Isaiah 40-66*, 429.

[14] 4Q201 col. v preserves fragments of *1 Enoch* 10:3-4, 4Q202 col. iv preserves fragments of *1 Enoch* 10:8-12, and 4Q204 col. v preserves portions of *1 Enoch* 10:13-19.

[15] The Greek text derives from the sixth-century Gizeh Fragment, or Codex Panopolitanus (P. Cairo 10759). For the text of 10:13-14 I have consulted the transcriptions in U. Bouriant, "Fragments grecs du livre d'Énoch," in U. Bouriant et al. (eds.), *Mémoires publiés par les membres de la Mission archéologique française au Caire* 9/1 (Paris: Ernest Leroux, 1892), 107; R. H. Charles, *The Ethiopic Version of the Book of Enoch, Edited from Twenty-three MSS., Together with the Fragmentary Greek and Latin Versions*, AnOx (Oxford: Clarendon Press, 1906), 29; M. Black (ed.), *Apocalypsis Henochi Graece*, PVTG 3 (Leiden: Brill, 1970), 25–6.

should be condemned[16] and destroyed henceforth will be bound with them until the consummation of their generation.[17]

(*1 Enoch* 10:13-14)

The Aramaic text preserved at Qumran (4Q204 col. v, lines 1–2) agrees with the Greek, so far as can be observed.[18]

The passage envisions an eschatological judgment of fire that will destroy the fallen angels and the giants (*1 Enoch* 10:4-15). It is possible that this place of fire is Gehenna, the place of judgment into which wicked humans will be cast. R. H. Charles thinks it is equating the "fiery abyss" of *1 Enoch* 10:13-14 with "the lake of fire and brimstone" (ἡ λίμνη τοῦ πυρός καὶ θείου) of Rev 20:10, 14-15, into which the Devil, the Beast (i.e., the Antichrist), all of Hell (or Hades), and anyone whose name is not written in the Book of Life will be cast on the day of judgment.[19] This is the same fiery place mentioned in Matt 25:41, where the enthroned Son of Man, or messianic King, will say to the wicked, "Depart from me, you cursed ones, into the eternal fire [τὸ πῦρ τὸ αἰώνιον] prepared for the Devil and his angels" (RSV,

---

[16] Reading κατακριθῇ. Black (*Apocalypsis Henochi Graece*, 26) reads κατακαυθῇ, "be burned up," while Charles (*Ethiopic Version*, 29) reads κατακαυσθῇ, but in a note (29 n. 5) he states the word is "Corrupt for κατακριθῇ." See also J. T. Milik, *The Books of Enoch: Aramaic Fragments of Qumrân Cave Four* (with collaboration of M. Black; Oxford: Clarendon Press, 1976), 190 (with comments on lines 1–2); G. W. E. Nickelsburg, *1 Enoch 1: A Commentary on the Book of 1 Enoch, Chapters 1-36; 81-108*, Hermeneia (Minneapolis: Fortress, 2001), 218 n. 14a.

[17] Translation based on Nickelsburg, *1 Enoch*, 215. The Ethiopic manuscripts of Enoch (*maṣḥafa ḥēnok*) read only slightly differently. Ephraim Isaac translates the Ethiopic text as follows: "In those days they will lead them into the bottom of the fire—and in torment—in the prison (where) they will be locked up forever.[14] And at the time when they will burn and die, those who collaborated with them will be bound together with them from henceforth unto the end of (all) generations." See. E. Isaac, "1 (Ethiopic Apocalypse of) Enoch," in *OTP* 1:18. In a note Isaac comments that the last part of the verse is corrupt. See also Nickelsburg, *1 Enoch*, 213.

[18] For the text of 4Q204, see Milik, *The Books of Enoch*, 189; F. García Martínez and E. J. C. Tigchelaar, *The Dead Sea Scrolls Study Edition. Volume One: 1Q1–4Q273* (Leiden: Brill, 1997), 414.

[19] In pre-Christian literature and tradition the idea of a lake in the underworld is relatively rare. According to Plato, "those who are found to have lived neither well nor ill go to the Acheron [Ἀχέροντα] and … arrive at the lake [εἰς τὴν λίμνην]; there they dwell and are purified"; but those found to be incorrigible are cast into Tartarus (Plato, *Phaedo* 113DE). One magical text includes a poem, in which reference is made to underworld imagery, including "the Acherusian lake of Hades [Ἀχερουσίατε λίμνη Ἀΐδου]" (*PGM* IV.1462-1463). Another refers to "the sacred lake called Abyss [τῇ ἱερᾷ τῇ λίμνῃ τῇ καλουμένῃ ἀβύσσῳ]" (*PGM* VII.517).

9. The Fiery Origins of Gehenna 147

modified).²⁰ Charles could be correct, but Nickelsburg calls for caution in light of what appears to be *two* places of fiery judgment described in *1 Enoch* 21:7-10 and 27:2-3 (=90:24-27). It is late texts, Nickelsburg notes, such as Revelation 20 and Matthew 25, that speak of a single place of fiery judgment.²¹

However, the Matthean Jesus himself apparently interprets *1 Enoch* 10 as Charles suggests. In the parable of the Marriage Feast (Matt 22:2-14) the wrathful king commands his servants with respect to the guest who lacks appropriate attire: "Bind him hand and foot, and cast him into the outer darkness [δήσαντες αὐτοῦ πόδας καὶ χεῖρας ἐκβάλετε αὐτὸν εἰς τὸ σκότος τὸ ἐξώτερον]; there men will weep and gnash their teeth" (22:13, RSV). The command clearly echoes the language of *1 Enoch* 10:4, where God commands the archangel Raphael: "Bind Azael foot and hand, and cast him into the darkness [δῆσον τὸν Ἀζαὴλ ποσὶν καὶ χερσίν, καὶ βάλε αὐτὸν εἰς τὸ σκότος], and open the desert that is in the Dadouel, and cast him in."²² This parallel could suggest that in the dominical tradition and perhaps in other roughly contemporaneous Jewish traditions the abyss of fire in *1 Enoch* 10, into which the fallen angels and their offspring will be cast, is Gehenna, the place of future judgment for the wicked of humanity.

Another interesting feature is the use of the word χάος, which in the context of *1 Enoch* means abyss. The word can mean, of course, "chaos," usually in reference to the primordial state of the Cosmos (LSJ). A very old example of this meaning is found in Hesiod, which is quoted by pagan, Jewish, and Christian authors.²³ The pagan idea of primordial chaos is similar to the ancient near eastern concept, as expressed in Gen 1:2: "The earth was invisible and unformed, and darkness was over the abyss" (LXX). Here "abyss" is not χάος but ἄβυσσος.²⁴ χάος can also mean "chasm" (cf. Mic 1:6; Zech 14:4).

---

[20] R. H. Charles, *The Book of Enoch, or 1 Enoch, Translated from the Editor's Ethiopic Text* (Oxford: Clarendon Press, 1912), 25.

[21] Nickelsburg, *1 Enoch*, 225.

[22] For compelling arguments in support of seeing *1 Enoch* 10:4 echoed in the Matthean parable, see D. C. Sim, "Matthew 22.13a and 1 Enoch 10.4a: A Case of Literary Dependence?" *JSNT* 47 (1992): 3–19. The "desert" (ἔρημος) that is to be opened up is to the south of Jerusalem, where the Valley of Hinnom is located. Nickelsburg (*1 Enoch*, 221) thinks it is probably Sheol. On the derivation and meaning of Dadouel (Δαδουήλ), see Nickelsburg, *1 Enoch*, 222.

[23] We find examples in Aristotle, who, quoting Hesiod (cf. *Theogonia*, 116–117), says chaos (χάος) was made first, then Earth (*Metaphysica* 1.984b; also quoted in Pausanias, *Graeciae descriptio* 9.27.2). The tradition appears in Christian (Theophilus, *Ad Autolycum* 2.6) and Jewish (Philo, *De aeternitate mundi* 17–18) writers. Elsewhere Aristotle says that "chaos or night [χάος ἢ νύξ] did not endure for an infinite time" (12.1072a; cf. 14.1091b, where χάος is said to be "one of the original forces").

[24] In the Jewish scriptures ἄβυσσος is usually associated with water (e.g., Gen 7:11; 8:2; Deut 33:13; Pss 32:7; 70:20-21; Prov 3:20; 8:24; Job 38:16).

In the book of *Jubilees* χάος and ἄβυσσος appear together in the retelling of creation:

> For on the first day he made the uppermost heavens, the earth, the waters, from which are snow and ice and hailstones and frost and dew. The spirits that minister before him are as follows: angels before (his) face, and angels of glory, and angels of the spirits of winds, angels of clouds and darkness, snow and hailstones and frost, angels of sounds, thunders, lightnings, cold, heat, winter, autumn, spring and summer; and all of the spirits of his creatures that are in the heavens and on the earth, the deeps, the (region) beneath the earth, and the chasm, and the darkness [τὰς ἀβύσσους, τήν τε ὑποκάτω τῆς γῆς, καὶ τοῦ χάους, καὶ σκότος], evening and night, the light of day and early morning.[25]
>
> (*Jub.* 2:2)

It is important to note the appearance of καὶ τοῦ χάους, "and the chasm," which lacks a corresponding element in the shorter, simpler Hebrew version preserved at Qumran (i.e., 4Q216 col. v, lines 9-10). The Greek translator evidently does not view the χάος as simply another way of referring to the ἄβυσσοι.[26] The ἄβυσσοι, "depths," reflect the "depth" of the Hebrew version (תהום).[27] The appearance of the χάος introduces a new element in the creation account, perhaps as part of the underworld. In the translation above, τοῦ χάους is rendered "the chasm," but it may, in fact, refer to hell or Gehenna. In later Christian tradition the χάος is linked to Tartaros itself, as we read in a second-century addition to the *Sibylline Oracles*: "And then the yawning earth will show Tartarean chaos [Ταρτάρεον δὲ χάος]" (*Sib. Or.* 8:241).

Assembling, editing, and composing his wisdom around 180 BCE Yeshua ben Sira exhorts the wise (according to the Hebrew version) to avoid pride: "More and more, humble your pride; what awaits man is the worm [רמה]" (Sir 7:17; quoted in *m. 'Abot* 4.4). The Hebrew version is based on mss A and C from the Cairo Genizah.[28] Ben Sira's morbid reference to the worm may be an allusion to

---

[25] The partially preserved Hebrew text contains fewer elements and so is closer to the MT than to the lengthier Greek. The relevant words in 4Q216 are התהו[מות] מאפלה ("depths, darkness"). There is no equivalent of καὶ τοῦ χάους.

[26] Although it is possible that χάος of Greek *Jub.* 2:2 reflects *tohū* of Gen 1:2, this is suggested in R. H. Charles, *The Book of Jubilees, or the Little Genesis*, with Introduction by G. H. Box, Translations of Early Documents I. Palestinian Jewish Texts 4 (London: SPCK; New York: Macmillan, 1917), 41 n. 1.

[27] "Depths" is plural in Ps 135:6. See also 1QH[a] col. ix, lines 13–14.

[28] The reconstructed Hebrew text of ben Sira can be found in I. Lévi, *The Hebrew Text of the Book of Ecclesiasticus*, SSS 3 (Leiden: Brill, 1904), 9; M. Segal, *The Book of Ben-Sira Completum* [Hebrew] (Jerusalem: Bialik, 1953), 44; and P. C. Beentjes, *The Book of Ben Sira in Hebrew: A Text Edition of all Extant Hebrew Manuscripts and a Synopsis of all Parallel Hebrew Ben Sira Texts*, VTSup 68 (Leiden: Brill, 1997), 30. The relationship of the several Hebrew mss and the Greek and Syriac translations is a complicated one.

Job 25:6: "how much less man, who is a maggot [רִמָּה], and the son of man, who is a worm [תּוֹלֵעָה / σκώληξ]!" (RSV). The ancient sage seems to have had in mind no more than death and decay, the fate that awaits all mortals.[29]

However, in the Greek translation produced by ben Sira's grandson (c. 132 BCE) the worm takes on a more sinister meaning. The text is rendered: "Humble yourself greatly, for the punishment of the ungodly is fire and worm [ἐκδίκησις ἀσεβοῦς πῦρ καὶ σκώληξ]" (Sir 7:17 RSVA).[30] The grandson has introduced the explicit theme of judgment with the word ἐκδίκησις, "punishment."[31] His πῦρ καὶ σκώληξ, "fire and worm," is an unmistakable allusion to the worm and fire of Isa 66:24 (ὁ σκώληξ ... καὶ τὸ πῦρ). The translator no doubt found warrant for this paraphrase because of what is said in the previous verse (v. 16): "Do not count yourself among the crowd of sinners; remember that wrath [עכרון / ὀργή] does not delay" (Sir 7:16 RSVA). Verses 16 and 17 would have been understood as synonymous parallelism, so that one might infer that the wrath of v. 16 and the worm of v. 17 speak of judgment and punishment, not simply death and decay (as in Job). Hence the worm of corruption becomes the fiery worm of punishment.

We have another relevant text from the book of *Enoch*, probably composed sometime between ben Sira's original Hebrew version and his grandson's Greek version. It reads:

> [24] And judgment was exacted first on the stars, and they were judged and found to be sinners. And they went to the place of judgment, and they threw them into an abyss.[32] [25] And those seventy shepherds were judged and found to be sinners, and they were thrown into that fiery abyss.[26] And I saw at that time that an abyss like it was opened in the middle of the earth, which was full of fire. And they brought those blinded sheep, and they were all judged and found to be sinners. And they were thrown into that fiery abyss, and they were burned. And that abyss was to the south of that house.[27] And I saw those sheep burning and their bones burning.[33]
>
> (*1 Enoch* 90:24-27)

---

[29] Post-mortem rewards and punishments are not entertained in the Wisdom of ben Sira. See P. W. Skehan and A. A. Di Lella, *The Wisdom of Ben Sira*, AB 39 (Garden City: Doubleday, 1987), 83–7.

[30] Vg: *quoniam vindicta carnis impii ignis et vermes*, "for the vengeance on the flesh of the impious is fire and worms."

[31] The Greek translation reflects the relatively recent development of ideas about post-mortem retribution and rewards. On this point, see G. H. Box and W. O. E. Oesterley, "Sirach," in *APOT* 1: 340; Skehan and Di Lella, *The Wisdom of Ben Sira*, 201–2. The change in thinking may have been due to the pogroms and persecution inaugurated by Antiochus IV (d. 164 BCE), as suggested by J. G. Snaith, *Ecclesiasticus* (The Cambridge Bible Commentary on the New English Bible; Cambridge: Cambridge University Press, 1974), 43.

[32] Nickelsburg (*1 Enoch 1*, 403) emends 'emuq ("deep") to 'emaq ("depth" or "abyss").

[33] Translation from Nickelsburg, *1 Enoch 1*, 402. *1 Enoch* 90 is dated to 165–161 BCE in Isaac, "1 (Ethiopic Apocalypse of) Enoch," 7. See 4 Macc 6:26 "burned to his very bones."

The "fiery abyss," which is "full of fire" and "south of that house," that is, south of either the city of Jerusalem or the temple, is Gehenna, even if the name itself does not appear.[34] This fire, which burns so hot that even the bones of the wicked are burned, is probably the unquenchable fire described in Isa 66:24.[35]

We may have an allusion to the worms of Isa 66:24 in the graphic description of the death of Antiochus IV Epiphanes in the highly theological and apologetic work known as 2 Maccabees, a work that dates to about 140 BCE.[36] After his blasphemies and threats against the people of Israel, the king is fatally stricken (cf. 2 Macc 9:5 "an incurable and unseen blow"). We are told that "the ungodly man's body swarmed with worms [σκώληκας ἀναζεῖν], and while he was still living in anguish and pain, his flesh rotted away, and because of his stench the whole army felt revulsion at his decay [βαρύνεσθαι τὴν σαπρίαν]" (2 Macc 9:9, RSVA).

A number of commentators suspect an allusion to the worm of Isa 66:24.[37] Gonzalo Aranda Pérez, for example, says, "This form of death is a foretaste of the later destiny of Antiochus" and then references Isa 66:24.[38] I am inclined to agree, but in his Anchor Bible Commentary Jonathan Goldstein objects because the evil king is not a corpse eaten by worms but is still living.[39] He and several others rightly note that worms and death as judgment against the powerful and arrogant constitute a well-known motif in late antiquity.[40] (On this point he is quite correct;

---

[34] So A. Dillmann, *Das Buch Henoch* (Leipzig: Vogel, 1853), 284; Montgomery, "The Holy City and Gehenna," 38–40; G. H. Schodde, *The Book of Enoch: Translated from the Ethiopic, with Introduction and Notes* (Andover: Warren F. Draper, 1911), 240; R. H. Charles, *The Book of Enoch, or 1 Enoch* (Oxford: Clarendon Press, 1912), 213; Nickelsburg, *1 Enoch 1*, 404: "south of the city of Jerusalem." Dillmann also explicitly identifies the fiery abyss as Gehenna; and Schodde and Nickelsburg ("Valley of Hinnom").

[35] Charles, *The Book of Enoch*, 213. Patrick Tiller agrees. See P. A. Tiller, *A Commentary on the Animal Apocalypse of I Enoch*, SBLEJL 4 (Atlanta: Scholars Press, 1993), 368, 372. Supposing that the burning of the bones is nonsense, Charles thinks the original text read differently. I think an emendation is unnecessary, in light of what is said in 4 Macc 6:26. The language is hyperbolic.

[36] D. R. Schwartz, *2 Maccabees* (Commentaries on Early Jewish Literature; Berlin: de Gruyter, 2008), 11–15. T. Fischer (*ABD* 4:447) suggests 125 BCE.

[37] N. J. McEleney, "1-2 Maccabees," in R. E. Brown et al. (eds.), *The New Jerome Biblical Commentary* (Englewood Cliffs, NJ: Prentice Hall, 1990), 444; R. Doran, "2 Maccabees," in M. Goodman (ed.), *The Apocrypha* (The Oxford Bible Commentary; Oxford: Oxford University Press, 2001), 175.

[38] G. Aranda Pérez, "2 Maccabees," in W. R. Farmer et al. (eds.), *The International Bible Commentary: A Catholic and Ecumenical Commentary for the Twenty-first Century* (Collegeville: Liturgical Press, 1998), 747.

[39] J. Goldstein, *II Maccabees*, AB 41A (Garden City: Doubleday, 1983), 354. The worms of Isa 66:24 have to do with corpses, not living persons.

[40] T. W. Africa, "Worms and the Death of Kings: A Cautionary Note on Disease and History," *ClAnt* 1 (1982): 1–17; A. Keaveney and J. A. Madden, "Phthiriasis and Its Victims," *Symbolae Osloenses* 57 (1982): 87–99; W. Nestle, "Legenden vom Tod der Gottesverächter," *ARW* 33 (1936): 246–69.

a few examples will be mentioned below.) The language of 2 Macc 9:9, like that of the original Hebrew version of Sira 7:17, has probably been influenced by Job 2:9; 7:5; 25:6; and Isa 14:11—not necessarily Isa 66:24.[41] Goldstein and company make a good point.

Admittedly, the reference to "worms" alone is not enough to permit the conclusion that we have an allusion to Isa 66:24 in 2 Macc 9:9, but the repeated references to the "stench" (ὀσμή, vv. 9, 10, 12) of the king's decaying flesh and the reference to "revulsion" (βαρύνεσθαι), *along with reference to the worms*, make us think of the corpses of the wicked, which in Isa 66:24 the righteous view and find "abhorrent" (דראון). The miserable description of the king's condition does seem intended to bring to mind his gruesome and fearful post-mortem destiny, as Aranda Pérez suggested.

The wormy demise of tyrants and the arrogant is commonplace in late antiquity. A few examples will suffice. After brutalizing the people of Barca, Queen Pheretima of Cyrene fled to Egypt and died a horrible death, "her body seething with maggots while still living"; which showed, says Herodotus, that excess "excites the anger of the gods" (Herodotus, *Historiae* 4.205).[42] After his murderous excesses, Cassander was infected with "worms while he was yet living" (Pausanias, *Graeciae descriptio* 9.7.2; cf. Marcus Junianus Justinus, *Liber Historiarum Philippicarum* 16.2.5). The avaricious Roman Sulla and others in ancient times died of worms, reports Plutarch (*Sulla* 36.2-4). According to Josephus, Herod the Great died miserably suffering from gangrene and worms (*J.W.* 1.656; *Ant.* 17.169). Herod's grandson Agrippa I, after killing the Apostle James, arresting the Apostle Peter, and accepting praise that should be given to God, "was eaten by worms [γενόμενος σκωληκόβρωτος] and died" (Acts 12:23; cf. Josephus, *Ant.* 19.346-350, who mentions several days of suffering but does not mention worms).

Lucian of Samosata (*c.* 180) tells us that the charlatan Alexander "met a most wretched end before the age of seventy," contrary to the latter's prophecy that he would live to the age of 150 and be carried off by a dramatic lightning strike (as had been Asclepius, the mortal doctor who afterward became a god). Instead, Alexander's "leg became infected all the way to the groin and was infested with worms [σκωλήκων ζέσας]." Soon after, he died miserably (Lucian, *Alexander pseudomantis* 59). In later apocryphal tradition, it is prophesied that Delilah the Philistine, who seduced and deceived Samson, "will rot away ... while living upon the earth, and worms will come out of her body [*vermes exient de corpore eius*]" (*LAB* 44:9). Commenting on the Hebrews who during the wilderness sojourn

---

[41] 2 Macc 9:9's σκώληκας ("worms") and τὴν σαπρίαν ("rot") may derive from Job 2:9[c], "You sit in the rot of worms [ἐν σαπρίᾳ σκωλήκων]," 7:5, "my body is defiled with the rot of worms [ἐν σαπρίᾳ σκωλήκων]," and Isa 14:11, "your glory has descended into Hades ... they will spread decay [σῆψιν] beneath you, and a worm [σκώληξ] will be your covering," while 2 Macc 9:10's τῶν οὐρανίων ἄστρων may echo τῶν ἄστρων τοῦ οὐρανοῦ of Isa 14:13.

[42] On the likelihood that the queen's condition was exaggerated, under the influence of the theme of divine retribution against the cruel and high-handed, see D. Asheri, A. Lloyd, and A. Corcella, *A Commentary on Herodotus Books I–IV* (ed. O. Murray and A. Moreno; Oxford: Oxford University Press, 2007), 721.

spread evil rumors and died of plague (Num 14:36-37), rabbinic tradition says "worms issued from their tongue" and eventually killed them (*b. Sotah* 35a).

Many examples of gruesome deaths are narrated by Lactantius (c. 240–c. 320) in his lurid tractate *De mortibus persecutorum*, whose purpose is to show that the exalted and powerful who persecuted and murdered Christians met with sorry ends themselves. Perhaps the most spectacular of these accounts is the death of the hated Emperor Galerius (d. 30 April 311), whose flesh, we are told, became putrid, gave off a horrific stench, and became infested with worms (Lactantius, *De mortibus persecutorum* 33.8-9; cf. Eusebius, *Hist. eccl.* 8.16.3-5 "a multitude of worms and a deadly stench").[43]

A number of potentially relevant passages in the book of *Enoch* are found in materials that date to about 105 BCE. The first speaks of a chasm and fire:

> And I saw a flaming fire. [10] And beyond these mountains is a place, the edge of the great earth; there the heavens come to an end. [11] And I saw a great chasm [χάσμα μέγα] among pillars of heavenly fire. And I saw in it pillars of fire descending; and they were immeasurable toward the depth and toward the height. [12] Beyond this chasm [τοῦ χάσματος τούτου] I saw a place where there was neither firmament of heaven above, nor firmly founded earth beneath it. Neither was there water upon it, nor bird; but the place was desolate and fearful [ἀλλὰ τόπος ἦν ἔρημος καὶ φοβερός].[44]
>
> (*1 Enoch* 18:9-12)

The second passage speaks of fire and abyss:

> From there I traveled to another place, more terrible than this one. And I saw terrible things—a great fire burning and flaming there [πῦρ μέγα ἐκεῖ καιόμενον καὶ φλεγόμενον]. And the place had a narrow cleft (extending) to the abyss [τῆς ἀβύσσου], full of great pillars of fire [πλήρης στύλων πυρὸς μεγάλου], borne downward. Neither the measure nor the size was I able to see or to estimate.[45]
>
> (*1 Enoch* 21:7)

The "flaming fire" that Enoch sees (in *1 Enoch* 18:9) is "the fire of the divine presence."[46] Beyond the heavenly fire lies a chasm and beyond the chasm is a waterless, desolate, fearful place (v. 12). It is the place of punishment.[47] The "pillars of fire" (18:11; 21:7) could refer to the angels themselves or to a place where the

---

[43] For discussion of Lactantius and Eusebius (*Vita Constantinii*), see E. Muehlberger, *Moment of Reckoning: Imagined Death and Its Consequences* (Oxford: Oxford University Press, 2019), 27–64.

[44] Translation based on Nickelsburg, *1 Enoch 1*, 276.

[45] Ibid., 297.

[46] Nickelsburg, *1 Enoch 1*, 286.

[47] Ibid., 288.

fallen angels will be punished.⁴⁸ The foreboding place is beyond the human ability to measure or even estimate.

The next two passages refer to the place of punishment for wicked humans:

> Woe to you, unrighteous, when you afflict the righteous on a day of hard anguish, and burn them in fire; for you will be recompensed according to your deeds. … in the heat of blazing fire you will burn.⁴⁹
>
> (*1 Enoch* 100:7-9)

> Know that down to Hades [εἰς ᾅδου]⁵⁰ they will lead your souls; and there they will be in great distress, and in darkness and in a snare and in burning flame [ἐν φλογὶ καιομένῃ]. Into great judgment your souls will enter, and the great judgment will be for all the generations of eternity [ἐν πάσαις ταῖς γενεαῖς τοῦ αἰῶνος].⁵¹
>
> (*1 Enoch* 103:7-8)

The prophecy of *1 Enoch* 100:7 concerning the wicked who afflicted the righteous and burned them with fire may allude to the fearsome tortures described in 2 Maccabees 6-7 (e.g., 6:11; 7:3-5; 4 Macc 5:30, 32; 6:24-27; 8:13).⁵² They who have done these things will be judged accordingly. The brothers about to be martyred tell the tyrant that he will "deservedly undergo the divine justice," which is "eternal torment by fire" (4 Macc 9:9). Although Gehenna is not mentioned by name, nor is Isa 66:24 alluded to, it is to this judgment, which is "eternal" (τοῦ αἰῶνος), that 4 Maccbees and the passages in *1 Enoch* refer.⁵³

Another important passage is found in Judith. After the death of Holofernes and the rout of his army, the courageous and righteous Judith utters a thanksgiving psalm (Jdt 16:2-17). The final verse alludes to Isa 66:24:

---

⁴⁸ Dillmann, *Das Buch Henoch*, 118; Schodde, *Book of Enoch*, 97; Nickelsburg, *1 Enoch 1*, 287. Cf. Charles, *The Book of Enoch*, 42; idem, "Book of Enoch," in *APOT* 2:200.

⁴⁹ Translation based on Nickelsburg, *1 Enoch 1*, 503.

⁵⁰ Nickelsburg (*1 Enoch 1*, 511) translates "Sheol"; so also L. T. Stuckenbruck, *1 Enoch 91-108* (Commentaries on Early Jewish Literature; Berlin: de Gruyter, 2007), 535. Stuckenbruck (536) rightly comments that both the righteous and wicked descend into Sheol at death, but "it is the resurrection of the righteous from Sheol (103:4a) that leaves the wicked behind which will make the abode into a place of punishment," that is, Hell. The Hebrew "Sheol" (שְׁאוֹל) is often translated "Hades" (ᾅδης) in the Old Greek (e.g., Gen 37:35; 44:29, 31; Num 16:30; Deut 32:22; passim).

⁵¹ Translation based on Nickelsburg, *1 Enoch 1*, 288. Nickelsburg also discusses the possibility of textual dislocations involving sections of *1 Enoch* 18 and 19.

⁵² Dillmann, *Das Buch Henoch*, 315; Schodde, *Book of Enoch*, 268; Charles, *Book of Enoch*, 250–1; cf. 257 (on *1 Enoch* 103:7).

⁵³ Nickelsburg, *1 Enoch 1*, 525; Stuckenbruck, *1 Enoch 91-108*, 453.

> Woe to the nations that rise up against my people! The Lord Almighty will take vengeance on them in the day of judgment; fire and worms he will give to their flesh [πῦρ καὶ σκώληκας εἰς σάρκας αὐτῶν]; they shall weep in pain for ever [κλαύσονται ἐν αἰσθήσει ἕως αἰῶνος].
>
> (Jdt 16:17, RSVA).

Judith's πῦρ καὶ σκώληκας almost certainly echoes ὁ σκώληξ and τὸ πῦρ of Isa 66:24, even as does the older Greek translation of ben Sira's wisdom at Sir 7:17.[54] The book of Judith probably dates to about 100 BCE.[55] Although the precise occasion and purpose for writing are debated, most would agree that Judith was written to encourage Jewish resistance against Gentile (i.e., Hellenistic) encroachment at a time when the Hasmonean leadership was itself pursuing an aggressive policy of re-Judaizing Israel's ancient territories.[56] Judith's psalm ends on a harsh, judgmental note, declaring that the nations that rise up against Israel will someday find themselves in the fires of Gehenna, where they shall "weep in pain for ever."

In Enochic materials usually dated to the first century BCE we find a reference (again) to a "deep and dry valley [φάραγγα βαθεῖαν καὶ ξηράν]" (1 Enoch 26:4). Enoch asks, "Why does this accursed valley [αὐτὴ δὲ ἡ φάραγξ κεκατηραμένη] exist?" (27:1). The Lord answers:

> ² The accursed valley [γῆ[57] κατάρατος] is for the ones cursed forever. Here all the accursed will be gathered together, whoever will speak with their mouth against the Lord (in) an unsuitable voice, and concerning his glory will say harsh things. Here they will be gathered together, and here will be (their) dwelling [ὧδε ἔσται τὸ οἰκητήριον], ³ in the last ages [ἐπ' ἐσχάτοις αἰῶσι], in the days of the true judgment [ἐν ταῖς ἡμέραις τῆς κρίσεως τῆς ἀληθινῆς], before the righteous for all time here [εἰς τὸν ἅπαντα χρόνον ὧδε]. The impious will bless the Lord of glory, the eternal king. ⁴ In the days of their judgment [ἐν ταῖς ἡμέραις τῆς κρίσεως αὐτῶν] they will bless on account of mercy, as it is apportioned to them.[58]
>
> (1 Enoch 27:2-4)

The "accursed valley" is almost certainly the Valley of Hinnom, or Gehenna.[59] The idea of the wicked being judged "before (or in the presence of) the righteous"

---

[54] C. A. Moore, *Judith*, AB 40B (Garden City: Doubleday, 1985), 251; L. M. Wills, *Judith: A Commentary on the Book of Judith*, Hermeneia (Minneapolis: Fortress Press, 2019), 382. Moore rightly calls attention to the Greek version of Sir 7:17, as well as 2 Macc 9:9.

[55] Moore, *Judith*, 67–70; Wills, *Judith*, 5–9.

[56] For a current overview, see Wills, *Judith*, 5–17.

[57] See Nickelsburg, *1 Enoch*, 317. The word is not γῆ, "earth," as "accursed earth," but γή, which transliterates גיא, "valley." So the correct reading is "accursed valley." In *1 Enoch* 26:4 and 27:1 the Greek φάραγξ, "valley," is used.

[58] My translation.

[59] Dillmann, *Das Buch Henoch*, 131–2; Schodde, *Book of Enoch*, 108; Charles, *Book of Enoch*, 56; Nickelsbury, *1 Enoch*, 319.

probably reflects Isa 66:24, when the righteous look upon the rotting, burning corpses of the wicked and continue to do so until they say, "We have seen enough" (*Tg.*).

First-century CE materials, the last to become part of the book of *Enoch*, refer to the fires of Gehenna. Two of the passages are found in the *Similitudes* (chapters 37-71). In the first we are told that "on the day of their tribulation" the wicked will be burned "as straw in the fire before the face of the holy" or righteous (48:8-9). We again probably have an allusion to Isa 66:24, in which the righteous look upon the fiery destruction of the wicked.[60] In the second passage Enoch sees "a deep valley with burning fire" (54:1) and the archangels seize the fallen angels "and cast them on that day into the burning furnace ... " (54:6). This "deep valley" seems to be the fiery place of judgment reserved for the fallen angels (as in *1 Enoch* 18:10-11; 19:1-2; 21:7-10). If so, it is not Gehenna, the place where the wicked of human will be cast.[61]

And finally, we have a third passage from the later additions to *Enoch*. The seer says: "And flames of fire I saw burning gloriously, and something like glorious mountains were turning over and quaking to and fro ... there is no heaven, but only flames of fire that are burning and the sound of weeping and crying and groaning and severe pain"[62] (*1 Enoch* 108:4-5). The "sound of weeping and crying" recalls Jdt 16:17, where the wicked receive fire and worms and will "weep in pain for ever." We find reference to weeping and gnashing of teeth in dominical tradition (e.g., Matt 18:11-12 // Luke 13:28; Matt 13:42, 50; 22:13; 24:51; 25:30) and elsewhere.[63] The place of this weeping is fiery Gehenna, here, as elsewhere, viewed as the place where both the fallen angels and the wicked of humanity will be confined.[64]

We have a few passages from texts composed at the end of the first century or beginning of the second. The first is found in Pseudo-Philo. Regarding Doeg the Syrian, who murdered Ahimelech and the priests (cf. 1 Sam 22:9, 18), "behold the time will come soon and a fiery worm [*vermis igneus*] will go up into his tongue and make him rot away, and his habitation will be with Jair in the inextinguishable fire forever [*in igne inextinguibili semper*]"[65] (*Liber Antiquitatum Biblicarum* 63:4).

---

[60] Charles, *Book of Enoch*, 95; G. W. E. Nickelsburg and J. C. VanderKam, *1 Enoch 2: A Commentary on the Book of 1 Enoch, Chapters 37 82*, Hermeneia (Minneapolis: Fortress, 2012), 175.

[61] Nickelsburg and VanderKam, *1 Enoch*, 201. It has already been noted that in later traditions the fiery abyss into which the fallen angels are cast and Gehenna seem to merge as a single fiery lake into which all the wicked—human and angelic—are cast.

[62] Translation based on Nickelsburg, *1 Enoch 1*, 551.

[63] VanderKam, *1 Enoch 91-108*, 708–9. VanderKam also cites *3 Bar.* 16:4; *Apoc. Abr.* 15:7; Greek *Apoc. Ezra* 5:27.

[64] Nickelsburg, *1 Enoch 1*, 555.

[65] H. Jacobson, *A Commentary on Pseudo-Philo's Liber Antiquitatum Biblicarum, with Latin Text and English Translation*, AGJU 31, 2 vols. (Leiden: Brill, 1996), 1: 58 (Latin text), 192 (English).

It is speculated that the text is problematic, in that it either originally read "worm and fire" or that "fiery" slipped into the text because of the words *in igne* ("in fire") two lines below.[66] Perhaps. But I think the "fiery worm" echoes the undying worm of Isa 66:24, which gnaws at the wicked dead in a fire that is never extinguished. It was noted above that the idea of a destructive worm entering the tongue of the wicked comes to expression in later rabbinic tradition (*b. Sotah* 35a).

The idea of weeping in Gehenna is also found in *2 Enoch*. The patriarch Enoch says that he wrote down everything he saw, including "the depth to the lowermost hell, and the place of condemnation, and the supremely large hell, open and weeping. And I saw how the prisoners were in pain, looking forward to endless punishment … "[67] (40:12-13).

In the work that became known as *4 Ezra*, also written about the end of the first century CE, which in its augmented Christian form is usually called 2 Esdras (and the nomenclature is actually more complicated than that),[68] we find one reference to Gehenna in a passage (i.e., 7:36-105) that in the Medieval period was apparently deliberately suppressed because of its teaching against offering up prayers for the dead (i.e., v. 105).[69] In 1875 Robert Bensly published what in his time was a recently discovered Latin ms that contained the missing verses.[70] The relevant verse reads: *et apparebit lacus* [ms reads *locus*] *tormenti, et contra illum erit locus requietionis, et clibanus gehennae ostendetur, et contra eum* [ms reads *eam*] *iocunditatis paradisus*,[71] "and the pit of torment shall appear, and opposite it shall be the place of rest; and the furnace of Gehenna shall be disclosed, and opposite it the paradise of delight" (7:36).

---

[66] Jacobson, *A Commentary on Pseudo-Philo's Liber Antiquitatum Biblicarum*, 2: 1200–1.

[67] Translation based on F. I. Andersen, "2 (Slavonic Apocalypse of) Enoch," in *OTP* 1:166.

[68] The work was originally written in Aramaic or, more probably, in Hebrew. It was translated into Greek, of which only a small fragment survives (P.Oxy 1010), and then into several other languages, including Latin. For an assessment of which parts of 2 Esdras are Jewish and which are Christian, see P. Riessler, *Altjüdisches Schrifttum ausserhalb der Bibel* (Augsburg: Benno Filser, 1928), 1273.

[69] B. M. Metzger (ed.), *The Apocrypha of the Old Testament* (New York: Oxford University Press, 1977), 38. Metzger notes that the missing verses are now found in the Syriac, Ethiopic, Arabic, and Armenian versions, and in two Latin mss as well.

[70] R. L. Bensly, *The Missing Fragment of the Latin Translation of the Fourth Book of Ezra* (Cambridge: Cambridge University Press, 1875). Metzger corrects the claim that Bensly was the first to publish the "lost" part of 2 Esdras 7 by pointing out that it had in fact been found and published in two German editions of the Bible some 150 years earlier. See B. M. Metzger, "The 'Lost' Section of II Esdras (= IV Ezra)," *JBL* 76 (1957): 153–7.

[71] Bensly, *The Missing Fragment*, 55; idem, *The Fourth Book of Ezra: The Latin Version Edited from the MSS*, Texts and Studies III/2 (ed. J. A. Robinson; Cambridge: Cambridge University Press, 1895), 28; cf. B. Violet, *Die Esra-Apokalypse (IV Esra)*, vol. 1: *Die Überlieferung*, GCS 18 (Leipzig: Hinrichs, 1910), 145–6; R. Weber, *Biblia Sacra iuxta Vulgatam Versionem*, 2 vols. (3rd ed., Stuttgart: Deutsche Bibelgesellschaft, 1985), 2:1945.

Prior to the discovery and publication of the "missing fragment" of Latin *4 Ezra*, Adolf Hilgenfeld published a retroversion of how he thought the original Greek probably read: καὶ φανήσεται ὁ κόλπος τῶν βασάνων, κατέναντι δὲ αὐτοῦ ὁ τόπος τῆς ἀναπαύσεως· ἀποκαλυφθήσεται ὁ κλίβανος τῆς γεέννης, κατέναντι δὲ αὐτοῦ πάλιν ὁ παράδεισος τῶν τρυφῶν,[72] "And the vale of torments will appear, and opposite it the place of rest; the furnace of Gehenna will be revealed, and opposite it again the Paradise of luxuries." Apart from κόλπος ("bosom," "vale"),[73] his retroversion could well be correct.

The idea of Gehenna and Paradise lying opposite one another seems to be presupposed in the dominical parable of the Rich Man and the Poor Man (Luke 16:19-30), specifically: "The rich man also died and was buried; [23] and in Hades [ἐν τῷ ᾅδῃ], being in torment [ἐν βασάνοις], he lifted up his eyes, and saw Abraham far off and Lazarus in his bosom.[24] And he called out, 'Father Abraham, have mercy upon me, and send Lazarus to dip the end of his finger in water and cool my tongue; for I am in anguish in this flame [ἐν τῇ φλογὶ ταύτῃ]'" (vv. 22-24). Being "in Hades" (or Gehenna), "in torment," and "in the flame" reflects some of the key Gehenna imagery, especially in roughly contemporaneous texts. That the rich man can actually see the poor man resting with Abraham the great patriarch and can even converse with Abraham reflects what seems to be described in *4 Ezra* 7:36, when it says Paradise and Gehenna are "opposite" (*contra* / κατέναντι) one another. Also, in v. 28 the rich man refers to Hades as "this place of torment" (τὸν τόπον τοῦτον τῆς βασάνου / vg *locum hunc tormentorum*),[74] which echoes descriptions of Hades and Gehenna in the literature that we have reviewed. Moreover, Abraham tells the wretched man that no one can cross from Paradise to Hades, or the reverse, because the two realms are separated by "a great chasm [χάσμα μέγα]" (v. 26). This description reflects ideas we have found in texts considered above. In fact, the exact expression, χάσμα μέγα, is found in *1 Enoch* 18:10.

In the Syriac version of *2 Baruch* we are told what the angel revealed to Baruch, Jeremiah the prophet's secretary, as follows: "But then also he showed to him the measure of the fire, and also the depths of the abyss … and the mouth of Gehenna [*ghn'*], and the place of vengeance … and the likeness of future torment … and the flaming hosts"[75] (59:5, 10, 11). Whereas *2 Enoch*'s "lowermost hell" might

---

[72] A. Hilgenfeld, *Messias Judaeorum* (Leipzig: Reisland, 1869), 65.

[73] Bensly (*Missing Fragment*, 57) finds the proposed κόλπος retroversion (based on one Syriac ms) wholly unsatisfactory. In the recovered Latin fragment the reading is *locus* ("place"), likely a misreading of *lacus* ("pit" or "lake"), and so the original Greek was probably λάκκος, "lake" or "pit" of suffering, etc.

[74] Luke may explain why *lacus tormenti* reads *locus tormenti* in some mss of 4 Ezra 7:36.

[75] Translation based on D. M. Gurtner, *Second Baruch: A Critical Edition of the Syriac Text, with Greek and Latin Fragments, English Translation, Introduction, and Concordances*, JCT 5 (London and New York: T&T Clark International, 2009), 103; see also R. H. Charles, *The Apocalypse of Baruch: Translated from the Syriac* (London: Adam and Charles Black, 1896), 101-2.

presuppose a series of levels, whether in heaven or below the earth,[76] *2 Baruch*'s "Gehenna" refers to the by-now standard subterranean hell.[77] In *2 Baruch* 83 we find a series of comments about aspects of this life "turning into" this or that. In v. 10 health will turn into diseases, in v. 11 strength and power will turn into weakness and impotence, and so on. But in vv. 18 and 20 we hear of judgment and torment. At v. 15 some Syriac mss read "rejection and corruption,"[78] others read "worms and corruption,"[79] which may recall the references to worms in Job (2:9; 7:5; 25:6), not Gehenna or the undying worm of Isa 66:24. But the fires of Gehenna are likely in view in *2 Bar.* 85:13, where it is explained to Baruch: "For there there is the sentence of judgment concerning the way of fire, and the path that leads to burning coals [*lgwmr'*]."[80] One Syriac ms reads "to the realm of death,"[81] again, a likely reference to Gehenna.

In the first major Christian addition to 4 Ezra (i.e., 2 Esdras 1-2), which probably dates to the middle of the second century CE, we find another reference to Gehenna: *manus meae tegent te, ne filii tui gehennam videant*, "My hands will cover you, that your sons may not see Gehenna" (2 Esdras 2:29).[82] One Latin ms reads: *me tremunt omnia; oculi mei geennam vident*, "all tremble because of me; my eyes shall see Gehenna."[83] The "sons" who will "not see Gehenna" refer to Christians (cf. 2:42-48) who, in contrast with apostate Israel, have remained faithful. Their "mother" (i.e., Jerusalem) is assured that God will bring her sons "out from their tombs," because God recognizes his "name in them" (2:16). Accordingly, these faithful sons, having been brought forth from their tombs, will "not see Gehenna."

Reference to unquenchable fire and Gehenna in an Egyptian magic charm against demons may provide us with an important clue as to how the Gehenna tradition developed. Because the charm apparently assumes the temple in Jerusalem is still standing, it could date to a time prior to 70 CE. The relevant portion reads: ὁρκίζω τὸν ἐν τῇ καθαρᾷ Ἱεροσολύμῳ, ᾧ τὸ ἄσβεστον πῦρ διὰ παντὸς αἰῶνος προσπαράκειται

---

[76] So N. Forbes and R. H. Charles, "The Book of the Secrets of Enoch," in *APOT* 2:456. That this hell might be in heaven, rather than below the earth, is suggested in Andersen, "2 (Slavonic Apocalypse of) Enoch," 166.

[77] Charles, *The Apocalypse of Baruch*, 102. Charles reminds us of *1 Enoch* 27:2-3; 62:12; etc.

[78] Followed by Gurtner, *Second Baruch*, 136–7.

[79] Followed by Charles, *The Apocalypse of Baruch*, 146–7.

[80] Translation based on Gurtner, *Second Baruch*, 145. Charles (*The Apocalypse of Baruch*, 164) reads *lghn'* and so translates, "There is the sentence of corruption, the way of fire, and the path which bringeth to Gehenna."

[81] As noted by A. F. J. Klijn, "2 (Syriac Apocalypse of) Baruch," in *OTP* 1:652. There are several variant readings among the Syriac mss.

[82] Bensly, *The Fourth Book of Ezra*, 5; cf. Weber, *Biblia Sacra*, 2:1933.

[83] J. M. Myers, *I and II Esdras: Introduction, Translation and Commentary*, AB 42 (Garden City: Doubleday, 1974), 146. The curious reading is not mentioned in the apparatus of *Biblia Sacra*.

[or προσπαρακάεται] (*PGM* IV.3069-3071a).[84] Morton Smith accepts the bracketed verb προσπαρακάεται, "burns," as the original reading and so translates the lines as follows: "I conjure you by him <who dwells> in the pure <city of> of Jerusalem, beside whom burns forever the unquenchable fire <of the Temple altar>."[85]

I find Smith's translation, which inserts a number of implied words and phrases, wholly plausible. The ἄσβεστον πῦρ is in reference to the fire on the altar of the Jerusalem temple, which according to Lev 6:13 "shall not be extinguished" (οὐ σβεσθήσεται). The reference in the charm is to Yahweh in his temple in Jerusalem, beside the altar on which the unquenchable fire burns. But the magic charm goes on to say: τῷ ὀνόματι αὐτοῦ τῷ ἁγίῳ Ιαεωβαφρενεμουν, λό[γος]· ὃν τρέμει Γέννα πυρὸς ⋯, "with his holy name, Iaeōbaphrenemoun[86] (for[mula]), the one before whom the Gehenna of fire trembles … " (*PGM* IV.3071b-72).

Given the eclectic and syncretistic nature of magic materials, it is not surprising to find two types of fire—one sacred and the other hellish—juxtaposed in a single incantation. However, the connection between the unquenchable fire of the altar and the unquenchable fire of Gehenna that we see in the Pibechis Charm may reflect a much older association that might explain the origins of Isa 66:24 itself. I hasten to add that I am not proposing that an ancient Jewish interpretation somehow remained intact and found its way into a first-century Egyptian magical text. All I am suggesting is that the fires of the altar and of Gehenna could be related, as appears to be the case in *PGM* IV.3069-3072, and that this relationship may explain the appearance of Isa 66:24 in the charm.

Origins of the Fire of Judgment

The imagery of unquenchable fire *as judgment* seems to have begun with Israel's first temple prophets. Amos (mid-eighth century BCE) rails against Israel, warning

---

[84] The "tested charm" is found in the Paris Magical Papyrus (*PGM* IV.3007-3086) and is said to derive from legendary Egyptian magician Pibechis. For text, see K. Preisendanz (ed.), *Papyri Graecae Magicae: Die Griechischen Zauberpapyri*, 2 vols. (Leipzig: B. G. Teubner, 1928-31; rev. ed., 1973; repr. Munich and Leipzig: K. G. Saur, 2001), 1:170-73 (with German translation).

[85] M. Smith, *Jesus the Magician* (San Francisco: Harper & Row, 1978), 113. The reading προσπαρακάεται is proposed in K. Preisendanz, "Zum großen Pariser Zauberpapyrus," *ARW* 17 (1914): 347-8; cf. idem (ed.), *Papyri Graecae Magicae*, 1:172; and is followed by most, including A. Deissmann, *Light from the Ancient East* (London: Hodder & Stoughton; New York: George H. Doran, 1927), 258. Deissmann and Smith believe the language of the charm supports a pre-70 CE date. I cautiously accept this conclusion.

[86] Iaeō is derived from the divine name Yahweh. The name Iaeōbaphrenemoun is a shortened version of a lengthy magical name. Its full form and meaning are explained in H. D. Betz (ed.), *The Greek Magical Papyri in Translation, Including the Demotic Spells: Volume One: Texts* (2nd ed., Chicago: The University of Chicago Press, 1992), 335.

the kingdom of coming judgment. "Seek the Lord and live," says the prophet, "lest he break out like fire in the house of Joseph, and it devour, with none to quench [אֵין־מְכַבֶּה / οὐκ ἔσται ὁ σβέσων] it" (Amos 5:6, RSV). A generation later Isaiah speaks of the decline of Judah, the southern kingdom: "And the strong shall become tinder, and his work a spark, and both of them shall burn together, with none to quench [אֵין־מְכַבֶּה / οὐκ ἔσται ὁ σβέσων] them" (Isa 1:31, RSV modified). The language of "none to quench" may have been formulaic,[87] or Isaiah may be echoing Amos.[88] Elsewhere the prophet Isaiah says the Lord's "fire is in Zion, and his furnace is in Jerusalem" (31:9b). The original reference may have been to the altar and its unquenchable fire,[89] but in later rabbinic interpretation it was applied to Gehenna.[90] In the seventh century BCE Huldah the prophetess speaks against Israel for burning incense to other gods, saying that Yahweh's wrath "will be kindled against this place, and it will not be quenched [לֹא תִכְבֶּה / οὐ σβεσθήσεται]" (2 Kgs 22:17). The same language is found in Jeremiah (at 4:4; 7:20; 17:27) and Ezekiel (at 21:3).

It is the way these two prophets—Jeremiah and Ezekiel—make use of the language of unquenchable fire that calls for comment. Both prophets warn of the impending capture of Jerusalem and the destruction of the first temple. Through Jeremiah the Lord warns the people of Jerusalem to repent, "lest my wrath go forth like fire [אֵשׁ / πῦρ], and burn with none to quench [אֵין מְכַבֶּה / οὐκ ἔσται ὁ σβέσων] it, because of the evil of your doings" (Jer 4:4). Jeremiah says the Lord commanded him to "stand in the gate of the Lord's house, and proclaim there this word" (7:2). What follows is a diatribe against the temple establishment and the elite who pass through the gates to offer sacrifice and mistakenly believe that the mere existence of the temple will protect them. On the contrary, warns Jeremiah, the temple will be destroyed (v. 12). Says the Lord: "Behold, my anger and my wrath will be poured out on this place … it will burn and not be quenched [בָעֲרָה וְלֹא תִכְבֶּה / καυθήσεται καὶ οὐ σβεσθήσεται]" (7:20). The prophet expands on this theme in chapter 17,

---

[87] As suggested by H. Wildberger, *Isaiah 1-12: A Continental Commentary* (Minneapolis: Fortress, 1991), 78.

[88] However, Amos 5:6 could be a later gloss, perhaps from the time of Josiah, which reflects the earlier references to the devouring fire (Amos 1:4, 7; 2:2). So H. W. Wolff, *Joel and Amos*, Hermeneia (Philadelphia: Fortress, 1977), 240; cf. W. Holladay, *Jeremiah 1: A Commentary on the Book of the Prophet Jeremiah Chapters 1-25*, Hermeneia (Philadelphia: Fortress, 1986), 130. If Wolff is correct, then the oldest attestation of the judgmental use of unquenchable fire is found in Isa 1:31, a fragment of a very old, authentic oracle by the late-eighth-century BCE prophet Isaiah, as argued in Childs, *Isaiah*, 22-3; Wildberger, *Isaiah 1-12*, 75-6.

[89] The matter is debated. See H. Wildberger, *Isaiah 28-39: A Continental Commentary* (Minneapolis: Fortress, 2002), 226-8.

[90] See *Mekilta, Baḥodeš* §9 (on Exod 20:18), where Gen 15:17 ("smoking furnace") is linked to Isa 31:9 ("his furnace in Jerusalem"), which is said to refer to Gehenna. So also *b. ʿErubin* 19a; *Gen. Rab.* 6.6. (on Gen 1:17).

again warning that God will burn the palaces of Jerusalem with a fire that will not be quenched (esp. v. 27).[91] Similarly Ezekiel warns that because the people of Judah offer up sacrifices and offerings to idols, God will ignite a fire among them that will not be quenched (Ezek 21:3[E 20:47]).[92]

It seems Jeremiah and Ezekiel have applied the cultic language of the unquenchable fire, commanded in Lev 6:12-13, and resignified it to describe God's fiery judgment against his people and their temple that they foolishly imagine guarantees their security (see Jer 7:4, 8, 10). But the people's wickedness, which includes burning their sons and daughters in the Valley of Hinnom (vv. 32-33), will result in judgment. Commenting on Jer 4:44 and related passages Jack Lundbom wonders if the concept of unquenchable fire might have been encouraged by Deut 32:22.[93] According to this text, Yahweh says, "A fire is kindled by my anger, and it burns to the depths of Sheol [עַד־שְׁאוֹל / ἕως ᾅδου]." A fire that "burns to the depths of Sheol" would easily conjure up the fire of Gehenna—the unquenchable fire—and, indeed, result in a gloss that becomes the last verse of the book of Isaiah.

Claus Westermann believes the appearance of דרא, "abomination" or "abhorrence," in Isa 66:24 and Dan 12:2, the latter of which was probably composed *c*. 160 BCE, "suggests that the addition [of Isa 66:24] is very late."[94] I think he is correct. The oldest materials that resemble Isa 66:24 date no earlier than 200 BCE. These materials include *1 Enoch* 10, which refers to an abyss of fire; *1 Enoch* 90:24-27, which refers to a fiery abyss south of Jerusalem, which is the traditional location of the Valley of Hinnom, or Gehenna; and Greek Sir 7:17, dating to about 132 BCE, which speaks of "fire and worm." Traditions from the first century BCE and first century CE make use of these elements and thus testify to the continuing currency of the Gehenna understanding of Isa 66:24. The Targum's addition of "Gehenna" (*c*. 100 CE) did not change the meaning of Isa 66:24; it only made explicit how late antique Jewish interpreters of Scripture, including Jesus of Nazareth, understood the verse. Because Isa 66:24 appears in Qumran's Great Isaiah Scroll (i.e., 1QIsaiah[a]), which dates to about 150 BCE, the verse could not have been added much after 200 BCE. The collocation of fire, abyss, and worm, therefore, seems to have formed about 200 BCE, perhaps a bit earlier.

The evidence suggests that Isa 66:24, with its reference to fire and worm, understood in reference to the final judgment of the wicked, represents the earliest extant form of this tradition and because of its incorporation into the prestigious

---

[91] In the OG the passage reads: "It shall be, if you do not listen to me ... I will also kindle a fire [ἀνάψω πῦρ] in its gates, and it shall devour the quarters of Jerusalem and shall not be quenched [οὐ σβεσθήσεται]."

[92] In the OG the passage reads: "Hear a word of the Lord ... Behold, I am kindling a fire in you [ἐγὼ ἀνάπτω ἐν σοὶ πῦρ] ... the kindled flame shall not be quenched [οὐ σβεσθήσεται ἡ φλὸξ ἡ ἐξαφθεῖσα]."

[93] J. R. Lundbom, *Jeremiah 1-20: A New Translation with Introduction and Commentary*, AB 21A (New York: Doubleday, 1999), 330.

[94] Westermann, *Isaiah 40-66*, 428. See the comments in Blenkinsopp, *Isaiah 56-66*, 317.

book of Isaiah it became very influential, as the subsequent history of the tradition bears witness. The Gehenna interpretation of Isa 66:24 continues in John, Jesus, and other Jewish interpreters, including the Rabbis, though—as we shall see— these interpreters may have added a new element to its meaning. To these late antique interpreters we now turn.

Gehenna in John the Baptist, Jesus, and the Rabbis

In the Christian tradition, John the Baptist seems to have been the first to allude to the fire of Isa 66:24. He is remembered to have said to those who went to him for baptism:[95]

> You brood of vipers! Who warned you to flee from the wrath to come?[8] Bear fruit that befits repentance,[9] and do not presume to say to yourselves, 'We have Abraham as our father'; for I tell you, God is able from these stones to raise up children to Abraham.[10] Even now the axe is laid to the root of the trees; every tree therefore that does not bear good fruit is cut down and thrown into the fire.[11] I baptize you with water for repentance, but he who is coming after me is mightier than I, whose sandals I am not worthy to carry; he will baptize you with the Holy Spirit and with fire.[12] His winnowing fork is in his hand, and he will clear his threshing floor and gather his wheat into the granary, but the chaff he will burn with unquenchable fire [κατακαύσει πυρὶ ἀσβέστῳ].
>
> (Matt 3:7b-12, RSV; cf. Luke 3:7b-9, 16b-17)

John's angry denunciation (directed against Pharisees and Sadducees in Matt 3:7a, but against the general populace in Luke 3:7a) at points echoes the ancient prophetic tradition. Some of John's language is probably drawn from Malachi (e.g., Mal 3:2 "he is like a refiner's fire"; 4:1 "the day comes, burning like an oven, when all the arrogant and all evildoers will be stubble; the day that comes shall burn them up") and perhaps also Jeremiah (e.g., Jer 22:7 "they shall cut down your choicest cedars, and cast them into the fire"). The prophetic oracles, reviewed above, that use the language of "unquenchable fire" may well have contributed to John's warning. But John's threat that God will burn the chaff "with unquenchable

---

[95] The historical John almost certainly was a preacher of coming judgment. Not only do we have three separate strands of tradition in the New Testament (i.e., Mark, Q, and the fourth Gospel), we also have the testimony of Josephus (*Ant.* 18.116-119), notwithstanding his efforts to mask much of the eschatological element. Although Josephus takes pains to present John as a preacher of good behavior and righteousness, the real point of his preaching is hinted at when we are told that tetrarch Herod Antipas became alarmed when he realized that John's preaching could lead "to sedition" (ἐπὶ στάσει). I think the right balance is struck in R. L. Webb, *John the Baptizer and Prophet: A Socio-historical Study*, JSNTSup 62 (Sheffield: JSOT Press, 1991).

fire" (πυρὶ ἀσβέστῳ) is probably an allusion to Isa 66:24.[96] This is likely for two reasons: (1) the judgment of which John speaks is eschatological and (2) his associate and successor, Jesus of Nazareth, also appeals to the unquenchable fire *and undying worm* (Mark 9:43, 48), an unmistakable allusion to Isa 66:24.[97]

Jesus warns his disciples of the danger of being cast into hell for causing people to stumble in faith. The earliest form of this teaching seems to be preserved in Mark 9:43-48:

> [43] And if your hand causes you to sin, cut it off; it is better for you to enter life maimed than with two hands to go to Gehenna [εἰς τὴν γέενναν], to the unquenchable fire [εἰς τὸ πῦρ τὸ ἄσβεστον].[45] And if your foot causes you to sin, cut it off; it is better for you to enter life lame than with two feet to be thrown into Gehenna [βληθῆναι εἰς τὴν γέενναν].[47] And if your eye causes you to sin, pluck it out; it is better for you to enter the kingdom of God with one eye than with two eyes to be thrown into Gehenna [βληθῆναι εἰς τὴν γέενναν],[48] where their worm does not die, and the fire is not quenched [ὁ σκώληξ αὐτῶν οὐ τελευτᾷ καὶ τὸ πῦρ οὐ σβέννυται].
>
> (Mark 9:43, 45, 47-48, RSV, modified)[98]

Luke does not make use of this material. However, Matthew does, and in two places:

> And if your hand or your foot causes you to sin, cut it off and throw it away; it is better for you to enter life maimed or lame than with two hands or two feet to be thrown into the eternal fire [βληθῆναι εἰς τὸ πῦρ τὸ αἰώνιον].[9] And if your eye causes you to sin, pluck it out and throw it away; it is better for you to enter life

---

[96] A number of Old Testament texts, including Isa 66:24, are noted in D. C. Allison Jr. and W. D. Davies, *A Critical and Exegetical Commentary on the Gospel according to Saint Matthew.* Volume I: *Introduction and Commentary on Matthew I–VII*, ICC (Edinburgh: T & T Clark, 1988), 319. See esp. R. T. France, *The Gospel of Matthew*, NICNT (Grand Rapids: Eerdmans, 2007), 115–16: "Such language derives from the vivid imagery of Isa 66:24."

[97] We should assume that Jesus, who was baptized by John (Mark 1:9; Matt 3:14), inherited some tradition from the Baptist. Jesus' parable of the unfruitful tree (Luke 13:6-9 "if it bears fruit ... well and good; but if not, you can cut it down") may reflect John's warning that "the axe is laid to the root of the trees" (Matt 3:10). In the parable Jesus has implied that the people have a little more time to repent (" ... until next year"). So Allison and Davies, *Matthew*, 309–10. Likewise, Jesus's reference to "unquenchable fire" in Mark 9 probably reflects John's language. Elsewhere in his public teaching Jesus refers to John (cf. Matt 9:14-17; 11:2-19; Luke 7:18-35). The public, including the tetrarch Antipas, compared Jesus to John (Matt 14:1-2; Mark 6:14-16; Luke 9:7-9).

[98] The RSV rightly omits vv. 44 and 46, which are glosses based on v. 48. Verses 44 and 46 are not found in ℵ B C L W Δ Ψ f^1 and many other authorities, but A D K Θ Π f^{13} and other authorities do include them.

with one eye than with two eyes to be thrown into the Gehenna of fire [βληθῆναι εἰς τὴν γέενναν τοῦ πυρός].

(Matt 18:8-9, RSV modified)

If your right eye causes you to sin, pluck it out and throw it away; it is better that you lose one of your members than that your whole body be thrown into Gehenna [βληθῇ εἰς γέενναν].[30] And if your right hand causes you to sin, cut it off and throw it away; it is better that you lose one of your members than that your whole body go into Gehenna [εἰς γέενναν ἀπέλθῃ].

(Matt 5:29-30, RSV modified)

Source-critical analysis of the larger parallel passages, that is, Mark 9:42-50, Matt 18:5-9 + 5:29-30, and Luke 17:1-2 + 14:34, is somewhat complicated. However, the priority of Mark (or perhaps proto-Mark), with some overlapping Q tradition, remains the best solution. Luke knows Mark and Q, but chooses to retain only the sayings about the millstone (Luke 17:2 = Mark 9:42), the inevitability of temptations (Luke 17:1 = Matt 18:7), and salt (Luke 14:34 = Mark 9:50 = Matt 5:13). The evangelist Luke, apparently, has no use for Mark 9:43-48.[99] Matthew follows Mark's hand–eye sequence in Matt 18:8-9, but in 5:29-30 the sequence is reversed, probably because the point of the passage is on *looking* at a woman with lust (5:28). Matthew also abbreviates (as the evangelist often does) Mark's "into the fire that is unquenchable" (Mark 9:43), reading instead "eternal fire" (Matt 18:8), and Mark's "thrown into Gehenna, where their worm does not die, and the fire is not quenched" in Mark 9:47-48 becomes in Matt 18:9 "thrown into the Gehenna of fire."

What is of interest is Mark's three references to Gehenna (translated "hell" in the RSV),[100] accompanied by references to the unquenchable fire:

v. 43 ἀπελθεῖν εἰς τὴν γέενναν, εἰς τὸ πῦρ τὸ ἄσβεστον
v. 45 βληθῆναι εἰς τὴν γέενναν
v. 47 βληθῆναι εἰς τὴν γέενναν
v. 48 ὅπου ὁ σκώληξ αὐτῶν οὐ τελευτᾷ καὶ τὸ πῦρ οὐ σβέννυται

The reference to being "cast into Gehenna, into the unquenchable fire" in v. 43 anticipates the quotation of Isa 66:24 in v. 48. The original reading of the material in Mark 9:43-48 creates an *inclusio*, with the opening and closing references alluding to unquenchable fire and the closing reference appealing to scriptural authority (i.e., Isa 66:24).

---

[99] For source-critical analysis of these materials, see D. C. Allison Jr. and W. D. Davies, *A Critical and Exegetical Commentary on the Gospel according to Saint Matthew. Volume II: Commentary on Matthew VIII–XVIII*, ICC (Edinburgh: T & T Clark, 1991), 752–3; J. A. Fitzmyer, *The Gospel according to Luke X–XXIV*, AB 28A (Garden City: Doubleday, 1985), 1136–7; J. Nolland, *Luke 9:21-18:34*, WBC 35B (Dallas: Word, 1993), 835–6.

[100] In Luther's translation εἰς τὴν γέενναν is regularly rendered *in die Hölle*.

The graphic imagery of this material seems inspired by the gruesome accounts of the seven sons of the Jewish woman tortured to death by agents of Antiochus IV Epiphanes for refusing to submit to the tyrant's decrees against the observance of the law of Moses (e.g., 2 Macc 7:4, where hands and feet are cut off). The courageous brothers would rather lose limbs than lose their souls.[101] This seems to be the principal point of the dominical tradition: if a hand, foot, or eye leads to temptation, better to remove it and go into eternal life maimed than go into eternal fire whole.[102]

One will recall that in the story of 2 Maccabees the seven martyred brothers warn Antiochus that judgment would befall him (e.g., 7:9, 14, 17, 19). It did, in the form of worms and decay (9:9, 28). It was suggested above that the king's suffering from worms anticipated his post-mortem judgment of unquenchable fire and the undying worm. Jesus' teaching in Mark 9, where terrible physical injuries and the worm and fire of Gehenna are found together, supports that interpretation.

As already noted, the dominical tradition in Mark 9:47-48 quotes a portion of Isa 66:24. We may compare versions:

Mark: ὅπου ὁ σκώληξ αὐτῶν οὐ τελευτᾷ καὶ τὸ πῦρ οὐ σβέννυται
"where their worm does not die and the fire is not quenched"
Isa (MT): תוֹלַעְתָּם לֹא תָמוּת וְאִשָּׁם לֹא תִכְבֶּה
"their worm does not die and their fire is not quenched"[103]
Isa (LXX): ὁ γὰρ σκώληξ αὐτῶν οὐ τελευτήσει, καὶ τὸ πῦρ αὐτῶν οὐ σβεσθήσεται
"for their worm will not die, and their fire will not be quenched"
Isa (Vulg): *vermis eorum non morietur et ignis eorum non extinguetur*
"their worm will not die and their fire will not be extinguished"
Isa (Targ): נִשְׁמָתְהוֹן לָא יְמוּתָן וְאִשָּׁתְהוֹן לָא תִטְפֵי וִיהוֹן מִידְּדָנִין רַשִׁיעַיָּא בְּגֵיהִנָּם
"their breaths will not die and their fire will not be extinguished, and the wicked shall be judged in Gehenna"

The quotation of Isa 66:24 in Mark 9:48 follows the Hebrew closely. The imperfect verbs of Isaiah are rendered as futures in the LXX and in the Vulgate and Targum. Mark's present tense forms of the verbs suggest the Markan version is independent of the LXX. The appearance of γέεννα in Mark 9:47 further suggests that the

---

[101] B. M. F. Van Iersel, "Mark 9,43 in a Martyrological Perspective," in A. A. R. Bastiaensen et al. (eds.), *Fructus Centesimus: Mélanges offerts à Gerard J. M. Bartelink à l'occasion de son soixante-cinquième anniversaire*, Instrumenta patristica 19 (Steenbrugge: Sint-Pietersabdij/Dordrecht: Kluwer, 1989), 333–41; idem, "Failed Followers in Mark: Mark 13:12 as a Key for the Identification of the Intended Readers," *CBQ* 58 (1996): 244–63, 252; Mark 9:43-48 "is best understood against the background of the story of the Maccabean brothers."

[102] The hand-foot-eye sequence refers to temptation and sin in general, not specifically to sexual sins. On this point, see J. Marcus, *Mark 8-16*, AB 27A (New Haven and London: Yale University Press, 2009), 695–8.

[103] Apart from minor spelling variations, the text of the MT matches 1QIsa^a LIV 17–18.

underlying dominical utterance originally intersected with the emerging Aramaic tradition, which is now preserved in the later Targum, where the worm and fire of Isa 66:24 are explicitly linked to judgment "in Gehenna" (בְּגֵיהִנָּם). Coherence between dominical utterances and the Aramaic paraphrase of Scripture, especially the book of Isaiah, has been observed.[104]

A few of the Rabbis of late antiquity had some things to say about Gehenna. In a midrash concerned with when to recite blessings Rabbi Yosé states that "the fire of Gehenna [אש גיהינם] was created on the second day (of creation) and will never be extinguished [כבת לעולם אינה], as it says, 'their fire will not be extinguished'" (*t. Ber.* 5.31; quoting Isa 66:24).[105] Yosé's midrash apparently presupposes targumic tradition, for he has linked Gehenna with Isa 66:24. The fire of Gehenna will never be extinguished, says the rabbi, because of what Isaiah says about the fire, namely, that it is unquenchable (אינה כבת).

But there is more. Jewish interpreters appealed to Isa 66:23, the verse that immediately precedes the last verse of Isaiah. Interpreters believed that Isa 66:23, which in the Hebrew reads, "From new moon to new moon, and from sabbath to sabbath, all flesh shall come to worship before me, says the Lord," hints at how long the wicked will suffer in Gehenna. According to Rabbi Aqiba, a late-first-/ early-second-century authority, "the judgment of the wicked in Gehenna [בְּגֵיהִנָּם] is twelve months, as it is said, 'it will be from one month until the same month [a year later]' (Isa 66:23)" (*m. 'Eduyyot* 2:10). That is, Isaiah's "from new moon to new moon," or "from one month to the same month," implies a period of one year. The Hebrew allows for this interpretation, though it does not require it. The rabbi believed Isa 66:23 is relevant because Isa 66:24, as seen in the Aramaic paraphrase, speaks of fiery Gehenna.

One should also ask, Why must the time of suffering in Gehenna be limited? Because of what is said in Isa 66:23, "all flesh shall come to worship before me." If a portion of humanity is condemned to the fires of Gehenna for eternity, then the prediction of this verse will not come to pass; "all flesh" will not in fact worship before God. Therefore, even the wicked will not remain in Gehenna forever. So how long will the wicked suffer in Gehenna? Twelve months, according Rabbi Aqiba and others. Aqiba presents an exegetical argument, as we have seen. But the Mishnah's argument is also based on precedent (*m. 'Eduyyot* 2:10): the judgment on the generation of the flood lasted twelve months (Gen 7:11 + 8:14); the judgment on Job lasted twelve months (Job 7:3); the judgment on the Egyptians lasted twelve

---

[104] For discussion of Isa 66:24 in Mark 9:43-48, see B. D. Chilton, *A Galilean Rabbi and His Bible: Jesus' Use of the Interpreted Scripture of His Time*, GNS 8 (Wilmington: Glazier, 1984), 101–7; idem, *The Isaiah Targum* (ArBib 11; Wilmington: Glazier, 1987), 127–8. Chilton discusses other examples of coherence between dominical and targumic tradition. I briefly treat these and one or two additional instances in an Introduction I wrote for the reprint of Matthew Black's third edition of *An Aramaic Approach to the Gospels and Acts* (Oxford: Clarendon Press, 1967; repr. Peabody, MA: Hendrickson Publishers, 1998), v–xxv.

[105] Translation based on J. Neusner, *The Tosefta*, 6 vols. (Hoboken: Ktav, 1977–86), 1: 34.

months (Exod 4:12; that is, five weeks per plague); and the future judgment on Gog and Magog will last twelve months (Ezek 38:2-23).[106] Accordingly, the judgment on the wicked in Gehenna will only last twelve months.[107] The belief that judgment ends after twelve months, when the flesh has decayed thus permitting the wicked burial in a place of honor (cf. *m. Sanh.* 6.6; *b. Qidd.* 31b), reflects the same thinking.

The Rabbis formulated other exegetical approaches to support the idea that the wicked do not remain in Gehenna forever. To be sure, they associated Isa 66:24 with Gehenna (as in *b. ʿErubin* 19a; *b. Roš HaŠanah* 17a), but in reference to "valley" (as in Valley of Gehenna), they also say that Gehenna is a place where the wicked "weep and shed tears" (*b. ʿErubin* 19a)—but only for a season. How do they know this? "Passing through the valley of Baca" (Ps 84:7[6], lit. "valley of weeping"), say the Rabbis, means the wicked *pass through* Gehenna and suffer for a time. But "passing through" implies that their time in Gehenna, where they shed tears, is not eternal. No indeed, "our father Abraham comes, brings them up, and receives them" (*b. ʿErubin* 19a). The midrash goes on to say that "the thoroughly wicked will be inscribed as doomed to Gehenna, as it says" (Dan 12:2 is cited), but when the wicked go down to Gehenna, they "squeal and rise again, as it says" (Zech 13:9 is cited, "I will bring the third part through the fire," etc.).

In a midrash on Isa 26:2 ("Open the gates, that the righteous nation which keeps faith [שֹׁמֵר אֱמֻנִים] may enter in") in *Yalkut Shimeoni* the letters in the words שמר אמנים ("keeps faith") are broken up to read שאומרים אמן, "who say 'amen,'" which are interpreted to mean: "For the sake of a single 'Amen,' which the wicked answer in the midst of Gehenna, they are delivered from its midst" (*Yalkut Shimeoni* on Isa 26:2).[108] A similar midrash, also based on Isa 26:2, appears in *Seder Rabbi Amram*. In response to David's singing, the righteous in Paradise and the wicked in Gehenna answer, "Amen." God asks who have said this and the angels report, "The sinners of Israel." God immediately orders the opening of the gates of Paradise, appealing to the words of Isa 26:2.[109] In a similar midrash we are told that those in Gehenna—the wicked of Israel and the righteous of the nations—cry out "Amen" in response to the Qaddish. God gives the keys of Gehenna to the

---

[106] All of these "twelve month" judgments are derived from midrashic deductions, not obvious scriptural exegesis.

[107] I. J. Yuval, "All Israel Have a Portion in the World to Come," in F. E. Udoh, S. Heschel, M. Chancey, and G. Tatum (eds.), *Redefining First-century Jewish and Christian Identities: Essays in Honor of Ed Parish Sanders*, CJAS 16 (Notre Dame, IN: University of Notre Dame Press, 2008), 114–38, esp. 134 in reference to "twelve months."

[108] The midrash also appears in *Alphabet of Rabbi Aqiba* §7; cf. A. Jellinek, *Bet ha-Midrasch: Sammlung kleiner Midraschim und vermischter Abhandlungen aus der ältern jüdischen Literatur. Dritter Theil* (Leipzig: C. W. Vollrath, 1855), 27–9. The midrash is discussed in C. G. Montefiore, "Rabbinic Conceptions of Repentance," *JQR* 16 (1904): 209–57, here 240.

[109] Discussed in Montefiore, "Rabbinic Conceptions of Repentance," 240. The midrash also appears in *Tanna debe Eliyyahu Zuta* §20.

archangels Michael and Gabriel and orders them to lift up those who said "amen" (cf. *Semaḥot* 2.9 "he who confesses has a portion in the world to come"). None of this should come as a surprise, for God himself prays that his mercy "overcomes" his anger, so that he will judge according to mercy and not strict justice (*b. Mo'ed Qatan* 16b; *b. Ber.* 7a). God's merciful attitude toward sinners is in keeping with the rabbinic maxim, "There is nothing greater than repentance" (*Deut. Rab.* 2.24 [on Deut 4:30]).

Many Christian fathers were less optimistic, declaring that the undying (or unresting) worm and unquenchable fire of Isa 66:24, understood to refer to Gehenna (or hell), imply eternal torment of the wicked. In one of his homilies on 1 Corinthians John Chrysostom addresses the question many in his day were asking, "whether hell fire has any end." Chrysostom says that it has no end, because of what Jesus "declared when he said, 'Their fire shall not be quenched, and their worm shall not die'" (Mark 9:48). The church father goes on to add:

> As I said then; that it has no end, Christ has declared. Paul also says, in pointing out the eternity of the punishment, that the sinners "shall pay the penalty of destruction, and that for ever" (2 Thess 1:9). And again, "Be not deceived; neither fornicators. nor adulterers, nor effeminate, shall inherit the kingdom of God" (1 Cor 6:9). And also to the Hebrews he says, "Follow peace with all men, and the sanctification without which no man shall see the Lord" (Heb 12:14). And Christ also, to those who said, "In your name we have done many wonderful works," saith, "Depart from me, I know you not, you workers of iniquity" (Matt 7:22). And the maidens too who were shut out, entered in no more (Matt 25:10-12). And also about those who gave him no food, He says, "They shall go away into everlasting punishment" (Matt 25:46).[110]
>
> (*Homiliae in epistulam i ad Corinthios, Hom.* 9.1 [on 1 Cor 3:12-15]; cf. *Homiliae in Genesim, Hom.* 22.21; 42.22).

Augustine believed the same; the torment of the damned is everlasting (*De civitate Dei* 21.9).

But other Christian fathers were not so sure. In his commentary on Tatian's *Diatessaron* the Syrian scholar Ephraem seems to be aware of the interpretation that suffering in Gehenna was only temporary. Commenting on Matt 12:31-32 and Mark 3:29, where Jesus warns of committing blasphemy against the Holy Spirit, Ephraem states: "But this sin does not prevent a person's justification at the end. When one will have made retribution in Gehenna, (God) will reward him for this in the kingdom" (*Commentary on the Diatessaron* X §4).[111] Ephraem believes that

---

[110] Translation based on P. Schaff et al. (eds.), *Nicene and Post-Nicene Fathers*: Series I, vol. 12 (repr., Peabody, MA: Hendrickson, 1996), 48.

[111] Translation based on C. McCarthy, *Saint Ephrem's Commentary on Tatian's Diatessaron: An English Translation of Chester Beatty Syriac MS 709 with Introduction and Notes*, JSSSup 2 (Oxford: Oxford University Press, 1993), 167.

there is in fact a sin for which no forgiveness is possible. But it is interesting that he speaks of some sinners who "will have made retribution in Gehenna" and then are rewarded for this retribution and enter heaven. Ephraem does not elaborate, but he seems to envision some sinners cast into Gehenna, where after making retribution (which is not entirely clear), they are rewarded. For these sinners Gehenna is evidently temporary, as in the rabbinic exegesis of Isa 66:23. It is possible, but not provable, that Ephraem's belief was based on a similar understanding of Isa 66:23-24, as expressed in the Targum and in the Mishnah.

A similar hope is expressed in the interesting tradition of the talking skulls.[112] This late narrative seems to have begun in Jewish circles and then later was adapted in Christian and Islamic circles. Perhaps best known is the legend of Apa Macarius and the skull found in the desert.[113] The skull identifies itself as belonging to a dead Egyptian pagan high priest, who has been sent to Gehenna. The wretched man describes to Macarius what the place of torment is like. In another version the skull belongs to Arsanis, king of Egypt. In this version it is Jesus himself who finds the skull. After conversing with the skull, Jesus intercedes for the dead man and he is raised up to heaven.

Speculations about short-term suffering in or deliverance from hell presupposed the idea that Gehenna is little more than a place of final destruction. Its worm might not die—and so is ever ready to gnaw at the corpses that are cast into Gehenna—and its fire never goes out. But even the undying worm and unquenchable fire do not remain forever, for apparently Gehenna itself will be destroyed. According to the New Testament Apocalypse, the "beast" and "false prophet" will be cast into the "lake of fire" (εἰς τὴν λίμνην τοῦ πυρός), so also the "devil" (Rev 19:20; 20:10); then "Death and Hades" (ὁ θάνατος καὶ ὁ ᾅδης—probably to be understood as the Greek equivalent of the Semitic Gehenna), along with everyone whose name is not written in the book of life, will be cast into the lake of fire (20:14-15; 21:8). We are told, moreover, that "this" (οὗτος), presumably the lake of fire, "is the second death" (ὁ θάνατος ὁ δεύτερός ἐστιν). Following the vision of fiery destruction, John sees "a new heaven and a new earth" (21:1) and hears a loud voice announce that God "will wipe away every tear from their eyes, and death shall be no more, neither shall there be mourning nor crying nor pain any more, for the former things have passed away" (21:4). It is hard to see how weeping and pain will cease, if humans are in Gehenna consciously suffering fiery torment.

---

[112] Skulls were sometimes put to use for the purpose of necromancy, which is cognate to the tradition of the talking skulls. On magic use of skulls, see D. Levene, "Calvariae magicae: The Berlin, Philadelphia and Moussaieff Skulls (Tab. XXXVII–XLIX)," *Or* 75 (2006): 359–79; idem, "Amuletic Skull," in F. Vukosavovic (ed.), *Angels and Demons: Jewish Magic through the Ages* (Jerusalem: Bible Lands Museum, 2010), 150–5.

[113] The Greek version is found in PG 38:257C–260D. A Syriac version will be found in I. H. Hall, "The Story of Arsânîs," *Hebraica* 6 (1890): 81–8. I rely on the recent study by E. Grypeou, "Talking Skulls: Some Personal Accounts of Hell and Their Place in Apocalyptic Literature," *ZAC* 20 (2016): 109–26.

Concluding Remarks

The biblical data are diverse and ambiguous. The conclusion of the Apocalypse seems to imply that the wicked are no more. Only the righteous, who are admitted into the New Jerusalem, still live. It is no wonder that both Jewish and Christian interpreters held to differing and conflicting understandings of the relevant texts, for the relevant components of this doctrine are diverse and sometimes appear to be at odds.

But the text to which Jesus himself appealed was Isa 66:24, which he associated with Gehenna, as did the Aramaic version of Isaiah and various Jewish texts and traditions. One must wonder if Jesus not only agreed with Jewish interpreters that Gehenna was in view, but perhaps he also agreed with other aspects of Jewish interpretation (such as we find in the interpretation of Isa 66:23). This could include the understanding that the dead were cast into Gehenna and consumed and that if they suffered (as in "weeping, wailing, and gnashing teeth"), they did so only for a limited period of time. Describing the fire of Gehenna as "unquenchable" or "inextinguishable" and the worm as "undying" no doubt encouraged the idea that torment of the wicked will be forever. But the portrayal of the righteous who say, "It is enough" (at the end of Isa 66:24), seems to imply a limit. Moreover, God's prophecy that "all flesh shall come to worship before me" (Isa 66:23) may lend support to Jewish belief (or hopes?) that all will eventually be rescued from Gehenna, as though from purgatory, and stand before God redeemed and forgiven.

Chapter 10

VIOLENCE AND "MAGIC" TRADITION

Matthias R. Hoffmann

Introduction

At first consideration of the topic "magic" with regard to "religiously motivated violence" one will probably immediately think of violence against users of magic: especially the European witch-hunts around the sixth century and then massively between 1430 and 1780[1]—and maybe even in both Americas, specifically in the New England States around 1692[2]—as phenomena of mass hysteria which is at least

---

[1] Cf. for the duration and the progression of witch-hunts (enforced by either the church or institutions of individual countries) Wolfgang Behringer, *Hexen. Glaube, Verfolgung, Vermarktung*, Beck'sche Reihe 2082 (4th ed., Munich: C.H. Beck, 2005), 32–74; Rita Voltmer, *Hexen. Hexen. Wissen was stimmt*, Herder Spektrum 5868 (Freiburg: Herder, 2008), 24–6; Walter Rummel and Rita Voltmer, *Hexen und Hexenverfolgung in der Frühen Neuzeit*, Geschichte Kompakt (Darmstadt: Wissenschaftliche Buchgesellschaft, 2008), 36–57; Rainer Decker, *Hexenjagd in Deutschland*, Geschichte Erzählt (Darmstadt: Primus, 2006), 16–26; Rainer Decker, *Die Päpste und die Hexen. Aus den geheimen Akten der Inquisition* (2nd ed., Darmstadt: Primus, 2013), 17–154; Helmut Birkhan, *Magie im Mittelalter*, Beck'sche Reihe 1901 (Munich: C.H. Beck, 2010), 154–76; Marco Frenschkowski, *Die Hexen. Eine kulturgeschichtliche Analyse* (Wiesbaden: Marixverlag, 2012), 15–35; Brian P. Levack, *Hexenjagd. Die Geschichte der Hexenverfolgung in Europa* (4th ed., Munich: C.H. Beck, 2009), passim; Owen Davies, *Grimoires: A History of Magic Books* (Oxford and New York: Oxford University Press, 2009), 44–92; Malcolm Gaskill, *Witchcraft: A Very Short Introduction* (Oxford and New York: Oxford University Press, 2010), 13–26, 61–94; Keith Thomas, *Religion and the Decline of Magic: Studies in Popular Beliefs in Sixteenth- and Seventeenth-century England* (London: Penguin, 1991), esp. 517–698; Christoph Elsas, *Religionsgeschichte Europas. Religiöses Leben von der Vorgeschichte bis zur Gegenwart* (Darmstadt: Wissenschaftliche Buchgesellschaft, 2002), 180, 202–7; and Richard Kieckhefer, *Magie im Mittelalter* (Munich: Deutscher Taschenbuch Verlag, 1995), 207–32.

[2] Cf. Frenschkowski, *Die Hexen*, 157–61.

partially religiously motivated.³ Without doubt moral and theological skepticism toward witchcraft and magic, as expressed in certain passages of the New Testament and especially the Hebrew Bible (as for instance Exod 22:17⁴), has resulted in the persecution of suspected practitioners of magic. Accordingly, the resulting events that led to countless victims can be regarded as motivated and triggered by religion. Similarly, one may even consider the prohibition of druids by Roman authorities as an act of religiously motivated violence toward people who may have been regarded as practitioners of magic (as is reflected in Pliny, *Nat. hist.* 30.13) or at least of divination (combined with sacrifice of humans). However, since our "knowledge" of druids heavily depends on Roman sources which evaluate them very differently,⁵ we can hardly assume to have insight into a possible conflict between druids as

---

³ See for witch-hunts and their motivation also Christa Tuczay, *Magie und Magier im Mittelalter* (2nd ed., Munich: Deutscher Taschenbuch Verlag, 2003), 43–140, esp. 75–120; Voltmer, *Hexen*, 27–35; Renate Jost, "Zauberei und Gottesmacht. Überlegungen zu Gender, Magie und Hexenwahn im Zusammenhang von Ex 22, 17," in Marcel Nieden (ed.), *Hexenwahn. Eine theologische Selbstbesinnung*, TA 5 (Stuttgart: Kohlhammer, 2004), 11–33, esp. 12–16; Marco Frenschkowski, *Magie im antiken Christentum. Eine Studie zur Alten Kirche und ihrem Umfeld*, Standorte in Antike und Christentum 7 (Stuttgart: Hiersemann, 2016), 93–100; Behringer, *Hexen*, 7–31; Christoph Daxelmüller, *Zauberpraktiken. Die Ideengeschichte der Magie* (Düsseldorf: Patmos, 2001), 74–94; Thomas Grüter, *Magisches Denken. Wie es entsteht und wie es uns beeinflusst* (Frankfurt: Scherz, 2010), 137–59; Kieckhefer, *Magie im Mittelalter*, 202–32; and Johannes Dillinger, *Hexen und Magie. Eine historische Einführung*, Historische Einführungen 3 (Frankfurt and New York: Campus, 2007), 13–42. See also Dieter Becker, "Hexerei, Magie und Gewalt," in Marcel Nieden (ed.), *Hexenwahn. Eine theologische Selbstbesinnung*, TA 5 (Stuttgart: Kohlhammer, 2004), 173–85; Richard van Dülmen, *Historische Anthropologie. Entwicklung, Probleme, Aufgaben* (2nd ed., Cologne, Weimar, and Vienna: Böhlau Verlag, 2001), 61–6; Stephanie Irene Spoto, "Jacobean Witchcraft and Feminine Power," *Pacific Coast Philology* 45 (2010): 53–70; and Claus Priesner, *Dinge zwischen Himmel und Erde. Eine Kulturgeschichte des magischen Denkens* (Darmstadt: Wissenschaftliche Buchgesellschaft, 2020), 171–87. Also shamans have been persecuted as practitioners of witchcraft; cf. Klaus E. Müller, *Schamanismus. Heiler, Geister, Rituale*, Beck'sche Reihe 2072 (3rd ed., Munich: C.H. Beck, 2006), 121–4.

⁴ This passage is especially relevant in the context of persecution and condemnation of witches. Cf. also Jost, "Zauberei und Gottesmacht," 11–32. Even for Martin Luther this passage—next to other biblical texts such as Gen 6:1-4; Exod 7-8; Deut 18:10-11; 1 Sam 28; Isa 28:15; Matt 4; Gal 5:20—had a major influence on his views regarding magic and witchcraft. Cf. for this Jörg Haustein, *Martin Luthers Stellung zum Zauber- und Hexenwesen* MKS 2 (Stuttgart: Kohlhammer, 1990), 68–97, esp. 68. Cf. within this context also Joachim Track, "' … eine Zauberin sollst du nicht leben lassen … ' (M. Luther). Vom Umgang mit der Schuld in Kirche und Theologie," in Marcel Nieden (ed.), *Hexenwahn. Eine theologische Selbstbesinnung*, TA 5 (Stuttgart: Kohlhammer, 2004), 203–21.

⁵ Cf. Bernhard Maier, *Die Druiden*, Beck'sche Reihe 2466 (Munich: C.H. Beck, 2009), 11–72; and Tuczay, *Magie und Magier im Mittelalter*, 173–9.

representatives of Gaulish religion and Roman religion. Probably the alleged human sacrifices offered by druids constituted a major conflict in this case. We can only see that the attempt to resolve this conflict resulted in the prohibition of druidic religion under Emperors Augustus, Tiberius, and Claudius.

In general, it seems that societies have viewed with suspicion practitioners of magic. These practitioners have been stigmatized by various religious groups and often the practices have then been condemned by religious or juridical writings.[6] Laws against the use of harmful magic—often connected with a religious justification—are, for instance, already formulated in the Codex Hammurapi from the eighteenth century BCE (§2). Also Assyrian laws from the eleventh century BCE prohibit the practice of magic (§47).[7] In the Roman Twelve-Table-Law[8] from the fifth century BCE magic is not only outlawed, but harmful magic is even punishable by death. Also laws established by Sulla (81 BCE) threaten with death those who make and trade poisons and those who use magic.[9] During the reign of Diocletian (284–305) sorcerers and magicians using harmful magic were threatened to be burnt alive.[10] Similarly, witchcraft and magic and even the belief

---

[6] Cf. for a discussion on this topic, see also C. Robert Phillips III, "Nullum Crimen sine Lege: Socioreligious Sanctions on Magic," in Christopher A. Faraone and Dirk Obbink (eds.), *Magika Hiera: Ancient Greek Magic and Religion* (New York and Oxford: Oxford University Press, 1991), 260–83: and Frenschkowski, *Magie im antiken Christentum*, 275–87.

[7] Cf. for Codex Hammurapi and the Assyrian Laws Otto Kaiser (ed.), *Rechts- und Wirtschaftsurkunden. Historisch-chronologische Texte*, TUAT 1 (Gütersloher Verlagshaus: Gütersloh, 1982-5); and Marie-Louise Thomsen, *Zauberdiagnose und Schwarze Magie in Mesopotamien*, CNI Publikations 2 (Copenhagen: Museum Tusculanum Press, 1987).

[8] Cf. for the text Dieter Flach, *Das Zwölftafelgesetz. Leges XII Tabularum* (Darmstadt: Wissenschaftliche Buchgesellschaft, 2004).

[9] For juridical issues concerning magic in Graeco-Roman texts, see Derek Collins, *Magic in the Ancient Greek World* (Malden, MA: Blackwell Publishing, 2008), 132–65; Decker, *Hexenjagd*, 15; Matthew W. Dickie, *Magic and Magicians in the Greco-Roman World* (London and New York: Routledge, 2003), 142–61; Susan R. Garrett, *The Demise of the Devil: Magic and the Demonic in Luke's Writings* (Minneapolis: Fortress Press, 1989), 116; and Fritz Graf, *Gottesnähe und Schadenszauber. Die Magie in der griechisch-römischen Antike* (Munich: C.H. Beck, 1996), 41–57.

[10] For laws against the use of magic in the Christian Empire, see Dickie, *Magic and Magicians*, 251–72. Cf. for the suppression of magic and related ideas, see also Richard A. Horsley, *Jesus and Magic. Freeing the Gospel Stories from Modern Misconceptions* (Cambridge: James Clarke, 2015), 93–6. Surprisingly, Roman documents and texts dealing with magicians, sorcerers, or witches are rather common. For collections of relevant texts, see Daniel Ogden, *Magic, Witchcraft and Ghosts in the Greek and Roman Worlds. A Sourcebook* (Oxford: Oxford University Press, 2002); Georg Luck, *Arcana Mundi: Magic and the Occult in the Greek and Roman Worlds: A Collection of Ancient Texts Translated, Annotated, and Introduced* (Baltimore: Johns Hopkins University Press, 1985). For a detailed survey of laws against using magic in late antiquity, see Almuth Lotz, *Der Magiekonflikt in der Spätantike*, Habelts Dissertationsdrucke, Alte Geschichte 48 (Bonn: Habelt, 2005).

in these phenomena are punishable by death in Charlemagne's laws after defeating the Saxons (in *Capitulatio de partibus Saxoniae* §6).[11] The willingness to use violence and torture against practitioners of magic is also demonstrated openly in well-known writings such as Heinrich Kramer's *Malleus Maleficarum* ("Der Hexenhammer" from 1486)[12] or Jean Bodin's *De la Démonomanie des sorciers* (from 1580). Moreover, even the opponents of the witch trials—as for instance the Protestant reverend Anton Praetorius in *Gründlicher Bericht von Zauberey und Zauberern* (from 1598),[13] the Jesuit Friedrich Spee in his writing *Cautio criminalis seu de processibus contra Sagas Liber* (from 1631), Christian Thomasius in *De Crimine Magiae* (from 1701) and *Processus Inquisitorii contra Sagas* (from 1712),[14] Johann Weyer in his writing *De praestigiis daemonum* (from 1563),[15] and Reginald Scot in *The Discoverie of Witchcraft* (from 1584)[16]—describe and condemn the massive use of violence employed against the accused.[17] Daunting examples of juridical trials against those who allegedly used magic and have to expect major punishment are already provided in late antiquity by Apuleius (in *De magia* 26-65)[18] and Pliny (in *Nat. hist.* 18.41-43).[19]

However, not only users of magic have to be considered as being subject to violence: these days we may at first glance think about harmful practices in Occultism,[20]

---

[11] On this and the use of magic in Germanic culture, see Rudolf Simek, *Götter und Kulte der Germanen*, Beck'sche Reihe 2335 (3rd ed., Munich: C.H. Beck, 2009), 99–108. In contrast to the *Capitulatio*, the use of violence is rather restricted in the ninth-century *Canon episcopi* of the church, see Decker, *Die Päpste und die Hexen*, 11–15.

[12] Cf. Decker, *Die Päpste und die Hexen*, 47–54.

[13] Cf. Hartmut Hegeler, "Der evangelische Pfarrer Anton Praetorius. Mit der Bibel gegen Folter und Hexenprozesse," in Marcel Nieden (ed.), *Hexenwahn. Eine theologische Selbstbesinnung* TA 5 (Stuttgart: Kohlhammer, 2004), 153–72.

[14] For the text, see Rolf Lieberwirth (ed.), *Christian Thomasius. Vom Laster der Zauberei. Über die Hexenprozesse. De Crimine Magiae. Processus Inquisitorii contra Sagas* (2nd ed., Munich: Deutscher Taschenbuch Verlag, 1987).

[15] Cf. Decker, *Die Päpste und die Hexen*, 100–1.

[16] For the text, see Reginald Scot, *The Discoverie of Witchcraft* (London: John Rodker, 1930).

[17] Cf. also Gaskill, *Witchcraft*, 56–60.

[18] Cf. further Francesca Lamberti, "De magia als rechtsgeschichtliches Dokument," in Jürgen Hammerstadt et al. (eds.), *Apuleius. De Magia—Über die Magie. Lateinisch und deutsch*, Sapere 5 (2nd ed., Darmstadt: Wissenschaftliche Buchgesellschaft, 2008), 331–50. See also Kimberly B. Stratton, *Naming the Witch: Magic, Ideology, and Stereotype in the Ancient World* (New York: Columbia University Press, 2007), 115–16 and Hans G. Kippenberg and Kocku von Stuckrad, *Einführung in die Religionswissenschaft. Gegenstände und Begriffe* (Munich: C.H. Beck, 2003), 158–60.

[19] Cf. Graf, *Gottesnähe und Schadenszauber*, 58–82.

[20] Cf. Sabine Doering-Manteufel, *Okkultismus. Geheimlehren, Geisterglaube, magische Praktiken*, Beck'sche Reihe 2713 (Munich: C.H. Beck, 2011), 85–93.

Satanism,²¹ or even Voodoo,²² when we relate religiously motivated violence and magic to each other. Taking Occultism or Voodoo into account when talking about violent forms of magic is not without problems, since it needs to be remembered that both phenomena exist in various forms. Further, Voodoo needs to be regarded as religion or at least a form of religion and, in addition, does not always concur with prejudices regarding the use of so-called black magic and voodoo dolls.²³

In turn, we may rather find the use of spells and magic causing harm and using violence in antiquity. It is remarkable that in recent discussions concerning magic the topic "violence" often plays a significant role, as long as (alleged) practitioners, for instance, witches, have become victims of violence. At the same time, it needs to be questioned whether or not some willingness to employ violence²⁴ in magical spells and other magic traditions can be detected in texts describing magic.

The Inner Perspective: Violence and Religious Elements in Magical Texts

Especially with the above made reference to Voodoo in mind, one might expect a large number of magical texts such as the *PGM*, the *PDM*,²⁵ collections of Curse

---

²¹ Notably, people allegedly involved with Satanism tend to become either being regarded as those who harm others or victims. On this, see the recent study of Jean La Fontaine, *Witches and Demons: A Comparative Perspective on Witchcraft and Satanism*, Studies in Public and Applied Anthropology 10 (New York and Oxford: Berghahn, 2016), esp. 45–58.

²² For this, see Astrid Reuter, *Voodoo und andere afroamerikanische Religionen*, Beck'sche Reihe 2316 (Munich: C.H. Beck, 2003), passim.

²³ For voodoo dolls as means of employing sympathetic magic, see Owen Davies, *Magic: A Very Short Introduction* (Oxford and New York: Oxford University Press, 2012), 83–4.

²⁴ A distinction between magic and religion is often based on the use of "duress" by those who employ magic: within the boundaries of these discussions "duress" is regarded as a category for defining magic (since Gods or other entities are forced to do the magician's will), whereas Gods are prayed to in religious systems. For examples, see Hans-Josef Klauck, *Die religiöse Umwelt des Urchristentums I. Stadt- und Hausreligion, Mysterienkulte, Volksglaube*, Studienbücher Theologie 9,1 (Stuttgart: Kohlhammer, 1995), 174–5 and William J. Goode, "Magic and Religion: A Continuum," *Ethnos* 14 (1949): 172–82. Cf. further David E. Aune, "Magic in Early Christianity," in *ANRW* II.23.2 (1980): 1507–57; reprinted in David E. Aune (ed.), *Apocalypticism, Prophecy, and Magic in Early Christianity. Collected Essays*, WUNT 199 (Tübingen: Mohr Siebeck, 2006; reprinted in Grand Rapids: Baker Academic, 2008), 368–420, esp. 376–7. The focus of this study is, however, not on this rather debatable category for distinguishing magic and religion, but rather on the actual use of violence in magical texts. For more on this discussion, see also Attilio Mastrocinque, *From Jewish Magic to Gnosticism*, STAC 24 (Tübingen: Mohr Siebeck, 2005), 206–11.

²⁵ For the texts cf. Hans Dieter Betz (ed.), *The Greek Magical Papyri in Translation, Including the Demotic Spells* (2nd ed., Chicago and London: Chicago University Press, 1992); Karl Preisendanz (ed.), *Papyri Graecae Magicae. Die Griechischen Zauberpapyri I*. (2nd ed., Stuttgart: Teubner, 1973); and Karl Preisendanz (ed.), *Papyri Graecae Magicae. Die Griechischen Zauberpapyri II* (2nd ed., Stuttgart: Teubner, 1974).

Tablets or collections of *defixiones* to include countless material which displays the willingness of practitioners of magic to widely employ violence.[26] However, the opposite seems to be the case. Furthermore, especially a connection between the employment of religious elements within violent aims of spells is relatively rarely found.

Numerous spells or magical texts even attempt to circumvent or avoid violence. In certain spells from the *PGM* we can even find attempts to use magical means to avoid anger: *PGM* XII.179-181 represents the attempt to cease someone being angry with the caster of the spell. Other spells, such as *PGM* VII.940-968; *PGM* X.24-35; *PGM* XXXVI.161-177; *PGM* XXXVI.1-34; *PGM* LXXIX.1-7; and *PGM* LXX.1-5, were even supposed to restrain or avoid anger. In *PGM* IV.467-470; IV.824; and IV.831-832 the casters tried to suppress anger (quoting Homer, *Iliad* 10.193) by referring to Zeus ("Will you dare to raise your mighty spear against Zeus?"), thus embedding slightly religious connotations to these spells.

Further, certain spells refer to the power of those who died a violent and untimely death[27]: for instance, *PGM* IV.2006-2125 and IV.2145-2240 suggest the location of a spell to be at burial site. In *PGM* II.64-185 the effectiveness of the spell depends on material from someone "who has died violently" (cf. *PGM* XIXb.4-18 and LXVII.1-24). Similarly, the love spell *PGM* IV.1390-1495 works with help of a

---

[26] The focus of this study is on violence with regard to human beings. However, it needs to be emphasized that forms of violence can naturally also be directed against animals in magical texts (e.g., in reference to animal sacrifices). For this topic, see Sarah Iles Johnston, "Sacrifice in the Greek Magical Papyri," in Paul Mirecki and Marvin Meyer (eds.), *Magic and Ritual in the Ancient World*, RGRW 141 (Leiden: Brill, 2002), 344–58 and Michael D. Swartz, "Sacrificial Themes in Jewish Magic," in Paul Mirecki and Marvin Meyer (eds.), *Magic and Ritual in the Ancient World*, RGRW 141 (Leiden: Brill, 2002), 303–15.

[27] The connection of references to people who met a violent death and magic is often attested in magic spells; cf. for this the thorough investigation in Helen Ingram, *Dragging Down Heaven: Jesus as Magician and Manipulator of Spirits in the Gospels* (PhD Dissertation; Birmingham: The University of Birmingham, 2007), 257–64 and Amina Kropp, "'Dann trag das Bleitäfelchen weg ans Grab eines vorzeitig Verstorbenen.' Antike Fluchtafeln und Ritualobjekte," in Annette Kehnel and Diamantis Panagiotopoulos (eds.), *Schriftträger—Textträger. Zur materialen Präsenz des Geschriebenen in frühen Gesellschaften*, Materiale Textkulturen (Berlin: de Gruyter, 2015), 73–101, here 75–6. For the connection of untimely death and pleas for vengeance, see also Fritz Graf, "Victimology or: How to Deal with Untimely Death," in Kimberly B. Stratton and Dayna S. Kalleres (eds.), *Daughters of Hecate. Women & Magic in the Ancient World* (Oxford and New York: Oxford University Press, 2014), 386–417 and Fritz Graf, "Untimely Death, Witchcraft, and Divine Vengeance: A Reasoned Epigraphical Catalog," *ZPE* 162 (2007): 139–50. For further evidence on the topic, see also Ogden, *Magic, Witchcraft and Ghosts in the Greek and Roman Worlds*, 146–61.

dead gladiator. Admittedly, these examples just relate to violence and the dead in order to be effective or at least enhance their effectiveness.[28]

Other texts may even relate to violence in very strange ways. For instance, the purpose of a part of *PGM* VII.167-186 was to compel two gladiators painted on a cup to fight with each other. In *PGM* III.1-164 one can find references to drowning a cat in water and a summons for an angel for "destroying." The purpose of *PGM* CXXVII.1-12 is to instigate a fight at a banquet.[29] Occasionally, references to violence appear somewhat obscured within these spells. For instance, *PGM* IV.1716-1870, the so-called Sword of Dardanos, has the purpose to bend someone's soul to the will of the caster. However, this spell is addressed to Aphrodite and aims to make someone fall in love with the caster. Similar features like this can also be found in various other love spells: the "Wondrous spell for binding a lover" (*PGM* IV.296-466) involves making figurines[30] of wax (one in the shape of Ares) in order to make the target of the spell fall in love with the caster. The plea to the "god of the dead" is to drag the target by her hair, her heart, and her soul. In most cases, though, love spells have the focus on binding another person to the caster, as in the "Binding love spell of Astrapsoukos"[31] (*PGM* VIII.1-63) and often refer to "fire," in order to invoke burning love of the spell's target, for instance, in the "love spells

---

[28] Occasionally, the references to the deceased or to the underworld can be obscure, as can possibly be seen in "Griechischer Liebeszauber aus Ägypten auf zwei Bleitafeln des Heidelberger Archäologischen Instituts." For the text, see Franz Boll, *Griechischer Liebeszauber aus Ägypten auf zwei Bleitafeln des Heidelberger Archäologischen Instituts. Mit 2 Lichtdrucktafeln,* Sitzungsberichte der Heidelberger Akademie der Wissenschaften. Philosophisch-historische Klasse Bd. 1. (Heidelberg: C. Winter, 1910.)

[29] The content of this spell is rather strange, since the person using this spell is advised to throw something bitten by a dog in the middle of a banquet. Maybe one can regard the content as an analogy to certain descriptions of banquets ending in a brawl, such as Lucian's Symposium where certain philosophers behave in rather cynical and disorderly ways while drunk.

[30] For the text (*PGM* IV.296-466) and the figurine, see also Reinhold Merkelbach (ed.), *Abrasax. Ausgewählte Papyri religiösen und magischen Inhalts. Traumtexte,* Papyrologica Coloniensia XVII.5 (Kleve: Westdeutscher Verlag, 2001), 95–112. For the use of figurines for binding spells, see also Daniel Ogden, "Binding Spells: Curse Tablets and Voodoo Dolls in the Greek and Roman Worlds," in Bengt Ankarloo and Stuart Clark (eds.), *Witchcraft and Magic in Europe: Ancient Greece and Rome* (Philadelphia: University of Pennsylvania Press, 1999), 1–90; Ogden, *Magic, Witchcraft, and Ghosts in the Greek and Roman Worlds,* 245–60; Stephen Skinner, *Techniques of Graeco-Egyptian Magic* (Singapore: Golden Hoard Press, 2017), 148–53; and John G. Gager, *Curse Tablets and Binding Spells from the Ancient World* (New York and Oxford: Oxford University Press, 1992), 15–18.

[31] The name "Astrapsoukos" most likely refers to the famous magician Astrampsychos. On this point, see Franziska Naether, *Die Sortes Astrampsychi. Problemlösungsstrategien durch Orakel im römischen Ägypten,* ORA 3 (Tübingen: Mohr Siebeck, 2010), 66–8.

of attraction" (*PGM* XXXVI.69-101 or *PGM* XXXVI.187-210).³² In another one of these "love spells of attraction" (*PGM* XXXVI.295-311) we find references to Aphrodite and the God of Israel. The woman targeted by this spell is supposed to be enchanted so that she will fall in love (hence the reference to Aphrodite) and feel burning love, clearly alluding to God and his angels destroying Sodom and Gomorrah³³ with fire and sulfur and turning a woman (i.e., Lot's wife) into a pillar of salt.³⁴ Similar references to events narrated in the Hebrew Bible with a clearer involvement of violent contents we can otherwise mostly find in certain prayers for revenge or *defixiones* (see below).

Another distinctive allusion to violence can be found in the so-called "Spell of Pnouthis" (*PGM* I.42-195) which tries to enable the caster to summon an assistant who "kills and destroys." *PDM* XIV.675-694 (cf. *PGM* XIVc.16-27) provides an example how violence can be inflicted by illness: in case of this spell a victim is

---

³² For more details on violence in love spells, see John J. Winkler, "The Constraints of Eros," in Christopher A. Faraone and Dirk Obbink (eds.), *Magika Hiera. Ancient Greek Magic and Religion* (New York and Oxford: Oxford University Press, 1991), 214–43, here 230–4.

³³ Similar allusions to Sodom and Gomorrah appear frequently within love magic, as seen for instance in T-S K 1.73, p. 1, lines 11–14; cf. Joseph Naveh and Shaul Shaked, *Amulets and Magic Bowls. Aramaic Incantations of Late Antiquity* (Jerusalem: Magnes Press, 1985), 230–6 and Gager, *Curse Tablets*, 108. Allusions to Sodom and Gomorrah are also seen in T-S NS 322.20, p. 1a, lines 3–5, and in IM 9736 ("Incantation Bowl for Sowing Discord"). For these texts, see Ortal-Paz Saar, *Jewish Love Magic. From Late Antiquity to the Middle Ages*, Magical and Religious Literature of Late Antiquity 6 (Leiden: Brill, 2017), 185–7. Moreover, certain incantation bowls refer to the destruction of Sodom and Gomorrah in order to threaten demons and evil spirits. See the texts of bowl 2.6 and bowl 6.9-10 in Charles D. Isbell, *Corpus of the Aramaic Incantation Bowls*, SBLDS 17 (Missoula: Scholars Press, 1975), 19–20, 29–30. For references concerning the destruction of Sodom and Gomorrah in curses, see the discussion on the *Curse against Several Violent People* (Papyrus Lichačev) below. An allusion to Sodom and Gomorrah can further be seen in the *Sepher ha-Razim*, where a spell is described, which is supposed to fell a fortified wall and destroy it like Sodom and Gomorrah. For the text, see Michael A. Morgan, *Sepher Ha-Razim. The Book of Mysteries*, SBLTT 25: SBLPS 11 (Chico: Scholars Press, 1983), 28.

³⁴ A similar love spell which is supposed to make the victim feel "tormented by love" is "Die Traumsendung der Domitiana an Urbanus" (= DT 271). For the text, see Reinhold Merkelbach (ed.), *Abrasax. Ausgewählte Papyri religiösen und magischen Inhalts. Exorzismen und jüdisch/christlich beeinflusste Texte*. Papyrologica Coloniensia XVII.4 (Kleve: Westdeutscher Verlag, 1996), 111–22 and Saar, *Jewish Love Magic*, 45. This spell represents an invocation of a demonic spirit which is adjured by praying to God and praising his power, therefore alluding to numerous passages from the Hebrew Bible and also early Jewish prayers (e.g., the Prayer of Manasseh).

supposed to be struck by "chills and fever."[35] In some other spells violent aims are openly displayed: *PGM* XIII.1-343 (esp. 262) is intended to be used to kill a snake addressing it with the name Aphyphis (possibly an allusion to the Egyptian god Apophis[36]); in *PDM* XIV.739-740 camel's blood and dead man's blood is to be employed for killing humans,[37] thus using the "magic" of the spell like poison, and *PDM* XIV.741 is intended to make someone blind. Given the vast amount of spells within the *PGM* and *PDM* we can conclude that violence and bodily harm are relatively rare within this magic corpus.

More openly and more often violence seems to be displayed in *defixiones* and spells which work similarly.[38] For instance, "Apollo's charm to subject" (*PGM* X.36-50) involves writing certain names (among which there are angels' names, such as Gabriel, Raphael, or Michael,[39] and divine names, for instance, Adonai) on a metal lamella. A frog's tongue is then to be put into the plate and in the spell-caster's sandal. The target's tongue shall be trampled down in analogy to the names embedded in the charm.

Some similar spells actually share an interest in generally restraining an adversary (e.g., *PGM* VII.394-395; 396-404; 417-422; 429-458) or binding him (e.g., *PGM* V.304-369). Often only certain body parts of an opponent are intended to be affected and to be held down: *PGM* CXXIV.1-43 is supposed to inflict

---

[35] For the full text, see Joachim Friedrich Quack, "Texte aus Ägypten. 4. Demotische magische und divinatorische Texte," in Bernd Janowski and Gernot Wilhelm (eds.), *Omina, Orakel, Rituale und Beschwörungen*, TUAT N.F. 4 (Gütersloh: Gütersloher Verlagshaus, 2008), 331–85, here 349–50. The reference to "chills and fever" might be reminiscent of a terminology ("fever and chills") present in Deut 28:22, which also often occurs in magical texts; cf. David Lincicum, "Greek Deuteronomy's 'Fever and Chills' and Their Magical Afterlife," *VT* 58 (2008): 544–9. However, *PDM* XIV.675-694 (cf. *PGM* XIVc.16-27) refers to these words in a reversed order.

[36] Cf. Albrecht Dieterich, *Abraxas. Studien zur Religionsgeschichte des spätern Altertums* (Leipzig: Teubner, 1891), 189.

[37] Spells for making war, sending a plague, or making opponents kill each other are also preserved within the *Harba de-Moshe* ("Sword of Moses"). For the text, see Moses Gaster, *The Sword of Moses. An Ancient Book of Magic from an Unique Manuscript. With Introduction, Translation, an Index of Mystical Names, and a Facsimile* (London: D. Nutt, 1896).

[38] Cf. for a summary of such spells employing violence Skinner, *Techniques of Graeco-Egyptian Magic*, 244–5, 301–12. For curse tablets in general, see also Karl Preisendanz, "Fluchtafel (Defixion)," in *RAC* 8 (Stuttgart: Anton Hiersemann, 1972), cols. 1–29.

[39] Angelic names and especially the name of the angel Michael appear frequently in the *PGM*. See Thomas J. Kraus, "Angels in the Magical Papyri—The Classic Example of Michael, the Archangel," in Friedrich V. Reiterer, Tobias Nicklas, and Karin Schöpflin (eds.), *Angels. The Concept of Celestial Beings—Origins, Development and Reception*, DCL.Y 2007 (Berlin and New York: de Gruyter, 2007), 611–27 and Matthias Hoffmann. "Systematic Chaos or Chain of Tradition? References to Angels in Early Jewish and Early Christian Literature and Magical Writings," in Amsalu Tefera and Loren T. Stuckenbruck (eds.), *Representations of Angelic Beings in Early Jewish and in Christian Traditions*. WUNT 2.544 (Tübingen: Mohr Siebeck, 2021) 89–129.

blindness; and the purpose of *PGM* V.70-95 is to cause massive pain in the eyes of a thief.

In another *defixio* (ca. 350 BCE), displayed in the "Antikensammlung im Archäologischen Museum der WWU Münster,"[40] some opponents of the spell-caster at court are cursed referring to various gods which are associated with the underworld (e.g., Hermes Katochos, Persephone, and Hades[41]). Such judicial references can actually be found commonly among the *defixiones* which contain curses or curse-like features in order to influence opponents' deeds, or body parts,[42] or health and thus to have control over their actions. Many of the *defixiones* contain magic words or language and expressions (esp. the characteristic formula "I bind" or respectively δέω), in order to get the result the caster wishes to achieve.[43] In most cases, the metal plates containing the *defixiones* were buried in graves or thrown in wells (or in case of *PGM* VII.464-466 into the sea) in accordance with their connection to the gods of the underworld[44] that were asked for assistance.

Next to some spells from the body of *PGM* and *PDM* which may be characterized as *defixio* a vast amount of such spells, curses,[45] and prayers for

---

[40] For the text and similar *defixiones*, see Werner Peek, *Kerameikos. Ergebnisse der Ausgrabungen III: Inschriften, Ostraka, Fluchtafeln* (Berlin: de Gruyter, 1941).

[41] For references to gods of the underworld in *defixiones*, see Kai Brodersen, "Briefe in die Unterwelt: Religiöse Kommunikation auf griechischen Fluchtafeln," in Kai Brodersen (ed.), *Gebet und Fluch, Zeichen und Traum. Aspekte religiöser Kommunikation in der Antike* (Münster: Lit, 2001), 57–68; Frenschkowski, *Magie im antiken Christentum*, 124–5; and Kropp, 'Dann trag das Bleitäfelchen weg ans Grab eines vorzeitig Verstorbenen,' 92–4. For similar lists of chthonic deities, see also *PGM* IV.1390-1495; IV.2785-2890; *DTA* 102, 103, or *SGD* 44.

[42] Cf. also Christopher A. Faraone, "Magic and Medicine in the Roman Imperial Period: Two Case Studies," in Gideon Bohak, Yuval Harari, and Shaul Shaked (eds.), *Continuity and Innovation in the Magical Tradition*, Jerusalem Studies in Religion and Culture 15 (Leiden: Brill, 2011), 135–58, here 148–9.

[43] For content, language, and forms of *defixiones* in general, see also Peter Busch, *Magie in neutestamentlicher Zeit*, FRLANT 218 (Göttingen: Vandenhoeck & Ruprecht, 2006), 31–44; Robert Conner, *Magic in the New Testament. A Survey and Appraisal of the Evidence* (Oxford: Mandrake, 2010), 182–7; and Heinz Schreckenberg, *Ananke. Untersuchungen zur Geschichte des Wortgebrauchs*, ZMKA 36 (Munich: C.H. Beck, 1964), 135–9.

[44] Cf. Werner Riess, *Performing Interpersonal Violence. Court, Curse, and Comedy in Fourth-century BCE Athens*, MythosEikonPoiesis 4 (Berlin and Boston: Walter de Gruyter, 2012), 188; and Gager, *Curse Tablets*, 18–21.

[45] For various other examples of curses, especially from the Roman era, see also Alf Önnerfors (ed.), *Antike Zaubersprüche. Zweisprachig* (Stuttgart: Reclam, 1991), 44–53; Ogden, *Magic, Witchcraft and Ghosts in the Greek and Roman Worlds*, 210–18; and Esther Eidinow, *Oracles, Curses, & Risk among the Ancient Greeks* (Oxford and New York: Oxford University Press, 2007), 139–55, 352–455.

vengeance can be found in the collections[46] of *SGD* (*Survey of Greek Defixiones*),[47] *SEG* (*Supplementum Epigraphicum Graecum*),[48] *DT* (*Defixionum Tabellae*),[49] or *DTA* (*Defixionum Tabellae Atticae*).[50]

The intended aims of a majority of these texts are to influence (i.e., to bind) opponents in legal trials.[51] Mostly body parts which bear significance in courtrooms—mouth, tongue, soul, and mind—are the intended target of these curses. In *SGD* 95, for instance, the "tongues of Eukleês and Aristophanes ... and their advocates" shall be bound (cf. similarly *PGM* VII.925-939 and *DT* 49). Especially in judicial contexts examples for *defixiones* with an attempt to have control over an adversary and control his tongue are very common.[52]

Other spells and curses within this category have the purpose to weaken adversaries in athletic competitions, dancers,[53] and gladiators, on the one hand, or even craftsmen and manufacturers, on the other. These spells also often represent an attempt to have influence on body parts relevant for the corresponding activities, such as hands, arms, or legs. In *SGD* 139, for instance, a charioteer and his horses are subject to a curse in order to be incapable of running, jumping, or moving forward.[54] Similarly, *DT* 242 is supposed to have an effect on charioteers and

---

[46] For a short survey of collections of *defixiones*, see also Brodersen, "Briefe in die Unterwelt," 59–61.

[47] For the *SGD* text, see David R. Jordan, "Survey of Greek Defixiones Not Included in the Special Corpora," *GRBS* 26 (1985): 151–97.

[48] For the *SEG*, see Jacobus J. E. Hondius et al. (eds.), *Supplementum Epigraphicum Graecum* (Leiden: Sijthoff, 1923–71); New Series: Henk W. Pleket, Ronald S. Stroud, Johan H. M. Strubbe et al. (eds.), *Supplementum Epigraphicum Graecum* (Alphen: Sijthoff; Amsterdam: Gieben; Leiden: Brill, 1976–).

[49] For the *DT*, see Auguste Audollent, *Defixionum tabellae quotquot innotuerunt tam in Graecis Orientis quam in totius Occidenti partibus praeter Atticas in Corpore Inscriptionum Atticarum editas* (Paris: A. Fontemoing, 1904).

[50] For the *DTA* text, see Richard Wünsch, *Defixionum Tabellae Atticae*, IG III,3 (Berlin: Reimer, 1897).

[51] For the different categories of curse tablets, see also Riess, *Performing Interpersonal Violence*, 167.

[52] For curses and *defixiones* in judicial scenarios, see also Gager, *Curse Tablets*, 116–50.

[53] For an example, see Attilio Mastrocinque, "A Defixio from Caesarea Maritima against a Dancer," in Celia Sánchez Natalías (ed.), *Litterae Magicae. Studies in Honour of Roger S.O. Tomlin* Supplementa MHNH 2 (Zaragoza: Libros Pórtico, 2019), 59–76.

[54] Cf. Hendrik S. Versnel, *Fluch und Gebet: Magische Manipulation versus religiöses Flehen? Religionsgeschichtliche und hermeneutische Betrachtungen über antike Fluchtafeln*, Hans-Lietzmann-Vorlesungen 10 (Berlin and New York: de Gruyter, 2009), 8–9. Generally speaking, spells with the purpose of binding any opposition (animals or humans) in the context of competition within theater or circus are widespread. Cf. Gager, *Curse Tablets*, 42–77.

horses making a victory in the circus impossible[55] (cf. similarly *DT* 233 exclusively targeting the horses). In *DTA* 74 we find an example of craftsmen being bound on tongue, body, and affairs of business.[56]

A fourth group[57] of these spells and curses deals with matters of sexuality and erotic affairs.[58] In curses such as *SGD* 152-156 people are enchanted in order to be incapable of having intercourse with any other person than the spell-caster.[59]

It is remarkable, though, that in most cases of these *defixiones* and curses adversaries are just "bound" by magic and the hostile effect often has only a temporal effect which is restricted to certain body parts. Therefore, one can probably hardly argue that *defixiones* are violent in general. Their limited (temporal and) areal effect does probably not allow for assumptions concerning bodily harm and violence to play a significant role.[60]

In turn, more willingness to employ violence becomes apparent in so-called[61] Prayers for Justice and Pleas for Vengeance. Notably, within these texts help from gods, demons, and other entities is frequently asked for.[62] An interest in inflicting harm on others can for instance be seen in *SGD* 21, where thieves are cursed and "handed over" to Pluto, Persephone, the Furies, and Hekate, in order to have their hearts cut out. That thieves are a welcome target for curses can further be seen in *SGD* 58, where some Syrian Gods (Lord Gods Sukonaioi and Lady Goddess Syria) are asked to punish and direct their anger against a thief (cf. also *PGM*

---

[55] For the text, see Gager, *Curse Tablets*, 62-4 and Merkelbach, *Abrasax*, 47–57. For various similar examples of curses against charioteers and their horses, see Christopher A. Faraone, "Cursing Chariot Horses Instead of Drivers in the Hippodromes of the Eastern Roman Empire," in Celia Sánchez Natalías (ed.), *Litterae Magicae. Studies in Honor of Roger S.O. Tomlin* (Zaragoza: Libros Pórtico, 2019), 83–101.

[56] Cf. further Gager, *Curse Tablets*, 151–74.

[57] Cf. for these categories also Versnel, *Fluch und Gebet,* 8–9 and Silke Trzcionka, *Magic and the Supernatural in Fourth-Century Syria* (London and New York: Routledge, 2007), 38–99.

[58] For evidence, see Gager, *Curse Tablets*, 78–115; Ogden, *Magic, Witchcraft and Ghosts in the Greek and Roman Worlds*, 227–36; Eidinow, *Oracles, Curses, & Risk among the Ancient Greeks*, 206–24; Peter Hasenfratz, *Die antike Welt und das Christentum. Menschen, Mächte, Gottheiten im Römischen Weltreich* (Darmstadt: Wissenschaftliche Buchgesellschaft, 2004), 58–66; and Christopher A. Faraone, *Ancient Greek Love Magic* (Cambridge, MA: Harvard University Press, 2009), 41–131.

[59] For the examples above, see also Versnel, *Fluch und Gebet*, 8–10.

[60] Cf. also Versnel, *Fluch und Gebet*, 6–14 and Riess, *Performing Interpersonal Violence,* 189–222.

[61] It is problematic to distinguish clearly between different categories of different forms of magical texts. On this, see Versnel, *Fluch und Gebet*, 14–15. This problem becomes even more apparent comparing some early Jewish prayers and prayers for justice which possibly have a Jewish background. On this, see the discussion below.

[62] Cf. Gager, *Curse Tablets*, 175.

III.483-488). Various similar curses against thieves have notably also been found in England: in these curses[63] certain gods are also asked for assistance in punishing thieves and doing them harm. Another commonplace and cause for placing curses is connected to disturbing burial grounds. In some Greek Epitaphs[64] one can see that grave-robbers and disturbers of graves are cursed with either being destroyed by Zeus, or being guilty in the eyes of Leto, with death (circumscribed as leaving orphaned children) and losing all their goods by fire, or simply meet an untimely death.[65]

Certain other Prayers and Pleas for Justice share these features with the purpose of causing bodily harm with the intervention of divine entities. Notably though, they allude to some well-known biblical traditions:

On a lead tablet from Megara (first or second century CE) people are cursed on "body, spirit, soul, mind, thought, feeling, life, heart—with Hekatean words and Hebrew oaths (ὁρκίσμασί τε αβραϊκοῖς)" and "commanded by the holy names and oaths of the Hebrews (ὑπὸ τῶν ἱερῶν ὀνομάτων αβραϊκῶν τε ὁρκισμάτων)."[66] In this curse we can only suspect some sort of Jewish influence. Within other curses, though, such a form of influence and syncretism becomes more apparent. An inscription from Chalcis (second century) with the purpose of protecting property reveals an interesting detail: the curse against those who trespass includes the warning that God may "strike this person with trouble and chills and itch and drought and insanity and blindness and mental fits," thus clearly quoting from Deut 28:22-28.[67] In addition, the inscription also includes blessings for the person who protects the property: "may he fare well and enjoy a good reputation with everyone; may his house prosper by the birth of children and the enjoyment of his

---

[63] Cf. also Gager, *Curse Tablets*, 194–8. For more examples for prayers for justice, see also Ogden, *Magic, Witchcraft and Ghosts in the Greek and Roman Worlds*, 219–22.

[64] For these curses, see also Gager, *Curse Tablets*, 178.

[65] Examples for the punishment of those who disturb a final resting place by magic are innumerable and can be found all over the Mediterranean world. For a detailed survey on the protection of graves with magic, see Christoffer Theis, *Magie und Raum. Der magische Schutz ausgewählter Räume im alten Ägypten nebst einem Vergleich zu angrenzenden Kulturbereichen*, ORA 13 (Tübingen: Mohr Siebeck, 2014), 433–590; idem, "Inschriften zum Schutz der Grabstätte im Raum Syrien-Palästina," UF 45 (2014): 73–295; and Johan H. M. Strubbe, "Cursed Be He That Moves My Bones," in Christopher A. Faraone and Dirk Obbink (eds.), *Magika Hiera. Ancient Greek Magic and Religion* (New York and Oxford: Oxford University Press, 1991), 33–59.

[66] For the text, see Gager, *Curse Tablets*, 183–4 and Richard Wünsch. *Antike Fluchtafeln*, Kleine Texte für Vorlesungen und Übungen 20 (2nd ed., Bonn: A. Marcus und E. Weber, 1912), 4–7.

[67] Cf. Gager, *Curse Tablets*, 184–5 and Lincicum, "Fever and Chills," 547–8. Curses from Deuteronomy also appear in certain incantation bowls, as for instance Deut 28:22, 28; 28:35; 29:19. For the text (on bowl 9), see Naveh and Shaked, *Amulets and Magic Bowls*, 174–9 and Gager, *Curse Tablets*, 205–7.

crops; and may Grace and Health watch over him." This blessing might represent an allusion to Deut 11:26.[68] The curses from Deuteronomy also occur on a burial inscription from Acmonia in Asia Minor (248/249 CE). Anyone who disturbs the grave or buries another corpse in it shall be subject to "the curses written in Deuteronomy" (ἐν τῷ Δευτερονομίῳ). A similar reference can be found in "Apa Victor's curse against Alo" (Michigan 3565), where the "curses of the Law and Deuteronomy" are descending on the victim of the curse.[69]

These references to the curses from Deuteronomy can be assumed to represent some kind of Jewish influence; however, a definite statement on this matter can hardly be made. Apa Victor's curse has to be considered as Christian, since the title "Apa" (= "abbott") seems to reflect a monastic background. However, there are no other traces within the text suggesting a Christian background. The inscription from Acmonia has been found near other gravestones which are Jewish in origin; therefore, it is probable that this inscription can be considered to be Jewish as well.[70] Moreover, on the lead tablet from Megara we can find hints which point to a Jewish origin of the curse: the targets of the curse are anathematized by the use of the word ἀναθηματίζειν which exclusively occurs in Jewish (and Christian) writings (for instance in Deut 13:15 LXX; 1 Cor 12:3; 16:22; Gal 1:8; and Rom 9:3).[71] In the case of the curse from Chalcis there also seems to be little doubt of Jewish influence, since the phrasing of the actual curse only refers to Deuteronomy and one single god, whereas other elements occurring in curses seem to have been eliminated. Possibly the originator of the curse, Amphicles, was an aristocrat or significant person who can be identified as "judaizing" gentile who came in touch with biblical texts and considered them to be a powerful element of a curse.[72]

A similar inclusion of several biblical phrases and the call for justice to God can also be observed in the "Prayer for Justice from Rheneia."[73] This curse from

---

[68] Cf. Gager, *Curse Tablets*, 185 n. 28.

[69] Cf. for the text Marvin Meyer and Richard Smith (eds.), *Ancient Christian Magic. Coptic Texts of Ritual Power* (Princeton: Princeton University Press, 1999), 211–12. See also Hans-W. Fischer-Elfert (ed.), *Altägyptische Zaubersprüche* (Stuttgart: Reclam, 2005), 126.

[70] Cf. Gager, *Curse Tablets*, 191.

[71] Ibid., 183 n. 14.

[72] Ibid., 184–5.

[73] An interesting parallel for this prayer for vengeance possibly occurs in the *Runestone of Sjonhem Kyrka* from Gotland (11th cent.) and also on some other runestones from the Viking era; cf. Janine Köster, "Sterbeinschriften auf wikingerzeitlichen Runensteinen," *RGA-E* 89 (2014): 102–3. Similar to the content of the "Prayer for Justice from Rheneia" the relatives of a deceased request God to take vengeance for a certain Rodfos on the *Runestone from Sjonhem Kyrka*: They plead to God that he may help Rodfos' soul and to punish those by betrayal who betrayed Rodfos. For text and translation, see Sune Lindqvist, *Gotlands Bildsteine*, vol. I–II (Stockholm: Wahlström & Widstrand, 1941–2), I, fig. 146; and II, p. 111; and Sven B. F. Jansson, *Runes in Sweden* (Stockholm: Gidlunds, 1987), 63. Since this runestone also depicts a cross it is without doubt Christian in origin. Therefore, one may wonder if it was simply the significance in certain Nordic heroic tales which have led to

epitaphs from Rheneia near Delos has been preserved in two almost identical forms: only the names of the person for whom vengeance is pleaded for vary, on one epitaph the deceased woman has the name Heraklea, on the other the name is Marthina.[74] Both prayers ask for God's (and his angels'[75]) assistance, in order to

the manifestation of vengeance in this inscription (for discussion, see Stephen Gundry, *Miscellaneous Studies towards the Cult of Óðinn* [New Haven: The Troth, 2014], 7), or if one can rather see a general feature of a (Christian) prayer for vengeance here. In other words, both texts probably represent an attempt to avoid personal revenge in a social context which otherwise displays a certain willingness to employ violent revenge. In case of the *Runestone of Sjonhem Kyrka* we might, therefore, see the attempt to solve a problem without taking personal revenge and instead calling for divine aid. Similarly, the "Prayer for Justice from Rheneia" might reflect solving the problem referred to by asking for God's intercession rather than taking personal revenge which could possibly be perceived as a more predominant solution in Hellenism. For the use of violence in Hellenism, see Hans-Joachim Gehrke, "Die Griechen und die Rache. Ein Versuch in historischer Psychologie," *Saeculum* 38 (1987): 121–49. The reason to circumvent violence seems to have rather obvious religious reasons in both texts. In any case, the change of attitude toward vengeance is not only reflected in Swedish texts such as the *Runestone of Sjonhem Kyrka*, but also in other Scandinavian legal texts, as for instance in the Norwegian *Landslov* or the Islandic *Jónsbók* (13th cent.) which are also influenced by Christian ideas. For the Christian influence on Scandinavian legal texts and literature in general, see Rudolf Simek, *Religion und Mythologie der Germanen* (2nd ed., Darmstadt: Theiss, 2014), 213–27.

More significantly, texts such as the "Prayer for Justice from Rheneia" and the *Runestone of Sjonhem Kyrka* raise the question whether or not it is justified to regard prayers for vengeance as almost magical in content and so consequently displaying a divergent form of religion. On the contrary, one may probably assume that these prayers oppose the concept of personal revenge and express a biblically influenced worldview in which revenge is forbidden to humans and is exclusively the right of God himself. In the case of the "Prayer for Justice from Rheneia" one observes explicit allusions to Mal 2:17 and 3:5 (see also below), as well as allusions to Deut 32:35; Rom 12:19; Matt 5:38-39; 18:12; Heb 10:30 (cf. also *2 Enoch* 50:1-4). Such prayers for vengeance could (regarding the exclusive divine right to take revenge) represent forms of texts in complete coherence with holy scripture (*despite* possibly giving an impression of almost being "magical" in character), rather than being deviant to the religious contexts in which they are obviously written. Therefore, texts like prayers for vengeance provide a good reason for being extremely cautious with categories such as "deviance," in order to establish a clear-cut distinction between "magical" and "religious" texts.

[74] For the text, see Gager, *Curse Tablets*, 185–7. See also Loren T. Stuckenbruck, *Angel Veneration and Christology: A Study in Early Judaism and in the Christology of the Apocalypse of John*, WUNT II/70 (Tübingen: Mohr Siebeck, 1995), 183–5.

[75] On the significance of angelic participation in God's revenge in the "Prayer for Justice from Rheneia," see Loren T. Stuckenbruck, "'Angels' and 'God': Exploring the Limits of Early Jewish Monotheism," in Loren T. Stuckenbruck and Wendy E. S. North (eds.), *Early Jewish and Christian Monotheism*, JSNTSup 263 (London and New York: T&T Clark, 2004), 45–70, here 53–4.

avenge the dead women's innocent blood and punish the people responsible for their deaths in order to meet the same end.⁷⁶ Whether or not one can consider these curses to be magical in character is difficult to decide. The invocation of God with the expression ἐπικαλοῦμαι, for instance, can also be frequently found in spells from the *PGM* (e.g., *PGM* IV.1215-1220; IV.1981; XVIIb.1-23). However, the same expression also occurs regularly in the Septuagint.⁷⁷ Nevertheless, evidence for a magical background of the "Prayer for Justice from Rheneia" can be provided. The topic of these epitaphs connecting a *prayer* with vengeance may be considered as unusual, although such invocations of gods or other entities with a plea for revenge also occur frequently within the *PGM*: In *PGM* LI.1-27 a demon of the dead is asked for assistance in a trial in order to avenge the spell-caster. A closer parallel to the "Prayer for Justice from Rheneia" can be found in *PGM* XL.1-18, where Oserapis is called by a certain Artemisia, in order to protect her husband's grave from grave-robbers.⁷⁸ Especially curses against those who disturb the resting places of the dead are commonly connected with invocations toward certain gods (such as Katachthonios, Selene, Hekate, or Helios).⁷⁹ Similar to the "Prayer for Justice from Rheneia" some magic texts have also been formulated as prayers: For instance, *PGM* XXIX.1-10 constitutes a prayer for good winds in an almost poetical form (although without addressing a god). In *PGM* I.195-222 the "first-born god" is asked for deliverance. *PGM* XII.21-48 is a prayer for curing a disease and in *PGM* XVIIb.1-23 Hermes is asked for assistance in affairs of divination.

A notable analogy between the "Prayer for Justice from Rheneia" in lines 12–13 and magic texts may be constituted by the reference to the effect of the prayer to

---

⁷⁶ Prayers for Justice, as provided here by the example of the "Prayer for Justice from Rheneia," do not necessarily result in asking God to act in violence: The "Communual Prayer" (Pap. Egerton 5) 20 is directed to God, in order to avoid acting in wrath against mortals. Moreover, the "Prayer for Justice from Rheneia" probably represents an exception for Jewish "magic" texts, since aggressive and violent magic is rarely attested in early Judaism; cf. Gideon Bohak, *Ancient Jewish Magic: A History* (Cambridge: Cambridge University Press, 2008), 123–35. Possibly the deliberate abstinence from violence is also displayed in Josephus' account on the miracle-worker Ḥoni and his refusal to curse fellow Jews in *Ant.* 14.22-24; cf. Bohak, *Ancient Jewish Magic*, 128–30.

⁷⁷ Cf. Gen 4:26; Deut 4:7; Amos 4:12; Joel 2:32; Jonah 1:6; or Sir 6:5. For this expression, see Pieter van der Horst and Judith H. Newman, *Early Jewish Prayers in Greek*, CEJL (Berlin and New York: de Gruyter, 2008), 139.

⁷⁸ For the text and its interpretation, see also Andrea Jördens, "Griechische Texte aus Ägypten," in Bernd Janowski and Gernot Wilhelm (eds.), *Omina, Orakel, Rituale und Beschwörungen*, TUAT N.F. 4 (Gütersloh: Gütersloher Verlagshaus, 2008), 417–45, here 429–30.

⁷⁹ Cf. Strubbe, "Cursed be he that moves my bones," 33–59; Gager, *Curse Tablets*, 175–99; and Hasenfratz, *Die antike Welt und das Christentum*, 64. For chthonic gods, see also *DT* 18, 22, 24, 26-27, 29-33, 35, 37-38, 74-75, 242.

work "as quickly as possible" (τὴν ταχίστην). Analogies for this reference (i.e., a fast intervention by a god or a demon) can also be found in various other magic texts (mostly at the end of the text) such as *PGM* III.123-124; IV.1245, 1594, 1924, 2037, 2098 (ἤδη ἤδη ταχύ ταχύ).[80] Also such references can be regularly found in some early Christian curses (e.g., in "A widow's Curse against Shenoute" [Munich Coptic Papyrus 5], the "Curse against Several Violent People" [Papyrus Lichačev], the "Curse against Perjurers" [Berlin 10587], and the "Curse of a Mother against her Son's Female Companion" [London Oriental Manuscript 6172]).[81]

Whether or not all the analogies between these Jewish prayers for vengeance and *defixiones* and magic curses allow for a designation of these texts as magic text may be questioned: the occurrence of elements of prayers in magic texts does naturally not indicate that prayers are generally magical in nature, because they contain similar elements as magic writings. In case of the "Prayer for Justice from Rheneia" unambiguous proof allowing for classifying it as magic writing, such as magic words and language cannot be provided.

A detail which possibly deserves attention is the reference to the cause of death of Heraklea ("Prayer for Justice from Rheneia" 8): the untimely death of Heraklea is described with a form of φαρμακεύειν (φαρμακεύσαντας). A translation of this expression is difficult here, since the word could refer to the woman's death either by poison or by magic. A clear identification of the cause of death is unfortunately impossible. The unspecific reason given here can certainly not be identified as magic by a general statement that φαρμακεύειν "was used just as frequently, if not more so, with reference to the casting of spells."[82] Evidence for such an assumption can hardly be provided.

The combination of φαρμακεύειν and a fast intervention of God to restore justice as such is also notable: a connection between the topic of vengeance (cf. especially "Prayer for Justice from Rheneia" 12) and God's swift intervention (cf. ibid. 13) and φαρμακεύειν (cf. ibid. 8) may possibly also exist in Malachi. The question where the God of righteousness is (ποῦ ἐστιν ὁ θεὸς τῆς δικαιοσύνης) raised in Mal 2:17 is answered in Mal 3:5 where God is described as a swift witness against those who committed various crimes amongst which also a reference to φάρμακοι

---

[80] Cf. also van der Horst and Newman, *Early Jewish Prayers*, 143 and David E. Aune, "The Apocalypse of John and Graeco-Roman Revelatory Magic," in Aune's collected works, *Apocalypticism, Prophecy and Magic in Early Christianity*, 347–67, here 366–7. For more on this issue, see Rodney L. Thomas, *Magical Motifs in the Book of Revelation*, LNTS 416 (London and New York: T&T Clark, 2010), 100–6.

[81] For the texts, see Meyer and Smith (eds.), *Ancient Christian Magic*, 188–97; and Angelicus M. Kropp, *Ausgewählte Koptische Zaubertexte*. vol. 2: *Übersetzungen und Anmerkungen* (Brussels: Édition de la Fondation Égyptologique Reine Élisabeth, 1931), 229–42.

[82] Gager, *Curse Tablets*, 187 n. 38. Cf. also van der Horst and Newman, *Early Jewish Prayers*, 140.

can be found (ἔσομαι μάρτυς ταχὺς ἐπὶ τὰς φαρμακούς).[83] The list of crimes provided in this context is reminiscent of similar catalogues of sins containing references to φαρμακεία, as can for instance be found in Gal 5:20; Rev 9:21; 18:23; 21:8; 22:15; or *Ascension of Isaiah* 2:5. However, an interpretation of φαρμακεία (and derivatives) as magic remains uncertain and therefore does not help to define the cause of death in the texts from Rheneia.[84] However, the presence of an allusion to Malachi might already suggest some form of strong Jewish background of the "Prayers from Rheneia."[85]

Moreover, the "Prayers from Rheneia" share very similar features with the curses and other prayers for vengeance mentioned above. Similar to some of the other curses we also find allusions to various passages—or at least certain expressions—from the Septuagint within the "Prayers from Rheneia": as stated above, the expression for calling God (ἐπικαλοῦμαι) occurs several times in the Septuagint (see above). In case of the "Prayers from Rheneia" the word is connected with referring to God as "the highest" (ὕψιστος) is also used in Ben Sira 46:5 (cf. also Mark 5:7 and *Test. Sol.* 11:6). This designation alone is common in the Septuagint (cf. Num 24:16; Mic 6:6; Ps 81:6).[86] Further, the salutation of God as "Lord of the Spirits and of all flesh" has been quite literally adopted from Num 16:22 and 27:16. Similarly one can find parallels for the description of God as "Lord, you who oversees all things" in the Septuagint (namely in 2 Macc 7:35; 12:22; 15:2; 3 Macc 2:21).[87] Also the phrase, "for whom every soul humbles itself on the present day with supplication," strongly points to influence of the Septuagint here: similar expressions can for instance be seen in Lev 16:29, 31; 23:27; and Ps 34(35):13 (cf. also Pr Man 4 and Pr Azariah 3:38-39). A more direct influence, however, can be found in Lev 23:29 and the reference to the Day of Atonement. Accordingly, both "Prayers for Vengeance from Rheneia" are probably texts asking for divine

---

[83] Cf. for the combination of God establishing swift justice against those who kill by poison (regarding Malachi as a considerable parallel for the Book of Revelation) also Thomas, *Magical Motifs*, 23.

[84] A solid example for death caused by magic is provided by the inscription on the gravestone of the boy Jucundus (*CIL* VI.3 19474), where the boy's death is brought about by witches. The content of the inscription on the gravestone is a warning and an accusation concerning the witch, however, in contrast to the "Prayers from Rheneia," a call for vengeance is not explicitly made. For the text, see Jens Schröter and Jürgen K. Zangenberg (eds.), *Texte zur Umwelt des Neuen Testaments*, UTB 3663 (3rd ed., Tübingen: Mohr Siebeck, 2013), 360 and Graf, *Gottesnähe und Schadenszauber*, 148.

[85] If one can consider the passages from Malachi as significant influence for this writing, it seems consequently questionable to regard the prayers as Samaritan, as proposed for instance by Gager, *Curse Tablets*, 186.

[86] Cf. van der Horst and Newman, *Early Jewish Prayers*, 139.

[87] Cf. van der Horst and Newman, *Early Jewish Prayers*, 141 and Gager, *Curse Tablets*, 187 n. 43.

intervention on Yom Kippur and therefore strongly indicate their use within a Jewish community.[88]

The tendency to allude to the Septuagint can also be seen in the description of the punishment of this prayer: the idea that the cursed person shall suffer along with his children possibly alludes to Exod 20:5 and Num 14:18.[89] Moreover, the spilling of "innocent blood" is reminiscent of Deut 19:10; 21:8-9; 2 Kgs 24:4; and Sus (θ) 62.[90] In addition, the expression, "avenge and requite her innocent blood," in lines 12–13 could correspond with Septuagint language, as preserved in Gen 9:5; 42:22; Deut 17:8; or Joel 4:21.[91] Therefore, we find massive evidence that the "Prayers from Rheneia" as well as the other curses mentioned above are certainly Jewish in origin or at least display strong Jewish influences by frequent allusions and quotations from the Hebrew Bible and especially the Septuagint.

Subsequently, we can summarize at this point that violence represents an element that can be observed in many texts which are considered to be magical in character. However, the number of spells and curses describing violent effects is rather limited compared to the amount of texts available in various collections. Especially in the *PGM* and *PDM* harmful magic is admittedly rare. The spells within this collection indicate a very limited use of violence and if harm is the intended target of spells the effects are often restricted to certain body parts and having an effect for limited time only. Exceptions from this observation possibly describe a kind of magic which either prevents damage (by killing a harmful snake) or can be considered as an act of poisoning (by killing someone with probably harmful substances).

In various *defixiones* a tendency to employ violence in order to solve certain conflicts is displayed more often. However, such an assessment is not unproblematic, since an undisputed clear-cut definition of what constitutes a *defixio* does not exist.[92] Despite the lack of such a definition, it is commonly agreed on the use of *defixiones* and similar writings: the purpose of many *defixiones* to have a harmful effect on targets can be considered rather typical for magic spells. However, it is debatable if one can simply assume violence as openly displayed feature: clearly a

---

[88] Cf. van der Horst and Newman, *Early Jewish Prayers*, 142 and Gager, *Curse Tablets*, 187 n. 44.

[89] Cf. van der Horst and Newman, *Early Jewish Prayers*, 140 and Gager, *Curse Tablets*, 187 n. 42.

[90] Cf. van der Horst and Newman, *Early Jewish Prayers*, 140 and Gager, *Curse Tablets*, 187 n. 40.

[91] Cf. van der Horst and Newman, *Early Jewish Prayers*, 143 and Gager, *Curse Tablets*, 187 n. 45.

[92] Cf. Versnel, *Fluch und Gebet*, 14; and Hendrik S. Versnel, "Beyond Cursing: The Appeal to Justice in Judicial Prayers," in Christopher A. Faraone and Dirk Obbink (eds.), *Magika Hiera. Ancient Greek Magic and Religion* (New York and Oxford: Oxford University Press, 1991), 60–106, here 60–2. For a possible definition, see Collins, *Magic in the Ancient Greek World*, 64–7.

judicial background of these attempts to take control of certain situations or the purpose to achieve justice has to be kept in mind for understanding the use of such texts. Consequently, it can be concluded that the evidence for the aim to cause harm and employ violence is rather limited in the magic texts from *PGM* and *PDM*. A massive amount of these magic texts deal with affairs of daily life. As is commonly known, in many communities harmful magic (so-called *Schadenszauber*) was often prohibited. Therefore, we may assume that such prohibitions are reflected in the limited amount of spells that were supposed to cause harm and injuries.

As a matter of fact, we probably also have to take the caster's personal situation and especially his own conscience into consideration: A person who attempts to curse another human being is obviously sharing a point of view, in which magic presents itself as part of such an individual's "reality." Therefore, for him practicing such dark and harmful magic obviously constitutes an effective instrument for having major power over others in the user's worldview. Subsequently, the (occasionally violent) effects that are aimed at must also have been regarded as a realistic threat. Within the context of cursing others many practitioners might therefore have been confronted with a dilemma: if the caster of a spell or curse with violent means believes to set certain effects in motion by which he harms others, he is confronted with the problem that such a process might—within the framework of the system of his belief—possibly not be stopped and might even be irreversible. A certain degree of reversibility (or at least a deliberately limited duration of an effect) might be assumed in cases of magical curses, when they are addressed to certain deities; however, without involvement of gods or God a termination or reversal of the curse might have appeared to be problematic. Accordingly, we may have to consider a certain amount of carefulness and remorse of the practitioner to employ lethal forms of violence as ultimate means to achieve certain targets by the use of such magic.

In contrast to other spells, in *defixiones* and prayers for vengeance[93] a larger willingness to employ violence can be seen. This willingness may be explained by a number of reasons: Firstly, in the majority of *defixiones* the originator remains anonymous and, therefore, has no need to be afraid of laws and prohibition.[94] The secrecy of the caster is further enhanced by the deployment of a *defixio*, because the metal plate with the written text is often placed underneath the earth, in wells or at burial sites which correspond with the entities which are asked for assistance. Moreover, a justification which could allow for an identification of the originator attempting to curse others is not necessarily provided. If reasons for cursing someone are provided, they are commonly related to justice and the reconstitution of justice respectively.[95] Secondly, the damage which is aimed for is

---

[93] A clear-cut distinction between a prayer and a *defixio* can hardly be made. On this point, see Graf, *Gottesnähe und Schadenszauber*, 192–203.
[94] Cf. further Versnel, "Beyond Cursing," 62–3 and idem, *Fluch und Gebet*, 13.
[95] Cf. Versnel, "Beyond Cursing," 64–5.

often restricted to certain body parts (tongue, mouth, soul, mind),[96] thus indicating the functionality of these curses: The main purpose is the paralyzation of body parts corresponding to a certain scenario the originator attempts to influence, e.g., the tongue in judicial contexts, sexual organs in love affairs or hands in matters of craftsmanship. Although we could evaluate such attempts as forms of violence, a permanent and painful effect is rarely asked for.[97] Thirdly, curses and *defixiones* are often addressed to gods (or God); therefore, it seems plausible to consider the practitioner's situation as well: by asking for divine help in the process of cursing others the originator might possibly also consider to have means for stopping this process (namely by addressing the corresponding deities again). Subsequently, we may possibly assume that such an opportunity for reversing a magical process might constitute a possible further reason for employing violence more openly.

Moreover, the curses frequently aim for an effect in order to manipulate the future: especially in judicial contexts such an intervention for keeping others from bearing witness or accusing the originator of the curse is obvious. In many cases, deities or other entities are simply instructed to carry out the demand of the caster. Accordingly, we can probably not assume the existence of a generally religious *stimulation* for these curses, but rather a religious figure is simply asked for assistance.

In contrast to the curses from the *defixiones*, prayers for vengeance display less hesitation when employing violence. On the contrary, the physical harm mentioned in these prayers is often rather radical and is intended to have a permanent and irreversible effect on an opponent, occasionally even along with his offspring. The punishment of the curse corresponds with an offense or guilt the target has taken upon himself.[98] Since the damage which has allegedly been done by the target is mostly irreparable, the curse operates accordingly and the effects are also often irreversible. The main purpose of these prayers for vengeance can be best described as re-establishing justice. Subsequently, we can assume that the prayers for vengeance represent an almost juridical issue: Affairs which cannot be settled by legal administration and trials any more are taken to a second level of

---

[96] Cf. Versnel, *Fluch und Gebet*, 7 and also Graf, *Gottesnähe und Schadenszauber*, 191. An interesting example for a curse with an effect on various body parts is also provided in Meyer and Smith (eds.), *Ancient Christian Magic*, 199–202; and Kropp, *Ausgewählte Koptische Zaubertexte*. vol. 2: *Übersetzungen und Anmerkungen*, 243–7: In "Abdallah's curses to weaken Mouflehalpahapani" (Berlin 8503) the victim of the curse shall be affected on hands, feet, eyes, ears, nose, mouth, and heart, so that he becomes like an idol made by human beings. The reference to an idol together with the reference to the different body parts recalls the biblical critique of idols being lifeless, immobile, mute, and deaf; cf., Deut 4:28; Ps 115:4-7, 135:15-17; Hab 2:18; 1 Cor 12:2; and Rev 9:20. A similar variety of human body parts is also referred to in *SEG* 40.266, where hands, feet, tongue, mind, and soul of the victim are bound.

[97] Cf. Versnel, *Fluch und Gebet*, 11–12.

[98] For evidence, see Versnel, "Beyond Cursing," 70.

jurisdiction. In case of these prayers we can be certain that this is in most cases gods or God rather than entities simply associated with the underworld. The divine judges are often addressed with more complex formulas (occasionally involving familiar curse language) and are not coerced to do the will of the originator, but rather asked politely. Therefore, many prayers for justice add certain expressions of supplication to the invocation of the addressed deities. Further, certain well-known phrases associated with the corresponding god can be added, as can clearly be seen in some of the examples provided above. The location for the prayers of vengeance also seems to differ slightly in comparison to *defixiones*: the prayers are not secretly placed in locations associated with the underworld, but are apparently openly displayed at places relating to the deity they are addressing or near the victims the gods are supposed to avenge. Therefore, prayers of vengeance have often been found at temples or near the graves of those who were innocent victims in need of revenge. In contrast to *defixiones* the prayers of vengeance also often include the name of the person demanding justice.[99]

However, there may be other reasons for the employment of attempting violent effects with prayers for justice than just calling for help to a higher authority as a worldly tribunal. The gods (or God) who are addressed in these prayers are undoubtedly held in high regards and are considered to be very potent in the communities addressing them in prayers and prayers for vengeance. Therefore, the integration of elements from curses related with gods could possibly have a deterrent effect on those who are aware of them. Further, the formulas related to well-known gods and to religious curses probably link a socially accepted religion with (almost) magic elements and the cursing of others. Subsequently, this form of invoking the help of a god in the process of cursing others who might even have acted against the will of gods also becomes a practice which is socially accepted. The recourse to explicitly religious elements might actually even circumvent especially magic components anathematized in communities by camouflaging curses in prayers for vengeance as religious practices, although in some of these texts elements normally appearing in magical contexts can still be seen. If this consideration is correct, this procedure could almost be understood as an absorption of a once magical practice into a religious social system. (Possibly we can observe a similar absorption of magic terminology in early Judaism in Sir 38:1-15 or in Tobit [S] 6:1-9; 8:2-3; and 11:11-12 and in early Christianity in the writing of Ignatius of Antioch who refers to the Eucharist as φάρμακον ἀθανασίας [*Eph.* 20:2], using the word φαρμακεία which is otherwise often occurring in the pejorative sense relating to magic.[100])

---

[99] For this, also see Raquel Martín Hernández, "Appealing for Justice in Christian Magic," in Sofía Torallas Tovar and Juan Pedro Monferrer-Sala (eds.), *Cultures in Context. Transfer of Knowledge in the Mediterranean Context: Selected Papers* (Córdoba: Ingeniero Torres Quevedo, 2013), 27–41.

[100] Cf. also Frenschkowski, *Magie im antiken Christentum*, 249–56.

In any case, we may regard the violent aims of curses and prayers for vengeance as means to achieve a certain amount of re-establishment of justice, which either takes the nonsocial perspective into account and therefore has to happen secretly, or circumvents socially unacceptable behavior, thus integrating socially accepted forms of revenge as known from religious contexts. Therefore, we can probably assume that violence is not religiously motivated in the prayers for vengeance, but rather that allusions and quotations from religious texts have become a way to bypass possible suspicions of employing magic and comparable practices which have otherwise been prohibited by legal or religious restrictions.

Some Coptic Christian curses seem to support these assumptions: the "Widow's Curse against Shenoute" (Munich Coptic Papyrus 5 from the seventh century CE),[101] for instance, provides elements familiar from magical texts, *defixiones*, and prayers for justice including numerous allusions to passages from the Bible. This papyrus contains magical language, like the usual accumulation of vowels and abbreviations of "holy names," for example, Χ Μ Γ, possibly meaning "Christ, Michael, Gabriel."[102] Since the papyrus "for vengeance" is supposed to be buried together with mummies in order to be effective, we also encounter a connection to the underworld commonly present in a *defixio*. Further, the reason for God and his angels to intervene on behalf of justice, as encountered in some *defixiones* and especially prayers for vengeance, is provided. Moreover, especially elements normally occurring in prayers for vengeance are displayed in this papyrus: God is invoked in order to re-establish justice and to avenge the helpless. This purpose is substantiated by stressing the injustice of Shenoute, the target of the curse and also mentioning the helplessness of the originator, an anonymous "widow with orphaned children." The plea for help is then even further supported by numerous references to God as known from biblical writings: God is addressed as the creator of Adam, who already accepted the offering of Abel, the one who crowned Stephen, the first martyr, the one who saved Noah from the flood, the one who saved Lot in Sodom, the one who liberated Daniel from the lions' den and who gave Job power to endure his trials—accordingly providing reasons that God will also accept the plea of the widow. Consequently, we can regard this call for a divine intervention as a prayer with curse elements including various allusions to biblical narratives.

A similar example for a combination of these elements is also provided by the "Curse against several violent people" (Papyrus Lichačev from the fourth to

---

[101] Cf. for the text Meyer and Smith (eds.), *Ancient Christian Magic*, 188–90 and Kropp, *Ausgewählte Koptische Zaubertexte*. vol. 2: *Übersetzungen und Anmerkungen*, 229–31.

[102] The identification of Χ Μ Γ as abbreviations of the names Christ, Michael, and Gabriel is, however, not certain: It is also possible to interpret the letters as an abbreviation of the sentence Χριστὸν Μαρία γεννᾷ (= "Mary gives birth to Christ"). For this possibility, see Meyer and Smith (eds.), *Ancient Christian Magic*, 390 and Preisendanz (ed.), *Papyri Graecae Magicae. II*, 210 and 216.

fifth century).¹⁰³ Also in this curse we encounter an appeal to God with juridical language: God is praised, next to several angels and his son and he is asked to bring his anger upon certain people who committed acts of violence as he has already brought his anger upon "Somorha and Komorha" (meaning Sodom and Gomorrah). He is further asked to bring the "vengeance of Enoch" against these people (maybe alluding to the first chapter of *1 Enoch*, but more likely referring to Gen 4:17-18¹⁰⁴) and to avenge innocent blood like the blood of Abel.

In both curses it seems that the allusions to biblical (and parabiblical) narratives are certainly employed in order to establish the power of the curses. Furthermore, though, the use of biblical examples for God as an avenger might also have led to an acceptance of these curses in a Christian group where such concepts might otherwise have been prohibited as magic.

The integration of normally forbidden practices¹⁰⁵ by relating them to a kind of in-group language could represent a phenomenon we possibly also encounter in the world of narrative texts: a prominent example for an awareness of the problem of the possibility to conflate magic and prayer is probably also displayed in the Acts of Peter where Simon's magic is portrayed as destructive, whereas Peter's miracles are exclusively described as beneficial.¹⁰⁶ Within this narrative

---

[103] For the text, see Meyer and Smith (eds.), *Ancient Christian Magic*, 190–1 and Kropp, *Ausgewählte Koptische Zaubertexte*. vol. 2: *Übersetzungen und Anmerkungen*, 232–4.

[104] The reference to Enoch within the context of the curse is rather strange: one could assume that the topic of vengeance is connected to God's punishment of worldly powers, for instance, reflected by the vengeance taken by Raguel in *1 En* 20:4. Moreover, one may possibly doubt the identity of Enoch as the person from *1 Enoch*. In turn, the connection of the reference to Enoch and Abel's blood could possibly indicate that the "curse against several violent people" is actually alluding to Enoch, the son of Cain (Gen 4:17-18) and Cain's punishment. This identification of "Enoch" could be interpreted as coherent with the concept of vengeance as God's exclusive right (cf. also footnote 73 above): since it is God taking revenge for Abel's blood (Gen 4:10-16; cf. Heb 12:24), the composer of the "curse against several violent people" is asking for God's intercession in analogy to this biblical narrative and consequently does not carry out revenge himself.

[105] On this problem, see also Christoph Markschies, *Das antike Christentum. Frömmigkeit, Lebensformen, Institutionen*, Beck'sche Reihe 1692 (Munich: C.H. Beck, 2006), 125.

[106] Cf. also Matthias Reinhard Hoffmann, "'Die Stadt ist zu klein für uns beide!' (Wunder des Petrus und Zauberei Simons)—ActPetr 4-15," in Ruben Zimmermann et al. (eds.), *Kompendium der frühchristlichen Wundererzählungen*. vol. 2: *Die Wunder der Apostel* (Gütersloh: Gütersloher Verlagshaus, 2017), 601–24; Martin G. Ruf, "Missglückte Himmelfahrt (Letzte Auseinandersetzung mit Simon)—ActPetr 30-32," in Ruben Zimmermann et al. (eds.), *Kompendium der frühchristlichen Wundererzählungen*. vol. 2: *Die Wunder der Apostel* (Gütersloh: Gütersloher Verlagshaus, 2017), 672–81; and Kasper Dalgaard, "Peter and Simon in the Acts of Peter: Between Magic and Miracles," in Helen R. Jacobus, Anne Katrine de Hemmer Gudme, and Philippe Guillaume (eds.), *Studies on Magic and Divination in the Biblical World*, Biblical Intersections 11 (Piscataway: Gorgias Press, 2013), 169–80.

the confrontation between Peter and Simon the Magician reaches its climax when Simon demonstrates his magical powers by flying above Rome (*Acts of Peter* 32).[107] The final confrontation is simply ended by Peter who prays to Christ in order to have the flying magician Simon fall out of the sky and break his leg.[108] This episode may demonstrate more than the Christian perspective on magic being inferior to prayer and Christian religion as such.[109] The meaning of Peter's prayer may also indicate that the course to protect the Christian belief justifies asking Christ for help, even by committing an act of violence through prayer. In this case Peter is asking for Christ's intervention by explaining that previous miracles could become implausible by Simon's performance. Accordingly, Simon shall be deprived of his powers and fall down, not in order to kill him, but rather to make him ineffective. The elements of protecting the community and establishing justice by causing harm (without being mortal) can probably also be regarded as comparable to elements we otherwise rather expect in curses. Form (prayer) and aim (protection of the community and establishing justice) are certainly supposed to demarcate a border to magical practice here.

A similar display of violence against those who are blamed of leading people astray and preventing them to accept the Christian faith can also be found in the Acts of John: In this narrative the apostle John enters the Temple of Artemis in Ephesus and threatens to kill all unbelievers present within by calling for God's assistance. As many of them beg him to spare their lives John prays to God asking him to demonstrate his powers and show mercy on the people, but to punish those who deceive by sorcery. The prayer is answered by the destruction of the altar and seven idols and half of the temple, killing the priest (*Acts of John* 37-42). Admittedly, the willingness to employ violence by prayer is slightly more limited

---

[107] Cf. also Hans-Josef Klauck, *Apokryphe Apostelakten. Eine Einführung* (Stuttgart: Katholisches Bibelwerk, 2005), 112–13; ET: H.-J. Klauck, *The Apocryphal Acts of the Apostles: An Introduction* (Waco, TX: Baylor University Press, 2008), 100–1.

[108] The reference to Simon's broken leg bears significance with regards to the content: In *Acts of Peter* 31 Simon has the title "the Standing One" (maybe also alluded to in his description as standing in or before the crowd in *Acts of Peter* 4 and 32; cf. further for the use of this title Clement of Alexandria, *Strom.*2.11.52.2; Hippolytus, *Ref.* 6.9, 13, 17.1, and 18; or Ps.-Clementines, *Hom.* 2.22; *Rec.* 2.7). The title "Standing One" seems to be an expression of immortality or immutability; cf. Jarl Fossum. *The Name of God and the Angel of the Lord: Samaritan and Jewish Concepts of Intermediation and the Origin of Gnosticism*, WUNT 36 (Tübingen: Mohr Siebeck, 1985), 112–29 or Jaan Lahe, *Gnosis und Judentum. Alttestamentliche und jüdische Motive in der gnostischen Literatur und das Ursprungsproblem der Gnosis*, NHMS 75 (Leiden: Brill, 2012), 136–7. Due to his broken leg he has to be carried out of Rome, clearly mocking the inflated claim that he is the "Standing One." Cf. Hoffmann, "Die Stadt ist zu klein für uns beide!" 618–19.

[109] Cf. Tamás Adamik, "The Image of Simon Magus in the Christian Tradition," in Jan N. Bremmer (ed.), *The Apocryphal Acts of Peter. Magic, Miracles and Gnosticism*, Studies in the Apocryphal Acts of the Apostles 3 (Leuven: Peeters, 1998), 52–64, here 62–4.

than in the examples provided above: not only is the number of victims reduced from all people present in the temple to the only victim being the priest of Artemis, but also is the priest reanimated by John's miraculous works afterward. Still, this episode might also be considered to be evidence that prayers with violent aims have been well known in early Christianity. Further, this narrative provides a parallel description to the events depicted in the Acts of Peter above: in both narratives people are led astray by sorcery and magic. The representatives of those who use magic or sorcery (i.e., Simon and the priest of Artemis) are punished by a prayer of the apostles leading to the return of the doubtful people to the Christian faith.

Traces of violence of Christian rites often considered to be magic in nature can further be seen in exorcisms in relation to baptism: In the *PGM* and *PDM* numerous examples of exorcisms have been preserved. Such practices are similarly preserved in biblical and parabiblical narratives where rituals possibly once considered magic have also been absorbed into corresponding religious contexts. In magical texts as well as in the early Jewish and New Testament tradition the exorcisms are directed against the demons possessing humans (or animals) and aim to drive the demons out of those who are possessed. However, in the early Church we can also encounter exorcisms as a part of baptisms. In some descriptions of these baptism exorcisms rather surprisingly the use of violence plays a major role: such practices are already mentioned by Hippolytus of Rome (*Traditio Apostolica* 20-21) referring to confessions of the candidate of the baptism to an exorcist who was supposed to liberate the person to be baptized from demons causing his sins. Similarly other authorities of the early Church, such as Cyprianus of Carthage (*Ad Demetrium* 15), Lactantius (*Divinae Institutiones* II 15.3), or Minucius Felix (*Octavius* 27.2-7), describe the confessions of the candidates and especially their demons within by the interrogation of the exorcist as rather metaphorical whiplashes against the devil and demons.[110] Also in these cases the violence seems to be restricted to being used against the powers opposing God (namely the demons and non-Christian deities), although the interrogations, confessions, and homologies expected of reflect a certain amount of unpleasantness directed against those who were involved in the process of baptism.[111] Nevertheless, although we find some use of mostly nonphysical violence in these baptism exorcisms of the second and third centuries, the more unlimited descriptions of violence in regards to magical traditions and religious contexts seem to be restricted to curses and prayers for vengeance.

---

[110] Cf. Merkelbach, *Abrasax*, 9–28; cf. also Christa Agnes Tuczay, *Geister, Dämonen—Phantasmen. Eine Kulturgeschichte* (Wiesbaden: Marixverlag, 2015), 124–6.

[111] Cf. for evidence also Eric Sorensen, *Possession and Exorcism in the New Testament and Early Christianity*, WUNT II/157 (Tübingen: Mohr Siebeck, 2002), 209–14 and Merkelbach, *Abrasax*, 9–19.

Conclusion

Violence against humans is not only employed against users of magic, but is also commonly used by practitioners of magic in late antiquity. However, the frequency of displaying violence and the degree in which human opponents are subjected to violence in magical context depend on certain sociological parameters: the more "harmful magic" is rejected or even forbidden by societies, be it by legal or by religious commandments, the more such magic becomes secret and is therefore often connected with chthonic gods and the underworld. The combination of violence within a forbidden act of magic and addressing gods from the underworld often resulted in a subsequent placement of such spells in graves, wells, or other places associated with the underworld where the performance of such a magical act would remain secret. A connection of forbidden magic with the underworld is especially visible in the so-called *defixiones*. Although violence against other humans is very common in such spells, the amount of physical damage the caster wishes to inflict is often limited to certain body parts which are supposed to be weakened or made useless in analogy with the purpose of the curse.

Similarly, violence is also employed in prayers for vengeance and other Christian curses where religious prohibition of carrying out revenge personally leads toward praying to God and asking him to avenge the praying (or related) person instead. In curses and prayers for vengeance the violence displayed is not necessarily religiously motivated, but rather indicate that divine intervention is pleaded for because opponents are either unknown (or in case of threatening with a curse, as for instance in case of disturbing graves, opponents have not committed an offense yet) or otherwise out of reach. Violence seems to be less restricted in curses and prayers for vengeance. Such a tendency probably derives from biblical (and occasionally parabiblical) *Vorlagen* which influenced the worldviews of the writer of such magical writings. Despite certain analogies between magical texts and curses and prayers (and to some degree also exorcisms in the context of baptism), form (religiously accepted prayers) and aim (protection of the community or an individual follower of God and begging God to carry out justice instead of carrying out a forbidden act of taking personal revenge) establish a clear-cut demarcation from magical practices apparently turning curses and prayers for vengeance into socially accepted expressions of behavior.

BIBLIOGRAPHY

Primary Literature

Alexander, Philip J. "3 (Hebrew Apocalypse of) Enoch." Pages 259–60 in *The Old Testament Pseudepigrapha*, vol. 1. Edited by James H. Charlesworth. New York: Doubleday, 1983.
Audollent, Auguste. *Defixionum tabellae quotquot innotuerunt tam in Graecis Orientis quam in totius Occidenti partibus praeter Atticas in Corpore Inscriptionum Atticarum editas.* Paris: A. Fontemoing, 1904.
Betz, Hans Dieter, ed. *The Greek Magical Papyri in Translation, Including the Demotic Spells.* Second ed. Chicago and London: Chicago University Press, 1992.
Duling, D. C. "Testament of Solomon." Pages 945–56 in *The Old Testament Pseudepigrapha*. vol. 1. Edited by James H. Charlesworth. New York: Doubleday, 1983.
Ehrman, Bart D. *The Apostolic Fathers*, vol. 2. LCL 25. Cambridge, MA: Harvard University Press, 2003.
Fischer-Elfert, Hans-W., ed. *Altägyptische Zaubersprüche*. Stuttgart: Reclam, 2005.
Flach, Dieter. *Das Zwölftafelgesetz. Leges XII Tabularum.* Darmstadt: Wissenschaftliche Buchgesellschaft, 2004.
García Martínez, Florentino, and Eibert J. C. Tigchelaar, eds. *The Dead Sea Scrolls: Study Edition*, 2 vols. Leiden: Brill, 1997.
Gaster, Moses. *The Sword of Moses. An Ancient Book of Magic from an Unique Manuscript. With Introduction, Translation, an Index of Mystical Names, and a Facsimile.* London: D. Nutt, 1896.
Hare, D. R. A. "The Lives of the Prophets: A New Translation and Introduction." Pages 379–400 in *The Old Testament Pseudepigrapha*, vol. 2. Edited by James H. Charlesworth. New York: Doubleday, 1985.
Harrington, Daniel J. "Pseudo-Philo: A New Translation and Introduction." Pages 297–377 in *The Old Testament Pseudepigrapha*. vol. 2: *Expansions of the "Old Testament" and Legends*. ABRL. Edited by James H. Charlesworth. Garden City, NY: Doubleday, 1985.
Holmes, Michael W. *The Apostolic Fathers*. Second Edition. Grand Rapids: Baker, 1989.
Isbell, Charles D. *Corpus of the Aramaic Incantation Bowls*. Missoula: Scholars Press, 1975.
Johnson, M. D. "Life of Adam and Eve." Pages 249–95 in *The Old Testament Pseudepigrapha*. ABRL. vol. 2. Edited by James H. Charlesworth. New York: Doubleday, 1985.
Kropp, Angelicus M. *Ausgewählte Koptische Zaubertexte*. Vol. 2: *Übersetzungen und Anmerkungen*. Brussels: Edition de la Fondation Egyptologique Reine Elisabeth, 1931.
Kugel, James L. "Testaments of the Twelve Patriarchs." Pages 1697–855 in *Outside the Bible: Ancient Jewish Writings Related to Scripture*, vol. 2. Edited by Louis H Feldman, James L. Kugel, and Lawrence H. Schiffman. Philadelphia: Jewish Publication Society, 2013.
Landau, Brent. *Revelation of the Magi: The Lost Tale of the Wise Men's Journey to Bethlehem*. New York: HarperOne, 2010.
Lightfoot, Joseph Barber, and J. R. Harmer. *The Apostolic Fathers*. London: Macmillan, 1891.
Mason, Steve. *Judean War 2*. vol. 1b of *Flavius Josephus: Translation and Commentary*. Edited by Steve Mason. Leiden: Brill, 2008.
McCown, C. C. *The Testament of Solomon*. Leipzig: J. C. Hinrichs, 1922.

Merkelbach, Reinhold, ed. *Abrasax. Ausgewählte Papyri religiösen und magischen Inhalts. Exorzismen und jüdisch/christlich beeinflusste Texte*. Papyrologica Coloniensia XVII.4. Kleve: Westdeutscher Verlag, 1996.

Merkelbach, Reinhold, ed. *Abrasax. Ausgewählte Papyri religiösen und magischen Inhalts. Traumtexte*. Papyrologica Coloniensia XVII.5. Kleve: Westdeutscher Verlag, 2001.

Meyer, Marvin, and Richard Smith, eds. *Ancient Christian Magic. Coptic Texts of Ritual Power*. Princeton: Princeton University Press, 1999.

Migne, Jacques-Paul. *Joannis Chrysostomi opera omnia quae exstant*. PG 56. Paris: Garnier, 1859.

Morgan, Michael A. *Sepher Ha-Razim. The Book of Mysteries*. SBLTT 25. SBLPS 11. Chico, CA: Scholars Press, 1983.

Naveh, Joseph, and Shaul Shaked. *Amulets and Magic Bowls. Aramaic Incantations of Late Antiquity*. Jerusalem: Magnes Press, 1985.

Önnerfors, Alf, ed. Antike Zaubersprüche. Zweisprachig. Stuttgart: Reclam, 1991.

Philo, *On the Cherubim, The Sacrifices of Abel and Cain, The Worse Attacks the Better, On the Posterit and Exile of Cain, and On the Giants*. Loeb Classical Library 227. Translated by F. H. Colson and G. H. Whitaker. Cambridge, MA: Harvard University Press, 1929.

Philo. *On Flight and Finding, On the Change of Names, and On Dreams*. Loeb Classical Library 275. Translated by F. H. Colson and G. H. Whitaker. Cambridge, MA: Harvard University Press, 1934.

Preisendanz, Karl, ed. *Papyri Graecae Magicae. Die Griechischen Zauberpapyri I*. Second ed. Stuttgart: Teubner, 1973.

Preisendanz, Karl, ed. *Papyri Graecae Magicae. Die Griechischen Zauberpapyri II*. Second ed. Stuttgart: Teubner, 1974.

Robinson, Stephen E. "Testament of Adam: A New Translation and Introduction." Pages 1: 989–95 in vol. 1. in *The Old Testament Pseudepigrapha*, 2 vols. ABRL. Edited by James H. Charlesworth. Garden City, NY: Doubleday, 1983–5.

Rousseau, Adelin, with Bertrand Hemmerdinger, Louis Doutreleau, and Charles Mercier, eds. *Irénée de Lyon, Contra les hérésies, Livre IV*. Sources chrétiennes 100. Paris: Cerf, 1965.

Schermann, Theodor. *Prophetarum Vitae Fabulosae*. Leipzig: B. G. Teubner, 1907.

Schröter, Jens, and Jürgen Zangenberg, eds. *Texte zur Umwelt des Neuen Testaments*. UTB 3663. Third ed. Tübingen: Mohr Siebeck, 2013.

Stone, Michael E., Benjamin G. Wright, and David Satran, eds. *The Apocryphal Ezekiel*. SBLEJL 18. Atlanta: Scholars Press, 2000.

Toepel, Alexander. "The Apocryphon of Seth: A New Translation and Introduction." Pages 33–9 in *Old Testament Pseudepigrapha: More Noncanonical Scriptures*. Edited by Richard Bauckham, James R. Davila, and Alexander Panayotov. Grand Rapids: Eerdmans, 2013.

Torrey, Charles C. *The Lives of the Prophets: Greek Text and Translation*. SBLMS 1. Philadelphia: Society of Biblical Literature and Exegesis, 1946.

Tullberg, Otto F. *Dionysii Telmahharensis Chronici liber primus: Textum e codice ms. Syriaco Bibliothecae Vaticanae*. Uppsala: Regiae Academiae Typographi, 1850.

van Banning, Joop. *Opus imperfectum in Matthaeum: Praefatio*. CCSL 87B. Turnhout: Brepols, 1988.

van den Broek, Roelof. *Pseudo-Cyril of Jerusalem On the Life and the Passion of Christ: A Coptic Apocryphon*. VCSup 118. Leiden: Brill, 2013.

van der Horst, Pieter, and Judith Newman. *Early Jewish Prayers in Greek*. CEJL. Berlin; New York: de Gruyter, 2008.

Ward, Benedicta. *The Sayings of the Desert Fathers*. CSS 59. Kalamazoo: Cistercian Publications, 1975.
Wünsch, Richard. *Antike Fluchtafeln*. Kleine Texte für Vorlesungen und Übungen 20. Second ed. Bonn: A. Marcus und E. Weber's Verlag, 1912.
Wünsch, Richard. *Defixionum Tabellae Atticae*. IG III, 3. Berlin: Reimer, 1897.
Yadin, Yigael. *The Scroll of the War of the Sons of Light against the Sons of Darkness*. Translated by Batya Rabin and Chaim Rabin. Oxford: Oxford University Press, 1962.

Secondary Literature

Adamik, Tamás. "The Image of Simon Magus in the Christian Tradition." Pages 52–64 in *The Apocryphal Acts of Peter: Magic, Miracles and Gnosticism*. Studies in the Apocryphal Acts of the Apostles 3. Edited by Jan N. Bremmer. Leuven: Peeters, 1998.
Adamik, Tamás. "The Serpent in the *Acts of Thomas*." Pages 115–24 in *The Apocryphal Acts of Thomas*. Edited by J.N. Bremmer. Leuven: Peeters, 2001.
Adelman, Rachel. "Midrash, Myth and Bakhtin's Chronotope: The Itinerant Well and the Foundation Stone in *Pirqe de-Rabbi Eliezer*." *Journal of Jewish Thought and Philosophy* 17.2 (2009): 143–76.
Alexander, Philip J. "Contextualizing the Demonology of the Testament of Solomon." Pages 613–35 in *Die Dämonen—Demons: The Demonology of Israelite-Jewish and Early Christian Literature in Context of Their Environment*. Edited by A. Lange, H. Lichtenberger, and K. F. Diethard Römheld. Tübingen: Mohr Siebeck, 2003.
Alexander, Philip J. "The Evil Empire: The Qumran Eschatological War Cycle and the Origins of Jewish Opposition to Rome." Pages 17–31 in *Emanuel: Studies in Hebrew Bible Septuagint and Dead Sea Scrolls in Honor of Emanuel Tov*. Edited by Shalom M. Paul, Robert A. Kraft, Lawrence H. Schiffman, and Weston W. Fields, with the assistance of Eva Ben-David. VTSup 94. Leiden: Brill, 2003.
Alexander, Philip J. "The Cultural History of the Ancient Bible Versions: The Case of Lamentations." Pages 78–102 in *Jewish Reception of Greek Bible Versions*. Texts and Studies in Medieval and Early Modern Judaism 23. Edited by Nicholas Robert Michael De Lange, Julia G. Krivoruchko, and Cameron Boyd-Taylor. Tübingen: Mohr Siebeck, 2009.
Anderson, Gary A. "The Penitence Narrative in the *Life of Adam and Eve*." Pages 3–42 in *Literature on Adam and Eve: Collected Essays*. Studia in Veteris Testamenti Pseudepigrapha 15. Edited by Gary Anderson, Michael Stone, and Johannes Tromp. Leiden: Brill, 2000.
Applebaum, Shimon. "Josephus and the Economic Causes of the Jewish War." Pages 237–64 in *Josephus, the Bible, and History*. Edited by Louis H. Feldman and Gohei Hata. Detroit: Wayne State University Press, 1989.
Aranda Pérez, Gonzalo. "2 Maccabees." Pages 739–50 in *The International Bible Commentary: A Catholic and Ecumenical Commentary for the Twenty-first Century*. Edited by William Reuben Farmer et al. Collegeville: Liturgical Press, 1998.
Arndt, William, Frederick W. Danker, and Walter Bauer. *A Greek-English Lexicon of the New Testament and Other Early Christian Literature*. Chicago: University of Chicago Press, 2000.
Assan-Dhôte, Isabelle, and Jacqueline Moatti-Fine. *Baruch, Lamentations, Lettre de Jérémie*. La Bible d'Alexandrie 25.2. Paris: Editions du Cerf, 2005.

Assefa, Daniel. *L'Apocalypse des animaux (1 Hen 85–90): une propogande militaire? Approches narrative, historico-critique, perspectives théologiques*. JSJSup 120. Leiden: Brill, 2007.

Atkinson, Kenneth. "Perception of the Temple Priests in the Psalms of Solomon." Pages 79–96 in *The Psalms of Solomon: Language, History, Theology*. EJL 40. Edited by Eberhard Bons and Patrick Pouchelle. Atlanta: SBL Press, 2015.

Attridge, Harold W. *The Interpretation of Biblical History in the Antiquities Judaicae of Flavius Josephus*. HDR 7. Missoula: Scholars Press, 1976.

Attridge, Harold W. *The Epistle to the Hebrews*. Hermeneia. Philadelphia: Fortress, 1989.

Aune, David E. "The Apocalypse of John and Graeco-Roman Revelatory Magic." Pages 347–67 in *Apocalypticism, Prophecy and Magic in Early Christianity: Collected Essays*. WUNT 199. Tübingen: Mohr Siebeck, 2006. Repr. Grand Rapids: Baker Academic, 2008.

Aune, David E. "Magic in Early Christianity." Pages 368–420 in *Apocalypticism, Prophecy and Magic in Early Christianity: Collected Essays*. WUNT 199. Tübingen: Mohr Siebeck, 2006. Repr. Grand Rapids: Baker Academic, 2008.

Aune, David E. *Prophecy in Early Christianity and the Ancient Mediterranean World*. Grand Rapids: Eerdmans, 1983.

Aviam, Mordechai. "Distribution Maps of Archaeological Data from the Galilee: An Attempt to Establish Zones Indicative of Ethnicity and Religious Affiliation." Pages 115–32 in *Religion, Ethnicity, and Identity in Ancient Galilee: A Region in Transition*. WUNT 210. Edited by Jürgen Zangenburg, Harold W. Attridge, and Dale B. Martin. Tübingen: Mohr Siebeck, 2007.

Barclay, John M. G. "The Empire Writes Back: Josephan Rhetoric in Flavian Rome." Pages 315–32 in *Flavius Josephus and Flavian Rome*. Edited by Jonathan Edmondson, Steve Mason, and James Rives. Oxford: Oxford University Press, 2005.

Barnett, Paul W. "The Jewish Sign Prophets—A.D. 40–70: Their Intentions and Origin." *NTS* 27 (1981): 679–97.

Barthélemy, Dominique. *Les Devanciers d'Aquila: Premiere Publication Integrale du Texte des Fragments du Dudodecapropheton*. VTSup 10. Leiden: Brill, 1963.

Batovici, Dan. "Hermas in Clement of Alexandria." Pages 41–51 in *Studia Patristica* LXVI. vol. 14. Edited by Markus Vinzent. Leuven: Peeters, 2013.

Batovici, Dan. "Hermas' Authority in Irenaeus' Works: A Reassessment." *Aug* 55 (2015): 5–31.

Batovici, Dan. "A New Hermas Papyrus Fragment in Paris." *APF* 62 (2016): 20–36.

Batovici, Dan. "The *Shepherd of Hermas* in Recent Scholarship on the Canon: A Review Article." *ASE* 34 (2017): 89–105.

Becker, Adam H., and Annette Yoshiko Reed, eds. *The Ways That Never Parted: Jews and Christians in Late Antiquity and the Early Middle Ages*. TSAJ 95. Tübingen: Mohr Siebeck, 2003.

Becker, Dieter. "Hexerei, Magie und Gewalt." Pages 173–85 in *Hexenwahn. Eine theologische Selbstbesinnung*. TA 5. Edited by Marcel Nieden. Stuttgart: Kohlhammer, 2004.

Becking, Bob. "Do the Earliest Samaritan Inscriptions Already Indicate a Parting of the Ways?" Pages 213–22 in *Judah and the Judeans in the Fourth Century BCE*. Edited by Oded Lipschits, Gary N. Knoppers, and Rainer Albertz. Winona Lake, IN: Eisenbrauns, 2007.

Behringer, Wolfgang. *Hexen. Glaube, Verfolgung, Vermarktung*. Beck'sche Reihe 2082. Fourth ed. Munich: C.H. Beck, 2005.

Berger, Klaus. "Die königlichen Messiastraditionen des Neuen Testaments." *NTS* 20 (1974): 1–44.

Bergsma, John S. "The Persian Period as Penitential Era: The 'Exegetical Logic' of Daniel 9.1–27." Pages 50–64 in *Exile and Restoration Revisited*. Edited by Gary N. Knoppers, Lester L. Grabbe, and Deirdre N. Fulton. London: T&T Clark, 2009.

Bernat, David. "Phinehas' Intercessory Prayer: A Rabbinic and Targumic Reading of the Baal Peor Narrative." *JJS* 58.2 (2007): 263–82.

Bernstein, Moshe J. "Scriptures: Quotation and Use." Pages 839–72 in *Encyclopedia of the Dead Sea Scrolls*. Edited by Lawrence H. Schiffman and James C. VanderKam. New York: Oxford University Press, 2000.

Bilde, Per. *Flavius Josephus between Jerusalem and Rome: His Life, His Works, and Their Importance*. Sheffield: Sheffield Academic, 1988.

Bissinger, H. G. *Friday Night Lights: A Town, A Team, A Dream*. Philadelphia: Da Capo Press, 1990.

Birkhan, Helmut. *Magie im Mittelalter*. Beck'sche Reihe 1901. Munich: C.H. Beck, 2010.

Bitton-Ashkelony, Brouria. *Encountering the Sacred: The Debate on Christian Pilgrimage in Late Antiquity*. Berkeley: University of California Press, 2005.

Black, Matthew. "Judas of Galilee and Josephus's 'Fourth Philosophy.'" Pages 45–54 in *Josephus Studien: Untersuchungen zu Josephus, dem antiken Judentum und dem Neuen Testament: Otto Michel zum 70. Geburtstag gewidmet*. Edited by Otto Betz, Klaus Haacker, and Martin Hengel. Göttingen: Vandenhoeck & Ruprecht, 1974.

Bloch, René. "Philo and Jeremiah: A Mysterious Passage in *De Cherubim*." Pages 438–42 in *Jeremiah's Scriptures: Production, Reception, Interaction, and Transformation*. Edited by Hindy Najman and Konrad Schmid. JSJSup 173. Leiden: Brill, 2016.

Bockmuehl, Markus. *The Remembered Peter in Ancient Reception and Modern Debate*. WUNT 262. Tübingen: Mohr Siebeck, 2010.

Bohak, Gideon. *Ancient Jewish Magic: A History*. Cambridge: Cambridge University Press, 2007.

Boll, Franz. *Griechischer Liebeszauber aus Ägypten auf zwei Bleitafeln des Heidelberger Archäologischen Instituts. Mit 2 Lichtdrucktafeln*, Sitzungsberichte der Heidelberger Akademie der Wissenschaften. Philosophisch-historische Klasse Bd. 1. Heidelberg: Carl Winter's Universitätsbuchhandlung, 1910.

Bongie, Elizabeth Bryson and Mary Schaffer. *The Life and Regimen of the Blessed and Holy Syncletica*, 2 vols. Eugene, OR: Wipf and Stock, 2005.

Bons, Eberhard and Patrick Pouchelle, eds. *The Psalms of Solomon: Language, History, Theology*. EJL 40. Atlanta: SBL Press, 2015.

Bourgel, Jonathan. "The Destruction of the Samaritan Temple by John Hyrcanus: A Reconsideration." *JBL* 135 (2016): 505–23.

Boustan, Raanan, and Michael Beshay. "Sealing the Demons, Once and for All: The Ring of Solomon, the Cross of Christ, and the Power of Biblical Kingship." *ARG* (2015): 99–129.

Boyarin, Daniel. *Intertextuality and the Reading of Midrash*. Bloomington, IN: Indiana University Press, 1990.

Brakke, David. "The Problematization of Nocturnal Emissions in Early Christian Syria, Egypt, and Gaul." *JECS* 3 (1995): 419–60.

Brakke, David. *Demons and the Making of the Monk: Spiritual Conflict in Early Christianity*. Cambridge, MA: Harvard University Press, 2009.

Bremmer, Jan N. "Man, Magic, and Martyrdom in the Acts of Andrew." Pages 15–34 in *The Apocryphal Acts of Andrew*. Studies on the Apocryphal Acts of the Apostles 5. Edited by Jan N. Bremmer. Leuven: Peeters, 2000.
Bright, John. "A Prophet's Lament and Its Answer: Jeremiah 15:10–21." *Int* 28 (1974): 59–74.
Brock, Sebastian P. "Jewish Traditions in Syriac Sources." *JJS* 30 (1979): 212–32.
Brock, Sebastian P. "Greek into Syriac and Syriac into Greek." Pages 11–14 in *Syriac Perspectives on Late Antiquity*. London: Variorum Reprints, 1984.
Brock, Sebastian P. "An Archaic Syriac Prayer over Baptismal Oil." Pages 3–12 in *Studia Patristica: Papers Presented at the Fourteenth International Congress on Patristic Studies Held in Oxford 2003*. Edited by Francis M. Young, Mark J. Edwards, and Paul M. Parvis. Leuven: Peeters, 2006.
Brodersen, Kai. "Briefe in die Unterwelt: Religiöse Kommunikation auf griechischen Fluchtafeln." Pages 57–68 in *Gebet und Fluch, Zeichen und Traum. Aspekte religiöser Kommunikation in der Antike*. Edited by Kai Brodersen. Münster: Lit, 2001.
Brooke, George G. "Moving Mountains: From Sinai to Jerusalem." Pages 73–89 in *The Significance of Sinai: Traditions about Sinai and Divine Revelation in Judaism and Christianity*. TBN 12. Edited by George J. Brooke, Hindy Najman, and Loren T. Stuckenbruck. Leiden: Brill, 2008.
Brooks, James A. "Clement of Alexandria as a Witness to the Development of the New Testament Canon." *SecCent* 9 (1992): 41–55.
Brown, Derek. *The God of This Age: Satan in the Churches and Letters of the Apostle Paul*. WUNT II/409. Tübingen: Mohr Siebeck, 2015.
Brown, Peter. *Society and the Holy in Late Antiquity*. Berkeley: University of California Press, 1982.
Brown, Peter. *The Body and Society: Men, Women, and Sexual Renunciation in Early Christianity*. New York: Columbia University Press, 1988.
Brown, Raymond E. *The Birth of the Messiah: A Commentary on the Infancy Narratives in the Gospels of Matthew and Luke*. ABRL. New York: Doubleday, 1993.
Brueggemann, Walter. "The Book of Jeremiah: Portrait of the Prophet." *Int* 37 (1983): 141–2.
Bucur, Bogdan Gabriel. "Revisiting Christian Oeyen: 'The Other Clement' on Father, Son, and the Angelomorphic Spirit." *VC* 61 (2007): 381–413.
Bucur, Bogdan Gabriel. "The Son of God and the Angelomorphic Holy Spirit: A Rereading of the Shepherd's Christology." *ZNW* 98 (2007): 120–42.
Bucur, Bogdan Gabriel. *Angelomorphic Pneumatology: Clement of Alexandria and Other Early Christian Witnesses*. VCSup 95. Leiden: Brill, 2009.
Busch, Peter. *Das Testament Salomos: Die älteste christliche Dämonologie, kommentiert und in deutscher Erstübersetzung*. TUGAL 153. Berlin: de Gruyter, 2006.
Busch, Peter. *Magie in neutestamentlicher Zeit*. FRLANT 218. Göttingen: Vandenhoeck & Ruprecht, 2006.
Busch, Peter. "Solomon as a True Exorcist: The Testament of Solomon in Its Cultural Setting." Pages 183–95 in *The Figure of Solomon in Jewish, Christian and Islamic Tradition: King, Sage and Architect*. TBN 16. Edited by J. Verheyden. Leiden: Brill, 2013.
Cason, Thomas. "Cultural Features: Monstrosity and the Construction of Human Identity in the *Testament of Solomon*." *CBQ* 77 (2015): 263–79.
Cazeaux, Jacques. *Pseudo-Philon: Les antiquités bibliques*. I. *Introduction et text critiques*. SC 229. Paris: Éditions du Cerf, 1976.

Čéplö, Slavomir. "Testament of Solomon and Other Pseudepigraphical Material in Aḥkām Sulaymān (Judgment of Solomon)." Pages 21–37 in *The Canon of the Bible and the Apocrypha in the Churches of the East*. Edited by V. S. Hovhanessian. New York: Peter Lang, 2012.

Chabot, Jean-Baptiste. *Chronicon anonymum Pseudo-Dionysianum vulgo dictum*. CSCO 91. Scriptores Syri 3.1. Paris: E. Typographeo Reipublicae, 1927.

Chazon, Esther, with Yonatan Miller. "'At the Crossroads': Anti-Samaritan Polemic in a Qumran Text about Joseph." Pages 381–7 in *The "Other" in Second Temple Judaism: Essays in Honor of John J. Collins*. Edited by Daniel C. Harlow, Karina Martin Hogan, Matthew Goff, and Joel S. Kaminsky. Grand Rapids: Eerdmans, 2011.

Chester, Andrew. "Citing the Old Testament." Pages 145–6 in *It Is Written: Scripture Citing Scripture: Essays in Honour of Barnabas Lindars*. Edited by D. A. Carson and H. G. M. Williamson. Cambridge: Cambridge University Press, 1988.

Choat, Malcolm, and Rachel Yuen-Collingridge. "The Egyptian Hermas: The Shepherd in Egypt before Constantine." Pages 191–212 in *Early Christian Manuscripts: Examples of Applied Method and Approach*. TENTS 5. Edited by Thomas J. Kraus and Tobias Nicklas. Leiden: Brill, 2010.

Choufrine, Arkadi. *Gnosis, Theophany, Theosis: Studies in Clement of Alexandria's Appropriation of His Background*. Patristic Studies 5. Edited by Gerald Bray. New York: Peter Lang, 2002.

Clark, Elizabeth. "Foucault, The Fathers, and Sex." *JAAR* 56 (1988): 619–41.

Coggins, R. J. *Samaritans and Jews: The Origins of Samaritanism Reconsidered*. Atlanta: John Knox, 1975.

Coggins, R. J. "The Samaritans in Josephus." Pages 257–73 in *Josephus, Judaism, and Christianity*. Edited by Louis H. Feldman and Gohei Hata. Detroit: Wayne State University Press, 1987.

Cohen, Shaye J. D. "*Ioudaios, Iudaeus*, Judaean, Jew." Pages 69–106 in *The Beginnings of Jewishness*. Berkeley: University of California Press, 1999.

Collins, Derek. *Magic in the Ancient Greek World*. Malden, MA: Blackwell Publishing, 2008.

Collins, John J. "The Epic of Theodotus and the Hellenism of the Hasmoneans." *HTR* 73 (1980): 91–104.

Collins, John J. *Apocalypticism in the Dead Sea Scrolls*. London: Routledge, 1997.

Collins, John J. "The Expectation of the End in the Dead Sea Scrolls." Pages 74–90 in *Eschatology, Messianism, and the Dead Sea Scrolls*. Edited by Craig A. Evans and Peter W. Flint. Grand Rapids: Eerdmans, 1997.

Collins, John J. "The Zeal of Phinehas, the Bible, and the Legitimation of Violence." *JBL* 122 (2003): 3–22.

Collins, John J. *Magic: A Very Short Introduction*. Oxford; New York: Oxford University Press, 2012.

Conner, Robert. *Magic in the New Testament. A Survey and Appraisal of the Evidence*. Oxford: Mandrake, 2010.

Conybeare, Frederick C. "The Testament of Solomon." *JQR* 11 (1898): 1–45.

Coon, Lynda L. *Sacred Fictions: Holy Women and Hagiography in Late Antiquity*. Philadelphia: University of Pennsylvania Press, 1997.

Cosaert, Carl P. *The Text of the Gospels in Clement of Alexandria*. NTGF 9. Atlanta, GA: Society of Biblical Literature, 2008.

Cosentino, Augusto. "La tradizione del re Salomone come mago ed esorcista." Pages 41–59 in *Atti dell'incontro di studio: Gemme gonstiche e cultura ellenistica*. Edited by A. Mastrocinque. Bologna: Pàtron Editore, 2002.

Cowley, A. E. *Aramaic Papyri of the Fifth Century BCE* Oxford: Clarendon Press, 1923.

Crown, Alan D. "Another Look at Samaritan Origins." Page 140 in *Essays in Honour of G. D. Sexdenier: New Samaritan Studies of the Société d'études Samaritaines III & IV*. Sydney: Mandelbaum, 1995.

Czachesz, István. *The Grotesque Body in Early Christian Discourse: Hell, Scatology, and Metamorphosis*. Routledge: London, 2014.

Dalgaard, Kasper. "Peter and Simon in the Acts of Peter: Between Magic and Miracles." Pages 169–80 in *Studies on Magic and Divination in the Biblical World*. Biblical Intersections 11. Edited by Helen R. Jacobus, Anne Katrine de Hemmer Gudme, and Philippe Guillaume. Piscataway: Gorgias Press, 2013.

Darsey, James. *The Prophetic Tradition and Radical Rhetoric in America*. New York: New York University Press, 1997.

Davies, Philip R. "Eschatology at Qumran." *JBL* 104 (1985): 39–55.

Davila, James R. *The Provenance of the Pseudepigrapha: Jewish Christian, or Other?* Leiden: Brill, 2005.

Davis, Kipp. *The Cave 4 Apocryphon of Jeremiah and the Qumran Jeremianic Traditions: Prophetic Persona and the Construction of Community Identity*. STDJ 111. Leiden: Brill, 2014.

Davies, Owen. *Grimoires. A History of Magic Books*. Oxford; New York: Oxford University Press, 2009.

Daxelmüller, Christoph. *Zauberpraktiken. Die Ideengeschichte der Magie*. Düsseldorf: Patmos, 2001.

De Bruin, Tom. *The Great Controversy: The Individual's Struggle between Good and Evil in the Testaments of the Twelve Patriarchs and in their Jewish and Christian Contexts*. NTOA/SUNT 106. Göttingen: Vandenhoeck & Ruprecht, 2015.

De Bruyn, Theodore, and Jitse H. F. Dijkstra. "Greek Amulets and Formularies from Egypt Containing Christian Elements: A Checklist of Papyri, Parchments, Ostraka, and Tablets." *BASP* 48 (2011): 163–216.

Decker, Rainer. *Hexenjagd in Deutschland*. Geschichte erzählt 2. Darmstadt: Primus, 2006.

Decker, Rainer. *Die Päpste und die Hexen. Aus den geheimen Akten der Inquisition*. Second ed. Darmstadt: Primus, 2013.

De Jonge, Marinus. *Pseudepigrapha of the Old Testament as Part of Christian Literature*. SVTP 18. Leiden: Brill, 2003.

De Villard, Ugo Monneret. *Le leggende orientali sui Magi evangelici*. StT 163. Translated by Giorgio Levi Della Vida. Vatican City: Biblioteca Apostolica Vaticana, 1952.

Delcor, M. "Vom Sichem der hellenistischen Epoche zum Sychar des Neuen Testaments." *ZDPV* 78 (1962): 35–8.

DesCamp, Mary Therese. *Metaphor and Ideology: Liber Antiquitatum Biblicarum and Literary Methods through a Cognitive Lens*. BibInt 87. Leiden: Brill, 2007.

Dickie, Matthew W. *Magic and Magicians in the Greco-Roman World*. London and New York: Routledge, 2003.

Dieterich, Albrecht. *Abraxas. Studien zur Religionsgeschichte des spätern Altertums*. Leipzig: Teubner, 1891.

Dillinger, Johannes. *Hexen und Magie. Eine historische Einführung.* Historische Einführungen 3. Frankfurt and New York: Campus, 2007.
Doering, Lutz. *Ancient Jewish Letters and the Beginnings of Christian Epistolography.* WUNT 298. Tübingen: Mohr Siebeck, 2012.
Doering-Manteufel, Sabine. *Okkultismus. Geheimlehren, Geisterglaube, magische Praktiken.* Beck'sche Reihe 2713. Munich: C.H. Beck, 2011.
Dossey, Leslie. "Watchful Greeks and Lazy Romans: Disciplining Sleep in Late Antiquity." *JECS* 21 (2013): 208–39.
Duhaime, Jean. "War Scroll." Pages 86–7 in *The Dead Sea Scrolls: Hebrew, Aramaic, and Greek Texts with English Translations.* vol. 2: *Damascus Document, War Scroll, and Related Documents.* Edited by James H. Charlesworth. Louisville: Westminster John Knox, 1995.
Duhaime, Jean. *The War Texts: 1QM and Related Manuscripts.* London: T&T Clark, 2004.
Duling, D. C. "The Testament of Solomon: Retrospect and Prospect." *JSP* 2 (1988): 87–112.
Dušek, Jan. *Aramaic and Hebrew Inscriptions from Mt. Gerizim and Samaria between Antiochus III and Antiochus IV Epiphanes.* CHANE 54. Leiden: Brill, 2012.
Efthymiadis, Stephanos, ed. *The Ashgate Research Companion to Byzantine Hagiography.* Abingdon: Routledge, 2011.
Egger, Rita. *Josephus Flavius und die Samaritaner: Eine Terminologische Untersuchung zur Identitätsklärung der Samaritaner.* NTOA 4. Göttingen: Vandenhoeck & Ruprecht, 1986.
Egger, Rita. "Josephus Flavius and the Samaritans." Pages 109–14 in *Proceedings of the First International Conference of the Société d'études Samaritaines; Tel-Aviv, April 11–13, 1988.* Edited by Abraham Tal and Moshe Florentin. Tel Aviv: Chaim Rosenberg School for Jewish Studies, 1991.
Ego, Beate. "'Denn er liebt sie' (Tob 6, 15 Ms. 139). Zur Rolle des Dämons Asmodäus in der Tobit- Erzählung." Pages 309–17 in *Die Dämonen—Demons: Die Dämonologie der israelitisch-jüdischen und frühchristlichen Literatur im Kontext ihrer Umwelt—The Demonology of Israelite-Jewish and Early Christian Literature in Context of Their Environment.* Edited by A. Lange, H. Lichtenberger, and K. F. Diethard Römheld. Tübingen: Mohr Siebeck, 2003.
Ehrman, Bart D. "The New Testament Canon of Didymus the Blind." *VC* 37 (1983): 1–21.
Ehrman, Bart D., and Zlatko Pleše. *The Apocryphal Gospels.* Oxford: Oxford University Press, 2011.
Eidinow, Esther. *Oracles, Curses, and Risk among the Ancient Greeks.* Oxford and New York: Oxford University Press, 2007.
Elgvin, Torleif. *An Analysis of 4QInstruction.* PhD dissertation. Jerusalem: The Hebrew University of Jerusalem, 1997.
Elgvin, Torleif. "Texts on Messianic Reign from the Hasmonean Period: 4Q521 as Interpretation of Daniel 7." Pages 168–78 in *The Seleucid and Hasmonean Periods and the Apocalyptic Worldview.* LSTS 88. Edited by Lester L. Grabbe, Gabriele Boccaccini, and Jason M. Zurawksi. London: Bloomsbury T&T Clark, 2016.
Elgvin, Torleif. "Violence, Apologetics, and Resistance: Hasmonaean Ideology and Yaḥad Texts in Dialogue." Pages 319–40 in *The War Scroll, Violence, War and Peace in the Dead Sea Scrolls and Related Literature: Essays in Honour of Martin G. Abegg on the Occasion of His 65th Birthday.* STDJ 115. Edited by Kipp Davis, Kyung S. Baek, Peter W. Flint, and Dorothy M. Peters. Leiden: Brill, 2016.

Elgvin, Torleif. "Chasing the Hasmonean and Herodian Editors of the Song of Songs." Pages 71–98 in *The Song of Songs in Its Context. Words for Love, Love for Words*. Edited by Pierre van Hecke. BETL 310. Leuven: Peeters, 2020.

Elgvin, Torleif. *The Literary Growth of the Song of Songs during the Hasmonean and Early-Herodian Periods*. CBET 89. Leuven: Peeters, 2018.

Elior, Rachel. "On the Changing Significance of the Sacred." Pages 277–301 in *Israel's God and Rebecca's Children: Christology and Community in Early Judaism and Christianity. Essays in Honor of Larry W. Hurtado and Alan F. Segal*. Edited by David B. Capes, April DeConick, Helen K. Bond, and Troy A. Miller. Waco, TX: Baylor University Press, 2007.

Elliott, J. K. *A Synopsis of the Apocryphal Nativity and Infancy Narratives*. Second ed. Leiden: Brill, 2016.

Elm, Susanna. *"Virgins of God": The Making of Asceticism in Late Antiquity*. Oxford: Clarendon Press, 1994.

Elsas, Christoph. *Religionsgeschichte Europas. Religiöses Leben von der Vorgeschichte bis zur Gegenwart*. Darmstadt: Wissenschaftliche Buchgesellschaft, 2002.

Embry, Brad. "Solomon's Name as a Prophetic Hallmark in Jewish and Christian Texts." *Henoch* 28 (2006): 47–62.

Embry, Brad. "Some Thoughts on and Implications from Genre Categorization in the Psalms of Solomon." Pages 59–78 in *The Psalms of Solomon: Language, History, Theology*. Edited by Eberhard Bons and Patrick Pouchelle. EJL. Atlanta: SBL Press, 2015.

Emmel, Stephen. "Shenoute of Atripe and the Christian Destruction of Temple in Egypt: Rhetoric and Reality." Pages 161–202 in *From Temple to Church: Destruction and Renewal of Local Cultic Topography in Late Antiquity*. RGRW 163. Edited by J. Hahn, S. Emmel and U. Gotter. Leiden: Brill, 2008.

Epp, Eldon Jay. "The Oxyrhynchus New Testament Papyri: 'Not without Honor Except in Their Hometown'?" Pages 743–802 in *Perspectives On New Testament Textual Criticism: Collected Essays, 1962–2004*. NovTSup 116. Leiden: Brill, 2005.

Epp, Eldon Jay. "Issues in the Interrelation of New Testament Textual Criticism and Canon." Pages 595–640 in *Perspectives on New Testament Textual Criticism*. NovTSup 116. Leiden: Brill, 2005.

Eshel, Hanan. "The Prayer of Joseph, a Papyrus from Masada and the Samaritan Temple on ΑΡΓΑΡΙΖΙΝ." *Zion* 56 (1991): 125–36.

Eshel, Hanan. "The Damascus Document's 'Three Nets of Belial': A Reference to the Aramaic Levi Document?" Pages 243–55 in *Heavenly Tablets: Interpretation, Identity and Tradition in Ancient Judaism*. JSJSup 119. Edited by L. LiDonnici and A. Lieber. Leiden: Brill, 2007.

Eshel, Hanan. *Exploring the Dead Sea Scrolls*. Edited by Shani Tzoref and Barnea Levi Selavan. Göttingen: Vandenhoeck & Ruprecht, 2015.

Evans, Craig A. "Luke and the Rewritten Bible: Aspects of Lukan Historiography." Pages 170–201 in *The Pseudepigrapha and Early Biblical Interpretation*. JSPSup 14. SSEJC 2. Edited by James H. Charlesworth and Craig A. Evans. Sheffield: JSOT Press, 1993.

Evans, Craig A. "A Preliminary Survey of Christian Literature Found in Oxyrhynchus." Pages 26–51 in *"Non-Canonical" Religious Texts in Early Judaism and Early Christianity*. JCT 14. Edited by Lee Martin McDonald and James H. Charlesworth. London: T&T Clark, 2012.

Evans, Craig A. "Prophet, Sage, Healer, Messiah, and Martyr: Types and Identities of Jesus." Pages 1217–43 in *Handbook for the Study of the Historical Jesus*. Edited by Tom Holmén and Stanley E. Porter. Leiden: Brill, 2011.
Faraone, Christopher A. *Ancient Greek Love Magic*. Cambridge, London: Harvard University Press, 2009.
Faraone, Christopher A. "Magic and Medicine in the Roman Imperial Period: Two Case Studies." Pages 135–58 in *Continuity and Innovation in the Magical Tradition*. Jerusalem Studies in Religion and Culture 15. Edited by Gideon Bohak, Yuval Harari, and Shaul Shaked. Leiden: Brill, 2011.
Faraone, Christopher A. "Cursing Chariot Horses instead of Drivers in the Hippodromes of the Eastern Roman Empire." Pages 83–101 in *Litterae Magicae. Studies in Honor of Roger S.O. Tomlin*. Edited by Celia Sánchez Natalías. Zaragoza: Libros Pórtico, 2019.
Feldman, Jackie. *A Jewish Guide in the Holy Land: How Christian Pilgrims Made Me Israeli*. Bloomington: Indiana University Press, 2016.
Feldman, Louis. "Introduction." Page lxxvii in *Antiquities* [M. R. James]. Repr. New York: KTAV, 1971.
Feldman, Louis. "Josephus' Attitude toward the Samaritans: A Study in Ambivalence." Pages 34–9 in *Jewish Sects, Religious Movements, and Political Parties: Proceedings of the Third Annual Symposium of the Philip M. and Ethel Klutznick Chair in Jewish Civilization Held on Sunday-Monday, October 14–15,1990*. Omaha: Creighton University Press, 1992.
Feldman, Louis. "Josephus' Portrayal of the Hasmoneans Compared with 1 Maccabees." Pages 41–68 in *Josephus and the History of the Greco-Roman Period: Essays in Memory of Morton Smith*. StPB 41. Edited by Fausto Parente and Joseph Sievers. Leiden: Brill, 1994.
Ferguson, Everett. "Canon Muratori: Date and Provenance." *Studia Patristica* 48 (1982): 677–83.
Fewster, Gregory P. *Creation Language in Romans 8: A Study in Monosemy*. Linguistic Biblical Studies 8. Leiden: Brill, 2013.
Fiorenza, Elizabeth Schüssler. *Rhetoric and Ethic: The Politics of Biblical Studies*. Minneapolis: Fortress, 1999.
Fischer, Thomas, and Udo Rüterswörden. "Aufruf zur Volksklage in Kanaan (Jesaja 23)." *Welt de Orients* 13 (1982): 45–8.
Fishbane, Michael. "Use, Authority and Interpretation of Mikra At Qumran." Pages 339–77 in *Mikra: Texts, Translation, Reading and Interpretation of the Hebrew Bible in Ancient Judaism and Early Christianity*. CRINT 2.1. Edited by Martin J. Mulder and Harry Sysling. Assen: Van Gorcum, 1988.
Fitzmyer, Joseph A. "The Use of Explicit Old Testament Quotations in Qumran Literature and in the New Testament." *NTS* 7 (1960): 297–333.
Fitzmyer, Joseph A. "Tobit." Pages 1–76 in *Qumran Cave 4: XIV. Parabiblical Texts, Part 2*. DJD 19. Oxford: Clarendon Press, 1995.
Fitzmyer, Joseph A. *Tobit*. CEJL. Berlin: de Gruyter, 2003.
Fleck, Ferdinand Florens. "Testamentum Salomonis: Bibliothecae Regiae Parisinae ineditum." Pages 111–40 in *Wissenschaftliche Reise durch das südliche Deutschland, Italien, Sicilien und Frank-reich 2, 3*. Edited by F. F. Fleck. Leipzig: Barth, 1837.
Fossum, Jarl. "Jewish-Christian Christology and Jewish Mysticism." *VC* 37 (1983): 260–87.
Fossum, Jarl. *The Name of God and the Angel of the Lord. Samaritan and Jewish Concepts of Intermediation and the Origin of Gnosticism*. WUNT 36. Tübingen: Mohr Siebeck, 1985.

Foucault, Michel. *The Archaeology of Knowledge*. Translated by A. M. Sheridan Smith. Repr. London: Routledge Classics, 2002 (1969).

Fox, Michael V. *The Song of Songs and the Ancient Egyptian Love Songs*. Madison: University of Wisconsin Press, 1985.

Fraade, Steven D. "To Whom It May Concern: 4QMMT and Its Addressee(s)." *RevQ* 19 (2000): 507–26.

Fraade, Steven D. *Legal Fictions*. Leiden: Brill, 2011.

Frankfurter, David. "The Perils of Love: Magic and Countermagic in Coptic Egypt." *Journal of the History of Sexuality* 10 (2001): 480–500.

Frenschkowski, Marco. *Die Hexen. Eine kulturgeschichtliche Analyse*. Wiesbaden: Marixverlag, 2012.

Frenschkowski, Marco. *Magie im antiken Christentum. Eine Studie zur Alten Kirche und ihrem Umfeld*. Standorte in Antike und Christentum 7. Stuttgart: Hiersemann, 2016.

Fretheim, Thorstein. "In Defense of Monosemy." Pages 79–115 in *Pragmatics and the Flexibility of Word Meaning*. Edited by Németh T. Enikö and Károly Bibok. Amsterdam: Elsevier Science, 2001.

Freyne, Sean. "Behind the Names: Galileans, Samaritans, *Ioudaioi*." Pages 114–31 in *Galilee and Gospel: Collected Essays*. WUNT 125. Tübingen: Mohr Siebeck, 2000.

Frilingos, Christopher A. "No Child Left Behind: Knowledge and Violence in the *Infancy Gospel of Thomas*." *JECS* 17 (2009): 27–54.

Frilingos, Christopher A. "Parents Just Don't Understand: Ambiguity in Stories about the Childhood of Jesus." *HTR* 109 (2016): 33–55.

Fröhlich, Ida. "Evil in Second Temple Texts." Pages 23–50 in *Evil and the Devil*. LNTS 481. Edited by I. Fröhlich and E. Koskenniemi. London: T&T Clark, 2013.

Gager, John G. *Curse Tablets and Binding Spells from the Ancient World*. New York; Oxford: Oxford University Press, 1992.

Gallagher, Edmond L. "Is the Samaritan Pentateuch a Sectarian Text?" *ZAW* 127 (2015): 96–107.

Gamble, Harry. *The New Testament Canon: Its Making and Meaning*. Philadelphia: Fortress Press, 1985.

Gamble, Harry. "The New Testament Canon: Recent Research and the Status Quaestionis." Pages 267–94 in *The Canon Debate: On the Origins and Formation of the Bible*. Edited by Lee Martin McDonald and James A. Sanders. Peabody, MA: Hendrickson, 2004.

Garrett, Susan R. *The Demise of the Devil: Magic and the Demonic in Luke's Writings*. Minneapolis: Fortress Press, 1989.

Gaskill, Malcolm. *Witchcraft: A Very Short Introduction*. Oxford; New York: Oxford University Press, 2010.

Gehrke, Hans-Joachim. "Die Griechen und die Rache. Ein Versuch in historischer Psychologie." *Saeculum* 38 (1987): 121–49.

Gerstenberger, Erhard. "Jeremiah's Complaints: Observations on Jer 15:10–21." *JBL* 82 (1963): 393–408.

Gieschen, Charles. "The Divine Name in Ante-Nicene Christology." *VC* 57 (2003): 115–58.

Ginzberg, Louis. *The Legends of the Jews* IV. Philadelphia: Jewish Publication Society, 1968.

Gmirkin, Russell. "Historical Allusions in the War Scroll." *DSD* 5 (1998): 180–5.

Goff, Matthew. "The Foolish Nation That Dwells in Shechem: Ben Sira on Shechem and the Other Peoples in Palestine." Pages 173–88 in *The "Other" in Second Temple Judaism: Essays in Honor of John J. Collins*. Edited by Daniel C. Harlow, Karina Martin Hogan, Matthew Goff, and Joel S. Kaminsky. Grand Rapids: Eerdmans, 2011.

Goff, Matthew. "Warriors, Cannibals and Teachers of Evil: The Sons of the Angels in Genesis 6, the Book of the Watchers and the Book of Jubilees." *SEÅ* 80 (2015): 67–85.

Goff, Matthew. "The Diabolical Wisdom of Solomon: Assessing the Jewishness of the Testament of Solomon." In *Testamentum Salomonis: Editiones studiaque collegerunt edideruntque*. Parabiblica 1. Edited by F. Albrecht and J. Dochhorn. Tübingen: Mohr Siebeck, forthcoming.

Goldstein, Jonathan. *2 Maccabees: A New Translation with Introduction and Commentary*. AB 41A. Garden City: Doubleday, 1983.

Goode, William J. "Magic and Religion: A Continuum." *Ethnos* 14 (1949): 172–82.

Gooding, David W. "Problems of Text and Midrash in the Third Book of Reigns." *Textus* 7 (1969): 1–29.

Goodman, Martin. "The First Jewish Revolt: Social Conflict and the Problem of Debt." *JJS* 33 (1982): 417–27.

Goodman, Martin. *The Ruling Class of Judaea: The Origins of the Jewish Revolt against Rome A.D. 66–70*. Cambridge: Cambridge University Press, 1987.

Gonis, Nickolaos. "4705–4707. Hermas." Pages 1–17 in *The Oxyrhynchus Papyri Volume LXIX*. Graeco-Roman Memoirs. London: Egypt Exploration Society, 2005.

Grabbe, Lester L. "'The End of the Desolations of Jerusalem': From Jeremiah's 70 Years to Daniel's 70 Weeks of Years." Pages 67–72 in *Early Jewish and Christian Exegesis: Studies in Memory of William Hugh Brownlee*. Homage 10. Edited by Craig A. Evans and William F. Stinespring. Atlanta: Scholars Press, 1987.

Grabbe, Lester L. "Eschatology in Philo and Josephus." Pages 177–81 in *Death, Life-after-death, Resurrection and the World-to-come in the Judaisms of Antiquity*, vol. 4 of *Judaism in Late Antiquity*. HdO I/49. Edited by Alan J. Avery-Peck and Jacob Neusner. Leiden: Brill, 2000.

Graetz, Heinrich. *Schir Ha-Schirim oder das salomonische Hohelied*. Vienna: Braumüller, 1871.

Graf, Fritz. *Gottesnähe und Schadenszauber. Die Magie in der griechisch-römischen Antike*. Munich: C.H. Beck, 1996.

Graf, Fritz. "Untimely Death, Witchcraft, and Divine Vengeance. A Reasoned Epigraphical Catalog." *ZPE* 162 (2007): 139–50.

Graf, Fritz. "Victimology or: How to Deal with Untimely Death." Pages 386–417 in *Daughters of Hecate. Women and Magic in the Ancient World*. Edited by Kimberly B. Stratton and Dayna S. Kalleres. Oxford; New York: Oxford University Press, 2014.

Gray, Rebecca. *Prophetic Figures in Late Second Temple Jewish Palestine: The Evidence from Josephus*. New York: Oxford University Press, 1993.

Gregg, Robert C. *Shared Stories, Rival Tellings: Early Encounters of Jews, Christians and Muslims*. Oxford: Oxford University Press, 2015.

Grossman, Maxine L. "Reading 4QMMT: Genre and History." *RevQ* 20 (2001): 3–22.

Grossman, Maxine L. "Is Ancient Jewish Studies (Still) Postmodern (Yet)?" *CurBR* 13 (2015): 245–83.

Gruen, Erich S. *The Construct of Identity in Hellenistic Judaism*. DCLS 29. Berlin: de Gruyter, 2016.

Grüter, Thomas. *Magisches Denken. Wie es entsteht und wie es uns beeinflusst*. Frankfurt: Scherz, 2010.

Gundry, Stephen. *Miscellaneous Studies towards the Cult of Óðinn*. New Haven: The Troth, 2014.

Hacham, Noah. "3 Maccabees and Esther: Parallels, Intertextuality, and Diaspora Identity." *JBL* 126 (2007): 765–85.

Hacham, Noah. "Bigthan and Teresh and the Reason Gentiles Hate Jews." *VT* 62 (2012): 318–56.
Hacham, Noah. "Joseph and Aseneth: Loyalty, Traitors, Antiquity and Diasporan Identity." *JSP* 22 (2012): 53–67.
Haelewyck, Jean-Claude. "Le nombre des Rois Mages: Les hésitations de la tradition syriaque." Pages 25–37 in *Les (Rois) Mages*. Graphè 20. Edited by Jean-Marc Vercruysse. Arras: Artois presses université, 2011.
Hägg, Henny Fiskå. *Clement of Alexandria and the Beginnings of Christian Apophaticism*. OECS. Oxford: Oxford University Press, 2006.
Hahneman, Geoffrey Mark. "The Muratorian Fragment and the Origins of the New Testament Canon." Pages 405–39 in *The Canon Debate: On the Origins and Formation of the Bible*. Edited by Lee Martin McDonald and James A. Sanders. Peabody, MA: Hendrickson, 2004.
Halpern-Amaru, Betsy. "The Killing of the Prophets: Unraveling a Midrash." *HUCA* 54 (1983): 153–5.
Harrak, Amir. *The Chronicle of Zuqnīn: Parts III and IV: A.D. 488–775*. Mediaeval Sources in Translation 36. Toronto: Pontifical Institute of Mediaeval Studies, 1999.
Harrington, Daniel J. "The Original Language of Pseudo-Philo's Liber Antiquitatum Biblicarum." *HTR* 63 (1970): 503–14.
Harris, R. Laird. "Chronicles and the Canon in New Testament Times." *JETS* 33 (1990): 75–84.
Hartmann, A. T. "Über Charakter und Auslegung des Hohenliedes." *ZWT* 3 (1829): 397–448.
Hasenfratz, Hans-Peter. *Die antike Welt und das Christentum. Menschen, Mächte, Gottheiten im Römischen Weltreich*. Darmstadt: Wissenschaftliche Buchgesellschaft, 2004.
Hauck, Robert J. "The Great Fast: Christology in the Shepherd of Hermas." *AThR* 75 (1993): 187–99.
Hauge, Martin Ravndal. *Solomon the Lover and the Shape of the Song of Songs*. Sheffield: Sheffield Phoenix Press, 2015.
Haustein, Jörg. *Martin Luthers Stellung zum Zauber- und Hexenwesen*. MKS 2. Stuttgart: Kohlhammer, 1990.
Hays, J. Daniel. "The Persecuted Prophet and Judgment on Jerusalem: The Use of LXX Jeremiah in the Gospel of Luke." *BBR* 25 (2015): 453–73.
Head, P. M. "On the Christology of the Gospel of Peter." *VC* 46 (1992): 217–18.
Heal, Kristian S. "Review of Brent Landau, *Revelation of the Magi: The Lost Tale of the Wise Men's Journey to Bethlehem*." *Hug* 14 (2011): 294–8.
Heard, Warren J., and Yamazaki-Ransom, Kazuhiko. "Revolutionary Movements." Pages 789–99 in *Dictionary of Jesus and the Gospels*. Second Edition. Edited by Joel B. Green. Downers Grove: IVP Academic, 2013.
Hegedus, Tim. *Early Christianity and Ancient Astrology*. Patristic Studies 6. New York: Lang, 2007.
Hegeler, Hartmut. "Der evangelische Pfarrer Anton Praetorius. Mit der Bibel gegen Folter und Hexenprozesse." Pages 153–72 in *Hexenwahn. Eine theologische Selbstbesinnung*. TA 5. Edited by Marcel Nieden. Stuttgart: Kohlhammer, 2004.
Heinevetter, Hans-Josef. *"Komm nun, mein Liebster, dein Garten ruft dich!": Das Hohelied als programmatische Komposition*. Athenäums Monografien. Bodenheim: Athenäum, 1988.
Hellholm, David. "The Shepherd of Hermas." Pages 215–42 in *The Apostolic Fathers: An Introduction*. Edited by Wilhelm Pratscher. Waco, TX: Baylor University Press, 2010.
Hengel, Martin. *The Zealots: Investigations into the Jewish Freedom Movement in the Period from Herod I Until 70 A.D.* Translated by David Smith. Edinburgh: T&T Clark, 1989.

Henne, P. "Hermas, un pseudonym." *Studia Patristica* 24 (1993): 136–9.
Herzer, Jens. *4 Baruch (Paraleipomena Jeremiou)*. WGRW 22. Leiden: Brill, 2006.
Herzer, Jens. "Retelling the Story of Exile: The Reception of the Jeremiah Tradition in *4 Baruch* in the Perspective of the Jewish Diaspora." Pages 387–8 in *Jeremiah's Scriptures*. JSJSup 173. Edited by Hindy Najman and Konrad Schmid. Leiden: Brill, 2016.
Hill, Charles E. "'The Writing which Says …' The *Shepherd* of Hermas in the Writings of Irenaeus." Pages 127–38 in *The First Two Centuries: Apocrypha; Tertullian and Rhetoric; From Tertullian to Tyconius Studia*. Patristica LXV. vol. 13. Leuven: Peeters, 2013.
Himmelfarb, Martha. "The Parting of the Ways Reconsidered: Diversity in Judaism and Jewish Christian Relations in the Roman Empire—'a Jewish Perspective.'" Pages 47–61 in *Interwoven Destinies: Jews and Christians through the Ages*. Edited by Eugene J. Fisher. New York: Paulist Press, 1993.
Himmelfarb, Martha. "*3 Baruch* Revisited: Jewish or Christian Composition, and Why It Matters." *ZAC* 20 (2016): 41–62.
Hirschfeld, Yizhar. *En-Gedi Excavations II. Final Report (1996–2002)*. Jerusalem: Israel Exploration Society, 2007.
Hjelm, Ingrid. *The Samaritans and Early Judaism: A Literary Analysis*. JSOTSup 303. Sheffield: Sheffield Academic Press, 2000.
Hoffmann, Matthias Reinhard. "'Die Stadt ist zu klein für uns beide!' (Wunder des Petrus und Zauberei Simons)—ActPetr 4–15." Pages 601–24 in *Kompendium der frühchristlichen Wundererzählungen*. vol. 2: *Die Wunder der Apostel*. Edited by Ruben Zimmermann et al. Gütersloh: Gütersloher Verlagshaus, 2017.
Hoffmann, Matthias Reinhard. "Systematic Chaos or Chain of Tradition? References to Angels in Early Jewish and Early Christian Literature and Magical Writings." Pages 89–129 in *Representations of Angelic Beings in Early Jewish and in Christian Traditions*. Edited by Amsalu Tefera and Loren T. Stuckenbruck. WUNT 2.544. Tübingen: Mohr Siebeck, 2021.
Hogeterp, Albert L. A. *Expectations of the End: A Comparative Tradition-historical Study of Eschatological, Apocalyptic and Messianic Ideas in the Dead Sea Scrolls and the New Testament*. STDJ 83. Leiden: Brill, 2009.
Hondius, Jacobus J. E. et al., eds. *Supplementum Epigraphicum Graecum*. Leiden: Sijthoff, 1923–1971.
Hooker, Morna. *Endings: Invitations to Discipleship*. London: SCM Press, 2003.
Horbury, William. *Messianism among Jews and Christians: Biblical and Historical Studies*. London: T&T Clark, 2003.
Horbury, William. *Jewish War under Trajan and Hadrian*. New York: Cambridge University Press, 2014.
Horsley, Richard A. "Josephus and the Bandits." *JSJ* 10 (1979): 37–63.
Horsley, Richard A., and John S. Hanson. *Bandits, Prophets and Messiahs: Popular Movements at the Time of Jesus*. Edinburgh: T&T Clark, 1985.
Horsley, Richard A. "The Zealots: Their Origin, Relationships and Importance in the Jewish Revolt." *NovT* 28 (1986): 159–92.
Horsley, Richard A. *Jesus and Magic. Freeing the Gospel Stories from Modern Misconceptions*. Cambridge: James Clarke, 2015.
Hultgård, Anders. "The Magi and the Star—the Persian Background in Texts and Iconography." Pages 215–25 in *Being Religious and Living Through the Eyes: Studies in Religious Iconography and Iconology*. Acta Universitatis Upsaliensis: Historia religionum 14. Edited by Peter Schalk and Michael Stausberg. Uppsala: Uppsala University Library, 1998.

Hurtado, Larry. *One God, One Lord: Early Christian Devotion and Ancient Jewish Monotheism*. Third ed. Cornerstones. London; New York: Bloomsbury T&T Clark, 2015.

Ingram, Helen. *Dragging down Heaven: Jesus as Magician and Manipulator of Spirits in the Gospels*. PhD dissertation. Birmingham: The University of Birmingham, 2007.

Isenberg, Wesley W. "The Gospel of Philip." Pages 141–60 in *Nag Hammadi Codex II, 2–7*. NHS 20. Edited by Bentley Layton. Leiden: Brill, 1989.

Istrin, V. M. "Grieceski Spiski Zabesania Solomona." *Lietopis istoriko-philologetscheskago Obtchestva* 7 (1899): 49–98.

Jacobs, Andrew S. "A Family Affair: Marriage, Class, and Ethics in the Apocryphal Acts of the Apostles." *JECS* 7 (1999): 105–38.

Jacobson, Howard. *A Commentary on Pseudo-Philo's Liber Antiquitatum Biblicarum*. AGJU 31. Leiden: Brill, 1996.

Jacobson, Howard. "Theodotus, 'On the Jews.'" Page 724 in *Outside the Bible: Ancient Jewish Writings Related to Scripture*. Edited by Louis H. Feldman, James L. Kugel, and Lawrence H. Schiffman. Philadelphia: Jewish Publication Society, 2013.

Jansson, Sven B. F. *Runes in Sweden*. Stockholm: Gidlunds, 1987.

Japhet, Sara. *I & II Chronicles*. OTL London: SCM Press, 1993.

Jassen, Alexander P. *Mediating the Divine: Prophecy and Revelation in the Dead Sea Scrolls and Second Temple Judaism*. STDJ 68. Leiden: Brill, 2007.

Jassen, Alexander P. "The Dead Sea Scrolls and Violence: Sectarian Formation and Eschatological Imagination." *BibInt* 17 (2009): 12–44.

Johns, Loren L. "Identity and Resistance: The Varieties of Competing Models in Early Judaism." Pages 254–77 in *Qumran Studies: New Approaches, New Questions*. Edited by Michael Thomas Davis and Brent A. Strawn. Grand Rapids: Eerdmans, 2007.

Johnston, Sarah Iles. *Restless Dead: Encounters between the Living and the Dead in Ancient Greece*. Berkeley: University of California Press, 1999.

Johnston, Sarah Iles. "Sacrifice in the Greek Magical Papyri." Pages 344–58 in *Magic and Ritual in the Ancient World*. RGRW 141. Edited by Paul Mirecki and Marvin Meyer. Leiden: Brill, 2002.

Johnston, Sarah Iles. "The *Testament of Solomon* from Late Antiquity to the Renaissance." Pages 35–50 in *The Metamorphosis of Magic from Late Antiquity to the Modern Period*. Groningen Studies in Cultural Change. Edited by Jan N. Bremmer and Jan R. Veenstra. Leuven: Peeters, 2002.

Joosten, Jan. "The Impact of the Septuagint Pentateuch on the Greek Psalms." Pages 197–205 in *XIIIth Congress of the IOCS Ljubljana*. Edited by M. K. H. Peters. Atlanta: SBL Press, 2007.

Joosten, Jan. "Reflections on the Original Language of the Psalms of Solomon." Pages 31–47 in *The Psalms of Solomon: Language, History, Theology*. EJL. Edited by Eberhard Bons and Patrick Pouchelle. Atlanta: SBL Press, 2015.

Jordan, David R. "Survey of Greek Defixiones Not Included in the Special Corpora." *GRBS* 26 (1985): 151–97.

Jördens, Andrea. "Griechische Texte aus Ägypten." Pages 417–44 in *Omina, Orakel, Rituale und Beschwörungen*. TUAT N.F. 4. Edited by Bernd Janowski and Gernot Wilhelm. Gütersloh: Gütersloher Verlagshaus, 2008.

Jossa, Giorgio. "Josephus' Action in Galilee during the Jewish War." Pages 265–78 in *Josephus and the History of the Greco-Roman Period: Essays in Memory of Morton Smith*. Edited by Fausto Parente and Joseph Sievers. StPB 41. Leiden: Brill, 1994.

Jost, Renate. "Zauberei und Gottesmacht. Überlegungen zu Gender, Magie und Hexenwahn im Zusammenhang von Ex 22,17." Pages 11–33 in *Hexenwahn. Eine theologische Selbstbesinnung*. TA 5. Edited by Marcel Nieden. Stuttgart: Kohlhammer, 2004.

Jurgens, Blake. "The Figure of Solomon." Pages 157–76 in *Wiley Blackwell Companion to Wisdom Literature*. Edited by M. Goff and S. L. Adams. West Sussex: Blackwell, 2020.

Jurgens, Blake. "Demonic Decans: An Analysis of Chapter 18 of the *Testament of Solomon*." In *Testamentum Salomonis: Editiones studiaque collegerunt edideruntque*. Parabiblica 1. Edited by F. Albrecht and J. Dochhorn. Tübingen: Mohr Siebeck, forthcoming.

Kaiser, Otto. "'Our Forefathers Never Triumphed By Arms ... ': The Interpretation of Biblical History in the Addresses of Flavius Josephus to the Besieged Jerusalemites in Bell. Jud. V. 356–426." Pages 239–64 in *History and Identity: How Israel's Later Authors Viewed Its Earlier History*. Deuterocanonical and Cognate Literature Yearbook 2006. Edited by Núria Calduch-Benages and Jan Liesen. Berlin: de Gruyter, 2006.

Kaiser, Otto., ed. *Rechts- und Wirtschaftsurkunden. Historisch-chronologische Texte*. TUAT 1. Gütersloh: Gütersloher Verlagshaus, 1982–5.

Kalimi, Isaac. "The Murders of the Messengers: Stephen versus Zechariah and the Ethical Values of 'New' versus 'Old' Testament." *Australian Biblical Review* 56 (2008): 69–73.

Kalimi, Isaac. "Murder in Jerusalem Temple: The Chronicler's Story of Zechariah. Literary and Theological Features, Historical Credibility and Impact." *RB* 117 (2010): 200–9.

Kalmin, Richard. *Migrating Tales: The Talmud's Migrating Tales: The Talmud's Narratives and Their Historical Context*. Oakland: University of California Press, 2014.

Kampen, John. "The Books of the Maccabees and Sectarianism in Second Temple Judaism." Pages 11–30 in *The Books of the Maccabees: History, Theology, Ideology*. JSJSup 118. Edited by Géza G. Xeravits and József Zsengellér. Leiden: Brill, 2007.

Kartveit, Magnar. *The Origins of the Samaritans*. VTSup 128. Leiden: Brill, 2009.

Kartveit, Magnar. "Who Are the Fools in 4QNarrative and Poetic Composition^{a-c}." Pages 119–33 in *Northern Lights on the Dead Sea Scrolls*. STDJ 80. Edited by Anders Klostergaard Petersen. Leiden: Brill, 2009.

Kellerman, James A. *Incomplete Commentary on Matthew* (Opus imperfectum). Ancient Christian Texts. Downers Grove, IL: IVP Academic, 2010.

Kerkeslager, Allen. "Jewish Pilgrimage and Jewish Identity in Hellenistic and Early Roman Egypt." Pages 99–225 in *Pilgrimage and Holy Space in Late Antique Egypt*. RGRW 134. Edited by David Frankfurter. Leiden: Brill, 1998.

Kieckhefer, Richard. *Magie im Mittelalter*. Munich: Deutscher Taschenbuch Verlag, 1995.

King, Karen L. "The Place of the *Gospel of Philip* in the Context of Early Christian Claims about Jesus' Marital Status." *NTS* 59 (2013): 565–87.

Kippenberg, Hans Gerhard. *Garizim und Synagoge: Traditionsgeschichtliche Untersuchungen zur samaritanischen Religion der aramäischen Periode*. RVV 30. Berlin: de Gruyter, 1971.

Kippenberg, Hans G., and Kocku von Stuckrad. *Einführung in die Religionswissenschaft. Gegenstände und Begriffe*. Munich: C.H. Beck, 2003.

Kister, Menahem. "Metamorphoses of Aggadic Traditions." *Tarbiz* 60.2 (1991): 179–224.

Kister, Menahem. "A Common Heritage: Biblical Interpretation at Qumran and Its Implications." Pages 101–11 in *Biblical Perspectives: Early Use and Interpretation of the Bible in Light of the Dead Sea Scrolls. Proceedings of the First International Symposium of the Orion Center, May 12–14, 1996*. STDJ 28. Edited by Michael E. Stone and Esther G. Chazon. Leiden: Brill, 1998.

Klauck, Hans-Josef. *Die religiöse Umwelt des Urchristentums I. Stadt- und Hausreligion, Mysterienkulte, Volksglaube.* Studienbücher Theologie 9,1. Stuttgart: Kohlhammer, 1995.
Klauck, Hans-Josef. *Apokryphe Apostelakten. Eine Einführung.* Stuttgart: Katholisches Bibelwerk, 2005.
Klijn, A. F. J. *Seth in Jewish, Christian and Gnostic Literature.* NovTSup 46. Leiden: Brill, 1977.
Klijn, A. F. J. *The Acts of Thomas: Introduction, Text, and Commentary.* Second ed. NovTSup 58. Leiden: Brill, 2003.
Klutz, Todd E. "The Archer and the Cross: Chorographic Astrology and Literary Design in the *Testament of Solomon*." Pages 219–44 in *Magic in the Biblical World: From the Rod of Aaron to the Ring of Solomon.* JSNTSup 245. Edited by T. Klutz. London: T&T Clark, 2003.
Klutz, Todd E. *Rewriting the Testament of Solomon: Tradition, Conflict and Identity in a Late Antique Pseudepigraphon.* LSTS 53. London: T&T Clark, 2005.
Knibb, Michael A. "Christian Adoption and Transmission of Jewish Pseudepigrapha: The Case of 1 Enoch." *JSJ* 32 (2001): 396–415.
Knibb, Michael A. *Essays on the Book of Enoch and Other Early Jewish Texts and Traditions.* SVTP 22. Leiden: Brill, 2009.
Knoppers, Gary. *Jews and Samaritans: The Origins and History of Their Early Relations.* New York: Oxford University Press, 2013.
Knowles, Michael. *Jeremiah in Matthew's Gospel: The Rejected Prophet Motif in Matthaean Redaction.* JSNTSup 68. Sheffield: Sheffield Academic Press, 1993.
Knust, Jennifer Wright. *Abandoned to Lust: Sexual Slander and Ancient Christianity.* New York: Columbia University Press, 2005.
Koch, Klaus. "Is Daniel Also among the Prophets?" *Int* 39 (1985): 117–30.
Koehler, Ludwig, and Walter Baumgartner. *The Hebrew and Aramaic Lexicon of the Old Testament.* Leiden: Brill, 1996.
Koester, Craig R. *Revelation: A New Translation with Introduction and Commentary.* AB 38A. New Haven: Yale University Press, 2014.
Kolenkow, Anitra Bingham. "The Literary Genre 'Testament.'" Pages 266–7 in *Early Judaism and Its Modern Interpreters.* BMI 2. Edited by Robert A. Kraft and George W. E. Nickelsburg. Atlanta: Scholars Press, 1986.
Korsvoll, Nils Hallvard. *Reconsidering "Christian:" Context and Categorisation in the Study of Syriac Amulets and Incantation Bowls.* PhD dissertation. Oslo: MF Norwegian School of Theology, 2017.
Köster, Janine. *Sterbeinschriften auf wikingerzeitlichen Runensteinen.* RGA-E 89. Berlin; Boston: de Gruyter, 2014.
Kraft, Robert A. "In Search of 'Jewish Christianity' and Its 'Theology': Problems of Definition and Methodology." *RSR* 60 (1972): 80–92.
Kraft, Robert A. "The Pseudepigrapha in Christianity." Pages 55–86 in *Tracing the Threads: Studies in the Vitality of Jewish Pseudepigrapha.* SBLEJL 6. Edited by John C. Reeves. Atlanta: Scholars, 1994.
Kraft, Robert A. *Exploring the Scripturesque.* Leiden: Brill, 2009.
Kraft, Robert A., and George Nickelsburg. *Early Judaism and Its Modern Interpreters.* Philadelphia: Fortress, 1986.
Kraus, Thomas J. "Angels in the Magical Papyri—The Classic Example of Michael, the Archangel." Pages 611–27 in *Angels. The Concept of Celestial Beings—Origins, Development and Reception.* DCLY 2007. Edited by Friedrich V. Reiterer, Tobias Nicklas, and Karin Schöpflin. Berlin; New York: de Gruyter, 2007.

Krawiec, Rebecca. *Shenoute and the Women of the White Monastery: Egyptian Monasticism in Late Antiquity*. Oxford: Oxford University Press, 2002.

Kropp, Amina. "'Dann trag das Bleitäfelchen weg ans Grab eines vorzeitig Verstorbenen.' Antike Fluchtafeln und Ritualobjekte." Pages 73–101 in *Schriftträger—Textträger. Zur materialen Präsenz des Geschriebenen in frühen Gesellschaften*. Materiale Textkulturen. Edited by Annette Kehnel and Diamantis Panagiotopoulos. Berlin: de Gruyter, 2015.

Kugel, James L. *Traditions of the Bible*. Cambridge, MA: Harvard University Press, 1998.

Kugler, Robert A. "Joseph at Qumran." Pages 261–78 in *Studies in the Hebrew Bible, Qumran, and the Septuagint Presented to Eugene Ulrich*. VTSup 101. Edited by Peter W. Flint, Emanuel Tov, and James C. VanderKam. Leiden: Brill, 2006.

La Fontaine, Jean. *Witches and Demons: A Comparative Perspective on Witchcraft and Satanism*. Studies in Public and Applied Anthropology 10. New York; Oxford: Berghahn, 2016.

Lahe, Jaan. *Gnosis und Judentum. Alttestamentliche und jüdische Motive in der gnostischen Literatur und das Ursprungsproblem der Gnosis*. NHMS 75. Leiden: Brill, 2012.

Lamberti, Francesca. "De magia als rechtsgeschichtliches Dokument." Pages 331–50 in *Apuleius De Magia – Über die Magie. Lateinisch und deutsch*. Sapere 5. Second ed. Edited by Jürgen Hammerstadt et al. Darmstadt: Wissenschaftliche Buchgesellschaft, 2008.

Lampe, G. W. H. *A Patristic Greek Lexicon*. Oxford: Clarendon Press, 1961.

Landau, Brent. "The Revelation of the Magi in the Chronicle of Zuqnin." *Apocrypha* 19 (2008): 182–201.

Landau, Brent. *The Sages and the Star-Child: An Introduction to the Revelation of the Magi, An Ancient Christian Apocryphon*. ThD dissertation. Harvard University, 2008.

Landau, Brent. "'One Drop of Salvation from the House of Majesty': Universal Revelation, Human Mission and Mythical Geography in the Syriac *Revelation of the Magi*." Pages 83–103 in *The Levant: Crossroads of Late Antiquity*. McGill University Monographs in Classical Archaeology and History 22. Edited by Ellen B. Aitken and John M. Fossey. Leiden: Brill, 2014.

Landau, Brent. "The Coming of the Star-Child: The Reception of the Revelation of the Magi in New Age Religious Thought and Ufology." *Gnosis* 1 (2016): 196–217.

Landau, Brent. "The *Revelation of the Magi*: A Summary and Introduction." Pages 19–38 in *New Testament Apocrypha: More Noncanonical Scriptures*. Edited by Tony Burke and Brent Landau. Grand Rapids: Eerdmans, 2016.

Lanfranchi, Pierluigi. *L'Exagoge d'Ezéchiel le Tragique*. SVTP 21. Leiden: Brill, 2006.

Lappenga, Benjamin J. "'Speak, Hannah, and Do Not Be Silent': Pseudo-Philo's Deconstruction of Violence in *Liber Antiquitatum Biblicarum* 50–51." *JSP* 25 (2015): 91–110.

Lappenga, Benjamin J. *Paul's Language of* Ζῆλος: *Monosemy and the Rhetoric of Identity and Practice*. BibInt 137. Leiden: Brill, 2016.

Leibner, Uzi. "The Origins of Jewish Settlement in the Second Temple Period: Historical Sources and Archaeological Data." *Zion* 77 (2012): 437–70.

Levack, Brian P. *Hexenjagd. Die Geschichte der Hexenverfolgung in Europa*. Fourth ed. Munich: C.H. Beck, 2009.

Levenson, Jon D. *Sinai and Zion: An Entry into the Jewish Bible*. San Francisco: HarperOne, 1985.

Levison, John R. *Portraits of Adam in Early Judaism: From Sirach to 2 Baruch*. JSPSup 1. Sheffield: JSOT Press, 1988.

Liddell, Henry George, Robert Scott, Henry Stuart Jones, and Roderick McKenzie. *A Greek-English Lexicon*. Oxford: Clarendon Press, 1996.
Lieberwirth, Rolf, ed. *Christian Thomasius. Vom Laster der Zauberei. Über die Hexenprozesse. De Crimine Magiae. Processus Inquisitorii contra Sagas*. Second ed. Munich: Deutscher Taschenbuch Verlag, 1987.
Lied, Liv Ingeborg. *The Other Lands of Israel: Imaginations of the Land in 2 Baruch*. JSJSup 129. Leiden: Brill, 2008.
Lietzmann, Hans. *Das Muratorische Fragment und die Monarchianischen Prologue zu den Evangelien*. KlT 1. Bonn: A. Marcus and E. Weber, 1902. Second ed. Berlin: de Gruyter, 1933.
Lieu, Judith M. "'The Parting of the Ways': Theological Construct or Historical Reality?" *JSNT* 17 (1994): 101–19.
Lincicum, David. "Greek Deuteronomy's 'Fever and Chills' and Their Magical Afterlife." *VT* 58 (2008): 544–9.
Lindner, Helgo. *Die Geschichtsauffassung Des Flavius Josephus Im Belud Judaicum: Gleichzeitig ein Beitrag zur Quellenfrage*. AGJU 12. Leiden: Brill, 1972.
Lindqvist, Sune. *Gotlands Bildsteine*. vols. I–II. Stockholm: Wahlström & Widstrand, 1941–2.
Loader, William. *The Pseudepigrapha on Sexuality: Attitudes towards Sexuality in Apocalypses, Testaments, Wisdom, and Related Literature*. Grand Rapids: Eerdmans, 2011.
Lotz, Almuth. *Der Magiekonflikt in der Spätantike*. Habelts Dissertationsdrucke. Reihe Alte Geschichte 48. Bonn: Habelt, 2005.
Luck, Georg. *Arcana Mundi: Magic and the Occult in the Greek and Roman Worlds: A Collection of Ancient Texts Translated, Annotated, and Introduced* (Baltimore: Johns Hopkins University Press, 1985).
Magen, Yitzhak. "The Dating of the First Phase of the Samaritan Temple on Mount Gerizim in Light of the Archaeological Evidence." Pages 157–211 in *Judah and the Judeans in the Fourth Century BCE*. Edited by Oded Lipschits, Gary N. Knoppers, and Rainer Albertz. Winona Lake, IN: Eisenbrauns, 2007.
Magen, Yitzhak. *Mount Gerizim Excavations*. vol. II: *A Temple City*. Jerusalem: Israel Antiquities Authority, 2008.
Magen, Yitzhak, Haggai Misgav, and Levana Tsfania. *Mount Gerizim Excavations*. vol. I: *The Aramaic, Hebrew, and Samaritan Inscriptions*. Jerusalem: Israel Antiquities Authority, 2004.
Maier, Bernhard. *Die Druiden*. Beck'sche Reihe 2466. Munich: C.H. Beck, 2009.
Marcus, Joel. "The *Testaments of the Twelve Patriarchs* and the *Didascalia Apostolorum*: A Common Jewish Christian Milieu?" *JTS* 61 (2010): 596–626.
Markschies, Christoph. *Das antike Christentum. Frömmigkeit, Lebensformen, Institutionen*. Beck'sche Reihe 1692. Munich: C.H. Beck, 2006.
Martin, Dale. *The Corinthian Body*. New Haven: Yale University Press, 1995.
Martín Hernández, Raquel. "Appealing for Justice in Christian Magic." Pages 27–41 in *Cultures in Context. Transfer of Knowledge in the Mediterranean Context. Selected Papers*. Edited by Sofía Torallas Tovar and Juan Pedro Monferrer-Sala. Córdoba: Ingeniero Torres Quevedo, 2013.
Mason, Steve. "Of Audience and Meaning: Reading Josephus' *Bellum Judaicum* in the Context of a Flavian Audience." Pages 71–100 in *Josephus and Jewish History in Flavian Rome and Beyond*. JSJSup 104. Edited by Joseph Sievers and Gaia Lembi. Leiden: Brill, 2005.

Mason, Steve. "Being Earnest, Being Playful: Speech and Speeches in Josephus and Acts." *Sapientia Logos* 3 (2011): 101–82.

Mason, Steve. "Why Did Judaeans Go to War with Rome in 66–67 CE? Realist-Regional Perspectives." Pages 126–206 in *Jews and Christians in the First and Second Centuries: How to Write Their History*. CRINT 13. Edited by Peter J., Tomson and Joshua Schwartz. Leiden: Brill, 2014.

Mastrocinque, Attilio. "A Defixio from Caesarea Maritima against a Dancer." Pages 59–76 in *Litterae Magicae. Studies in Honour of Roger* S.O. *Tomlin*. Supplementa MHNH 2. Edited by Celia Sánchez Natalías. Zaragoza: Libros Pórtico, 2019.

Mastrocinque, Attilio. *From Jewish Magic to Gnosticism*. STAC 24. Tübingen: Mohr Siebeck, 2005.

McCabe, Matt Jackson, ed. *Jewish Christianity Reconsidered: Rethinking Ancient Groups and Texts*. Minneapolis: Fortress Press, 2007.

McDonald, Lee Martin. *The Biblical Canon: Its Origin, Transmission, and Authority*. Peabody, MA: Hendrickson Publishers, 2007.

McDonald, Lee Martin. *Forgotten Scriptures: The Selection and Rejection of Early Religious Writings*. Louisville: Westminster John Knox Press, 2009.

McDonald, Lee Martin. "What Do We Mean by Canon? Ancient and Modern Questions." Pages 8–40 in *Jewish and Christian Scriptures: The Function of "Canonical" and "Non-Canonical" Religious Texts*. JCT 14. Edited by James H. Charlesworth and Lee M. McDonald. New York: T&T Clark, 2010.

McKane, William. *A Critical and Exegetical Commentary on Jeremiah*. ICC. Edinburgh: T&T Clark, 1986.

McLaren, James S. "Constructing Judaean History in the Diaspora: Josephus's Accounts of Judas." Pages 90–108 in *Negotiating Diaspora: Jewish Strategies in the Roman Empire*. LSTS 45. Edited by John M. G. Barclay. London: T&T Clark, 2004.

McLaren, James S. "Theocracy, Temple and Tax: Ingredients for the Jewish-Roman War of 66–70 CE." Paper presented at the Annual Meeting of the SBL, San Antonio, TX, 2004.

McLaren, James S. "Delving into the Dark Side: Josephus' Foresight as Hindsight." Pages 49–67 in *Making History: Josephus and Historical Method*. JSJSup 110. Edited by Zuleika Rodgers. Leiden: Brill, 2007.

McLaren, James S. "Resistance Movements." Pages 1135–40 in *The Eerdmans Dictionary of Early Judaism*. Edited by John J. Collins and Daniel C. Harlow. Grand Rapids: Eerdmans, 2010.

McLaren, James S. "Going to War against Rome: The Motivation of the Jewish Rebels." Pages 129–53 in *The Jewish Revolt against Rome: Interdisciplinary Perspectives*. JSJSup 154. Edited by Mladen Popović. Leiden: Brill, 2011.

Merling, David. "The 'Pools of Heshbon': As Discovered by the Heshbon Expedition." Pages 211–23 in *Hesban After 25 Years*. Edited by David Merling and Lawrence T. Geraty. Berrien Springs, MI: Andrews University, 1994.

Merrills, A. H. "Monks, Monsters, and Barbarians: Re-Defining the African Periphery in Late Antiquity." *JECS* 12 (2004): 217–44.

Metzger, Bruce M. *The Canon of the New Testament: Its Origin, Development, and Significance*. New York: Clarendon Press and Oxford University Press, 1987.

Millar, Fergus. "Linguistic Co-existence in Constantinople: Greek and Latin (and Syriac) in the Acts of the Synod of 536 C.E." *JRS* 99 (2009): 92–103.

Miller, Marvin Lloyd. *Performances of Ancient Jewish Letters*. JAJSup 20. Göttingen: Vandenhoeck & Ruprecht, 2015.

Minov, Sergey. "Satan's Refusal to Worship Adam: A Jewish Motif and Its Reception in Syriac Christian Tradition." Pages 230–71 in *Tradition, Transmission, and Transformation from Second Temple Literature through Judaism and Christianity in Late Antiquity*. STDJ 113. Edited by M. Kister, H. Newman, M. Segal, and R. Clements. Leiden: Brill, 2015.

Mor, Menachem. "The Samaritans in Transition from the Persian to the Greek Period." Pages 191–8 in *Judah between East and West: The Transition from Persian to Greek Rule (ca. 400–200 BCE)*. LSTS 90. Edited by L. L. Grabbe and O. Lipschits. London: T&T Clark, 2011.

Morag, Shlomo. "Language and Style in Miqsat Maase Ha-Torah: Did Moreh ha-Sedeq Write This Document?" *Tarbiz* 65 (1996): 209–23.

Mroczek, Eva. *The Literary Imagination in Jewish Antiquity*. Oxford: Oxford University Press, 2016.

Müller, Klaus E. *Schamanismus. Heiler, Geister, Rituale*. Beck'sche Reihe 2072. Third ed. Munich: C.H. Beck, 2006.

Murphy, Frederick J. *Pseudo-Philo: Rewriting the Bible*. New York: Oxford University Press, 1993.

Naether, Franziska. *Die Sortes Astrampsychi. Problemlösungsstrategien durch Orakel im römischen Ägypten*. ORA 3. Tübingen: Mohr Siebeck, 2010.

Najman, Hindy. *Seconding Sinai: The Development of Mosaic Discourse in Second Temple Judaism*. JSJSup 77. Leiden: Brill, 2003.

Najman, Hindy. *Past Renewals: Interpretative Authority, Renewed Revelation and the Quest for Perfection in Jewish Antiquity*. JSJSup 53. Leiden: Brill, 2010.

Newman, Judith H. "Confessing in Exile: The Reception and Composition of Jeremiah in (Daniel and) Baruch." Pages 231–52 in *Jeremiah's Scriptures*. JSJSup 173. Edited by Hindy Najman and Konrad Schmid. Leiden: Brill, 2016.

Nickelsburg, George W. E. "Good and Bad Leaders in Pseudo-Philo's *Liber Antiquitatum Biblicarum*." Pages 49–65 in *Ideal Figures in Ancient Judaism: Profiles and Paradigms*. SBLSCS 12. Edited by John J. Collins and George W. E. Nickelsburg. Chico: Scholars, 1980.

Nickelsburg, George W. E. *1 Enoch 1: A Commentary on the Book of 1 Enoch, Chapters 1–36; 81–108*. Hermeneia. Minneapolis: Fortress Press, 2001.

Nickelsburg, George W. E. *Jewish Literature between the Bible and the Mishnah*. Minneapolis: Fortress, 2005.

Nickelsburg, George W. E. and James C. VanderKam. *1 Enoch: The Hermeneia Translation*. Minneapolis: Fortress Press, 2012.

Nielsen, David. "The Place of the *Shepherd of Hermas* in the Canon Debate." Pages 162–76 in *"Non-Canonical" Religious Texts in Early Judaism and Early Christianity*. Edited by Lee Martin McDonald and James H. Charlesworth. JCT 14. London: T&T Clark, 2012.

Nikiprowetzky, Valentin. "Josephus and the Revolutionary Parties." Pages 196–216 in *Josephus, the Bible, and History*. Edited by Louis H. Feldman and Gohei Hata. Translated by Angela Armstrong. Detroit: Wayne State University Press, 1988.

Nikolsky, Ronit. "The History of the Rechabites: The History of the Rechabites and the Jeremiah Literature." *JSP* 13 (2002): 185–207.

Nikolsky, Ronit. "Ishmael Sacrificed Grasshoppers." Pages 243–62 in *Abraham, the Nations, the Hagarites: Jewish, Christian, and Islamic Perspectives on Kinship with Abraham*. TBN 13. Edited by M. Goodman, G. H. Van Kooten, and J. T. A. G. M. Van Ruiten. Leiden: Brill, 2010.

Nitzan, Bilha. *Qumran Prayer and Religious Poetry*. Translated by Jonathan Chipman. STDJ 12. Leiden: Brill, 1994.

Ogden, Daniel. "Alexander, Agathos Daimon, and Ptolemy: The Alexandrian Foundation Myth in Dialogue." Pages 129–50 in *Foundation Myths in Ancient Societies: Dialogues and Discourses*. Edited by Naoíse Mac Sweeney. Philadelphia: University of Pennsylvania Press, 2015.

Ogden, Daniel. "Binding Spells: Curse Tablets and Voodoo Dolls in the Greek and Roman Worlds." Pages 1–90 in *Witchcraft and Magic in Europe: Ancient Greece and Rome*. Edited by Bengt Ankarloo and Stuart Clark. Philadelphia: University of Pennsylvania Press, 1999.

Ogden, Daniel. *Magic, Witchcraft and Ghosts in the Greek and Roman Worlds. A Sourcebook*. Oxford: Oxford University Press, 2002.

Ogden, Daniel. *Drakon: Dragon Myth and Serpent Cult in the Greek and Roman Worlds*. Oxford: Oxford University Press, 2013.

Olson, Daniel C. *A New Reading of the Animal Apocalypse of 1 Enoch: "All Nations Shall be Blessed."* SVTP 24. Leiden: Brill, 2013.

Orlov, Andrei. *The Enoch-Metatron Tradition*. TSAJ 107. Tübingen: Mohr Sieback, 2005.

O'Rourke, Sean, and Mary Stuckey. "Civility, Democracy, and National Politics." *Rhetoric and Public Affairs* 17 (2014): 711–36.

Osiek, Carolyn. *The Shepherd of Hermas: A Commentary*. Edited by Helmut Koester. Hermeneia. Minneapolis: Fortress, 1999.

Parlagi, Gáspár. "The City without(?) Women: Approach to the Female in Early Monastic Literature." Pages 246–62 in *Religion and Female Body in Ancient Judaism and Its Environments*. Edited by G. G. Xeravits. Berlin: de Gruyter, 2015.

Pastis, Jacqueline Z. "Dating the Dialogue of Timothy and Aquila: Revisiting the Earlier Vorlage Hypothesis." *HTR* 95 (2002): 169–95.

Patera, Maria. *Figures grecques de l'épouvante de l'antiquité au présent: peurs enfantines et adultes*. Mnemosyne Supplements 376. Leiden: Brill, 2014.

Peek, Werner. *Kerameikos. Ergebnisse der Ausgrabungen III: Inschriften, Ostraka, Fluchtafeln*. Berlin: de Gruyter, 1941.

Phillips III, C. Robert. "Nullum Crimen sine Lege: Socioreligious Sanctions on Magic." Pages 260–83 in *Magika Hiera. Ancient Greek Magic and Religion*. Edited by Christopher A. Faraone and Dirk Obbink. New York; Oxford: Oxford University Press, 1991.

Piovanelli, Pierluigi. "Scriptural Trajectories through Early Christianity, Late Antiquity, and Beyond: Christian Memorial Traditions in the *longue durée*." Pages 100–1 in *Forbidden Texts on the Western Frontier: Christian Apocrypha in North American Perspectives: Proceedings from the 2013 York University Christian Apocrypha Symposium*. Edited by Tony Burke. Eugene, OR: Cascade, 2015.

Pleket, Henk W., Ronald S. Stroud, Johan H. M. Strubbe et al., eds. *Supplementum Epigraphicum Graecum*. Alphen: Sijthoff; Amsterdam: Gieben; Leiden: Brill, 1976–.

Poorthuis, Marcel. "The Infallibility of the Prophets and the Fallible Jesus in Islam: On the Transformation of a Jewish Story into an Islamic Anti-Christian Polemic." Pages 260–74 in *Religious Stories in Transformation. Conflict, Revision and Reception*. JCPS 31. Edited Alberdina Houtman, Tamar Kadari, Marcel Poorthuis, and Vered Tohar. Leiden: Brill, 2016.

Portier-Young, Anathea E. *Apocalypse against Empire: Theologies of Resistance in Early Judaism*. Grand Rapids: Eerdmans, 2011.

Popović, Mladen. "Anthropology, Pneumatology, and Demonology in Early Judaism: The Two Spirits Treatise (1QS 3: 13–4:26) and Other Texts from the Dead Sea Scrolls." Pages 1029–67 in *Sibyls, Scriptures, and Scrolls: John Collins at Seventy*. JSJSup 175. Edited by J. Baden, H. Najman, and E. Tigchelaar. Leiden: Brill, 2016.

Preisendanz, Karl. "Fluchtafel (Defixion)." Columns 1–29 in *RAC* 8. Stuttgart: Anton Hiersemann, 1972.

Price, Jonathan J. "The Provincial Historian in Rome." Pages 101–18 in *Josephus and Jewish History in Flavian Rome and Beyond*. Edited by J. Sievers and G. Lembi. JSJSup 104. Leiden: Brill, 2005.

Price, Jonathan J. "Revolt, First Jewish." Pages 1146–7 in *The Eerdmans Dictionary of Early Judaism*. Edited by John J. Collins and Daniel C. Harlow. Grand Rapids: Eerdmans, 2010.

Procter, Everett. *Christian Controversy in Alexandria: Clement's Polemic against the Basilideans and Valentinians*. New York: Peter Lang, 1995.

Pummer, Reinhard. "Genesis 34 in Jewish Writings of the Hellenistic and Roman Periods." *HTR* 75:2 (1982): 184–5.

Pummer, Reinhard. "The Modern Invention of 'Old Testament Pseudepigrapha.'" *JTS* 60 (2009): 403–36.

Pummer, Reinhard. *The Samaritans in Flavius Josephus*. TSAJ 129. Tübingen: Mohr Siebeck, 2009.

Pummer, Reinhard. "Review of *Revelation of the Magi: The Lost Tale of the Wise Men's Journey to Bethlehem* by Brent Landau. *Sino-Platonic Papers* 208 (2011): 43–7.

Quack, Joachim Friedrich. "Texte aus Ägypten. 4. Demotische magische und divinatorische Texte." Pages 331–85 in *Omina, Orakel, Rituale und Beschwörungen*. TUAT N.F. 4. Edited by Bernd Janowski and Gernot Wilhelm. Gütersloh: Gütersloher Verlagshaus, 2008.

Ray, Paul J. *Tell Hesban and Vicinity in the Iron Age*. Berrien Springs, MI: Andrews University Press, 2001.

Rayo, Agustín. "A Plea for Semantic Localism." *Noûs* 47 (2013): 647–79.

Reed, Annette Yoshiko. "'Jewish Christianity' as Counter-History? The Apostolic Past in Eusebius' Ecclesiastical History and the Pseudo-Clementine Homilies." Pages 173–216 in *Antiquity in Antiquity: Jewish and Christian Pasts in the Greco-Roman World*. TSAJ 123. Edited by Gregg Gardner and Kevin Osterloh. Tübingen: Mohr Siebeck, 2008.

Reeves, John C. *Heralds of That Good Realm: Syro-Mesopotamian Gnosis and Jewish Traditions*. NHMS 41. Leiden: Brill, 1996.

Reinink, Gerrit J. "Das Problem des Ursprungs des Testamentes Adams." *OrChrAn* 197 (1972): 387–99.

Reinink, Gerrit J. "Das Land 'Seiris' (Šīr) und das Volk der Serer in jüdischen und christlichen Traditionen." *JSJ* 6 (1975): 72–85.

Reuter, Astrid. *Voodoo und andere afroamerikanische Religionen*. Beck'sche Reihe 2316. Munich: C.H. Beck, 2003.

Reynolds, Bennie H. "Adjusting the Apocalypse: How the *Apocryphon of Jeremiah C* Updates the Book of Daniel." Pages 279–94 in *The Dead Sea Scrolls in Context*. VTSup 140. Edited by Armin Lange, Emanuel Tov, and Matthias Weigold. Leiden: Brill, 2011.

Rhoads, David M. *Israel in Revolution: 6–74 C.E. A Political History Based on the Writings of Josephus*. Philadelphia: Fortress, 1976.

Rice, Bradley N. "From the Watchers to the Sethites to the Magi: Reinterpretations of Genesis in the Syriac *Revelation of the Magi*." *Henoch* 41 (2019): 226–42.

Riess, Werner. *Performing Interpersonal Violence. Court, Curse, and Comedy in Fourth-century BCE Athens*. MythosEikonPoiesis 4. Berlin: de Gruyter, 2012.
Roberts, Colin H. *Manuscript, Society and Belief in Early Christian Egypt*. London: Oxford University Press, 1979.
Robertson, R. G. *The Dialogue of Timothy and Aquila: A Critical Text, Introduction to the Manuscript Evidence, and an Inquiry into the Sources and Literary Relationships*. ThD dissertation. Harvard University, 1986.
Robinson, Stephen E. *The Testament of Adam: An Examination of the Syriac and Greek Traditions*. SBLDS 52. Chico, CA: Scholars Press, 1982.
Rosen-Zvi, Ishay. "Bilhah the Temptress: The Testament of Reuben and 'The Birth of Sexuality.'" *JQR* 96 (2006): 65–94.
Roth, Cecil. "The Zealots in the War of 66–73." *JSS* 4 (1959): 332–55.
Ruf, Martin G. "Missglückte Himmelfahrt (Letzte Auseinandersetzung mit Simon)—ActPetr 30–32." Pages 672–81 in *Kompendium der frühchristlichen Wundererzählungen*. vol. 2: *Die Wunder der Apostel*. Edited by Ruben Zimmermann et al. Gütersloh: Gütersloher Verlagshaus, 2017.
Ruhl, Charles. *On Monosemy: A Study in Linguistic Semantics*. Albany: State University of New York, 1989.
Rummel, Walter, and Rita Voltmer. *Hexen und Hexenverfolgung in der Frühen Neuzeit*. Geschichte Kompakt. Darmstadt: Wissenschaftliche Buchgesellschaft, 2008.
Runia, David T. "Clement of Alexandria and the Philonic Doctrine of the Divine Power[s]." *VC* 58 (2004): 256–76.
Ruzer, Serge. "Jesus' Crucifixion in Luke and Acts: The Search for a Meaning vis-à-vis the Biblical Pattern of Persecuted Prophet." Pages 173–91 in *Judaistik und neutestamentliche Wissenschaft. Standorte—Grenzen—Beziehungen*. FRLANT 226. Edited by Lutz Doering, Hans-Günther Waubke, and Florian Wilk. Göttingen: Vandenhoeck & Ruprecht, 2008.
Saar, Ortal-Paz. *Jewish Love Magic. From Late Antiquity to the Middle Ages*. MRLLA 6. Leiden; Boston: Brill, 2017.
Sacks, Steven Daniel. *Midrash and Multiplicity. Pirke de-Rabbi Eliezer and the Renewal of Rabbinic Interpretive Culture*. SJ 48. Berlin: de Gruyter, 2009.
Samkutty, V. J. *The Samaritan Mission in Acts*. LNTS 328. London: T&T Clark, 2006.
Sanders, James A. "Canon: Hebrew Bible." Pages 837–52 in vol. 1 in *Anchor Bible Dictionary*. Edited by David Noel Freedman, Gary A. Herion, David F. Graf, John David Pleins, and Astrid B. Beck. 6 vols. New York: Doubleday, 1992.
Satran, David. "The Lives of the Prophets." Pages 56–9 in *Jewish Writings of the Second Temple Period*. CRINT 2.2. Edited by Michael E. Stone. Assen: van Gorcum, 1984.
Satran, David. *Biblical Prophets in Byzantine Palestine*. SVTP 11. Leiden: Brill, 1995.
Schaper, Joachim. *Eschatology in the Greek Psalter*. WUNT II/76. Tübingen: Mohr Siebeck, 1995.
Schenker, A. "Le Seigneur choisira-t-il le lieu de son nom ou l'a-t-il choisi? L'apport de la Bible grecque ancienne à l'histoire du texte samaritain et massorétique." Pages 339–51 in *Scripture in Transition*. JSJSup 126. Edited by Anssi Voitila and Jutta Jokiranta. Leiden: Brill, 2008.
Schiffman, Lawrence H. "The Samaritans in Tannaitic Halakhah." *JQR* 75 (1985): 323–50.
Schiffman, Lawrence H. "The Concept of Restoration in the Dead Sea Scrolls." Pages 203–21 in *Restoration: Old Testament, Jewish, and Christian Perspectives*. Edited by James M. Scott. JSJSup 72. Leiden: Brill, 2001.

Schmidt, Francis. *How the Temple Thinks: Identity and Social Cohesion in Ancient Judaism.* BibSem 78. Translated by J. Edward Crowley. Sheffield: Sheffield Academic Press, 2001.

Scholem, Gershom. *Major Trends in Jewish Mysticism.* New York: Schocken, 1961.

Schorch, Stefan. "The Construction of Samari(t)an Identity from the Inside and from the Outside." Pages 135–49 in *Between Cooperation and Hostility: Multiple Identities in Ancient Judaism.* JAJSup 11. Edited by Rainer Albertz and Jakob Wöhrle. Gottingen: Vandenhoeck & Ruprecht, 2013.

Schreckenberg, Heinz. *Ananke. Untersuchungen zur Geschichte des Wortgebrauchs.* ZMKA 36. Munich: C.H. Beck, 1964.

Schreiber, Stefan. "Am Rande Des Krieges: Gewalt Und Gewaltverzicht Bei Jesus Von Nazaret." *BN* 145 (2010): 91–112.

Schroeder, Caroline. "Prophecy and *Porneia* in Shenoute's Letters: The Rhetoric of Sexuality in a Late Antique Egyptian Monastery." *JNES* 65 (2006): 81–97.

Schroeder, Caroline. *Monastic Bodies: Discipline and Salvation in Shenoute of Atripe.* Philadelphia: University of Pennsylvania Press, 2007.

Schroeder, Caroline. "Queer Eye for the Ascetic Guy? Homoeroticism, Children, and the Making of Monks in Late Antique Egypt." *JAAR* 77 (2009): 333–47.

Schuller, Eileen. "4Q372 1: A Text about Joseph." *RevQ* 14 (1990): 349–76.

Schultz, Brian. *Conquering the World: The War Scroll (1QM) Reconsidered.* STDJ 76. Leiden: Brill, 2009.

Schwartz, Daniel R. "Rome and the Jews: Josephus on 'Freedom' and 'Autonomy.'" Pages 65–81 in *Representations of Empire: Rome and the Mediterranean World.* Edited by Alan K. Bowman, Hannah M. Cotton, Martin Goodman, and Simon Price. Oxford: Oxford University Press, 2002.

Schwartz, Daniel R. *2 Maccabees.* CEJL. Berlin: de Gruyter, 2008.

Schwartz, Daniel R. *Judeans and Jews: Four Faces of Dichotomy in Ancient Jewish History.* Toronto: University of Toronto Press, 2014.

Schwartz, Seth. "The 'Judaism' of Samaria and Galilee in Josephus's Version of the Letter of Demetrius I to Jonathan (*Antiquities* 13:48-57)." *HTR* 82 (1989): 377–91.

Schwartz, Seth. *Josephus and Judaean Politics.* CSCT 18. Leiden: Brill, 1990.

Schwartz, Seth. "John Hyrcanus I's Destruction of the Gerizim Temple and Judaean-Samaritan Relations." *JH* 7 (1993): 9–25.

Schwarz, Sarah L. *Building a Book of Spells: The So-Called Testament of Solomon Reconsidered.* PhD dissertation. Philadelphia: University of Pennsylvania, 2005.

Schwarz, Sarah L. "Reconsidering the Testament of Solomon." *JSP* 16 (2007): 203–37.

Schwemer, Anna Maria. *Studien zu den frühjüdischen Prophetenlegenden: Vitae Prophetarum.* TSAJ 50. Tübingen: Mohr Siebeck, 1995.

Scot, Reginald. *The Discoverie of Witchcraft.* London: John Rodker, 1930.

Scott, James M. *Geography in Early Judaism and Christianity: The Book of Jubilees.* SNTSMS 113. Cambridge: Cambridge University Press, 2002.

Shahar, Yuval. *Josephus Geographicus: The Classical Context of Geography in Josephus.* TSAJ 98. Tübingen: Mohr Siebeck, 2004.

Shalev-Eyni, Sarit. "Solomon, His Demons and Jongleurs: the Meeting of Islamic, Judaic and Christian Culture." *Al-Masāq* 18 (2006): 145–60.

Sheppard, Gerald T. "Canon." Pages 62–9 in *The Encyclopedia of Religion*, vol. 3. Edited by Mircea Eliade. New York: Macmillan, 1987.

Sheridan, Mark. "The Modern Historiography of Early Egyptian Monasticism." Pages 197–220 in *Il Monachesimo tra Eredità e Aperture. Atti del simposio «Testi e temi nella tradizione del monachesimo cristiano» per il 50 anniversario dell'Instituto Monastico di*

Sant'Anselmo. Edited by M. Bielawski and D. Hombergen. Rome: Pontificio Ateneo S. Anselmo, 2004.

Simek, Rudolf. *Götter und Kulte der Germanen*. Beck'sche Reihe 2335. Third ed. Munich: C.H. Beck, 2009.

Simek, Rudolf. *Religion und Mythologie der Germanen*. Second ed. Darmstadt: Theiss, 2014.

Skinner, Stephen. *Techniques of Graeco-Egyptian Magic*. Singapore: Golden Hoard Press, 2017.

Slusser, Michael. "The Heart of Irenaeus's Theology." Pages 133–9 in *Irenaeus: Life, Scripture, Legacy*. Edited by Sara Parvis and Paul Foster. Minneapolis: Fortress, 2012.

Smith, Gregory A. "How Thin Is a Demon?" *JECS* 16 (2008): 479–512.

Sorensen, Eric. *Possession and Exorcism in the New Testament and Early Christianity*. WUNT II/157. Tübingen: Mohr Siebeck, 2002.

Spilsbury, Paul. "Reading the Bible in Rome: Josephus and the Constraints of Empire." Pages 209–27 in *Josephus and Jewish History in Flavian Rome and Beyond*. JSJSup 104. Edited by Joseph Sievers and Gaia Lembi. Leiden: Brill, 2005.

Spoto, Stephanie Irene. "Jacobean Witchcraft and Feminine Power." *Pacific Coast Philology* 45 (2010): 53–70.

Standhartinger, Angela. "Jesus, Elija und Mose auf dem Berg: Traditionsgeschichtliche Überlegungen zur Verklärungsgeschichte (Mk 9, 2–8)." *BZ* 47 (2003): 66–85.

Steenberg, M. C. "Irenaeus on Scripture, *Graphe*, and the Status of *Hermas*." *SVTQ* 53 (2009): 29–66.

Steenberg, M. C. "Tracing the Irenaean Legacy." Pages 199–211 in *Irenaeus: Life, Scripture, Legacy*. Edited by Sara Parvis and Paul Foster. Minneapolis: Fortress, 2012.

Sterling, Gregory E. "Jeremiah as Mystagogue: Jeremiah in Philo of Alexandria." Pages 417–30 in *Jeremiah's Scriptures*. JSJSup 173. Edited by Hindy Najman and Konrad Schmid. Leiden: Brill, 2016.

Stern, David. *Parables in Midrash: Narrative and Exegesis in Rabbinic Literature*. Cambridge, MA: Harvard University Press, 1991.

Steudel, Annette. "The Eternal Reign of the People of God—Collective Expectations in Qumran Texts (4Q246 and 1QM)." *RevQ* 17 (1996): 507–25.

Stone, Michael E. *Selected Studies in Pseudepigrapha and Apocrypha with Special Reference to the Armenian Tradition*. SVTP 9. Leiden: Brill, 1991.

Stone, Michael E. *A History of the Literature of Adam and Eve*. SBLEJL 3. Atlanta: Scholars Press, 1992.

Stone, Michael E. *Ancient Judaism: New Visions and Views*. Grand Rapids: Eerdmans, 2011.

Stone, Michael E., and Gary A. Anderson. *A Synopsis of the Books of Adam and Eve*. Second rev. ed. SBLEJL 17. Atlanta: Scholars Press, 1999.

Stratton, Kimberly B. *Naming the Witch: Magic, Ideology, and Stereotype in the Ancient World*. New York: Columbia University Press, 2007.

Strubbe, Johan H. M. "'Cursed Be He That Moves My Bones.'" Pages 33–59 in *Magika Hiera: Ancient Greek Magic and Religion*. Edited by Christopher A. Faraone and Dirk Obbink. New York; Oxford: Oxford University Press, 1991.

Stuckenbruck, Loren T. *Angel Veneration and Christology: A Study in Early Judaism and the Christology of the Apocalypse of John*. WUNT 70. Tübingen: Mohr Siebeck, 1995.

Stuckenbruck, Loren T. "'Angels' and 'God': Exploring the Limits of Early Jewish Monotheism." Pages 45–70 in *Early Jewish and Christian Monotheism*. JSNTSup 263. Edited by Loren T. Stuckenbruck and Wendy E. S. North. London; New York: T&T Clark, 2004.

Stuckenbruck, Loren T. *The Myth of Rebellious Angels: Studies in Second Temple Judaism and New Testament Texts*. WUNT 335. Tübingen: Mohr Siebeck, 2014.

Sundberg Jr., A. C. "Toward a Revised History of the New Testament Canon." *SE* IV (1964): 452–61.
Sundberg Jr., A. C. "Canon Muratori: A Fourth-Century List." *HTR* 66 (1973): 1–41.
Swartz, Michael D. "Sacrificial Themes in Jewish Magic." Pages 303–15 in *Magic and Ritual in the Ancient World*. RGRW 141. Edited by Paul Mirecki and Marvin Meyer. Leiden: Brill, 2002.
Syon, Danny. *Small Change in Hellenistic-Roman Galilee: The Evidence from Numismatic Site Finds as a Tool for Historical Reconstruction*. Jerusalem: Israel Numismatic Society, 2015.
Terian, Abraham. *The Armenian Gospel of the Infancy*. Oxford: Oxford University Press, 2008.
Termini, Cristina. *Le potenze di Dio: studio su dynamis in Filone di Alessandria*. Studie ephemeridis Augustinianum 71. Rome: Institutum patristicum Augustinianum, 2000.
Theis, Christoffer. "Inschriften zum Schutz der Grabstätte im Raum Syrien-Palästina." *UF* 45 (2014): 73–295.
Theis, Christoffer. *Magie und Raum. Der magische Schutz ausgewählter Räume im alten Ägypten nebst einem Vergleich zu angrenzenden Kulturbereichen*. ORA 13. Tübingen: Mohr Siebeck, 2014.
Thiessen, Matthew. "4Q372 1 and the Continuation of Joseph's Exile." *DSD* 15 (2008): 380–95.
Thomas, Keith. *Religion and the Decline of Magic. Studies in Popular Beliefs in Sixteenth- and Seventeenth-century England*. London: Penguin, 1991.
Thomas, Rodney L. *Magical Motifs in the Book of Revelation*. LNTS 416. London; New York: T&T Clark, 2010.
Thomsen, Marie-Louise. *Zauberdiagnose und schwarze Magie in Mesopotamien*. CNI Publikations 2. Copenhagen: Museum Tusculanum Press, 1987.
Tiller, Patrick A. *A Commentary on the Animal Apocalypse of I Enoch*. SBLEJL 4. Atlanta: Scholars Press, 1993.
Toepel, Alexander. *Die Adam- und Seth-Legenden im Syrischen Buch der Schatzhöhle: Eine quellenkritische Untersuchung*. CSCO 618: Subsidia 119. Louvain: Peeters, 2006.
Tomasino, Anthony J. *Daniel and the Revolutionaries: The Use of Daniel Tradition by Jewish Resistance Movements of Late Second-Temple Palestine*. PhD dissertation. Chicago: University of Chicago, 1995.
Tomasino, Anthony J. "Oracles of Insurrection: The Prophetic Catalyst of the Great Revolt." *JJS* 59 (2008): 86–111.
Tomson, Peter J. "The Song of Songs in the Teachings of Jesus and the Development of the Exposition on the Song." *NTS* 61 (2015): 429–47.
Torijano, Pablo A. *Solomon the Esoteric King: From King to Magus, Development of a Tradition*. JSJSup 73. Leiden: Brill, 2002.
Tov, Emanuel. "Three Strange Books of the LXX: 1 Kings, Esther, and Daniel Compared with Similar Rewritten Compositions from Qumran and Elsewhere." Pages 283–305 and 371–7 in *Hebrew Bible, Greek Bible, and Qumran: Collected Essays*. TSAJ 121. Tübingen: Mohr Siebeck, 2008.
Townsend, Philippa. "Who Were the First Christians? Jews, Gentiles and the *Christianoi*." Pages 212–30 in *Heresy and Identity in Late Antiquity*. TSAJ 119. Edited by Eduard Iricinschi and Holger M. Zellentin. Tübingen: Mohr Siebeck, 2008.
Track, Joachim. "' … eine Zauberin sollst du nicht leben lassen … ' (M. Luther). Vom Umgang mit der Schuld in Kirche und Theologie." Pages 203–21 in *Hexenwahn. Eine theologische Selbstbesinnung*. TA 5. Edited by Marcel Nieden. Stuttgart: Kohlhammer, 2004.

Trible, Phyllis. *Texts of Terror: Literary-Feminist Readings of Biblical Narratives*. Philadelphia: Fortress, 1997.
Trzcionka, Silke. *Magic and the Supernatural in Fourth-Century Syria*. London; New York: Routledge, 2007.
Tuczay, Christa Agnes. *Geister, Dämonen—Phantasmen. Eine Kulturgeschichte*. Wiesbaden: Marixverlag, 2015.
Tuczay, Christa Agnes. *Magie und Magier im Mittelalter*. First ed. Munich: Diedrichs, 1992; Second ed. Munich: Deutscher Taschenbuch Verlag, 2003.
van den Hoek, Annewies. *Clement of Alexandria and His Use of Philo in the Stromateis: An Early Christian reshaping of a Jewish Model*. VCSup 3. Leiden: Brill, 1988.
van den Hoek, Annewies. "The 'Catechetical' School of Early Christian Alexandria and Its Philonic Heritage." *HTR* 90 (1997): 59–87.
VanderKam, James C. *From Joshua to Caiaphas: High Priests after the Exile*. Minneapolis: Fortress, 2004.
VanderKam, James C. "Open and Closed Eyes in the Animal Apocalypse (1 Enoch 85–90)." Pages 279–92 in *The Idea of Biblical Interpretation: Essays in Honor of James L. Kugel*. JSJSup 83. Edited by Hindy Najman and Judith Newman. Leiden: Brill, 2004.
van der Kooij, Arie. "On the Place of Origin of the Old Greek of Psalms." *VT* 33 (1983): 67–74.
van der Kooij, Arie. "Authoritative Scriptures and Scribal Culture." Pages 5–71 in *Authoritative Scriptures in Ancient Judaism*. JSJSup 141. Edited by Mladen Popović. Leiden: Brill, 2010.
van der Vliet, Jacques. "Solomon in Egyptian Gnosticism." Pages 197–218 in *The Figure of Solomon in Jewish, Christian and Islamic Tradition: King, Sage and Architect*. TBN 16. Edited by J. Verheyden. Leiden: Brill, 2013.
van Dülmen, Richard. *Historische Anthropologie. Entwicklung, Probleme, Aufgaben*. Second ed. Cologne; Vienna: Böhlau Verlag, 2001.
van Henten, Jan Willem. "Commonplaces in Herod's Commander Speech in Josephus' A. J. 15.127–146." Pages 183–206 in *Josephus and Jewish History in Flavian Rome and Beyond*. Edited by Joseph Sievers and Gaia Lembi. JSJSup 104. Leiden: Brill, 2005.
Varneda, Pere Villalbai. *The Historical Method of Flavius Josephus*. ALGHJ 19. Leiden: Brill, 1986.
Varner, William. *Ancient Jewish-Christian Dialogues: Athanasius and Zacchaeus, Simon and Theophilus, Timothy and Aquila*. Lewiston; Queenston: Edwin Mellen Press, 2004.
Vermes, Geza. "Biblical Proof-texts in Qumran Literature." *JSS* 34 (1989): 493–508.
Versnel, Hendrik S. "Beyond Cursing: The Appeal to Justice in Judicial Prayers." Pages 60–106 in *Magika Hiera: Ancient Greek Magic and Religion*. Edited by Christopher A. Faraone and Dirk Obbink. New York; Oxford: Oxford University Press, 1991.
Versnel, Hendrik S. *Fluch und Gebet: Magische Manipulation versus religiöses Flehen? Religionsgeschichtliche und hermeneutische Betrachtungen über antike Fluchtafeln*. Hans-Lietzmann-Vorlesungen 10. Berlin; New York: de Gruyter, 2009.
Voltmer, Rita. *Hexen. Hexen. Wissen Was stimmt*. Herder Spektrum 5868. Freiburg: Herder, 2008.
Von Nordheim, Eckhard. *Die Lehre der Alten*, vol. 1: *Das Testament als Literaturgattung im Judentum der Hellenistisch Römischen Zeit*. ALGHJ 13. Leiden: Brill, 1980.
von Stuckrad, Kocku. *Das Ringen um die Astrologie: Judische und christliche Beitrage zum antiken Zeitverstandnis*. Berlin: de Gruyter, 2000.

Von Weissenberg, Hanne. *4QMMT: Reevaluating the Text: The Function and the Meaning of the Epilogue*. STDJ 82. Leiden: Brill, 2009.
Walker, Julia. "'God Is With Italy Now': Pro-Roman Jews and the Jewish Revolt." Pages 157–88 in *Jewish Identity and Politics between the Maccabees and Bar Kokhba: Groups, Normativity and Rituals*. JSJSup 155. Edited by Benedikt Eckhardt. Leiden: Brill, 2012.
Wei, Simon Lienyuah. "The Absence of Sin in Sexual Dreams in the Writings of Augustine and Cassian." *VC* 66 (2012): 362–78.
Wenthe, Dean O. "The Use of the Hebrew Scriptures in 1QM." *DSD* 5 (1998): 290–319.
Werline, Rodney A. "The Psalms of Solomon and the Ideology of Rule." Pages 69–88 in *Conflicted Boundaries in Wisdom and Apocalypticism*. SBLSymS 35. Edited by Benjamin G.Wright III and Lawrence M. Wills. Atlanta: Press, 2005.
Werline, Rodney A. "The Formation of the Pious Person in the Psalms of Solomon." Pages 133–54 in *The Psalms of Solomon: Language, History, Theology*. SBLEJL 40. Edited by Eberhard Bons and Patrick Pouchelle. Atlanta: SBL Press, 2015.
Werman, Cana. "Epochs and End-Time: The 490-Year Scheme in Second Temple Literature." *DSD* 13 (2006): 229–55.
Whitters, Mark F. "Jesus in the Footsteps of Jeremiah." *CBQ* 68 (2006): 229–47.
Widengren, Geo. *Iranisch-semitische Kulturbegegnung in parthischer Zeit*. Arbeitsgemeinschaft für Forschung des Landes Nordrhein-Westfalen: Geisteswissenschaften. Heft 70. Cologne: Westdeutscher Verlag, 1960.
Wilfong, Terry G. "'Friendship and Physical Desire': The Discourse of Female Homoeroticism in Fifth Century CE Egypt." Pages 304–29 in *Among Women: From the Homosocial to the Homoerotic in the Ancient World*. Edited by N. Sorkin Rabinowitz and L. Auanger. Austin: University of Texas Press, 2002.
Wilson, Robert R. "Resonances of Jeremiah in Daniel 9." Pages 1386–98 in *Sibyls, Scriptures, and Scrolls: John Collins at Seventy*. JSJSup 175. Edited by Joel Baden, Hindy Najman, and Eibert Tigchelaar. Leiden: Brill, 2017.
Winkler, John J. "The Constraints of Eros." Pages 214–43 in *Magika Hiera: Ancient Greek Magic and Religion*. Edited by Christopher A. Faraoneand Dirk Obbink. New York; Oxford: Oxford University Press, 1991.
Witakowski, Witold. *The Syriac Chronicle of Pseudo-Dionysius of Tel-Mahre: A Study in the History of Historiography*. AUUSSU 9. Uppsala: Uppsala University Press, 1987.
Witakowski, Witold. "Syryjska *Opowieść o Magach* (OpMag)." Pages 352–83 in vol. 1 in *Apokryfy Nowego Testamentu*, 3 vols. Edited by Marek Starowieyski. Krakow: Wydawnictwo WAM, 2003–8.
Witakowski, Witold. "The Magi in Syriac Tradition." Pages 809–43 in *Malphono w-Rabo d-Malphone: Studies in Honor of Sebastian P. Brock*. GECS 3. Edited by George A. Kiraz. Piscataway, NJ: Gorgias, 2008.
Wright, J. Edward. "Hebrews 11:37 and the Death of the Prophet Ezekiel." In *The Echoes of Many Texts: Reflections on Jewish and Christian Traditions: Essays in Honor of Lou H. Silberman*. BJS 313. Edited by William G. Dever and J. Edward Wright. Atlanta: Scholars, 1997.
Wright, N. T. *The New Testament and the People of God: Christian Origins and the Question of God*, vol. 1. Minneapolis: Fortress, 1992.
Xeravits, Géza G. "The Wonders of Elijah in the *Lives of the Prophets*." Pages 231–8 in *Biblical Figures in Deuterocanonical and Cognate Literature*. Edited by Hermann Lichtenberger, Friedrich V. Reiterer, and Ulrike Mittmann-Richert. Berlin: de Gruyter, 2009.

Zakovitch, Yair. "A Still Small Voice." *Tarbiz* 51 (1982): 335.
Zakovitch, Yair. "Inner-Biblical Interpretation." Pages 57–9 in *A Companion to Biblical Interpretation in Early Judaism*. Edited by Matthias Henze. Grand Rapids: Eerdmans, 2012.
Zamfir, Korinna. "Jeremian Motifs in the Synoptics' Understanding of Jesus." Pages 139–76 in *Prophets and Prophecy in Jewish and Early Christian Literature*. WUNT II/286. Edited by Joseph Verheyden, Korinna Zamfir, and Tobias Nicklas. Tübingen: Mohr Siebeck, 2010.
Zerbe, Gordon. *Non-Retaliation in Early Jewish and New Testament Texts: Ethical Themes in Social Contexts*. JSJSup 13. Sheffield: JSOT, 1993.
Zsengellér, József. "Maccabees and Temple Propaganda." Pages 186–7 in *The Books of the Maccabees: History, Theology, Ideology: Papers of the Second International Conference on the Deuterocanonical Books, Pápa, Hungary, 9–11 June, 2005*. Leiden: Brill, 2007.

INDEX OF REFERENCES

HEBREW BIBLE/OLD TESTAMENT
Genesis
1:2	147–8
1:17	160
1:26–28	64
2:23	62
3:5	63
3:15	63
4:10–16	194
4:17–18	194
4:26	186
6:1–4	172
7:11	147, 166
8:2	147
8:14	166
9:5	189
12:10–20	130
14:13–16	130
15:17	160
32:24–32	96
34	116–18, 121
34:7	120
37:35	153
42:22	189
44:29	153
44:31	153
49:9	9

Exodus
1–14	130
3:8	118
3:17	118
4:12	167
7–8	172
14:1–31	125
15:4	125
15:25–26	95
16:4–10	95
16:7	95
20:5	189
20:18	160
22:17	172
32:19	88

Leviticus
6:12–13	161
6:13	159
16:29	188
16:31	188
23:27	188
23:29	188

Numbers
10:9	124
14:18	189
14:36–37	152
16:22	188
16:30	153
24:16	188
24:17–19	126
24:17	52, 136
25	88–90
25:11	88
25:13	89
27:16	188

Deuteronomy
4:7	186
4:28	191
6:19	124
7:1	118
7:21–22	124
7:21	124
11:26	184
13:15	184
17:8	189
18:10–11	172
18:10	141
19:10	189
20:2–5	124
21:8–9	189
23:15	124

26:5	130	3:9	27
28:22–28	183	3:11–12	27
28:22	179, 183	3:13	27
28:28	183	4:32	6, 25
28:35	183	5:3–5	9
29:19	183	5:9–14	25
32	118, 121	8:13	9
32:21	118	8:46–52	12
32:22	153, 161	11:2–3	22–23
32:35	185		
33:13	147	2 Kings	
		16:3	141
Joshua		17	110–11, 115, 121
10	104	17:18	110
		17:23	110
Judges		17:25	111
11	83, 85	17:29–34	111
11:2	86	17:41	111
12:7	83	18:13–19:37	125, 130
17	87	19:35–36	130
19	87	21:6	141
20	87	22:17	160
20:21	87	23:10	141
20:25	87	24:4	189
20:28	87		
		1 Chronicles	
1 Samuel		5:22	125
4:1–7:1	130	28:11–18	11
12:7	83		
12:11	83	2 Chronicles	
17	91, 125	20:15	125
17:5	9	28:3	141
17:38	9	33:6	141
22:9	155		
22:18	91, 155	Ezra	
23:1–5	125	1:1–8	130
28	172	1:7–10	11
		9:2	118
2 Samuel			
2:17	7	Job	
5:17–25	125	1:6–12	90
8:1–14	125	2:9	151, 158
21:2	90	7:3	166
		7:5	151, 158
1 Kings		25:6	149, 151, 158
2:4–5	40	38:16	147
3	27		
3:5–28	25	Psalms	
3:5–15	27	2:7	49
3:6	27	2:9	11

2:10	9	1:2–4	19, 23
8:6	64	1:2	16, 21
32:7	147	1:3	18, 28
35:13	188	1:4	21–4
45:2–10	6	1:5	21, 24
45:10–15	22	1:5–17	19
45:11–16	5–6	1:12	21–4, 28
45:18	9	1:13–14	22
59:9–10	24	1:14	16
70:20–21	147	2:1–5:1	21
72	6, 25	2–4	21
72:4	9	2:1–17	18
72:8–11	6	2:1–6	19, 21
72:8	9–10	2:1	16, 18
72:15	6	2:4	21
72:17–19	9	2:7	19, 21
72:17	6, 9	2:8–5:1	17, 21
81:6	188	2:8–17	17
84:7	167	2:8–9	19
89	27	2:8	18, 22, 28
89:26	10	2:9–3:2	20
89:28	27	2:9–17	21
106:28–31	89	2:9–14	19, 21
107:9–10	24	2:9	17
110	9	2:10–13	28
110:2	11	2:15	20
110:4	9	2:16–17	19, 21
110:5–6	9	2:16	21
110:5	11	2:17	18, 22
115:4–7	191	3:1–5	17
135:6	148	3:1–2	19–21
135:15–17	191	3:2–4:5	19
		3:2–4:1	18
Proverbs		3:2–5	17, 21
2–7	23	3:2–4	21
3:20	147	3:2	18
6:23	72	3:4	21
7:18	16	3:5	21
8:24	147	3:6–11	16–17
		3:6	18–20, 22
Qohelet		3:7–11	16–17, 19–22, 28
1–2	6	3:7–8	22
		3:7	23
Canticles (Song of Solomon)		3:9	23
1:1–3:1	18	3:10	20
1–2	18	3:11	23
1:1–3:1	18	4:1–7	17, 19–21
1:1–7	18	4:1–3	21
1:1	18–19, 21–3	4:1	21
1:2–8:6	21	4:3	18, 20

4:5–6	20–2	8:14	22
4:6	18, 20, 22		
4:7	18	Isaiah	
4:8–5:1	17, 19, 21	1:31	160
4:8	16	10:33–34	136
4:10	16, 18	11:2–3	71
4:13–15	16	11:4	9–10
4:13	22	13:21–22	33
4:15	28	14:11	151
4:16	18, 22	14:13	151
5:1–4	16	23	121
5:1	17, 21–2	23:2–4	116
5:2–8:6	21	26:2	167
5:2–6:10	19, 21	28:15	172
5:2–6:3	21	29:16	63
5:2	28	31:8	125–6
5:7	21	31:9	160
5:8–9	21	40–55	144
5:16	21	40	142
6:1	21	40:5	142
6:2	16, 22	45:9	63
6:3	21	50:11	143–4
6:4–7	21	56–66	144
6:4	16	56–60	144
6:5	21	61–66	144
6:8–9	21–2	64:8	63
6:10	21	66:10	142
6:11–7:13	19	66:12	142
6:11	18	66:15–17	144
7:5	16, 21–2, 24	66:15–16	143–4
7:6	16	66:16	144
7:7	18	66:17	142–3
7:12–13	16	66:18–21	142
7:13	16	66:22–23	142
7:14	28	66:23–24	169
8	18	66:23	142, 166, 169–70
8:1–3	18–19		
8:4	18–19, 21	66:24	142–5, 149–51, 153–6, 159, 161–8, 170
8:5–6	18		
8:5	18–19, 22		
8:6	18–19, 21–2		
8:7–14	21–2	Jeremiah	
8:7	19, 21	4:4	160
8:8–10	18–19	4:44	161
8:11–12	16, 18–19, 21–3	7:2	160
		7:4	161
8:12	22	7:8	161
8:13–14	18–19, 21	7:10	161
8:13	28	7:12	160

7:20	160	Micah	
7:31	141	1:6	147
7:32–33	161	4:4	9–10
17	160	5:3–5	9
17:27	160–1	5:4–5	11
19:1–6	63	6:6	188
19:2–6	141		
19:5–6	141	Habakkuk	
19:5	83	2:18	191
22:7	162		
32:35	141	Zechariah	
41:4–8	111	4:10	71
50:39	33	9:10	9–10
51:37	33	12:6	126
		13:9	167
Lamentations		14:4	147
2:7	19		
2:8	19	Malachi	
2:18	19	2:17	185, 187
3:5	19	3:2	162
		3:5	185, 187
Ezekiel		4:1	162
16:8	16		
16:17	16	NEW TESTAMENT	
21:3	160–1	Matthew	
23:17	16	2:1–12	52
38:2–23	167	3:7–12	162
		3:7	162
Daniel		3:10	163
2:34	126	3:14	163
2:45	126	4	172
7	136	5:13	164
7:11	145	5:28	164
9:24–27	136	5:29–30	164
11:14	139	5:38–39	185
12:2	144–5, 161, 167	6:29	28
		7:22	168
Joel		9:14–17	163
2:32	186	9:32	33
4:21	189	10:24–25	63
		11:2–19	163
Amos		12:31–32	168
1:4	160	12:42	28
1:7	160	13:42	155
2:2	160	13:50	155
4:12	186	13:52	28
5:6	160	14:1–2	163
		18:5–9	164
Jonah		18:7	164
1:6	186	18:8–9	164

18:8	164	11:31	28
18:9	164	12:22	28
18:10	71	12:35–36	28
18:11–12	155	13:6–9	163
18:12	185	13:28	155
22:2–14	147	14:34	164
22:13	147, 155	16:19–30	157
24:51	155	16:22–24	157
25	147	16:26	157
25:1–12	28	16:28	157
25:10–12	168	17:1–2	164
25:30	155	17:1	164
25:41	146	17:2	164
25:46	168		
26:52	143	John	
		3:28–30	28
Mark		4:9	113
1:9	163	4:10–15	28
3:24	62	4:20	113
3:29	168	7:37–38	28
5:3	33	12:1–8	28
5:7	188	13:16	63
6:14–16	163	15:20	63
9	163		
9:14–18	33	Acts	
9:42–50	164	7:47	28
9:42	164	12:23	151
9:43–48	163–6		
9:43	163–4	Romans	
9:44	163	9:3	184
9:45	163–4	12:19	185
9:46	163		
9:47–48	163–5	1 Corinthians	
9:47	164–5	3:12–15	168
9:48	163–5, 168	5:5	33
9:50	164	6:9	168
13:28–29	28	7	33
14:3–72	28	7:5	33
16:18	63	10:20–21	33
		12:2	191
Luke		12:3	184
3:7–9	162	16:22	184
3:7	162		
3:16–17	162	Galatians	
4:27	33	1:8	184
7:18–35	163	5:20	172, 188
9:7–9	163		
9:37–42	33	2 Thessalonians	
10:19	63	1:9	168

1 Timothy		3:7	9
4:1	33	3:9	9
		5:62	7, 11
Hebrews		10:10–11	9
10:30	185	10:17–21	113
11:32	83	10:30	113
12:14	168	10:38	113
12:24	194	11:34–36	113
		11:34	113
Revelation		12:36	9
1:4	71	13:52	9
3:1	71	14:4–15	9
4:5	71	14:5–6	9
5:6	71	14:8	10
8:2	71	14:10	9
9:20	191	14:11	10
9:21	188	14:12	10
16:14	33	14:13	11
18:2–3	33	14:14	11
18:23	188	14:15	11
19:20	169	14:41	9, 11
20	147		
20:10	146, 169	2 Maccabees	
20:14–15	146, 169	5:22–23	111
21:1	169	6–7	153
21:4	169	6:11	153
21:8	169, 188	7:3–5	153
22:15	188	7:4	165
		7:9	165
APOCRYPHA		7:14	165
2 Esdras		7:17	165
1–2	158	7:19	165
2:16	158	7:35	188
2:29	158	9:5	150
2:42–48	158	9:9	150–1, 154, 165
7	156	9:10	151
		9:12	151
Judith		9:28	165
5:16	116–18	12:22	188
9:1–4	117	15:2	188
9:2	117		
16:2–17	153	3 Maccabees	
16:17	154–5	2:21	188
1 Maccabees		4 Maccabees	
2:24–28	7	5:30	153
2:26	8	5:32	153
2:54	7	6:24–27	153
3:3–9	9	6:26	149

8:13	153	6:12–24	14
9:9	153	7–9	15
		7:17–22	25
Prayer of Azariah		7:20	48
3:38–39	188	7:22–11:4	14
		8	14
Prayer of Manasseh		8:1–4	14
4	188	8:9–10	14
		8:16–21	14
Sirach		9:1–4	64
6:5	186	10	15
7:16	149	10:1–2	64
7:17	148–9, 151, 154, 161	11–19	14–15
17:2–4	64	PSEUDEPIGRAPHA	
36:1–19	6	*Apocalypse of Abraham*	
38:1–15	192	15:7	155
45:24–26	6		
45:25	6	*Apocalypse of Ezra*	
46:5	188	5:27	155
47	6		
47:11	7	*Aramaic Levi Document*	
47:12–22	6	2:1	117
47:14–17	6	12:6	117
47:22	7		
50	6	*Ascension of Isaiah*	
50:1–4	6	2:5	188
50:25–26	118		
50:25	116	*2 Baruch*	
51:13–21	14	59:5	157
		59:10	157
Susanna		59:11	157
62	189	83	158
		83:10	158
Tobit		83:11	158
6:1–9	192	83:13	158
6:15	32	83:15	158
8	43	83:18	158
8:2–3	192	83:20	158
8:3	43		
11:11–12	192	*3 Baruch*	
13:8–17	6	16:4	155
Wisdom of Solomon		*4 Baruch*	
1:1	14	8:1–12	111
1–6	14		
1:4	14	*Biblical Antiquities (LAB)*	
6–10	15	8.7	117
6–9	15	9.6	85
6:1–25	14	11.6	85

12	84	58	92
12.4–10	88, 92	58.1	85, 92
14.5	89	59.4	85
18.5	90	59.5	91
18.11	85	60	48
18.14	87–88	60.3	93
20.5	85	61.1	91
25–28	91	61.8	91–2
27.8–14	91	61.9	92
28.3	88	62.1	85, 91
32.1–2	90	62.4	91
32.1	85	62.8	93
32.2–4	90	62.11	85, 91, 93
32.2	85	63.2	91
39–40	84–5	63.3–4	87, 91
39.2	85–6	63.3	92
39.11	85, 89	64.2	93
40.1	85	64.8	85, 91
40.2	90	65.2–5	93
40.3	85, 90	65.5	95
40.4	85		
40.5	90	*1 Enoch*	
40.9	85	1–36	145
44–47	87	1:2	98
44	87	6:1	31
44.7	85, 87	7:3–6	31
44.9	151	8:1–2	31
44.10	85, 87	10	145, 147
45	91	10:3–4	145
45.6	85, 87–8	10:4–15	146
46.1	87	10:4	147
46.3	87	10:8–12	145
46.4	87	10:13–19	145
47	84, 87–8	10:13–14	145–6
47.1–3	87, 92	15:4	31
47.1	85, 87	18	153
47.3	88–9	18:9 12	152
47.4–8	91	18:9	152
47.7	85, 87–8	18:10–11	155
48–51	85	18:10	157
48.2	86	18:11	152
50–51	84	18:12	152
50	90	19	153
50.2	89	19:1–2	155
50.3	86	19:1	31
50.5	85–6, 89	20:4	194
51.2	89	21:7–10	147, 155
51.6	88	21:7	152
56–65	84, 90	26:4	154
56.3	92	27	144–5

27:1	154	89:74–75	102
27:2–4	154	89:74	102
27:2–3	147, 158	90	149
37–71	155	90:3	102
48:8–9	155	90:6	97–8, 102
54:1	155	90:7	98, 103
54:6	155	90:9–10	103–4
62:12	158	90:9	102–3
85–90	95	90:11	102
85:1	96	90:12–16	103
85:3	96	90:12	102
85:4	96	90:13	103
85:5	96	90:15	103
85:7	96	90:16	102–3
85:9	96	90:18	103–4
86:1	96	90:19	99, 103
86:2	96	90:24–27	145, 147, 149, 161
86:3	96	90:35–36	101
86:4	96	90:35	100, 105
87:1	96	100:7–9	153
87:2	96	100:7	153
87:4	96	103:4	153
88:1	96	103:7–8	153
88:3	96	103:7	153
89:2	96	108:4–5	155
89:3	96		
89:4	96	*2 Enoch*	
89:5	96	30:12	64
89:6	96	40:12–13	156
89:7	96	50:1–4	185
89:15	99–101		
89:16	97	*3 Enoch*	
89:19	96	5:1–6	65
89:21	96, 100	5:12–13	65
89:22	100		
89:24	100	*4 Ezra*	
89:27	96	6:53–54	64
89:28	95, 98–100, 102	7:36–105	156
89:30–31	100	7:36	156–7
89:30	100	7:105	156
89:39–45	98		
89:40	101, 105	*Joseph and Aseneth*	
89:41–45	101	23:14–15	117
89:46–50	98, 101		
89:51–58	98, 101	*Jubilees*	
89:57	101–2	2:2	148
89:58	101–2	2:14	64
89:59–90:6	98	5:1	31
89:68	102	7:27	31
89:69	102	10:1	31

10:2	31	17:4–6	11
10:3	31	17:4	12
10:7–8	31	17:21–46	12
11:4	31	18	12
11:5	31	18:1–9	12
12:20	31		
17:16	90	*Sibylline Oracles*	
18:12	90	8:241	148
30:3	117		
30:12–13	116	*Testament of Adam*	
30:12	117	1:1–2:12	62
30:18	117	3:1–7	62
		3:2	63
Life of Adam and Eve		3:3	63
14:1–3	64	3:4	63
16:1–3	64	3:5	63
		3:5	63
Martyrdom of Isaiah		3:6	63
2:4	34	3:7	63
3:28	34	4:1–8	62
		7:3–8	63
Psalms of Solomon		8:1–7	63
1–16	12	8:5	63
1	12	9:2–6	63
1:8	12	10:2	63
2	12		
2:2–3	12	*Testament of Issachar*	
2:11	13	4:4	34
2:13	13		
2:19–21	12	*Testament of Judah*	
3	12	13:4	34
4:4	13		
4:5	13	*Testament of Levi*	
5	12	5:3–4	116–17
7	12	6:6–8	116
7:1	12	6:8	117
8	12	6:9–10	117
8:9–10	13	7:1–3	117
8:11–12	12	7:1	117
8:22	12	7:2–3	119
9:1–2	12	7:3	116
10	12		
11	12	*Testament of Reuben*	
13	12	2:1–9	34
14	12	3:3	34
15	12	3:10–15	34
16	12	4:7	34
16:7–8	13	4:11	34
17	12	5:5–6	34

Testament of Solomon

1–15	46
1	40
2	39
2:2	39
2:3	40
3	41
3:2	39
4	41
4:2	41
4:5–6	42
4:5	42
5:7	42
5:8	44
5:9–11	43
6	45
6:4	45
11:6	188
12:4	48
14	44
14:4	44
16	45
16:2–3	45
16:2	45
17	44
18	46, 48, 50
24:5	48
26	49
26:2–3	49
26:4	49
26:5	49

QUMRAN

CD

4.13–18	32
7.19–21	127

1QIsaiah^a

col. LIV 17–18	165

1QH

6.29–30	128
9.13–14	148
11.19–36	127
14.29–32	128
14.29–30	127

1QM

1.1	128
1.2	128
1.6	128
1.8–9	128
1.9–10	127
1.10–13	128
1.14–16	128
1.14–15	128
3.8	128
4.12	128
4.13	128
6.5–6	125
6.17	127
7.6–7	125
8.8–9	128
8.16–18	128
9.1–2	128
cols. X–XIV	124
cols. X–XII	124
col. X	124
10.1–8	126
10.1–2	124
10.2–5	124
10.6–8	125
10.8–9	125
col. XI	124, 126–7
11.1–18	123–4, 129
11.1–4	126
11.1–2	125
11.1	125
11.2–5	125
11.2–3	125
11.2	125
11.3–4	125
11.4	125
11.5–7	126
11.7–9	126
11.9–12	126
11.9–10	125
11.10	126
11.11–12	125–6
11.13–14	126
11.17–19	127
12.7–9	125
12.11–12	128
12.16	128
13.13–14	125
13.14	125–6
14.4–15	125–6
15.8–9	125
15.13–14	128

16.7	128		4Q202	
16.9	128		col. IV	145
17.7–8	128			
17.12–13	128		4Q204	
18.1	128		col. V	145
19.1	125		col. V 1–2	146
19.3–4	128			
19.8	128		4Q216	
			col. V 9–10	148
1QS				
3.13–4.26	127		4Q246	
4.10	32		2.4	128
5.1	123		2.5–9	128
8.6–7	128			
8.10	128		4Q285	
9.23	123		frg. 6	127
1Q28b			4Q372	
5.24–25	127		ll. 11–14	119
5.27	127			
			4Q398	
1QapGen			frgs. 11–13 1–2	27
20.16–32	31			
			4QMMT	
1QpHab			B 8	5
5.3	128		C 10–11	5
5.4	128		C 18–19	27
4QCanticles[b]			4Q418	
col. I	18		frg. 81	27
col. II	18		frg. 81 5	27
col. III	18		frg. 81 6	27
col. IV	18		frg. 81 9	27
frg. 1	18			
			4Q423	
4Q161			frg. 5 5–6	27
frgs. 8–10	127		frg. 5 5	27
4Q171			4Q510	
2.14–15	127		1.5	31
2.18–19	127			
			6QCanticles	
4Q174			col. I	18
1.18–19	127		cols. I–II	18
			col. I 3	18
4Q197				
frg. 4 col. ii 9	32		11Q11	
			col. II	48
4Q201			col. II 2–7	25
col. V	145			

MISHNAH

'Abot
4.4	148

'Eduyyot
2.10	166

Sanhedrin
6.6	167

TOSEFTA

Berakot
5.31	166

Sanhedrin
12.10	28

BABYLONIAN TALMUD

Berakot
7a	168

'Erubin
19a	160, 167

Gittin
68a	43

Hullin
6a	115

Mo'ed Qatan
16b	168

Qiddushin
31b	167

Roš HaŠanah
17a	167

Sanhedrin
89b	90

Sotah
35a	152, 156

Yoma
69a	115

MINOR TRACTATES

Semaḥot
2.9	168

MIDRASH AND ANTHOLOGIES

Alphabet of Rabbi Aqiba
§7	167

Deuteronomy Rabbah
2.24 (on Deut 4:30)	168

Genesis Rabbah
3.1–5 (on Gen 1:3)	65
6.6 (on Gen 1:17)	160
19.7 (on Gen 3:7)	65
53.11 (on Gen 21:9)	49
55.4 (on Gen 22:1)	90
56.4 (on Gen 22:4)	90

Mekilta
Baḥodeš
§9	160

Seder Rabbi Amram
on Isa 26:2	167

Sifre Numbers
131	89

Tanna debe Eliyyahu Zuta
§20	167

Yalkut Shimeoni
on Isa 26:2	167

TARGUMS

Ps.-Jonathan
Numbers
25:8	89

Isaiah
66:24	155, 166

PHILO

De aeternitate mundi
17–18	147

Index of References

De migratione Abrahami
224	116

De mutatione nominum
193–195	116
199–200	117

JOSEPHUS
Antiquities
1.337–340	116
6.20–21	140
6.20	133
6.21	134
8.42–49	48
8.44–45	26
9.288–290	115
9.291	112
10.184	115
11.19–20	115
11.88	115
11.302–347	112
11.302	115
11.340–345	115
11.342–347	116
11.344	115
12.154–224	112
12.257–264	115
12.257	112, 115
12.303	133
13.45	113
13.172	126
13.198	133
13.254–256	113
13.255–256	115
13.256–258	7
13.256	115
13.275–281	113
13.275–279	113
13.318–319	7
13.380	16
13.395–397	7
14.22–24	186
14.77	133
17.169	151
18.7–9	139
18.9–10	132
18.10	134
18.18	126
18.23	133
18.24	133
18.25	135
18.29–30	113
18.116–119	162
19.346–350	151
20.97–99	137
20.97	137
20.118	113
20.120–121	113
20.125	113
20.167–172	137
20.167	137
20.168	137

Jewish War
1–3	138
1.10–11	132
1.27	132
1.63	7, 113
1.64–65	113
1.377–392	139
1.656	151
2.84	132
2.88	132
2.118	132
2.208	132
2.223–231	135
2.230	134
2.232–240	113
2.447	134
2.252–253	134
2.258–265	137
2.258	137
2.259	137
2.261	137
2.264	137
2.266	132
2.274	132
2.289–308	135
2.324	132
2.346	133
2.388–391	130
2.390	129
2.442	132
2.449–457	130
2.517–518	132
3.6	129
3.9	134
3.480	133

3.484	130	5.416	129
4.157	132	5.439	132
4.177	133	5.541	129
4.190–191	130	5.442–445	132
4.323	132	5.443	132
4.362	132	6.38	129
4.622	129	6.79	134
5.5	132	6.94	129
5.11	132	6.98	132
5.21	134	6.108–110	130
5.30	132	6.110	139
5.33	132	6.118	129
5.100	134	6.129	129, 132
5.114	129	6.143	132
5.261	129	6.249–251	130
5.325–326	129	6.286–288	137
5.362–419	129	6.286	137
5.362–374	130	6.312–313	136
5.365	133	6.365	129
5.367	129, 138	7.254–255	133
5.375	130	7.270	134
5.376–377	130	7.318–319	130
5.377	139	7.323–336	133
5.378	129, 139	7.327–332	130
5.379–390	123, 138	7.341–388	133
5.379–389	131, 139	7.358–359	130
5.379–381	130	7.389	134
5.381	138		
5.382–383	130	THEODOTUS THE SAMARITAN	
5.382	139–40	*Peri Ioudaiōn*	
5.383	139	frgs. 7–8	116–17
5.384–385	130	frg. 7	117
5.386	130		
5.387–388	130	APOSTOLIC FATHERS	
5.388	140	Ignatius	
5.389	130	*Ephesians*	
5.390–391	130	20:2	192
5.390	130, 139		
5.391–398	139	Shepherd of Hermas	
5.395	139	*Mandates*	
5.396	133	1.1	77
5.400	140		
5.402–403	130	*Similitudes*	
5.402	132	5.5.3	71
5.406	133	9.12.8	73
5.407–408	130	9.13	73–4
5.412	129, 132, 139	9.13.2	74
5.413	130	9.13.4	74

Visions

1.3	74
1.3.4	73
2	73
2.4.1	73
3	72–3
3.3	74
3.3.5	73
3.4	74
3.4.1	71
3.4.3	71, 73–5
3.5.1	75
3.8	73–4
3.8.5–8	73
3.8.6	74
3.8.7	74
3.8.9	74
3.13.4	72

CLASSICAL WRITERS/CHRISTIAN WRITERS

Acts of John

37–42	195

Acts of Peter

4–15	194
4	195
30–32	194
31	195
32	195

Acts of Thomas

30–33	36
42–50	36
44	36

Apuleius
The Golden Ass

4	44
4.33.1–2	44
5	44
5.17	44
5.22.2	44

De magia

26–65	174

Aristotle
Metaphysica

1.984b	147
12.1072a	147
14.1091b	147

Athanasius
Life of Antony

5–6	38
6	41
53	42

Augustine
De civitate Dei

21.9	168

Cave of Treasures

2.10–11	64
2.17–25	64

Clement of Alexandria
Stromata

1.178.1	72
1.181.1	71, 76
1.181.3	72
2.3.5	72
2.11.52.2	195
6.13.106	75
6.131.2	72

Dialogue of Timothy and Aquila

9	49
9.11–13	49

Cyprianus of Cathage
Ad Demetrium

15	196

Dioscorus
Historia Monarchorum

20	40

Ephrem
Commentarius in Diatessaron

X §4	168

Commentarius in epistolam ad Hebraeos

226–227	83

Eusebius
Historia ecclesiastica
8.16.3–5	152

Evagrius
Eight	*Spirits*
4–6	38

Eulogios
13	38
16	38
27	38

Excerpts
9	38

Praktikos
8	38

Talking Back
2	38
2.15	40
2.19	40
2.22–23	40
2.32	40

Herodotus
Historiae
4.205	151

Hesiod
Theogonia
116–117	147

Hippolytus
Refutatio omnium haeresium
6.9	195
6.13	195
17.1	195
18	195

Traditio apostolica
20–21	196

Homer
Iliad
10.193	176

Irenaeus
Adversus haereses
4.20.2	77

Jerome
Vita Pauli
8	42

John Cassian
Conferences
12	40
12.7.4	40

John Chrysostom
Homiliae epistulam i ad Corinthos
Hom. 9.1	168

Homiliae in Genesim
Hom. 22.21	168
Hom. 42.22	168

Justin Martyr
1 Apology
5	35
5.1	35
12	35
14.2	35
15	35
25	35
26	35
27–28	35

2 Apology
5	35

Lactantius
Divinae institutiones
II 15.3	196

De mortibus persecutorum
33.8–9	152

Lausaic History
16.4	44
59.2	44
63	44

Index of References

Lucian of Samosata
Alexander pseudomantis
59   151

Vera Historia
2.46   42

Marcus Junianus Justinus
Liber Historiarum
Philippicarum
16.2.5   151

Minucius Felix
Octavius
27.2–7   196

Muratorian Fragment
73–80   78
74–76   78–9

Opus imperfectum
in Matthaeum
Hom. 2 on Matt 2   59

Origen
Homilies on Joshua
15   38

Homilies on Ezekiel
6   38

Ovid
Heroides
8.117   88

Pausanius
Graeciae descriptio
9.7.2   151
9.27.2   147

Plato
Phaedo
113DE   146

Pliny the Elder
Naturalis historia
18.41–43   174
30.13   172

Plutarch
Parallela minora
29   42

Sulla
36.2–4   151

Ps.-Clementines
Homiliae
2.22   195

Libri recognitionum
2.7   195

Revelation of the Magi
1–5   57
1.1–3.6   56
1–2   52
1.1   59
2–4   52
2.3   57
2.4   60
2.5–6   60
2.5   63
3.1–7   60
3.2–7   63
3.2–3   53
3.2   63
3.3   63
3.4   63
3.5   63
3.6   63
3.7   63–4
4–10   52
4.1   63
4.2–3   60
4.7–9   60
4.7   60
4.10   60
5.1   60
5.9–10   60
5.10   60
6–10   53, 55
6.1–10.9   57
6
6.1–4   57–8
6.1   53, 57–8, 63

6.2–3	58, 64	21.10	58
6.2	53, 58	26–28	52
6.3	53, 64	27–32	56
6.4	53, 57–8	27–28	55–6, 58
7–10	58	27.3	58
7.1–10.7	57–8	27.7	58
7.1	53	28.4	56
7.2	53, 62, 64	29–32	52, 55, 58, 65
7.3–8	63	29.1	55, 57
7.3	53	29.2–3	55
7.4	53, 62	29.4	56
7.6	53, 58	29.5–6	56
7.7	53, 64	30.1	56
8.1–7	63	30.2–9	56
8.1	53, 58, 64	31.1–3	56
8.2–3	53	31.1	56
8.4	53	31.4–7	56
8.5	53, 58, 63–4	31.8–9	56
8.6	53, 64	31.10	56
8.7	53, 64	32.1	56
8.8	53, 58, 64	32.2–3	56
9.1–6	64	32.4	59
9.1	53		
9.2–6	63	Strabo	
9.2	53	*Geographica*	
9.3	53	5.4.5	142
9.4	53	13.4.14	142
9.5–6	53		
10.1–4	64	Suetonius	
10.1–2	54, 58	*Vespasianus*	
10.2	54, 63	4.5	136
10.3	54, 64		
10.4	54, 58, 64	Tacitus	
10.5–6	54, 64	*Historiae*	
10.7	54, 57, 64	5.13	136
10.8–9	57		
10.8	57, 63	Theophilus	
10.9	57–8	*Ad Autolycum*	
10.10	57	2.6	147
11–15	52		
11.7	58	NAG HAMMADI AND RELATED WRITINGS	
13.1	58	*Gospel of Philip*	
15.3–5	58	65.1–12	36
16–18	52	65.13–19	36
18–25	52		
18–21	52	INSCRIPTIONS AND PAPYRI	
19.1	58	Aramaic Incantation Bowls	
19.9	58	2.6	178
21.6	58	6.9–10	178
21.8	58	9	183

Index of References

Aramaic Papyri
30–34   111

Berlin 10587   187

Corpus Inscriptionum Latinarum
VI.3 19474   188

Defixionum Tabellae
18   186
22   186
24   186
26–27   186
29–33   186
35   186
37–38   186
49   181
74–75   186
233   182
242   181, 186
271   178

Defixionum Tabellae Atticae
74   182
102   180
103   180

Iraq Museum (magic texts)
9736   178

London Oriental Manuscript 6172   187

Munich Coptic Papyri
5   187, 193

Papyri Demoticae Magicae
XIV.675–694   178–9
XIV.739–740   179
XIV.741   179

Papyri Graecae Magicae
I.42–195   178
I.195–222   186
II.64–185   176
III.1–164   177
III.123–124   187
III.483–488   182–3
IV.296–466   177
IV.467–470   176
IV.824   176
IV.831–832   176
IV.1215–1220   186
IV.1245   187
IV.1390–1495   176, 180
IV.1462–1463   146
IV.1594   187
IV.1716–1870   177
IV.1924   187
IV.1981   186
IV.2006–2125   176
IV.2037   187
IV.2098   187
IV.2145–2240   176
IV.2785–2890   180
IV.3007–3086   159
IV.3069–3072   159
IV.3069–3071   159
IV.3071–3072   159
V.70–95   180
V.304–369   179
VII.167–186   177
VII.394–395   179
VII. 396–404   179
VII.417–422   179
VII.429–458   179
VII.464–466   180
VII.517   146
VII.925–939   181
VII.940–968   176
VIII.1–63   177
X.24–35   176
X.36–50   179
XII.21–48   186
XII.179–181   176
XIII.1–343   179
XIII.262   179
XIVc.16–27   178–9
XVIIb.1–23   186
XVIIb.12–13   186
XIXb.4–18   176
XXIX.1–10   186
XXXVI.1–34   176
XXXVI.69–101   178

XXXVI.161–177	176
XXXVI.187–210	178
XXXVI.295–311	178
XL.1–18	186
LI.1–27	186
LXVII.1–24	176
LXX.1–5	176
LXXIX.1–7	176
CXXIV.1–43	179
CXXVII.1–12	177

Papyrus Egerton 5
20	186

Supplementum epigraphicum graecum
40.266	191

Survey of Greek Defixiones
21	182
44	180
58	182
95	181
139	181
152–156	182

Taylor-Schechter Geniza Collection
T-S K 1.73	178
T-S NS 322.20	178

MISCELLANEOUS LITERATURE

Capitulatio de partibus Saxoniae
§6	174

Codex Hammurapi
§2	173
§47	173

Kebra Negest
63	49

"Prayer for Justice for Rheneia"
8	187
12–13	186, 189
12	187
13	187

Quran
34	26

Index of Modern Names

Adamik, Tamás 36, 195
Adams, Samuel L. 29
Africa, Thomas W. 150
Aitken, Ellen B. 61
Albertz, Rainer 108
Albrecht, Felix 45
Alexander, Philip S. 19, 47, 65, 127
Allison, Dale C., Jr. 163–4
Amit, David 16
Andersen, Francis I. 156, 158
Anderson, Gary A. 64
Ankarloo, Bengt 1, 177
Applebaum, Shimon 135
Aranda Pérez, Gonzalo 150–1
Armstrong, Angela 136
Asheri, David 151
Assan-Dhôte, Isabelle 19
Assefa, Daniel 97, 99
Atkins, Christopher 1, 67
Atkinson, Kenneth 11–12
Attridge, Harold W. 130
Auanger, Lisa 41
Audollent, Auguste 181
Aune, David E. 175, 187
Avery-Peck, Alan J. 136

Baden, Joel 32
Bailey, Lloyd R. 141
Barclay, John M. G. 131–2
Barnett, Paul W. 137
Barthélemy, Dominique 19
Bastiaensen, Antonius Adrianus Robertus 165
Batovici, Dan 68–72, 77
Bauckham, Richard 51
Becker, Dieter 172
Becking, Bob 108
Beentjes, Panc C. 148
Behringer, Wolfgang 171–2
Bensly, Robert Lubbock 156–7
Berger, Klaus 26, 28

Bernat, David 89
Bernstein, Moshe J. 124
Beshay, Michael 26, 50
Betz, Hans Dieter 159, 175
Betz, Otto 132
Bibok, Károly 84
Bielawski, Maciej 30
Bilde, Per 129, 132, 138–9
Birkhan, Helmut 171
Bissinger, Harry Gerard 96
Black, Matthew 132, 145–6, 166
Blenkinsopp, Joseph 144
Boccacini, Gabriele 9
Bohak, Gideon 26, 180, 186
Boll, Franz 177
Bongie, Elizabeth Bryson 44
Bons, Eberhard 11
Bourgel, Jonathan 108, 113
Bouriant, Urbain 145
Boustan, Ra'anan 26, 50
Bowman, Alan K. 133
Box, George Herbert 148–9
Boyd-Taylor, Cameron 19
Brakke, David 38, 40, 42, 44
Bremmer, Jan N. 29, 35–6, 195
Brock, Sebastian P. 56, 58, 61–2
Brodersen, Kai 180–1
Brooks, James A. 70
Brown, Derek 33
Brown, Peter 37
Brown, Raymond E. 52, 150
Bruin, Tom de 34
Bruyn, Theodore de 45
Bucur, Bogdan Gabriel 68, 70–2, 74–5
Burke, Tony 51
Busch, Peter 42, 44, 47–8, 180

Calduch-Benages, Núria 138
Carson, D. A. 124
Cason, Thomas 30
Cazeaux, Jacques 86

Čéplö, Slavomir 48
Chabot, Jean-Baptiste 51, 54–5
Chancey, Mark 167
Charles, Robert Henry 145–8, 150, 153, 155, 157–8
Charlesworth, James H. ix, 26, 47, 62, 69, 86, 126
Chazon, Esther 119
Chesnutt, Randall ix
Chester, Andrew 124, 126
Childs, Brevard S. 144, 160
Chilton, Bruce D. 143, 166
Chipman, Jonathan 124
Choat, Malcolm 67, 69
Choufrine, Arkadi 71, 76
Clark, Elizabeth 37
Clark, Stuart 177
Coggins, Richard J. 108–10, 116
Cohen, Shaye J. D. 108
Collins, Derek 173, 189
Collins, John J. 8, 85, 117, 119, 127–8, 131–2
Conner, Robert 180
Conybeare, Frederick C. 46
Corcella, Aldo 151
Cosaert, Carl P. 70
Cosentino, Augusto 29
Cowley, A. E. 111
Crowley, J. Edward 108
Crown, Alan D. 111
Czachesz, István 36

Dalgaard, Kasper 194
Danker, Frederick W.
Darsey, James 115
Davies, Owen 171, 175
Davies, Philip R. 128
Davies, William David 163–4
Davila, James R. 51
Davis, Kipp 24
Davis, Michael Thomas 125
Daxelmüller, Christoph 172
Decker, Rainer 171, 173–4
Deissman, G. Adolf 159
Delcor, Mathias 116
DesCamp, Mary Therese 85
Di Lella, Alexander A. 149
Dickie, Matthew W. 173
Dieterich, Albrecht 179
Dijkstra, Jitse H. F. 45

Dillinger, Johannes 172
Dillman, August 150, 153–4
Dochhorn, Jan 45
Doering-Manteufel, Sabine 174
Doran, Robert 150
Dossey, Leslie 40
Duhaime, Jean 125–6, 128
Duhm, Bernhard 143–5
Duling, Dennis C. 26, 40, 47–9
Dušek, Jan 108, 112–14, 116

Eckhardt, Benedikt 129
Edmondson, Jonathan 131
Edwards, Mark J. 56
Efrati, Shlomi 27
Egger, Rita 109, 116
Ego, Beate 32
Ehrlich, Arnold B. 16
Ehrman, Bart D. 67, 69, 75
Eidinow, Esther 180, 182
Elgvin, Torlief 1, 5, 9, 15, 18, 27, 29
Elm, Susanna 44
Elsas, Christoph 171
Embry, Brad 12
Emmel, Stephen 43
Enikö, Németh T. 84
Epp, Eldon Jay 67–8
Eshel, Hanan 32, 119
Evans, Craig A. ix, 2, 67, 128

Faraone, Christopher A. 173, 178, 180, 182–3, 189
Farmer, William Reuben 150
Feldman, Louis H. 93, 112, 116–17, 119, 133, 135–6
Ferguson, Everett 78
Fewster, Gregory P. 84
Fiorenza, Elizabeth Schüssler 114
Fischer, Thomas 116, 150
Fischer-Elfert, Hans-W. 184
Fishbane, Michael 124, 126
Fitzmyer, Joseph A. 32, 125–6, 164
Flach, Dieter 173
Fleck, Ferdinand Florens 46
Flint, Peter W. 119, 128
Florentin, Moshe 109
Forbes, Nevill 158
Fossey, John M. 61
Fossum, Jarl 73, 195
Foster, Paul 77

Fox, Michael V. 15–16, 23
France, Richard Thomas 163
Frankfurter, David 46
Frenschkowski, Marco 171–3, 180, 192
Fretheim, Thorstein 84
Freyne, Sean 112
Frölich, Ida 32

Gager, John G. 177–8, 180–9
Gallagher, Edward L. 108
Gamble, Harry 69, 77
Garrett, Susan R. 173
Garza, John 2
Gaskill, Malcolm 171, 174
Gaster, Moses 179
Gehrke, Hans-Joachim 185
Geraty, Lawrence T. 17
Geva, Hillel 17
Gieschen, Charles 73
Ginzberg, Louis 83
Gmirkin, Russell 125
Goff, Matthew 29, 31, 45, 47, 119
Goldstein, Jonathan 111, 113, 150–1
Gonis, Nikolaos 67
Goode, William J. 175
Gooding, David W. 27
Goodman, Martin 49, 113, 132, 135, 150
Gosse, Bernard 5
Gotter, Ulrich 43
Grabbe, Lester L. 9, 113, 136
Graetz, Heinrich 15
Graf, Fritz 173–4, 176, 190–1
Gray, Rebecca 137
Grüter, Thomas 172
Grypeou, Emmanouela 169
Guillaume, Philippe 194
Gundry, Stephen 185
Gurtner, Daniel M. 157–8

Haacker, Klaus 132
Haelewyck, Jean-Claude 55
Hägg, Henny Fiskå 74
Hahn, Johannes 43
Hahneman, Geoffrey Mark 79
Hall, Isaac Hollister 169
Hammerstadt, Jürgen 174
Hanson, John S. 137
Harari, Yuval 180
Harlow, Daniel C. 119, 131–2
Harmer, John Reginald 75

Harrak, Amir 59
Harrington, Daniel J. 84, 86
Hartmann, A. Th. 6
Hasenfratz, Peter 182
Hata, Gohei 116, 135–6
Hauck, Robert J. 68
Hauge, Martin Ravndal 23
Haustein, Jörg 172
Heal, Kristian S. 60
Heard, Warren J. 137
Hegedus, Tim 52
Hegeler, Hartmut 174
Heider, George C. 142
Heinevetter, Hans-Josef 15–17, 21, 23
Hellholm, David 67
de Hemmer Gudme, Anne Katrine 194
Hengel, Martin 132–34
Henne, Philippe 67
Hernández, Raquel Martín 192
Heschel, Susannah 167
Hilgenfeld, Adolf 157
Hill, Charles E. 77
Hirschfeld, Yizhar 16
Hjelm, Ingrid 108
Hoffmann, Matthias Reinhard 2, 179, 194–5
Hogan, Karina Martin 119
Hogeterp, Albert L. A. 127
Holladay, William 160
Holmes, Michael W. 73, 75
Hombergen, Daniël 30
Hondius, Jacobus J. E. 181
Hooker, Morna 94
Horbury, William 6, 133
Horsley, Richard A. 134, 137, 173
Hossfeld, Frank-Lothar 6
Hovhanessian, V. S. 48
Hultgård, Anders 54

Ingram, Helen 176
Isaac, Ephraim 146
Isbell, Charles D. 178
Isenberg, Wesley W. 36
Istrin, Vasilii Mikhailovich 46

Jacobs, Andrew S. 36
Jacobson, Howard 84, 86, 117, 155–6
Jacobus, Helen R. 194
James, M. R. 93
Janowski, Bernd 179, 186

Jansson, Sven B. F. 184
Japhet, Sara 141
Jassen, Alex 128
Jellinek, Adolph 167
Johns, Loren L. 125
Johnson, Marshall D. 64
Johnston, Sarah Iles 29, 42, 176
Jokiranta, Jutta 108
Joosten, Jan 11
Jordan, David R. 181
Jördens, Andrea 186
Jossa, Giorgio 138
Jost, Renate 172
Jurgens, Blake 1, 29

Kaiser, Otto 138, 173
Kalleres, Dayna S. 176
Kalmin, Richard 43
Kaminsky, Joel S. 119
Kartveit, Magnar 108, 118–19
Keaveney, Arthur 150
Kehnel, Annette 176
Kellerman, James A. 51
Kieckhefer, Richard 171–2
Kippenberg, Hans G. 119, 174
King, Karen L. 36
Kiraz, George A. 61
Klauck, Hans-Josef 175, 195
Klijn, Albertus Frederik Johannes 36, 64, 158
Klutz, Todd E. 30, 39, 44, 46, 48
Knoppers, Gary N. 108–9, 111–14
Knust, Jennifer Wright 35
Koester, Craig R. 33
Kolenkow, Anitra Bingham 63
Kooten, G. H. Van 49
Korsvoll, Nils Hallvard 26
Koskenniemi, Erkki 32
Köster, Janine 184
Kraft, Robert A. 63
Kraus, Thomas J. 67, 179
Krawiec, Rebecca 38
Krivoruchko, Julia G. 19
Kropp, Angelicus M. 187
Kropp, Amina 176, 180, 191, 193
Kugel, James L. 117–19
Kugler, Robert A. 119

La Fontaine, Jean 175
Lahe, Jaan 195

Lamberti, Francesca 174
Landau, Brent 51–2, 54–62
Lange, Armin 32
Lange, Nicholas R. M. de 19
Lankford, Rebecca 107
Lappenga, Benjamin J. 1–2, 83–84, 86, 88, 92
Lembi, Gaia 129–31
Levack, Brian P. 171
Levene, Dan 169
Lévi, Israel 148
Levison, John R. 64
Lichtenberger, Herman 32
LiDonnici, Lynn R. 32
Lieber, Andrea 32
Lieberwirth, Rolf 174
Liesen, Jan 138
Lietzmann, Hans 78
Lightfoot, Joseph Barber 75
Lincicum, David 179, 183
Lindner, H. 139
Lindqvist, Sune 184
Lipschits, Oded 108, 113
Lloyd, Alan 151
Loader, William 30, 40, 42, 45
Lotz, Almuth 173
Luck, Georg 173
Lundbom, Jack R. 141, 161

Madden, John A. 150
Magen, Yitzhak 108, 112
Maier, Bernhard 172
Marcus, Joel 34, 165
Markschies, Christoph 194
Martin, Dale 33
Martínez, Florentino García 125, 146
Mason, Steve 131–2, 135, 138
Mastrocinque, Attilio 29, 175, 181
McCarthy, Carmel 168
McCown, Chester C. 46–7
McDonald, Lee Martin 69, 79
McEleney, Neil J. 150
McLaren, James S. 131–5, 139
Merkelbach, Reinhold 177–8, 182, 196
Merling, David 17
Merrills, Andrew H. 42
Metzger, Bruce Manning 69, 77–8, 156
Meyer, Marvin A. 176, 184, 187, 191, 193–4

Migne, Jacques Paul 51
Milik, Józef Tadeusz 146
Millar, Fergus 61
Miller, Yonatan 119
Mirecki, Paul 176
Misgav, Haggai 108
Moatti-Fine, Jacqueline 19
Monferrer-Sala, Juan Pedro 192
Monneret de Villard, Ugo 54, 60–1
Montefiore, Claude Goldsmid 167
Montgomery, James A. 141–2, 150
Moore, Carey A. 154
Mor, Menachem 113
Morag, Schomo 5
Moreno, Alfonso 151
Morgan, Michael A. 178
Muehlberger, Ellen 152
Mulder, Martin J. 124
Müller, Klaus E. 172
Murphy, Frederick J. 85–6, 93–4
Murray, Oswyn 151
Myers, Jacob M. 158

Naether, Franziska 177
Najman, Hindy 24, 32, 96
Natalías, Celia Sánchez 181–2
Naveh, Joseph 178, 183
Nestle, Wilhelm 150
Neusner, Jacob 136, 166
Newman, Judith 96, 186–9
Nickel, Jesse P. 2, 123
Nickelsburg, George W. E. 63, 85, 95, 102–4, 146–7, 149–50, 152–5
Nicklas, Tobias 67
Nieden, Marcel 172, 174
Nielsen, David 69
Nikiprowetzky, Valentin 136
Nikolsky, Ronit 49
Nitzan, Bilha 124, 129
Nolland, John 164
North, Wendy E. S. 185

Obbink, Dirk 173, 178, 183, 189
Oesterley, William Oscar Emil 149
Ogden, Daniel 173, 176–7, 180, 182–3
Olson, Daniel C. 95, 102
Önnerfors, Alf 180
O'Rourke, Sean 115
Osiek, Carolyn 67–70, 75, 77

Panagiotopoulos, Diamantis 176
Panayotov, Alexander 51
Parente, Fausto 133, 138
Parlagi, Gáspár 42
Parvis, Paul M. 56
Parvis, Sara 77
Pastis, Jacqueline Z. 48
Patera, Maria 42
Paul, Shalom M. 127
Peek, Werner 180
Perrot, Charles 93
Petersen, Anders Klostergaard 118
Phillips, C. Robert III 173
Pleket, Henk W. 181
Piovanelli, Pierluigi 60
Popović, Mladen 24, 32, 133
Portier-Young, Anathea E. 96–9, 102, 104–5
Pouchelle, Patrick 11
Pratscher, Wilhelm 67
Preisendanz Karl 159, 175, 179, 193
Price, Jonathan J. 129–30, 132, 138–9
Priesner, Claus 172
Procter, Everett 74
Pummer, Reinhard 108–10, 116

Quack, Joachim Friedrich 179

Rabin, Batya 125
Rabin, Chaim 125
Rabinowitz, Nancy Sorkin 41
Ray, Paul J. 17
Rayo, Agustín 84
Reed, Annette Yoshiko 60
Reeves, John C. 58
Reinink, Gerrit 55, 62
Reiterer, Friedrich V. 179
Reuter, Astrid 175
Rhoads, David M. 126
Rice, Bradley N. 1, 51–2
Riess, Werner 180–2
Riessler, Paul 156
Rives, James 131
Roberts, Colin H. 67
Robertson, Robert G. 48
Robinson, J. Armitage 156
Robinson, Stephen E. 62–3
Rodgers, Zuleika 139
Römheld, K. F. Diethard 32

Rosen-Zvi, Ishay 34
Roth, Cecil 134
Rothschild, Clare K. 79
Rousseau, Adelin 77
Ruf, Martin G. 194
Ruhl, Charles 84
Ruiten, Jacques T. A. G. M. van 49
Rummel, Walter 171
Runia, David T. 70, 72–5
Rüterswörden, Udo 116

Saar, Ortal-Paz 178
Samkutty, V. J. 110, 115
Sanders, James A. ix, 69, 79
Schaff, Philip 168
Schaffer, Mary 44
Schalk, Peter 54
Schenker, Adrian 108
Schiffman, Lawrence H. 114, 117, 119, 124, 129
Schmidt, Francis 108, 111
Schodde, George H. 150, 153–4
Schöpflin, Karin 179
Schorch, Stefan 108
Schreiber, Stefan 135
Schrekenberg, Heinz 180
Schroeder, Caroline 37–8, 41
Schröter, Jens 188
Schuller, Eileen 119
Schultz, Brian 126
Schwartz, Daniel R. 133, 150
Schwartz, Joshua 135
Schwartz, Seth 108, 113, 131
Schwarz, Sarah L. 47
Scot, Reginald 174
Scott, James M. 129
Segal, Moses Z. 148
Shaked, Shaul 178, 180, 183
Shalev-Eyni, Sarit 29
Sheppard, Gerald T.
Sheridan, Mark 30
Sievers, Joseph 129–31, 133, 138
Sim, David C. 147
Simek, Rudolf 174, 185
Skehan, Patrick W. 149
Skinner, Stephen 177, 179
Slotki, Israel Wolf 142
Slusser, Michael 77
Smith, David 132

Smith, Gregory A. 37
Smith, Morton 159
Smith, Richard 184, 187, 191, 193–4
Snaith, John G. 149
Sorensen, Eric 33, 196
Spilsbury, Paul 131, 138–9
Spoto, Stephanie Irene 172
Starowieyski, Marek 54
Stausberg, Michael 54
Steenberg, Matthew C. 68, 77
Steudel, Annette 126, 128
Stone, Michael E. 64
Stratton, Kimberly B. 174, 176
Strawn, Brent A. 125
Stroud, Ronald S. 181
Strubbe, Johan H. M. 181, 183, 186
Stuckenbruck, Loren T. ix, 153, 179, 185
Stuckey, Mary 115
Sundberg, Albert C. Jr 79
Swartz, Michael D. 176
Sysling, Harry 124

Tal, Abraham 109
Talbert, Evan 107
Tatum, Gregory 167
Tefera, Amsalu 179
Termini, Cristina 71
Theis, Christoffer 183
Thiessen, Matthew 119
Thomas, Keith 171
Thomas, Rodney L. 187–8
Thomsen, Marie-Louise 173
Tigchelaar, Eibert J. C. 32, 125, 146
Tiller, Patrick A. 95, 101, 150
Toepel, Alexander 51, 54, 59
Tomasino, Anthony J. 135–7
Tomson, Peter J. 28, 135
Torijano, Pablo A. 29
Tov, Emanuel 27, 119
Tovar, Sofía Torallas 192
Trible, Phyllis 83, 94
Tromp, Johannes 64
Trzcionka, Silke 182
Tsfania, Levana 108
Tuczay, Christa Agnes 172, 196
Tullberg, Otto F. 51, 57
Tur-Sinai, Naftali Herz 22

Udoh, Fabian E. 167

van Banning, Joop 51, 61
van den Broek, Roelof 60
van den Hoek, Annewies 70, 72, 74–5
van der Horst, Pieter 186–9
van der Kooij, Arie 24
van Dülmen, Richard 172
van Hecke, Pierre 15
van Iersel, Bastian Martinus Franciscus 165
VanderKam, James C. 95–7, 111, 119, 124, 155
Varner, William 49
Veenstra, Jan R. 29
Vercruysse, Jean-Marc 55
Verheyden, Joseph 47
Vermes, Geza 126
Versnel, Hendrik S. 181–2, 189–91
Vida, Giorgio Levi Della 54
Villalbai Varneda, Pere 130
Violet, Bruno 156
Vliet, Jacques van der 48
Voitila, Anssi 108
Voltmer, Rita 171
von Nordheim, Eckhard 63
von Stuckrad, Kocku 39, 174
Vukosavovic, Filip 169

Walker, Julia 129, 132, 139
Ward, Benedicta 41
Wardle, Tim 2, 107, 111–12
Watson, Duane F. 141
Webb, Robert L. 162
Weber, Robert 156

Wei, Simon Lienyuah 40
Wenthe, Dean O. 124, 129
Werline, Rodney A. 11–12
Westermann, Claus 144–5, 161
Widengren, Geo 54, 58
Wildberger, Hans 160
Wilfong, Terry G. 41
Wilhelm, Gernot 179, 186
Willem van Henten, Jan 130
Williamson, Hugh G. M. 124
Wills, Lawrence M. 11, 154
Winkler, John J. 178
Witakowski, Witold 54, 58–9, 61
Wöhrle, Jakob 108
Wolff, Hans Walter 160
Wright, Benjamin G., III 11
Wright, N. T. 133
Wünsch, Richard 181, 183

Xeravits, G. G. 42

Yadin, Yigael 125
Yamazaki-Ransom, Kazuhiko 137
Young, Francis M. 56
Yuen-Collingridge, Rachel 67, 69
Yuval, Israel J. 167

Zakovitch, Yair 20
Zangenberg, Jürgen K. 188
Zenger, Erich 6
Zerbe, Gordon 128
Zimmermann, Ruben 194

Zsengellér, József 111